Existentialism

Modern Library
College Editions

The publisher will be pleased to send,
upon request, a brochure listing each volume in the
Modern Library College Editions.

Existentialism

*Edited with
an Introduction by*

Robert C. Solomon
University of Texas

The Modern Library
New York

For C.M.S.,
on his 60th,
with respect and affection

First Edition

© Copyright, 1974, by Random House, Inc.

All rights reserved under International and Pan-American Copyright Conventions. No part of this book may be reproduced in any form or by any means, electronic or mechanical, including photocopying, without permission in writing from the publisher. All inquiries should be addressed to Random House, Inc., 201 East 50th Street, New York, N.Y. 10022. Published in the United States by Random House, Inc., and simultaneously in Canada by Random House of Canada Limited, Toronto.

Library of Congress Cataloging in Publication Data

Solomon, Robert C   comp.
    Existentialism.

    (Modern Library college editions)
    1. Existentialism—Addresses, essays, lectures.
I.   Title.
B819.S576   142'.7   73-18150

The Modern Library is published by Random House, Inc.
Manufactured in the United States of America

Upon your conception of the single individual all your descriptions will be based, all your science established. For this reason, the human sciences, philosophy, ethics, psychology, politics, economics, can never be sciences at all. There can never be an exact science dealing with individual life. L'anatomia presuppone il cadavere; anatomy presupposes its corpse, says D'Annunzio. You can establish an exact science on a corpse, supposing you start with the corpse and don't try to derive it from a living creature. But upon life itself, or any instance of life, you cannot establish a science.

D. H. Lawrence, KANGAROO

TABLE OF CONTENTS

INTRODUCTION

1. It is a commonly accepted half-truth that existentialism is a revolt against traditional Western rationalistic philosophy. It is also a demonstrable half-truth that existentialist philosophy is very much a continuation and logical expansion of themes and problems in Descartes, Kant, Hegel, Marx, and Husserl. But two half-truths provide us with less than the truth. Existentialism is not simply a philosophy or a philosophical revolt. Existentialist philosophy is the explicit conceptual manifestation of an existential attitude—a spirit of "the present age." It is a philosophical realization of a self-consciousness living in a "broken world" (Marcel), an "ambiguous world" (de Beauvoir), a "dislocated world" (Merleau-Ponty), a world into which we are "thrown" and "condemned" yet "abandoned" and "free" (Heidegger and Sartre), a world which appears to be indifferent or even "absurd" (Camus). It is an attitude that recognizes the unresolvable confusion of the human world, yet resists the all-too-human temptation to resolve the confusion by grasping toward whatever appears or can be made to appear firm or familiar—reason, God, nation, authority, history, work, tradition, or the "other-worldly," whether of Plato, Christianity, or utopian fantasy. The existential attitude begins with a disoriented individual facing a confused world that he cannot accept. This disorientation and confusion is one of the by-products of the Renaissance, the Reformation, the growth of science, the decline of Church authority, the French Revolution, and the growth of mass militarism and technocracy. In philosophical terms, the new stress on "the individual" provides the key themes of the Enlightenment, the "Age of Reason," the philosophical rationalism of Descartes, Kant, and Hegel. In these authors, however, the theme of individual autonomy is synthesized and absorbed into a transcendental movement of reason. But in a culture that harps so persistently upon the themes of individual autonomy and freedom, there will always be individuals who carry these to their ultimate conclusion. Existentialism begins with the expression of a few such isolated individuals of genius, who find themselves cut adrift in the

dangerous abyss between the harmony of Hegelian reason and the romantic celebration of the individual, between the warmth and comfort of the "collective idea" and the terror of finding oneself alone. Existentialism is this self-discovery. Its presupposition is always the Cartesian *sum* (not the *cogito*). 2. So long as we think of philosophy as a set of (hopefully) true propositions, we will continue to be tempted by notions that philosophy can be a "science," that there is a *correct* way of doing philosophy, that a philosophical judgment or body of judgments can be *true*. If instead we allow ourselves to think of philosophy as *expression*, these rigid demands seem pointless or vulgar. Yet we surely do not want to reduce philosophy to *mere* expression, to autobiography or poetry, to "subjective truth" or psychic discharge. Although it is an expression of personal attitude, a philosophical statement is better compared to a piece of statuary than to a feeling or an attitude. The philosopher is a conceptual sculptor. He uses his language to give a shape to his prejudices and values, to give his attitudes a life of their own, outside of him, for the grasp of others. A philosophical statement, once made, is "in the world," free of its author, open to the public, a piece to be interpreted; it becomes universal. But "universal" does not mean "universally true."[1] Philosophical genius lies not in the discovery of universal truth, but in the seductiveness with which one molds his personal attitudes as universals for others. The philosopher builds insight onto insight, illustration into argument, joins metaphysical slogan to concrete observation, perhaps using himself as an example, his entire age as a foil. Nevertheless, the philosophy is never merely a personal statement; if it is the individual that has made existentialist philosophy possible, it is also the case that existentialism has deepened our individualism. Nor is philosophy ever merely an epiphenomenon of cultural attitudes; it gives them shape and direction, creates them as well as expresses them.
3. Existential philosophy, perhaps like all philosophies, typically finds itself going in circles, trying to prove axioms with theorems, converting premises into methodological rules, using repetition and restatement for argument and illustration for proof. Here "the individual" appears as a conclusion, there as

---

[1] *I follow Hegel here in distinguishing between "universally available" and "universally applicable."*

the presupposition, and there again as the rule. The existential attitude finds itself in syndromes, interpreting a feeling as a mark of identity, converting an insight about oneself into an interpretation of the world, resolving self-doubt by exaggerating the self in everything. The existential attitude is first of all an attitude of self-consciousness. One feels himself separated from the world, from other people. In isolation, one feels threatened, insignificant, meaningless, and in response demands significance through a bloated view of self. One constitutes himself as a hero, as an offense, as a prophet or anti-Christ, as a revolutionary, as unique. As a result of this self-exaggeration, the world becomes—whether apparently or "really" is irrelevant—more threatening. So one attacks the world, discovering, with both despair and joy, that its threats are themselves without ultimate meaning, that there are no moral facts, no good and evil, that "the highest values devalue themselves," and that the human world is typically, even essentially, a hypocritical world. And so one self-righteously finds himself as the creator of meaning, which heightens one's role as absurd hero, prophet, revolutionary, "underground man," rebel, saint—or buffoon. Then there is at least slight paranoia, me or us against the others, the authorities, the public, the herd, the bourgeoisie, the pharisees, the oppressors. As the world becomes more threatening, one is thrown into his exaggerated concept of self all the more; and as he becomes more self-conscious, the world becomes increasingly "his." Then one begins to feel impotent in the face of the responsibility for "his" world; it becomes more apparent how indifferent the world is, how contingent its events, how utterly absurd. One feels isolated from others, and in desperate loneliness one seeks comradery, through rebellion, through art, through writing existential philosophy. In the existential syndrome every tension increases self-consciousness, every increase in self-consciousness exaggerates the irresolvable tension with the world that is always there. As the existentialist becomes more sophisticated, as his feelings become formulated into ideas, as the existential attitude becomes philosophy, it becomes a mantra for similar attitudes in others. When those attitudes finally manifest themselves in the sardonic irony of Kierkegaard, the utter loneliness of Nietzsche's Zarathustra, the pathetic spitefulness of Dostoevsky's underground man, the struggle against nausea and "bad faith" in Sartre, the struggle for the heights in Camus's Sisyphus, these attitudes are no longer personal syndromes but universal meanings that we can accept as our own.

4. According to many existentialists, every act and every attitude must be considered a choice. Yet the existential attitude itself is apparently not chosen. One finds oneself in it. Dostoevsky tells us that self-consciousness is a "disease"; Nietzsche adds, in his discussion of "bad conscience," that it is "a disease—but as pregnancy is a disease." Although many existentialists speak of the universality of "the human condition," this universality is itself a view from within an attitude which is less than universal. Most existentialists, no less than Descartes, Kant, and Hegel, take self-consciousness to be the home of a universal first truth about all men. But self-consciousness itself is not universal, although once one becomes self-conscious, he cannot go back, no matter how he denies himself, drugs himself, *leaps* or *falls* away from himself (the terms, from Kierkegaard and Heidegger respectively, carry their evaluations with them). In *Utilitarianism*, John Stuart Mill argues for "quality" of pleasures by contrasting the dissatisfied Socrates with a satisfied pig. The first is preferable, Mill argues, because Socrates has experienced both Socratic pleasures and pig pleasures and he, like other men, has chosen to remain Socratic. Actually Socrates has no choice. He can *act like* a pig, but he cannot enjoy himself as one. Socrates can no more imagine the self-less indulgence of pig pleasure than the pig can appreciate the arguments of the *Apology*. Once expressed, the existential attitude appears as a universal condition, but only to those who can understand it. It is a peculiarly Western attitude, and talk of "the human condition" is as presumptuous as it is overdramatic. Perhaps that is why, for many of us, Hermann Hesse is convincing, even in the wild fantasies of the magic theater, but lyrically unpersuasive as he attempts to capture the selflessness of his Eastern Siddhartha. If we begin by understanding Siddhartha's quest, it is because we, like Hesse, understand quests. However, we may well have difficulty understanding the peace and satisfaction of Siddhartha's repetitive routine as a ferryman. Of course we, like Hesse, can moon for that selflessness as a dream, a nostalgia for something lost. But for us, even selflessness is something viewed self-consciously, something that would have to be striven for by each of us as an individual. The existential attitude is not universal, and existential philosophy is not a truth about the human condi-

tion. As Camus says, for many of us it is simply a necessity.
5. Most of us have experienced this existential attitude at several points in our lives. A threat of imminent death—or even a passing thought of our own mortality—is sufficient to wrench us out of our current involvements—even if but for a moment—and force us to look at our lives. Like Sartre's characters in hell in *No Exit*, it is perhaps every man's private dream to see his own funeral, to see his life after its completion. In life, however, there can be no such viewpoint, as Kierkegaard complains against Hegel, since "at no particular moment can I find the necessary resting place from which to understand [my life] backwards." Inevitably the thought of death prompts existential questions, What have I done? Who have I been? What have I wanted to be? Is there still time? But anxiety of death is only one preface to existential anxiety. As Camus tells us, "at any streetcorner the absurd can strike a man in the face." Imagine yourself involved in any one of those petty mechanical tasks which fill so much of our waking hours—washing the car, boiling an egg, changing a typewriter ribbon—when a friend appears with a new movie camera. No warning: "Do something!" he commands, and the camera is already whirring. A frozen shock of self-consciousness, embarrassment, and confusion. "Do something!" Well of course one was doing something, but that is now seen as insignificant. And one is doing something just standing there, or perhaps indignantly protesting like a housewife caught in curlers. At such moments one appreciates the immobilization of John Barth's Jacob Horner, that paralyzing self-consciousness in which no action seems meaningful. In desperation one *falls* back into his everyday task, or he *leaps* into an absurd posture directed only toward the camera. In either case, one feels absurd. One remains as aware of the camera as of his actions, and then of his actions viewed by the camera. It is the Kantian transcendental deduction with a 16mm lens: there is the inseparable polarity between self and object; but in this instance the self is out there, in the camera, but it is also the object. A *sum* (not a *cogito*) accompanies my every presentation. "How do I look?" No one knows the existential attitude better than a ham actor.
6. Enlarge this moment, so that the pressure of self-consciousness is sustained. Norman Mailer, for example, attempted in *Maidstone* a continuous five-day film of himself and others which did not use a developed script, leaving itself open to

the "contingencies of reality." His problem was, as ours now becomes, how to present oneself, how to live one's life, always playing to the camera, not just as one plays to an audience but as one plays to a mirror. One enjoys making love, but always with the consciousness of how one appears to be enjoying himself. One thinks or suffers, but always with the consciousness of the "outer" significance of those thoughts or sufferings. A film of one's life: would it be a comedy? a tragedy? thrilling? boring? heartrending? Would it be, as Kierkegaard suggests, the film of "a life which put on the stage would have the audience weeping in ecstasy"? Would it be a film you would be willing to see yourself? twice? infinitely? Or would eternal reruns force you to throw yourself down and gnash your teeth and curse this Nietzschean projectionist? And who would edit this extravagant film of every detail—of yet undetermined significances—cf your life? How would the credits be distributed? Each of us finds himself in his own leading role—the hero, the protagonist, the buffoon. John Barth tells us that Hamlet could have been told from Polonius' point of view: "He didn't think he was a minor character in anything."

What does one do? "Be yourself!" An empty script; *myself* sounds like a mere word that points at "me" along with the camera. One wants to "let things happen," but in self-conscious reflection nothing ever "just happens." One seizes a plan (one chooses a self), and all at once one demands controls unimaginable in everyday life. Every demand becomes a need, yet every need is also seen as gratuitous. During the filming of *Maidstone*, Mailer was attacked by one of his "co-stars" (Rip Torn), and his candid reaction exploded the film's pretense of reality. No one can be an existential hero and also accept fate, yet no one is more aware of contingencies. Camus tells us that Sisyphus is happy, but perhaps he is because his routine is settled. He can afford to have scorn because his mythical reality is entirely structured within its predictable contingencies. Could Sisyphus remain the absurd hero if he were alive? How much does Camus' absurd hero and the existential attitude require the routine and leisure of the bourgeoisie? Perhaps there are no existentialists in foxholes.

7. The hero? The buffoon? Does any of us really think of himself that way? As Odysseus, Beowulf, James Bond, Woody Allen, perhaps not. But as the center, the one who endows all else with meaning, that is an attitude we recognize easily. Yet

at the same instant we recognize ourselves as pelted by meanings, "sown on our path as thousands of little demands, like the signs which order us to keep off the grass" (Sartre). The existential attitude is the constant confusion of given meanings and our own. As this confusion becomes better formulated, one begins to suspect both. Today, I am Dr. Pangloss, and the world is spectacular; yesterday I was a Schopenhauerian fecal monist, grumbling over a fine wine in a rotten world. Each day values are given to me, but each day I find changes to explain how yesterday's differing values depended on differences in the world. (Yesterday I was there, now I'm here; yesterday she was friendly, today she insulted me.) My friends assure me, typically, that what has changed is only me, and that yesterday's depression was a symptom of a very real problem. It is today that is the illusion; my happiness is merely another symptom of my problem. But the values remain a problem, outside of me. Then, the exaggerated insight: It is all me (mine). No one can begin in the existential attitude without feeling sometime the hero, the megalomaniac (Nietzsche: "I am dynamite"). But again, one need not, should not, take this attitude for the truth. The realization that "I am the world" is a necessary step in the awakening of self-consciousness. In the existentialists' self-conscious sense, perhaps one has never existed if he has never once seen himself as everything.

8. What is self-consciousness? According to some recent existentialists, there is no *self* as such. And what is consciousness? "It is nothing," Sartre tells us, and for Heidegger it is scarcely worth mentioning. One looks at paradigm cases. One is self-conscious because of the camera, "he is self-conscious about his baldness." To be self-conscious is to be embarrassed, to be ill-at-ease. Or is that a peculiarly American paradigm? Descartes sees self-consciousness as a propositional attitude; consciousness of one's own existence seems in the light of reason to be not much different from a mathematical postulate. Hegel is centrally concerned with self-consciousness in his master-slave parable, but self-consciousness in Hegel carries with it a sense of dignity, pride, autonomy. We might well suspect that semantics is here becoming an ethology as well. What we begin to see, in our movie-making example as well as in Descartes and Hegel, is that self-consciousness is neither a subject aware nor an awareness of an object (the self) so much as it is a motivation, an attitude that illuminates the

world as well as the individual in the world. Self-consciousness is not, strictly speaking, awareness of self, for there is no self. Rather, self-consciousness in the existential sense is this very recognition that there is no self. The self is an ideal, a chosen course of action and values. Self-consciousness does not add anything to the world or to consciousness; it is neither a Lockean "turning back on itself" nor a Cartesian reflective substance. Self-consciousness robs the world of its authority, its given values, and it robs consciousness of its innocence. Self-consciousness is not a premise or an object for study. It is rather the perspective within which existentialism attempts to focus itself.

9. Existentialism is forced to be centrally concerned with problems of justification. In self-consciousness one holds all given values suspect. How much of reason might be no more than *our* reason, the anonymous consensus of "the public"? How many of our values might be no more than relics of dead authority or products of our weaknesses, our fears of isolation, failure, or meaninglessness? How many of our values are prejudices, how much reason mere rationalization? Nevertheless, to simply pronounce the nihilist thesis that the highest values are without justification is not sufficient. The problem, we hear from every author, is to live. And so we continue to seek courses of action. We look to Kant and try to act in a way that would universalize our principles of action for everyone. But that supposes that we can identify those features of our own action which would be so universalizable. And then, already caught in the existential attitude, each of us realizes that he is always an exception. I can accept moral principles by the tabletful, but I am always without the rule which teaches me to apply such principles to my own case. One is tempted to turn away from principles to the concrete—to his feelings and attitudes. Yet to do so, as Kant had already argued, is to give up morality. And which feelings can I trust? How does one build a way of life on a foundation of tenuous, passing feelings? How much does one value happiness? Pleasure? Self-interest? Feelings for others? Simple perversity and spite? Must my values change every time my feelings change? And how can decisions for the future always depend upon the undependability of passing whims, a bad night's sleep, too much coffee, or a hassle on the subway? To be consistent, in such a scheme, one must be impotent. Still, all of this supposes that there are feelings, that they are given—

with directions and instructions—like concrete and intuited moral principles of the moment. But a feeling does not have an identity or a direction before it is already made self-conscious. For one who is not yet self-conscious, a feeling can be a cause of behavior. In one who is self-conscious, a feeling is but an obscure text which requires an interpretation, and that presupposes a set of values. In one and the same situation I might be ashamed or embarrassed, depending on my own sense of responsibility, angry or afraid, depending on my sense of value, indignant or amused, depending on my sense of morality. One can always find values given, in his everyday tasks, by "the public," but the existential self-consciousness has already closed this escape behind itself. One can no longer turn to religion, for Kant has destroyed its authority and reduced it to a mere "postulate" of morality. So, one *creates* a criterion, "leaps" to a set of values, to a life of one's own. Camus calls this "philosophical suicide," for every such attempt to adopt a value is at the same time a pretense that the value is justified. However, no one can simply rest in the existential attitude of the absurd, any more than he can relax in Hegel's dialectic. Kierkegaard's "leap," like the lie in Kafka's *Trial*, becomes for existentialism a universal principle.

10. The existential attitude, as we have been describing it, is not merely a piece of psychology, much less psychopathology. Existential statements are at once both personal and general. Personal, however, is not autobiographical. The same Kierkegaard who complains of the lack of passion in his age is thus described by a friend: "There is nothing spontaneous about him: I am surprised he can eat and sleep." The Nietzsche one might have met in Sils Maria in 1886 was surely not the Dionysian epic hero one pictures from his writings. This is not hypocrisy. It is the mark of these great philosophers that their personal discomfort could be so brilliantly transformed into matters of universal concern and inspiration. Kierkegaard describes himself as a "stormy petrel" (a bird that appears "when, in a generation, storms begin to gather") and as "an epigram to make people aware." Nietzsche often feared that he would be considered either a saint or a buffoon. (Hesse remarked that "a nature such as Nietzsche's had to suffer the ills of our society a generation in advance"; his personal suffering was at the same time "the sickness of the times themselves.") And Camus gives us, not just *his* feelings of aliena-

tion, but "an absurd sensitivity that is widespread in our age." If these feelings are not universal, neither are they exceptional. What is exceptional is their expression in these authors and their ability to provoke others who hold these still unformed and unexpressed existential attitudes as personal failures and not yet as philosophical insights. Kierkegaard and Nietzsche wrote only for "the few": Camus and Sartre write to generations. Nevertheless, in each case the philosopher is not simply striving after merely the truth, but after converts as well. The philosopher becomes the seducer, the *provocateur*. The Socratic gadfly kept people annoyedly aware of reason. The existentialist Don Juan draws his power from desires, from loneliness, from feelings of inadequacy that we already share.

11. One might object that this sketch of the existential attitude and its philosophical expression has failed to give a definition of existentialism. But existentialism is not a dead doctrine to be bottled and labeled. It is a living attitude that is yet defining and creating itself. As Nietzsche warns us in his *Genealogy of Morals*, "Only that which has no history can be defined." And Sartre, rejecting an invitation to define existentialism, says, "It is in the nature of an intellectual quest to be undefined. To name it and define it is to wrap it up and tie the knot. What is left? A finished, already outdated mode of culture, something like a brand of soap, in other words, an idea" (*Search for a Method*). Although one might develop a working definition of one aspect of one twentieth-century existentialist "movement," namely that series of attempts to develop an existential phenomenology in extension of and reaction to Edmund Husserl's "transcendental phenomenology," existentialism is but a growing series of expressions of a set of attitudes which can be recognized only in a series of portraits. Therefore, I have made no attempts to define existentialism as such, and the selection of authors and works in this book can be justified only by their tenuous appeal to my own sympathies and perspectives on the origins, directions, and extensions of the existential attitude.[2] Existentialism is not a movement or a set of ideas or an established list of authors. It is an attitude which has found and is still finding philosophical expression in the most gifted writers of our

---

[2] *See my* From Rationalism to Existentialism (*New York: Harper and Row,* 1972).

times. But little more needs to be said *about* existentialism, for nothing could be further from the existential attitude than attempts to define existentialism, except perhaps a discussion *about* the attempts to define existentialism.

12. In conformity with my belief that philosophical statements are a form of conceptual sculpture, I have tried to arrange the following selections as in a gallery, with each author's works prefaced by a brief introduction to give the reader some orientation. Biographical material has been kept to bare essentials, namely, dates and native country (and, where different, country of residence).

Existentialism

Søren Kierkegaard

(1813–1855) ———————— DANISH

It is generally acknowledged that if existentialism is a "movement" at all, Søren Kierkegaard is its prime mover. Referring to himself as "that Individual," he directs his sarcastic wit and irony against the most powerful institutions of the day—the Lutheran Church, the press, and Hegel's philosophy. However, these indictments of the church and press and ad hominem attacks upon Hegel are but targets for his fundamental objection to the hyperreflectiveness, lack of passion, and collective contempt for the individual that Kierkegaard takes to be endemic of "the Present Age." In place of the search for science and objectivity that had motivated Kant and Hegel, Kierkegaard substitutes "subjective truth," choice and passion, and he turns our attention back to the individual and away from the "collective idea" and the philosophical system. In Either/Or, we are told that human existence (a very special notion for Kierkegaard and the later existentialists) is choice. Either/Or contains a dialogue between two life styles or "spheres of existence," the aesthetic life of pleasure, self-indulgence, and personal taste (represented by a young Don Juan) and the ethical life of moral principle and duty (represented by an elderly judge). The dialogue remains conscientiously without resolution, for it is the presupposition of Kierkegaard's existentialism that there is no "rational" resolution to such choices. Yet it is also clear that Kierkegaard wants to encourage the choice of the ethical. This paradox runs throughout the existentialists. It is central to their arguments that there is no "better" choice, yet each wants to defend and promote some particular position.

A similar crisis of decision between the secular ethical life and the religious life is dramatically exemplified in the Old Testament story of Abraham and Isaac retold and interpreted by Kierkegaard in the excerpt from Fear *and* Trembling *that follows. Kierkegaard's own choice of existence is a "leap" to the religious, that is, the Christian, way of life. After 1846*

3

Kierkegaard defines his efforts as "a Socratic task—to revise the conception of what it is to be a Christian." His harsh attacks upon Christendom—the secularized Christian public —are intended to dramatize just how opposed being a Christian in Christendom is to becoming a Christian in Kierkegaard's sense.

Kierkegaard's most systematic work, written pseudonymously, is his Concluding Unscientific Postscript. *In selections from that work included here, he explains his central notion of subjective truth, a concept that supports the earlier arguments in* Either/Or *and* Fear and Trembling. *The opening selection, from* The Present Age, *is a relatively late work (1846) which captures, as well as any other document of the existentialist movement, the temperament of personal revolt and sense of "untimeliness" that these thinkers share. And because so much of Kierkegaard's best writing is to be found in scattered entries in his notebooks and journals, I have placed a sampling of them among the longer selections.*

from
THE PRESENT AGE

Our age is essentially one of understanding and reflection, without passion, momentarily bursting into enthusiasm, and shrewdly relapsing into repose.

If we had statistical tables of the consumption of intelligence from generation to generation as we have for spirits, we should be astounded at the enormous amount of scruple and deliberation consumed by small, well-to-do families living quietly, and at the amount which the young, and even children, use. For just as the children's crusade may be said to typify the Middle Ages, precocious children are typical of the present age. In fact one is tempted to ask whether there is a single man left ready, for once, to commit an outrageous folly.

Nowadays not even a suicide kills himself in desperation.

From *The Present Age* by Søren Kierkegaard, translated by Alexander Dru and Walter Lowrie. Oxford University Press, 1962. Reprinted by permission of Alexander Dru.

Before taking the step he deliberates so long and so carefully that he literally chokes with thought. It is even questionable whether he ought to be called a suicide, since it is really thought which takes his life. He does not die *with* deliberation but *from* deliberation.

It would therefore be very difficult to prosecute the present generation in view of its legal quibbles: in fact, its ability, virtuosity, and good sense consist in trying to reach a judgement and a decision without ever going as far as action. If one may say of the revolutionary period that it runs wild, one would have to say of the present that it runs badly. Between them, the individual and his generation always bring each other to a standstill, with the result that the prosecuting attorney would find it next to impossible to get any fact admitted —because nothing really happens. To judge from innumerable indications, one would conclude that something quite exceptional had either just happened or was just about to happen. Yet any such conclusion would be quite wrong. Indications are, indeed, the only achievements of the age; and its skill and inventiveness in constructing fascinating illusions, its bursts of enthusiasm, using as a deceitful escape some projected change of form, must be rated as high in the scale of cleverness and of the negative use of strength as the passionate, creative energy of the revolution in the corresponding scale of energy. But the present generation, wearied by its chimerical efforts, relapses into complete indolence. Its condition is that of a man who has only fallen asleep towards morning: first of all come great dreams, then a feeling of laziness, and finally a witty or clever excuse for remaining in bed.

· · ·

A revolutionary age is an age of action; ours is the age of advertisement and publicity. Nothing ever happens but there is immediate publicity everywhere. In the present age a rebellion is, of all things, the most unthinkable.* Such an expression of strength would seem ridiculous to the calculating intelligence of our times. On the other hand a political virtuoso might bring off a feat almost as remarkable. He might write a manifesto suggesting a general assembly at which people should decide upon a rebellion, and it would be so

* *Written in 1846! (Editor's note.)*

carefully worded that even the censor would let it pass. At the meeting itself he would be able to create the impression that his audience had rebelled, after which they would all go quietly home—having spent a very pleasant evening.

. . .

This reflective tension ultimately constitutes itself into a principle, and just as in a passionate age *enthusiasm* is the unifying principle, so in an age which is very reflective and passionless *envy* is the negative unifying principle. This must not, however, be interpreted as an ethical charge; the idea of reflection is, if one may so express it, envy, and it is therefore twofold in its action: it is selfish within the individual and it results in the selfishness of the society around him, which thus works against him.

. . .

But the further it is carried the more clearly does the envy of reflection become a moral *ressentiment*. Just as air in a sealed space becomes poisonous, so the imprisonment of reflection develops a culpable *ressentiment* if it is not ventilated by action or incident of any kind. In reflection the state of strain (or tension as we called it) results in the neutralization of all the higher powers, and all that is low and despicable comes to the fore, its very impudence giving the spurious effect of strength, while protected by its very baseness it avoids attracting the attention of *ressentiment*.

It is a fundamental truth of human nature that man is incapable of remaining permanently on the heights, of continuing to admire anything. Human nature needs variety. Even in the most enthusiastic ages people have always liked to joke enviously about their superiors. That is perfectly in order and is entirely justifiable so long as after having laughed at the great they can once more look upon them with admiration; otherwise the game is not worth the candle. In that way *ressentiment* finds an outlet even in an enthusiastic age. And as long as an age, even though less enthusiastic, has the strength to give *ressentiment* its proper character and has made up its mind what its expression signifies, *ressentiment* has its own, though dangerous, importance. . . .

On the other side, the more reflection gets the upper hand and thus makes people indolent, the more dangerous *ressentiment* becomes, because it no longer has sufficient character to make it conscious of its significance. Bereft of that character reflection is cowardly and vacillating, and according to circumstances interprets the same thing in a variety of ways. It tries to treat it as a joke, and if that fails, to regard it as an insult, and when that fails, to dismiss it as nothing at all; or else it will treat the thing as a witticism, and if that fails then say that it was meant as a moral satire deserving attention, and if that does not succeed, add that it is not worth bothering about.

. . .

The *ressentiment* which is *establishing itself* is the process of levelling, and while a passionate age storms ahead setting up new things and tearing down old, raising and demolishing as it goes, a reflective and passionless age does exactly the contrary: it *hinders and stifles* all action; it levels. Levelling is a silent, mathematical, and abstract occupation which shuns upheavals.

. . .

In order that everything should be reduced to the same level it is first of all necessary to procure a phantom, its spirit, a monstrous abstraction, an all-embracing something which is nothing, a mirage—and that phantom is *the public*. It is only in an age which is without passion, yet reflective, that such a phantom can develop itself with the help of the press which itself becomes an abstraction. In times of passion and tumult and enthusiasm, even when a people desire to realize a fruitless idea and lay waste and destroy everything: even then there is no such thing as a public.

. . .

A public is everything and nothing, the most dangerous of all powers and the most insignificant: one can speak to a whole nation in the name of the public and still the public will be less than a single real man however unimportant. The qualification "public" is produced by the deceptive juggling of an age of reflection which makes it appear flattering to the individual who in this way can arrogate to himself this monster in comparison with which concrete realities seem poor. The public is the fairy story of an age of understanding which in imagination makes the individual into something even greater than a king above his people; but the public is also a gruesome abstraction through which the individual will receive his religious formation—or sink.

. . .

from
THE JOURNALS

People hardly ever make use of the freedom which they have, for example, freedom of thought; instead they demand freedom of speech as compensation.

The method which begins by doubting in order to philosophize is just as suited to its purpose as making a soldier lie down in a heap in order to teach him to stand up straight.

It is perfectly true, as philosophers say, that life must be understood backwards. But they forget the other proposition, that it must be lived forwards. And if one thinks over that proposition it becomes more and more evident that life can never really be understood in time simply because at no particular moment can I find the necessary resting place from which to understand it—backwards.

In relation to their systems most systematizers are like a man who builds an enormous castle and lives in a shack close by; they do not live in their own enormous systematic buildings. But spiritually that is a decisive objection. Spiritually speaking a man's thought must be the building in which he lives—otherwise everything is topsy-turvy.

Like Leporello learned literary men keep a list, but the point is what they lack; while Don Juan seduces girls and enjoys himself—Leporello notes down the time, the place and a description of the girl.

I always say: all honour to the sciences, etc.
But the thing is that bit by bit people have tried to popularize the scientific spirit, it has forced its way down among the people—true religiousness has gone to pot, and existential respect is lost.

From *The Journals* by Søren Kierkegaard, translated by Alexander Dru. Oxford University Press, 1938. Reprinted by permission of Alexander Dru.

I have just returned from a party of which I was the life and soul; wit poured from my lips, everyone laughed and admired me—but I went away—and the dash should be as long as the earth's orbit ——————————— and wanted to shoot myself.

. . . What I really lack is to be clear in my mind *what I am to do*, not what I am to know, except insofar as a certain understanding must precede every action. The thing is to understand myself, to see what God really wishes *me* to do; the thing is to find a truth which is true *for me*, to find *the idea for which I can live and die*. What would be the use of discovering so-called objective truth, of working through all the systems of philosophy and of being able, if required, to review them all and show up the inconsistencies within each system; what good would it do me to be able to develop a theory of the state and combine all the details into a single whole, and so construct a world in which I did not live, but only held up to the view of others; what good would it do me to be able to explain the meaning of Christianity if it had *no* deeper significance *for me and for my life*; what good would it do me if truth stood before me, cold and naked, not caring whether I recognized her or not, and producing in me a shudder of fear rather than a trusting devotion? I certainly do not deny that I still recognize an *imperative of understanding* and that through it one can work upon men, *but it must be taken up into my life*, and *that* is what I now recognize as the most important thing. . . .

THE ROTATION METHOD

Starting from a principle is affirmed by people of experience to be a very reasonable procedure; I am willing to humor them, and so begin with the principle that all men are bores.

From *Either/Or* by Søren Kierkegaard, Vol. I, translated by David F. Swenson and Lillian Marvin Swenson; Vol. II, translated by Walter Lowrie; both Vols. I and II with Revisions and a Foreword by Howard A. Johnson. Copyright 1944 © 1959 by Princeton University Press; Princeton Paperback, 1971. Reprinted by permission of Princeton University Press.

Surely no one will prove himself so great a bore as to contradict me in this. This principle possesses the quality of being in the highest degree repellent, an essential requirement in the case of negative principles, which are in the last analysis the principles of all motion. It is not merely repellent, but infinitely forbidding; and whoever has this principle back of him cannot but receive an infinite impetus forward, to help him make new discoveries. For if my principle is true, one need only consider how ruinous boredom is for humanity, and by properly adjusting the intensity of one's concentration upon this fundamental truth, attain any desired degree of momentum. Should one wish to attain the maximum momentum, even to the point of almost endangering the driving power, one need only say to oneself: Boredom is the root of all evil. Strange that boredom, in itself so staid and stolid, should have such power to set in motion. The influence it exerts is altogether magical, except that it is not the influence of attraction, but of repulsion.

. . .

The history of this can be traced from the very beginning of the world. The gods were bored, and so they created man. Adam was bored because he was alone, and so Eve was created. Thus boredom entered the world, and increased in proportion to the increase of population. Adam was bored alone; then Adam and Eve were bored together; then Adam and Eve and Cain and Abel were bored *en famille*; then the population of the world increased, and the peoples were bored *en masse*. To divert themselves they conceived the idea of constructing a tower high enough to reach the heavens. This idea is itself as boring as the tower was high, and constitutes a terrible proof of how boredom gained the upper hand. The nations were scattered over the earth, just as people now travel abroad, but they continued to be bored. Consider the consequences of this boredom. Humanity fell from its lofty height, first because of Eve, and then from the Tower of Babel. What was it, on the other hand, that delayed the fall of Rome, was it not *panis* and *circenses*?[1] And is anything being done now? Is anyone concerned about planning some means of diversion? Quite the contrary, the impending ruin is being proclaimed. It is proposed to call a constitutional assem-

[1] *Bread and circuses.*

bly. Can anything more tiresome be imagined, both for the participants themselves, and for those who have to hear and read about it? It is proposed to improve the financial condition of the state by practicing economy. What could be more tiresome? Instead of increasing the national debt, it is proposed to pay it off. As I understand the political situation, it would be an easy matter for Denmark to negotiate a loan of fifteen million dollars. Why not consider this plan? Every once in a while we hear of a man who is a genius, and therefore neglects to pay his debts—why should not a nation do the same, if we were all agreed? Let us then borrow fifteen millions, and let us use the proceeds, not to pay our debts, but for public entertainment. Let us celebrate the millennium in a riot of merriment. Let us place boxes everywhere, not, as at present, for the deposit of money, but for the free distribution of money. Everything would become gratis; theaters gratis, women of easy virtue gratis, one would drive to the park gratis, be buried gratis, one's eulogy would be gratis; I say gratis, for when one always has money at hand, everything is in a certain sense free. No one should be permitted to own any property. Only in my own case would there be an exception. I reserve to myself securities in the Bank of London to the value of one hundred dollars a day, partly because I cannot do with less, partly because the idea is mine, and finally because I may not be able to hit upon a new idea when the fifteen millions are gone. . . .

All men are bores. The word itself suggests the possibility of a subdivision. It may just as well indicate a man who bores others as one who bores himself. Those who bore others are the mob, the crowd, the infinite multitude of men in general. Those who bore themselves are the elect, the aristocracy; and it is a curious fact that those who do not bore themselves usually bore others, while those who bore themselves entertain others. Those who do not bore themselves are generally people who, in one way or another, keep themselves extremely busy; these people are precisely on this account the most tiresome, the most utterly unendurable.

. . .

Now since boredom, as shown above, is the root of all evil, what can be more natural than the effort to overcome it? Here, as everywhere, however, it is necessary to give the problem calm consideration; otherwise one may find oneself driven by the demoniac spirit of boredom deeper and deeper into the mire, in the very effort to escape. Everyone who feels bored cries out for change. With this demand I am in complete sympathy, but it is necessary to act in accordance with some settled principle.

My own dissent from the ordinary view is sufficiently expressed in the use I make of the word "rotation." This word might seem to conceal an ambiguity, and if I wished to use it so as to find room in it for the ordinary method, I should have to define it as a change of field. But the farmer does not use the word in this sense. I shall, however, adopt this meaning for a moment, in order to speak of the rotation which depends on change in its boundless infinity, its extensive dimension, so to speak.

This is the vulgar and inartistic method, and needs to be supported by illusion. One tires of living in the country, and moves to the city; one tires of one's native land, and travels abroad; one is *europamüde*, and goes to America, and so on; finally one indulges in a sentimental hope of endless journeyings from star to star. Or the movement is different but still extensive. One tires of porcelain dishes and eats on silver; one tires of silver and turns to gold; one burns half of Rome to get an idea of the burning of Troy. This method defeats itself; it is plain endlessness. And what did Nero gain by it? Antonine was wiser; he says: "It is in your power to review your life, to look at things you saw before, but from another point of view."

My method does not consist in change of field, but resembles the true rotation method in changing the crop and the mode of cultivation. Here we have at once the principle of limitation, the only saving principle in the world. The more you limit yourself, the more fertile you become in invention. A prisoner in solitary confinement for life becomes very inventive, and a spider may furnish him with much entertainment. One need only hark back to one's schooldays, when aesthetic considerations were ignored in the choice of one's instructors, who were consequently very tiresome: how fertile in invention did not one prove to be! How entertaining to catch a fly and hold it imprisoned under a nut shell, watching it run around the shell; what pleasure, from cutting a hole in the desk, putting a fly in it, and then peeping down at it through a piece of paper! How entertaining sometimes to listen to the monotonous drip of water from the roof! How close an observer does not one become under such circumstances, when not the least noise nor movement escapes one's attention! Here we have the extreme application of the method which seeks to achieve results intensively, not extensively.

. . .

. . . Your whole nature contradicts itself. But you can only get out of this contradiction by an either/or . . .

Now in case a man were able to maintain himself upon the pinnacle of the instant of choice, in case he could cease to be a man, in case he were in his inmost nature only an airy thought, in case personality meant nothing more than to be a kobold, which takes part indeed in the movements, but nevertheless remains unchanged; in case such were the situation, it would be foolish to say that it might ever be too late for a man to choose, for in a deeper sense there could be no question of a choice. The choice itself is decisive for the content of the personality, through the choice the personality immerses itself in the thing chosen, and when it does not choose it withers away in consumption. For an instant it is as if, for an instant it may seem as if the thing with regard to which a choice was made lay outside of the chooser, that he stands in no relationship to it, that he can preserve a state of indifference over against it. This is the instant of deliberation, but this, like the Platonic instant, has no existence, least of all in the abstract sense in which you would hold it fast, and the longer one stares at it the less it exists. That which has to be chosen stands in the deepest relationship to the chooser and, when it is a question of a choice involving a life problem, the individual must naturally be living in the meantime; hence it comes about that the longer he postpones the choice the easier it is for him to alter its character, notwithstanding that he is constantly deliberating and deliberating and believes that thereby he is holding the alternatives distinctly apart. When life's either/or is regarded in this way, one is not easily tempted to jest with it. One sees, then, that the inner drift of the personality leaves no time for thought-experiments, that it constantly hastens onward and in one way or another posits this alternative or that, making the choice the more difficult the next instant, because what has thus been posited must be revoked. Think of the captain on his ship at the instant when it has to come about. He will perhaps be able to say, "I can either do this or that"; but in case he is not a pretty poor navigator, he will be aware at the same time that the ship is all the while making its usual headway, and that therefore it is only an instant when it is indifferent whether he does this or that. So it is with a man. If he forgets to take account of the headway, there comes at last an instant when there no longer is any question of an either/or, not because he has chosen but because he has neglected to choose, which is equivalent to saying, because others have chosen for him, because he has lost his self.

. . .

What is it, then, that I distinguish in my either/or? Is it good and evil? No, I would only bring you up to the point where the choice between the evil and the good acquires significance for you. Everything hinges upon this. As soon as one can get a man to stand at the crossways in such a position that there is no recourse but to choose, he will choose the right. Hence if it should chance that, while you are in the course of reading this somewhat lengthy dissertation, you were to feel that the instant for choice had come, then throw the rest of this away, never concern yourself about it, you have lost nothing—but choose, and you shall see what validity there is in this act, yea, no young girl can be so happy in the choice of her heart as is a man who knows how to choose. So then, one either has to live aesthetically, or one has to live ethically. In this alternative, as I have said, there is not yet in the strictest sense any question of a choice; for he who lives aesthetically does not choose, and he who after the ethical has manifested itself to him chooses the aesthetical is not living aesthetically, for he is sinning and is subject to ethical determinants even though his life may be described as unethical. . . .

IS THERE SUCH A THING AS A TELEOLOGICAL SUSPENSION OF THE ETHICAL?

The ethical as such is the universal, it applies to everyone and the same thing is expressed from another point of view by saying that it applies every instant. It reposes immanently

From *Fear and Trembling* and *The Sickness Unto Death* by Søren Kierkegaard, translated by Walter Lowrie. Copyright 1941, 1954 by Princeton University Press; Princeton Paperback, 1968. Reprinted by permission of Princeton University Press.

in itself, it has nothing outside itself which is its *telos*, but is itself *telos* for everything outside it, and when this has been incorporated by the ethical it can go no further. Conceived immediately as physical and psychical, the particular individual is the particular which has its *telos* in the universal, and its task is to express itself constantly in it, to abolish its particularity in order to become the universal. As soon as the individual would assert himself in his particularity over against the universal he sins, and only by recognizing this can he again reconcile himself with the universal. . . .

Faith is precisely this paradox, that the individual as the particular is higher than the universal, is justified over against it, is not subordinate but superior—yet in such a way, be it observed, that it is the particular individual who, after he has been subordinated as the particular to the universal, now through the universal becomes the individual who as the particular is superior to the universal, *inasmuch as the individual as the particular stands in an absolute relation to the absolute*. This position cannot be mediated, for all mediation comes about precisely by virtue of the universal; it is and remains to all eternity a paradox, inaccessible to thought. And yet faith is this paradox. . . .

Now the story of Abraham contains such a teleological suspension of the ethical. . . . Abraham's relation to Isaac, ethically speaking, is quite simply expressed by saying that a father shall love his son more dearly than himself. Yet within its own compass the ethical has various gradations. Let us see whether in this story there is to be found any higher expression for the ethical such as would ethically explain his conduct, ethically justify him in suspending the ethical obligation toward his son, without in this search going beyond the teleology of the ethical.

. . .

The difference between the tragic hero and Abraham is clearly evident. The tragic hero still remains within the ethical. He lets one expression of the ethical find its *telos* in a higher expression of the ethical; the ethical relation between father and son, or daughter and father, he reduces to a sentiment which has its dialectic in the idea of morality. Here there can be no question of a teleological suspension of the ethical.

With Abraham the situation was different. By his act he overstepped the ethical entirely and possessed a higher *telos* outside of it, in relation to which he suspended the former.

For I should very much like to know how one would bring Abraham's act into relation with the universal, and whether it is possible to discover any connection whatever between what Abraham did and the universal—except the fact that he transgressed it. It was not for the sake of saving a people, not to maintain the idea of the state, that Abraham did this, and not in order to reconcile angry deities. If there could be a question of the deity being angry, he was angry only with Abraham, and Abraham's whole action stands in no relation to the universal; it is a purely personal undertaking. Therefore, whereas the tragic hero is great by reason of his moral virtue, Abraham is great by reason of a personal virtue. In Abraham's life there is no higher expression for the ethical than this, that the father shall love his son. Of the ethical in the sense of morality there can be no question in this instance. Insofar as the universal was present, it was indeed cryptically present in Isaac, hidden as it were in Isaac's loins, and must therefore cry out with Isaac's mouth, "Do it not! Thou art bringing everything to naught."

Why then did Abraham do it? For God's sake, and (in complete identity with this) for his own sake. He did it for God's sake because God required this proof of his faith; for his own sake he did it in order that he might furnish the proof. The unity of these two points of view is perfectly expressed by the word which has always been used to characterize this situation: it is a trial, a temptation (*Fristelse*). A temptation —but what does that mean? What ordinarily tempts a man is that which would keep him from doing his duty, but in this case the temptation is itself the ethical—which would keep him from doing God's will.

Here is evident the necessity of a new category if one would understand Abraham. Such a relationship to the deity paganism did not know. The tragic hero does not enter into any private relationship with the deity, but for him the ethical is the divine, hence the paradox implied in his situation can be mediated in the universal.

• • •

The story of Abraham contains therefore a teleological suspension of the ethical. As the individual he became higher than the universal: this is the paradox which does not permit of mediation. It is just as inexplicable how he got into it as it is inexplicable how he remained in it. If such is not the position of Abraham, then he is not even a tragic hero but a murderer. To want to continue to call him the father of faith, to talk of this to people who do not concern themselves with anything but words, is thoughtless. A man can become a tragic hero by his own powers—but not a knight of faith. When a man enters upon the way, in a certain sense the hard way of the tragic hero, many will be able to give him counsel; to him who follows the narrow way of faith no one can give counsel, him no one can understand. Faith is a miracle, and yet no man is excluded from it; for that in which all human life is unified is passion, and faith is a passion.

TRUTH IS SUBJECTIVITY

. . . In an attempt to make clear the difference of way that exists between an objective and a subjective reflection, I shall now proceed to show how a subjective reflection makes its way inwardly in inwardness. Inwardness in an existing subject culminates in passion; corresponding to passion in the subject the truth becomes a paradox; and the fact that the truth becomes a paradox is rooted precisely in its having a relationship to an existing subject. Thus the one corresponds to the other. By forgetting that one is an existing subject, passion goes by the board and the truth is no longer a paradox; the knowing subject becomes a fantastic entity rather than a human being, and the truth becomes a fantastic object for the knowledge of this fantastic entity.

When the question of truth is raised in an objective manner, reflection is directed objectively to the truth, as an object to which the knower is related. Reflection is not focussed upon the relationship, however, but upon the question of whether it is the truth to which the knower is related. If only the object to which he is related is the truth, the subject is accounted to be in the truth. When the question of the truth is raised subjectively, reflection is directed subjectively to the nature of the individual's relationship; if only the mode of this

From *Concluding Unscientific Postscript* by Søren Kierkegaard, translated by David F. Swenson and Walter Lowrie. Copyright 1941 © 1969 by Princeton University Press; Princeton Paperback, 1968. Reprinted by permission of Princeton University Press and the American Scandinavian Foundation.

*relationship is in the truth, the individual is in the truth even
if he should happen to be thus related to what is not true.*
Let us take as an example the knowledge of God. Objectively,
reflection is directed to the problem of whether this object is
the true God; subjectively, reflection is directed to the question
whether the individual is related to a something *in such
a manner* that his relationship is in truth a God-relationship.
On which side is the truth now to be found? Ah, may we not
here resort to a mediation, and say: It is on neither side, but
in the mediation of both? Excellently well said, provided we
might have it explained how an existing individual manages
to be in a state of mediation. For to be in a state of mediation
is to be finished, while to exist is to become. Nor can an existing
individual be in two places at the same time—he cannot
be an identity of subject and object. When he is nearest to
being in two places at the same time he is in passion; but
passion is momentary, and passion is also the highest expression
of subjectivity.

The existing individual who chooses to pursue the objective
way enters upon the entire approximation-process by which
it is proposed to bring God to light objectively. But this is in
all eternity impossible, because God is a subject, and therefore
exists only for subjectivity in inwardness. The existing
individual who chooses the subjective way apprehends instantly
the entire dialectical difficulty involved in having to
use some time, perhaps a long time, in finding God objectively;
and he feels this dialectical difficulty in all its painfulness,
because every moment is wasted in which he does not
have God. That very instant he has God, not by virtue of any
objective deliberation, but by virtue of the infinite passion of
inwardness. The objective inquirer, on the other hand, is not
embarrassed by such dialectical difficulties as are involved in
devoting an entire period of investigation to finding God—
since it is possible that the inquirer may die tomorrow; and
if he lives he can scarcely regard God as something to be
taken along if convenient, since God is precisely that which
one takes *a tout prix*, which in the understanding of passion
constitutes the true inward relationship to God.

It is at this point, so difficult dialectically, that the way
swings off for everyone who knows what it means to think,
and to think existentially; which is something very different
from sitting at a desk and writing about what one has never
done, something very different from writing *de omnibus dubi-*

tandum and at the same time being as credulous existentially as the most sensuous of men. Here is where the way swings off, and the change is marked by the fact that while objective knowledge rambles comfortably on by way of the long road of approximation without being impelled by the urge of passion, subjective knowledge counts every delay a deadly peril, and the decision so infinitely important and so instantly pressing that it is as if the opportunity had already passed.

Now when the problem is to reckon up on which side there is most truth, whether on the side of one who seeks the true God objectively, and pursues the approximate truth of the God-idea; or on the side of one who, driven by the infinite passion of his need of God, feels an infinite concern for his own relationship to God in truth (and to be at one and the same time on both sides equally, is as we have noted not possible for an existing individual, but is merely the happy delusion of an imaginary I-am-I): the answer cannot be in doubt for anyone who has not been demoralized with the aid of science. If one who lives in the midst of Christendom goes up to the house of God, the house of the true God, with the true conception of God in his knowledge, and prays, but prays in a false spirit; and one who lives in an idolatrous community prays with the entire passion of the infinite, although his eyes rest upon the image of an idol: where is there most truth? The one prays in truth to God though he worships an idol; the other prays falsely to the true God, and hence worships in fact an idol.

When one man investigates objectively the problem of immortality, and another embraces an uncertainty with the passion of the infinite: where is there most truth, and who has the greater certainty? The one has entered upon a never-ending approximation, for the certainty of immorality lies precisely in the subjectivity of the individual; the other is immortal, and fights for his immortality by struggling with the uncertainty. Let us consider Socrates. Nowadays everyone dabbles in a few proofs; some have several such proofs, others fewer. But Socrates! He puts the question objectively in a problematic manner: *if* there is an immortality. He must therefore be accounted a doubter in comparison with one of our modern thinkers with the three proofs? By no means. On this "if" he risks his entire life, he has the courage to meet death, and he has with the passion of the infinite so determined the pattern of his life that it must be found acceptable

—*if* there is an immortality. Is any better proof capable of being given for the immortality of the soul? But those who have the three proofs do not at all determine their lives in conformity therewith; if there is an immortality it must feel disgust over their manner of life: can any better refutation be given of the three proofs? The bit of uncertainty that Socrates had, helped him because he himself contributed the passion of the infinite; the three proofs that the others have do not profit them at all, because they are dead to spirit and enthusiasm, and their three proofs, in lieu of proving anything else, prove just this. A young girl may enjoy all the sweetness of love on the basis of what is merely a weak hope that she is beloved, because she rests everything on this weak hope; but many a wedded matron more than once subjected to the strongest expressions of love, has in so far indeed had proofs, but strangely enough has not enjoyed *quod erat demonstrandum*. The Socratic ignorance, which Socrates held fast with the entire passion of his inwardness, was thus an expression for the principle that the eternal truth is related to an existing individual, and that this truth must therefore be a paradox for him as long as he exists; and yet it is possible that there was more truth in the Socratic ignorance as it was in him, than in the entire objective truth of the System, which flirts with what the times demand and accommodates itself to *Privatdocents*.

The objective accent falls on WHAT is said, the subjective accent on HOW it is said. This distinction holds even in the aesthetic realm, and receives definite expression in the principle that what is in itself true may in the mouth of such and such a person become untrue. In these times this distinction is particularly worthy of notice, for if we wish to express in a single sentence the difference between ancient times and our own, we should doubtless have to say: In ancient times only an individual here and there knew the truth; now all know it, except that the inwardness of its appropriation stands in an inverse relationship to the extent of its dissemination. Aesthetically the contradiction that truth becomes untruth in this or that person's mouth, is best construed comically: In the ethico-religious sphere, accent is again on the "how." But this is not to be understood as referring to demeanor, expression, or the like; rather it refers to the relationship sustained by the existing individual, in his own existence, to the content of his utterance. Objectively the interest is focussed merely on the thought-content, subjectively on the inwardness. At its maximum this inward "how" is the passion of the infinite, and the passion of the infinite is the truth. But the passion of the infinite is precisely subjectivity, and thus subjectivity becomes the truth. Objectively there is no infinite decisiveness, and hence it is objectively in order to annul the difference between good and evil, together with the principle of contradiction, and therewith also the infinite difference between the true and the false. Only in subjectivity is there decisiveness, to seek objectivity is to be in error. It is the passion of the infinite that is the decisive factor and not its content, for its content is precisely itself. In this manner subjectivity and the subjective "how" constitute the truth.

But the "how" which is thus subjectively accentuated precisely because the subject is an existing individual, is also subject to a dialectic with respect to time. In the passionate moment of decision, where the road swings away from objective knowledge, it seems as if the infinite decision were thereby realized. But in the same moment the existing individual finds himself in the temporal order, and the subjective "how" is transformed into a striving, a striving which receives indeed its impulse and a repeated renewal from the decisive passion of the infinite, but is nevertheless a striving.

When subjectivity is the truth, the conceptual determination of the truth must include an expression for the antithesis to objectivity, a memento of the fork in the road where the way swings off; this expression will at the same time serve as an indication of the tension of the subjective inwardness. Here is such a definition of truth: *An objective uncertainty held fast in an appropriation-process of the most passionate inwardness is the truth*, the highest truth attainable for an *existing* individual. At the point where the way swings off (and where this is cannot be specified objectively, since it is a matter of subjectivity), there objective knowledge is placed in abeyance. Thus the subject merely has, objectively, the uncertainty; but it is this which precisely increases the tension of that infinite passion which constitutes his inwardness. The truth is precisely the venture which chooses an objective uncertainty with the passion of the infinite. I contemplate the order of nature in the hope of finding God, and I see omnipotence and wisdom; but I also see much else that disturbs my mind and excites anxiety. The sum of all this is an objective uncertainty. But it is for this very reason that the inwardness becomes as intense as it is, for it embraces this objective uncertainty with the entire passion of the infinite. In the case of a mathematical proposition the objectivity is given, but for this reason the truth of such a proposition is also an indifferent truth.

But the above definition of truth is an equivalent expression for faith. Without risk there is no faith. Faith is precisely the contradiction between the infinite passion of the individual's inwardness and the objective uncertainty. If I am capable of grasping God objectively, I do not believe, but precisely because I cannot do this I must believe. If I wish to preserve myself in faith I must constantly be intent upon holding fast the objective uncertainty, so as to remain out upon the deep, over seventy thousand fathoms of water, still preserving my faith.

It is impossible to exist without passion, unless we understand the word "exist" in the loose sense of a so-called existence. Every Greek thinker was therefore essentially a passionate thinker. I have often reflected how one might bring a man into a state of passion. I have thought in this connection that if I could get him seated on a horse and the horse made to take fright and gallop wildly, or better still, for the sake of bringing the passion out, if I could take a man who wanted to arrive at a certain place as quickly as possible, and hence already had some passion, and could set him astride a horse that can scarcely walk—and yet this is what existence is like if one is to become consciously aware of it. Or if a driver were otherwise not especially inclined toward passion, if someone hitched a team of horses to a wagon for him, one of them a Pegasus and the other a worn-out jade, and told him to drive—I think one might succeed. And it is just this that it means to exist, if one is to become conscious of it. Eternity is the winged horse, infinitely fast, and time is a worn-out jade; the existing individual is the driver. That is to say, he is such a driver when his mode of existence is not an existence loosely so called; for then he is no driver, but a drunken peasant who lies asleep in the wagon and lets the horses take care of themselves. To be sure, he also drives and is a driver; and so there are perhaps many who—also exist.

The way of objective reflection makes the subject accidental, and thereby transforms existence into something indifferent, something vanishing. Away from the subject the objective way of reflection leads to the objective truth, and while the subject and his subjectivity become indifferent, and this indifference is precisely its objective validity; for all interest, like all decisiveness, is rooted in subjectivity. The way of objective reflection leads to abstract thought, to mathematics, to historical knowledge of different kinds; and always it leads away from the subject, whose existence or non-existence, and from the objective point of view quite rightly, becomes infinitely indifferent. Quite rightly, since as Hamlet says, existence and non-existence have only subjective significance. . . .

In spite of all his exertion the subjective thinker enjoys only a meager reward. The more the collective idea comes to dominate even the ordinary consciousness, the more forbidding seems the transition to becoming a particular existing human being instead of losing oneself in the race, and saying "we," "our age," "the nineteenth century." That it is a little thing merely to be a particular existing human being is not to be denied; but for this very reason it requires considerable resignation not to make light of it. For what does a mere individual count for? Our age knows only too well how little it is, but here also lies the specific immorality of the age. Each age has its own characteristic depravity. Ours is perhaps not pleasure or indulgence or sensuality, but rather a dissolute pantheistic contempt for the individual man. In the midst of all our exultation over the achievements of the age and the nineteenth century, there sounds a note of poorly conceived contempt for the individual man; in the midst of the self-importance of the contemporary generation there is revealed a sense of despair over being human. Everything must attach itself so as to be a part of some movement; men are determined to lose themselves in the totality of things, in world-history, fascinated and deceived by a magic witchery; no one wants to be an individual human being. Hence perhaps the many attempts to continue clinging to Hegel, even by men who have reached an insight into the questionable character of his philosophy. It is a fear that if they were to become particular existing human beings, they would vanish tracelessly, so that not even the daily press would be able to discover them, still less critical journals, to say nothing at all of speculative philosophers immersed in world-history. As particular human beings they fear that they will be doomed to a more isolated and forgotten existence than that of a man in the country; for if a man lets go of Hegel he will not even be in a position to have a letter addressed to him.

ON BECOMING A CHRISTIAN

My only analogy is Socrates. My task is a Socratic task—to revise the conception of what it means to be a Christian.

(Attack upon Christendom)

What now is the absurd? The absurd is—that the eternal truth has come into being in time, that God has come into being, has been born, has grown up, and so forth, precisely like any other individual human being, quite indistinguishable from other individuals. . . .

(Concluding Unscientific Postscript)

. . . The absurd is precisely by its objective repulsion the measure of the intensity of faith in inwardness. Suppose a man who wishes to acquire faith; let the comedy begin. He wishes to have faith, but he wishes also to safeguard himself by means of an objective inquiry and its approximation-process. What happens? With the help of the approximation-process the absurd becomes something different; it becomes probable, it becomes increasingly probable, it becomes extremely and emphatically probable. Now he is ready to believe it, and he ventures to claim for himself that he does not believe as shoe-makers and tailors and simple folk believe, but only after long deliberation. Now he is ready to believe it; and lo, now it has become precisely impossible to believe it. Anything that is almost probable, or probable, or extremely and emphatically probable, is something he can almost know, or as good as know, or extremely and emphatically almost *know*—but it is impossible to *believe*. For the absurd is the object of faith, and the only object that can be believed.

* From *Attack upon Christendom*, 1854–1855, by Søren Kierkegaard, translated by Walter Lowrie. Copyright 1944 by Princeton University Press; Princeton Paperback, 1968. Reprinted by permission of Princeton University Press.

The two ways. One is to suffer; the other is to become a professor of the fact that another suffered.   *(Journals)*

. . . The objective faith, what does that mean? It means a sum of doctrinal propositions. But suppose Christianity were nothing of the kind; suppose on the contrary it were inwardness, and hence also the paradox, so as to thrust the individual away objectively, in order to obtain significance for the existing individual in the inwardness of his existence, in order to place him as decisively as no judge can place an accused person, between time and eternity in time, between heaven and hell in the time of salvation. The objective faith—it is as if Christianity also had been promulgated as a little system, if not quite so good as the Hegelian; it is as if Christ—aye, I speak without offense—it is as if Christ were a professor, and as if the Apostles had formed a little scientific society. Verily, if it was once difficult to become a Christian, now I believe it becomes increasingly difficult year by year, because it has now become so easy that the only ambition which stirs any competition is that of becoming a speculative philosopher. And yet the speculative philosopher is perhaps at the farthest possible remove from Christianity, and it is perhaps far preferable to be an offended individual who nevertheless sustains a relation to Christianity than a speculative philosopher who assumes to have understood it.

. . .

Suppose, on the other hand, that subjectivity is the truth, and that subjectivity is an existing subjectivity, then, if I may so express myself, Christianity fits perfectly into the picture. Subjectivity culminates in passion, Christianity is the paradox, paradox and passion are a mutual fit, and the paradox is altogether suited to one whose situation is, to be in the extremity of existence. Aye, never in all the world could there be found two lovers so wholly suited to one another as paradox and passion, and the strife between them is like the strife between lovers, when the dispute is about whether he first aroused her passion, or she his. And so it is here; the existing individual has by means of the paradox itself come to be placed in the extremity of existence. And what can be more splendid for lovers than that they are permitted a long time together without any alteration in the relationship between them, except that it becomes more intensive in inwardness? And this is indeed granted to the highly unspeculative understanding between passion and the paradox, since the whole of life in time is vouchsafed, and the change comes first in eternity.

. . .

Subjectively, what it is to become a Christian is defined thus:

The decision lies in the subject. The appropriation is the paradoxical inwardness which is specifically different from all other inwardness. The thing of being a Christian is not determined by the *what* of Christianity but by the *how* of the Christian. This *how* can only correspond with one thing, the absolute paradox. There is therefore no vague talk to the effect that being a Christian is to accept, and to accept, and to accept quite differently, to appropriate, to believe, to appropriate by faith quite differently (all of them purely rhetorical and fictitious definitions); but *to believe* is specifically different from all other appropriation and inwardness. *Faith is the objective uncertainty along with the repulsion of the absurd held fast in the passion of inwardness, which precisely is inwardness potentiated to the highest degree.* This formula fits only the believer, no one else, not a lover, not an enthusiast, not a thinker, but simply and solely the believer who is related to the absolute paradox. *(Concluding Unscientific Postscript)*

Can one prove from history that Christ was God? Let me first put another question: Is it possible to conceive of a more foolish contradiction than that of wanting to PROVE (no matter for the present purpose whether it be from history or from anything else in the wide world one wants to *prove* it) that a definite individual man is God? That an individual man is God, declares himself to be God, is indeed the "offense" κατ' ἐξοχήν. But what is the offense, the offensive thing? What is at variance with (human) reason. And such a thing as that one would attempt to prove! To "prove" is to demonstrate something to be the rational reality it is. Can one demonstrate that to be a rational reality which is at variance with reason? Surely not, unless one would contradict oneself. One can "prove" only that it is at variance with reason. The proofs which Scripture presents for Christ's divinity—His miracles, His Resurrection from the dead, His Ascension into heaven— are therefore only for faith, that is, they are not "proofs," they have no intention of proving that all this agrees perfectly with reason; on the contrary they would prove that it conflicts with reason and therefore is an object of faith.

(Training in Christianity)*

. . . So rather let us mock God, out and out, as has been done before in the world—this is always preferable to the disparaging air of importance with which one would prove God's existence. For to prove the existence of one who is present is the most shameless affront, since it is an attempt to make him ridiculous; but unfortunately people have no inkling of this and for sheer seriousness regard it as a pious undertaking. But how could it occur to anybody to prove that he exists, unless one had permitted oneself to ignore him, and now makes the thing all the worse by proving his existence before his very nose? The existence of a king, or his presence, is commonly acknowledged by an appropriate expression of subjection and submission—what if in his sublime presence one were to prove that he existed? Is that the way to prove it? No, that would be making a fool of him; for one proves his presence by an expression of submission, which may assume various forms according to the customs of the country—and thus it is also one proves God's existence by worship . . . not by proofs. A poor wretch of an author whom a later investigator drags out of the obscurity of oblivion may indeed be very glad that the investigator succeeds in proving his existence—but an omnipresent being can only by a thinker's pious blundering be brought to this ridiculous embarrassment.

(Concluding Unscientific Postscript)

To stand on one leg and prove God's existence is a very different thing from going on one's knees and thanking Him.

(Journals)

Christianity is certainly not melancholy, it is, on the contrary, glad tidings—for the melancholy; to the frivolous it is certainly not glad tidings, for it wishes first of all to make them serious.　　　　　　　　　　　　　　　　*(Journals)*

. . . *it is easier to become a Christian when I am not a Christian than to become a Christian when I am one* . . .

(Concluding Unscientific Postscript)

---

* From *Training in Christianity* by Søren Kierkegaard, translated by Walter Lowrie. Princeton University 1944; Princeton Paperback, 1967. Reprinted by permission of Princeton University Press.

The same thing happens to Christianity, or to becoming a Christian, as to all radical cures, one puts it off as long as possible. . . .   *(Journals)*

What Do I Want?

March 1855.

Quite simply: I want honesty. I am not, as well-intentioned people represent (for I can pay no attention to the interpretations of me that are advanced by exasperation and rage and impotence and twaddle), I am not a Christian severity as opposed to a Christian leniency.

By no means. I am neither leniency nor severity: I am—a human honesty.

The leniency which is the common Christianity in the land I want to place alongside of the New Testament in order to see how these two are related to one another.

Then, if it appears, if I or another can prove, that it can be maintained face to face with the New Testament, then with the greatest joy I will agree to it.

But one thing I will not do, not for anything in the world. I will not by suppression, or by performing tricks, try to produce the impression that the ordinary Christianity in the land and the Christianity of the New Testament are alike.

(Attack upon Christendom)

Ivan Turgenev

(1818–1883)   —————◆·◆·◆—————   RUSSIAN

*Turgenev was a Russian novelist and contemporary of Dosto-
evsky. In his best-known work,* Fathers and Sons, *he popularized the concept of nihilism, a concept he may have picked
up from Nadezhdin and other current Russian authors. The
term itself, however, goes at least as far back as Saint Augus-
tine, who used it to refer to unbelievers. Turgenev is very
likely the source for Nietzsche's adoption of the term, although the latter gives it a much more profound place in his
thought. In Turgenev, nihilism refers to lack of respect; in
Nietzsche, it refers to a philosophical problem of justification
as well as to the nihilistic attitudes exemplified by Turgenev's
Bazarov. On its release in Russia, Turgenev's book created
considerable admiration for him among the rebellious young,
although he then took pains to object that he had not at all
attempted a sympathetic defense of nihilism.*

from
FATHERS AND SONS

"What is Bazarov?" Arkady looked amused. "Shall I tell you
what he really is, Uncle?"

"Please do, nephew."

"He is a nihilist."

"A what?" Nikolai Petrovich asked, while Pavel Petrovich
stopped dead, his knife with a dab of butter on the tip
arrested in mid-air.

"He is a nihilist," Arkady repeated.

From *Fathers and Sons* by I. Turgenev, translated by B. Isaacs. Reprinted by
permission of Washington Square Press.

"A nihilist," Nikolai Petrovich said. "That's from the Latin *nihil*—nothing, as far as I can judge. Does that mean a person who . . . who believes in nothing?"

"Say, 'Who respects nothing,'" put in Pavel Petrovich, applying himself to the butter again.

"Who regards everything critically," Arkady observed.

"Isn't that the same thing?" asked Pavel Petrovich.

"No, it isn't. A nihilist is a person who does not look up to any authorities, who does not accept a single principle on faith, no matter how highly that principle may be esteemed."

"Well, and is that a good thing?" Pavel Petrovich broke in.

"It all depends, Uncle. It may be good for some people and very bad for others."

"I see. Well, this, I see, is not in our line. We are men of the old school—we believe that without principles" (he pronounced the word softly, in the French manner, whereas Arkady clipped the word and accentuated the first syllable) "—principles taken on faith, as you put it, one cannot stir a step or draw a breath. *Vous avez changé tout cela*, God grant you good health and a generalship, but we'll be content to look on and admire, *Messieurs les* . . . what do you call them?"

"Nihilists," Arkady said distinctly.

"Yes. We used to have *Hegelists*, now we have nihilists. We shall see how you manage to live in a void, in a vacuum. And now please ring the bell, brother Nikolai Petrovich. It's time for my cocoa."

. . .

"Who wants that logic? We get along without it."

"What do you mean?"

"What I say. You, I trust, don't need logic to put a piece of bread into your mouth when you are hungry. Of what use are these abstract ideas?"

Pavel Petrovich threw up his hands.

"I don't understand you. You insult the Russian people. I don't understand how one can deny principles, maxims! What do you believe in?"

"I've already told you, Uncle, that we don't recognize authorities," interposed Arkady.

"We believe in whatever we consider useful," Bazarov said. "These days negation is more useful than anything else—so we negate."

"Everything?"

"Yes, everything."

"What? Not only art, poetry, but even . . . it's too shocking to utter. . . ."

"Everything," Bazarov repeated with indescribable coolness.

Pavel Petrovich stared at him. He had not expected this. Arkady, on the other hand, flushed with pleasure.

"But, look here," Nikolai Petrovich broke in. "You negate everything or, to be more exact, you destroy everything. But who is going to do the building?"

"That's not our affair. The ground has to be cleared first."

. . .

"I see," Pavel Petrovich interrupted. "So you have convinced yourself of all this and have made up your mind not to tackle anything seriously?"

"And have made up our mind not to tackle anything," Bazarov echoed grimly. He was suddenly annoyed with himself for having loosened his tongue before this aristocrat.

"And do nothing but damn?"

"Do nothing but damn."

"And that's called nihilism?"

"That's called nihilism," Bazarov repeated, this time with pointed insolence.

Pavel Petrovich narrowed his eyes slightly.

"I see!" he said in a singularly calm voice. "Nihilism is to cure all our ills—and you, *you* are our deliverers and heroes. So. But what makes you take the others to task, the denouncers, for instance? Don't you go about ranting like the rest of them?"

"Whatever our faults, that is not one of them," Bazarov muttered.

"What then? Do you act? Do you intend to act?"

Bazarov did not answer. Pavel Petrovich controlled himself with an effort.

Feodor Dostoevsky

(1821–1881) ━━━━━◆━◆━━━━━ RUSSIAN

Freedom and rebellion are central themes in Dostoevsky's writings, from his early short novel The Double *to his last, great works. In* Notes from Underground *(a section of which is reprinted here) Dostoevsky's peculiar protagonist carries on a revolt in the extreme, not only against other people but against nature itself. He refuses to "obey" his own interests, according to the laws of nature. He refuses medical attention and he argues philosophically that nature has no bind on him. For as he becomes conscious of a law of nature, his very consciousness of it constitutes a new variable not accounted for by the law itself. He can then formulate a second-level law that takes knowledge of the first into account, but then his consciousness of this second-level law produces a variable not accounted for in the second law. And even though the laws in question might be laws of "human nature," laws which constitute one's own self-interest, the demand for freedom— or just plain spite—can always provide motivation to act against the natural law. For the man "underground" this hyperconsciousness becomes a disease that renders him incapable of the simplest actions. Equally destructive is the freedom of Stavrogin and Kirilov (of* The Possessed*), who both literally destroy themselves out of freedom. And Ivan Karamazov despairs, "If there is no God, everything is permitted," and goes mad. There are characters in Dostoevsky who are portrayed as both free and good, Alyosha in* The Brothers Karamazov*, Prince Myshkin in* The Idiot*. But Dostoevsky is inevitably more convincing in his voices of nihilism and despairing freedom than he is in the honeyed words of his good men. Purely "negative" freedom has plagued philosophers since Kant (and ultimately since Socrates) and will continue to be the central dilemma of existentialism.*

from
NOTES FROM UNDERGROUND

I am a sick man . . . I am a spiteful man. I am an unpleasant man. I think my liver is diseased. However, I don't know beans about my disease, and I am not sure what is bothering me. I don't treat it and never have, though I respect medicine and doctors. Besides, I am extremely superstitious, let's say sufficiently so to respect medicine. (I am educated enough not to be superstitious, but I am.) No, I refuse to treat it out of spite. You probably will not understand that. Well, but *I* understand it. Of course, I can't explain to you just whom I am annoying in this case by my spite. I am perfectly well aware that I cannot "get even" with the doctors by not consulting them. I know better than anyone that I thereby injure only myself and no one else. But still, if I don't treat it, it is out of spite. My liver is bad, well then—let it get even worse!

. . .

. . . But these are all golden dreams. Oh, tell me, who first declared, who first proclaimed, that man only does nasty things because he does not know his own real interests; and that if he were enlightened, if his eyes were opened to his real normal interests, man would at once cease to do nasty things, would at once become good and noble because, being enlightened and understanding his real advantage, he would see his own advantage in the good and nothing else, and we all know that not a single man can knowingly act to his own disadvantage. Consequently, so to say, he would begin doing good through necessity. Oh, the babe! Oh, the pure, innocent child! Why, in the first place, when in all these thousands of years has there ever been a time when man has acted only for his own advantage? What is to be done with the millions of facts that bear witness that men, *knowingly*, that is, fully understanding their real advantages, have left them in the background and have rushed headlong on another path, to risk, to chance, compelled to this course by nobody and by nothing, but, as it were, precisely because they did not want the beaten track, and stubbornly, wilfully, went off on another

From *Notes from Underground* and *The Grand Inquisitor* by Feodor Dostoevsky, translated by Ralph Matlaw. Copyright © 1960 by E. P. Dutton & Co., Inc., publishers. Reprinted by permission of E. P. Dutton.

difficult, absurd way seeking it almost in the darkness. After
all, it means that this stubbornness and wilfulness were more
pleasant to them than any advantage. Advantage! What is
advantage? And will you take it upon yourself to define with
perfect accuracy in exactly what the advantage of man consists of? And what if it so happens that a man's advantage
sometimes not only may, but even must, consist exactly in his
desiring under certain conditions what is harmful to himself
and not what is advantageous. And if so, if there can be such
a condition then the whole principle becomes worthless. What
do you think—are there such cases? You laugh; laugh away,
gentlemen, so long as you answer me: have man's advantages
been calculated with perfect certainty? Are there not some
which not only have been included but cannot possibly be
included under any classification? After all, you, gentlemen,
so far as I know, have taken your whole register of human
advantages from the average of statistical figures and scientific-
economic formulas. After all, your advantages are prosperity,
wealth, freedom, peace—and so on, and so on. So that a man
who, for instance, would openly and knowingly oppose that
whole list would, to your thinking, and indeed to mine too, of
course, be an obscurantist or an absolute madman, would he
not? But, after all, here is something amazing: why does it
happen that all these statisticians, sages and lovers of humanity, when they calculate human advantages invariably leave
one out? They don't even take it into their calculation in the
form in which it should be taken, and the whole reckoning
depends upon that. There would be no great harm to take it,
this advantage, and to add it to the list. But the trouble is,
that this strange advantage does not fall under any classification and does not figure in any list. For instance, I have a
friend. Bah, gentlemen! But after all he is your friend, too;
and indeed there is no one, no one, to whom he is not a friend!
When he prepares for any undertaking this gentleman immediately explains to you, pompously and clearly, exactly how
he must act in accordance with the laws of reason and truth.
What is more, he will talk to you with excitement and passion
of the real normal interests of man; with irony he will reproach the short-sighted fools who do not understand their
own advantage, for the true significance of virtue; and, within
a quarter of an hour, without any sudden outside provoca-
tion, but precisely through that something internal which is
stronger than all his advantages, he will go off on quite a

different tack—that is, act directly opposite to what he has just been saying himself, in opposition to the laws of reason, in opposition to his own advantage—in fact, in opposition to everything. I warn you that my friend is a compound personality, and therefore it is somehow difficult to blame him as an individual. The fact is, gentlemen, it seems that something that is dearer to almost every man than his greatest advantages must really exist, or (not to be illogical) there is one most advantageous advantage (the very one omitted of which we spoke just now) which is more important and more advantageous than all other advantages, for which, if necessary, a man is ready to act in opposition to all laws, that is, in opposition to reason, honor, peace, prosperity—in short, in opposition to all those wonderful and useful things if only he can attain that fundamental, most advantageous advantage which is dearer to him than all.

"Well, but it is still advantage just the same," you will retort. But excuse me, I'll make the point clear, and it is not a case of a play on words, but what really happens is that this advantage is remarkable from the very fact that it breaks down all our classifications, and continually shatters all the systems evolved by lovers of mankind for the happiness of mankind. In short, it interferes with everything. But before I mention this advantage to you, I want to compromise myself personally, and therefore I boldly declare that all these fine systems—all these theories for explaining to mankind its real normal interests, so that inevitably striving to obtain these interests, it may at once become good and noble—are, in my opinion, so far, mere logical exercises! Yes, logical exercises. After all, to maintain even this theory of the regeneration of mankind by means of its own advantage, is, after all, to my mind almost the same thing as—as to claim, for instance, with Buckle, that through civilization mankind becomes softer, and consequently less bloodthirsty, and less fitted for warfare. Logically it does not seem to follow from his arguments. But man is so fond of systems and abstract deductions that he is ready to distort the truth intentionally, he is ready to deny what he can see and hear just to justify his logic. I take this example because it is the most glaring instance of it. Only look about you: blood is being spilled in streams, and in the merriest way, as though it were champagne. Take the whole of the nineteenth century in which Buckle lived. Take Napoleon—both the Great and the present one. Take North

America—the eternal union. Take farcical Schleswig-Holstein. And what is it that civilization softens in us? Civilization only produces a greater variety of sensations in man—and absolutely nothing more. And through the development of this variety, man may even come to find enjoyment in bloodshed. After all, it has already happened to him. Have you noticed that the subtlest slaughterers have almost always been the most civilized gentlemen, to whom the various Attilas and Stenka Razins could never hold a candle, and if they are not so conspicuous as the Attilas and Stenka Razins it is precisely because they are so often met with, are so ordinary and have become so familiar to us. In any case if civilization has not made man more bloodthirsty, it has at least made him more abominably, more loathsomely bloodthirsty than before. Formerly he saw justice in bloodshed and with his conscience at peace exterminated whomever he thought he should. And now while we consider bloodshed an abomination, we nevertheless engage in this abomination and even more than ever before. Which is worse? Decide that for yourselves. It is said that Cleopatra (pardon the example from Roman history) was fond of sticking gold pins into her slave-girls' breasts and derived enjoyment from their screams and writhing. You will say that that occurred in comparatively barbarous times; that these are barbarous times too, because (also comparatively speaking) pins are stuck in even now; that even though man has now learned to see more clearly occasionally than in barbarous times, he is still far from having *accustomed* himself to act as reason and science would dictate. But all the same you are fully convinced that he will inevitably accustom himself to it when he gets completely rid of certain old bad habits, and when common sense and science have completely re-educated human nature and turned it in a normal direction. You are confident that man will then refrain from erring *intentionally*, and will, so to say, willy-nilly, not want to set his will against his normal interests. More than that: then, you say, science itself will teach man (though to my mind that is a luxury) that he does not really have either caprice or will of his own and that he has never had it, and that he himself is something like a piano key or an organ stop, and that, moreover, laws of nature exist in this world, so that everything he does is not done by his will at all, but is done by itself, according to the laws of nature. Consequently we have only to discover these laws of nature, and man will no longer be responsible for his actions, and life will become exceedingly easy for him. All human actions will then, of course, be tabulated according to these laws, mathematically, like tables of logarithms up to 108,000, and entered in a table; or better still, there would be published certain edifying works like the present encyclopedic lexicons, in which everything will be so clearly calculated and designated that there will be no more incidents or adventures in the world.

Then—it is still you speaking—new economic relations will be established, all ready-made and computed with mathematical exactitude, so that every possible question will vanish in a twinkling, simply because every possible answer to it will be provided. Then the crystal palace will be built. Then—well, in short, those will be halcyon days. Of course there is no guaranteeing (this is my comment now) that it will not be, for instance, terribly boring then (for what will one have to do when everything is calculated according to the table?) but on the other hand everything will be extraordinarily rational. Of course boredom may lead you to anything. After all, boredom even sets one to sticking gold pins into people, but all that would not matter. What is bad (this is my comment again) is that for all I know people will be thankful for the gold pins then. After all, man is stupid, phenomenally stupid. Or rather he is not stupid at all, but he is so ungrateful that you could not find another like him in all creation. After all, it would not surprise me in the least, if, for instance, suddenly for no reason at all, general rationalism in the midst of the future, a gentleman with an ignoble, or rather with a reactionary and ironical, countenance were to arise and, putting his arms akimbo, say to us all: "What do you think, gentlemen, hadn't we better kick over all that rationalism at one blow, scatter it to the winds, just to send these logarithms to the devil, and to let us live once more according to our own foolish will!" That again would not matter; but what is annoying is that after all he would be sure to find followers—such is the nature of man. And all that for the most foolish reason, which, one would think, was hardly worth mentioning: that is, that man everywhere and always, whoever he may be, has preferred to act as he wished and not in the least as his reason and advantage dictated. Why, one may choose what is contrary to one's own interests, and sometimes one *positively ought* (that is my idea). One's own free unfettered choice, one's own fancy, however wild it may be, one's own fancy worked up at times to frenzy—why that is that very "most advantageous advantage" which we have overlooked, which comes under no classification and through which all systems and theories are continually being sent to the devil. And how do these sages know that man must necessarily need a rationally advantageous choice? What man needs is simply *independent* choice, whatever that independence may cost and wherever it may lead. Well, choice, after all, the devil only knows . . .

"Ha! ha! ha! But after all, if you like, in reality, there is no such thing as choice," you will interrupt with a laugh. "Science has even now succeeded in analyzing man to such an extent that we know already that choice and what is called freedom of will are nothing other than—"

Wait, gentlemen, I meant to begin with that myself. I admit that I was even frightened. I was just going to shout that after all the devil only knows what choice deperds on, and that perhaps that was a very good thing, but I remembered the teaching of science—and pulled myself up. And here you have begun to speak. After all, really, well, if some day they truly discover a formula for all our desires and caprices— that is, an explanation of what they depend upon, by what laws they arise, just how they develop, what they are aiming at in one case or another and so on, and so on, that is, a real mathematical formula—then, after all, man would most likely at once stop to feel desire, indeed, he will be certain to. For who would want to choose by rule? Besides, he will at once be transformed from a human being into an organ stop or something of the sort; for what is a man without desire, without free will and without choice, if not a stop in an organ? What do you think? Let us consider the probability—can such a thing happen or not?

"H'm!" you decide. "Our choice is usually mistaken through a mistaken notion of our advantage. We sometimes choose absolute nonsense because in our stupidity we see in that nonsense the easiest means for attaining an advantage assumed beforehand. But when all that is explained and worked out on paper (which is perfectly possible, for it is contemptible and senseless to assume in advance that man will never understand some laws of nature), then, of course, so-called desires will not exist. After all, if desire should at any time come to terms completely with reason, we shall then, of course, reason and not desire, simply because, after all, it will be impossible to retain reason and *desire* something senseless, and in that way knowingly act against reason and desire to injure ourselves. And as all choice and reasoning can really be calculated, because some day they will discover the laws of our so-called free will—so joking aside, there may one day probably be something like a table of desires so that we really shall choose in accordance with it. After all, if, for instance, some day they calculate and prove to me that I stuck my tongue out at someone because I could not help sticking my tongue out at him and that I had to do it in that particular way, what sort of *freedom* is left me, especially if I am a learned man and have taken my degree somewhere? After all, then I would be able to calculate my whole life for thirty years in advance. In short, if that comes about, then, after all, we could do nothing about it. We would have to accept it just the same. And, in fact, we ought to repeat to ourselves incessantly that at such and such a time and under such and such circumstances, Nature does not ask our leave; that we must accept her as she is and not as we imagine her to be, and if we really aspire to tables and indices and well, even—well, let us say to the chemical retort, then it cannot be helped. We must accept the retort, too, or else it will be accepted without our consent."

Yes, but here I come to a stop! Gentlemen, you must excuse me for philosophizing; it's the result of forty years underground! Allow me to indulge my fancy for a minute. You see, gentlemen, reason, gentlemen, is an excellent thing, there is no disputing that, but reason is only reason and can only satisfy man's rational faculty, while will is a manifestation of all life, that is, of all human life including reason as well as all impulses. And although our life, in this manifestation of it, is often worthless, yet it is life nevertheless and not simply extracting square roots. After all, here I, for instance, quite naturally want to live, in order to satisfy all my faculties for life, and not simply my rational faculty, that is, not simply one-twentieth of all my faculties for life. What does reason know? Reason only knows what it has succeeded in learning (some things it will perhaps never learn; while this is nevertheless no comfort, why not say so frankly?) and human nature acts as a whole, with everything that is in it, consciously or unconsciously, and, even if it goes wrong, it lives. I suspect, gentlemen, that you are looking at me with compassion; you repeat to me that an enlightened and developed man, such, in short, as the future man will be, cannot knowingly desire anything disadvantageous to himself, that this can be proved mathematically. I thoroughly agree, it really can—by mathematics. But I repeat for the hundredth time, there is one case, one only, when man may purposely, consciously, desire what is injurious to himself, what is stupid, very stupid—simply in order *to have the right* to desire for himself even what is very stupid and not to be bound by an obligation to desire only what is rational. After all, this very stupid thing, after all, this caprice of ours, may really be more advantageous for us, gentlemen, than anything else on earth, especially in some cases. And in particular it may be more advantageous than any advantages even when it does us obvious harm, and contradicts the soundest conclusions of our reason about our advantage—because in any case it preserves for us what is most precious and most important—that is, our personality, our individuality. Some, you see, maintain that this really is the most precious thing for man; desire can, of course, if it desires, be in agreement with reason; particularly if it does not abuse this practice but does so in moderation, it is both useful and sometimes even praiseworthy. But very often, and even most often, desire completely and stubbornly opposes reason, and . . . and . . . and do you know that that, too, is useful and sometimes even praiseworthy? Gentlemen, let us suppose that man is not stupid. (Indeed, after all, one cannot say that about him anyway, if only for the one consideration that, if man is stupid, then, after all, who is wise?) But if he is not stupid, he is just the same monstrously ungrateful! Phenomenally ungrateful. I even believe that the best definition of man is—a creature that walks on two legs and is ungrateful. But that is not all, that is not his worst defect; his worst defect is his perpetual immorality, perpetual—from the days of the Flood to the Schleswig-Holstein period of human destiny. Immorality, and consequently lack of good sense; for it has long been accepted that lack of good sense is due to no other cause than immorality. Try it, and cast a look upon the history of mankind. Well, what will you see? Is it a grand spectacle? All right, grand, if you like. The Colossus of Rhodes, for instance, that is worth something. Mr. Anaevsky may well testify that some say it is the work of human hands, while others maintain that it was created by Nature herself. Is it variegated? Very well, it may be variegated too. If one only took the dress uniforms, military and civilian, of all peoples in all ages—that alone is worth something, and if you take the undress uniforms you will never get to the end of it; no historian could keep up with it. Is it monotonous? Very well. It may be monotonous, too; they fight and fight; they are fighting now, they fought first and they fought last—you will admit that it is almost too monotonous. In short, one may say anything about the history of the world—anything that might enter the most disordered imagination. The only thing one cannot say is that it is rational. The very word sticks in one's throat. And, indeed, this is even the kind of thing that continually happens. After all, there are continually turning up in life moral and rational people, sages, and lovers of humanity, who make it their goal for life to live as morally and rationally as possible, to be, so to speak, a light to their neighbors, simply in order to show them that it is really possible to live morally and rationally in this world. And so what? We all know that those very people sooner or later toward the end of their lives have been false to themselves, playing some trick, often a most indecent one. Now I ask you: What can one expect from man since he is a creature endowed with such strange qualities? Shower upon him every earthly blessing, drown him in bliss so that nothing but bubbles would dance on the surface of his bliss, as on a sea; give him such economic prosperity that he would have nothing else to do but sleep, eat cakes and busy himself with ensuring the continuation of world history and even then man, out of sheer ingratitude, sheer libel, would play you some loathsome trick. He would even risk his cakes and would deliberately desire the most fatal rubbish, the most uneconomical absurdity, simply to introduce into all this positive rationality his fatal fantastic element. It is just his fantastic dreams, his vulgar folly, that he will desire to retain, simply in order to prove to himself (as though that were so necessary) that men still are men and not piano keys, which even if played by the laws of nature themselves threaten to be controlled so completely that soon one will be able to desire nothing but by the calendar. And, after all, that is not all: even if man really were nothing but a piano key, even if this were proved to him by natural science and mathematics, even then he would not become reasonable, but would purposely do something perverse out of sheer ingratitude, simply to have his own way. And if he does not find any means he will devise destruction and chaos, will devise sufferings of all sorts, and will thereby have his own way. He will launch a curse upon the world, and, as only man can curse (it is his privilege, the primary distinction between him and other animals) then, after all, perhaps only by his curse will he attain his object, that is, really convince himself that he is a man and not a piano key! If you say that all this, too, can be calculated and tabulated, chaos and darkness and curses, so that the mere possibility of calculating it all beforehand would stop it all, and reason would reassert itself—then man would purposely go mad in order to be rid of reason and have his own way! I believe in that, I vouch for it, because, after all, the whole work of man seems really to consist in nothing but proving to himself continually that he is a man and not an organ stop. It may be at the cost of his skin! But he has proved it; he may become a caveman, but he will have proved it. And after that can one help sinning, rejoicing that it has not yet come, and that desire still depends on the devil knows what!

You will shout at me (that is, if you will still favor me with your shout) that, after all, no one is depriving me of my will, that all they are concerned with is that my will should somehow of itself, of its own free will, coincide with my own normal interests, with the laws of nature and arithmetic.

Bah, gentlemen, what sort of free will is left when we come to tables and arithmetic, when it will all be a case of two times two makes four? Two times two makes four even without my will. As if free will meant that!

Friedrich Nietzsche

(1844–1900) ———◆——— **GERMAN**
("EUROPEAN")

Nietzsche never read Kierkegaard, but there are remarkable parallels between them: their stress on the individual and disdain for the "herd" or "public"; their attacks on hypocritical Christendom and upon the bloated philosophical celebration of reason in Kant and Hegel; their hatred of personal weakness and anonymity. But Nietzsche will have no part of Kierkegaard's new Christian; indeed, he turns Kierkegaard on his head and defends the aesthetic life against both morality and Christianity. This defense, however, begins with the Dostoevskian premise that all of our claims—scientific, moral, and religious—are now without foundation. "God is dead," "the highest values devalue themselves," and the foundations of science are but errors ("necessary errors," perhaps, that is, necessary for the life of the species, yet not "true"). The negative, or "nihilistic," side of Nietzsche's philosophy consists of an attack on Christianity and Christian morality. On the one hand, the argument proceeds from the crumbling of the religious foundations and sanctions (the "death of God") to the invalidity of morality. More important, Nietzsche argues from a general thesis about values ("the value of value") to the rejection of both God and Christian morality. To do this, Nietzsche takes a naturalistic approach to moral reasoning. There are no a priori moral principles; there are only desires, all of them reducible to a single psychological drive, "the will to power." Values can be defended only insofar as they maximize one's power (in this regard, Nietzsche has in mind more the "spiritual" power of the artist or saint than political power). Christian morality, Nietzsche argues, is also a manifestation of the will to power, but the will of the weak, originating out of inferiority and ressentiment, a "slave morality" whose purpose is the preservation of the herd rather than the excellence of the strong. The positive side of Nietzsche's philosophy is more sketchy. Its three central doctrines are that of

43

the will to power, a conception Nietzsche was just beginning to fully develop when he was struck down by tragic illness; the Übermensch, the "more-than-human-all-too-human" who is to serve as our new ideal; and the "eternal recurrence," which is to serve as the test for that new ideal.

Nietzsche developed his critique of morality and Christianity in a remarkable series of aphorisms, essays and books during the last seven productive years of his life, 1882–1888. He begins with a slogan, "God is dead" (in The Joyful Wisdom,[1] *excerpted here), and he offers us a quasi-religious, quasi-autobiographical protagonist, Zarathustra (in* Thus Spake Zarathustra), *which immediately followed* Beyond Good and Evil, The Genealogy of Morals, Twilight of the Idols, The Antichrist, *and other philosophical expositions of the terse insights of Zarathustra. Nietzsche intended to systematize his philosophy in a grand opus entitled* The Will to Power, *but he never had the opportunity. Consequently, we possess only a brilliant series of preparatory notes of this period, a few of which are included here.*

from
THE JOYFUL WISDOM

The Madman.—Have you ever heard of the madman who on a bright morning lighted a lantern and ran to the market-place calling out unceasingly: "I seek God! I seek God!"—As there were many people standing about who did not believe in God, he caused a great deal of amusement. Why! is he lost? said one. Has he strayed away like a child? said another. Or does he keep himself hidden? Is he afraid of us? Has he taken a sea-voyage? Has he emigrated?—the people cried out laugh-

[1] Die Fröliche Wissenschaft, *also translated as* The Gay Science.

Excerpts from *The Joyful Wisdom* by Friedrich Nietzsche, from *The Complete Works of Friedrich Nietzsche*, edited by Oscar Levy, New York: Russell & Russell, 1964. Reprinted by permission of the publisher. (Editor's note: this acknowledgment covers all excerpts from *The Joyful Wisdom* appearing herein except the one on p. 77.)

ingly, all in a hubbub. The insane man jumped into their midst and transfixed them with his glances. "Where is God gone?" he called out. "I mean to tell you! *We have killed him,*— you and I! We are all his murderers! . . ."

What our Cheerfulness Signifies.—The most important of more recent events—that "God is dead," that the belief in the Christian God has become unworthy of belief—already begins to cast its first shadows over Europe. To the few at least whose eye, whose *suspecting* glance, is strong enough and subtle enough for this drama, some sun seems to have set, some old, profound confidence seems to have changed into doubt: our old world must seem to them daily more darksome, distrustful, strange and "old." In the main, however, one may say that the event itself is far too great, too remote, too much beyond most people's power of apprehension, for one to suppose that so much as the report of it could have *reached* them; not to speak of many who already knew *what* had taken place, and what must all collapse now that this belief had been undermined,—because so much was built upon it, so much rested on it, and had become one with it: for example, our entire European morality. This lengthy, vast and uninterrupted process of crumbling destruction, ruin and overthrow which is now imminent: who has realised it sufficiently to-day to have to stand up as the teacher and herald of such a tremendous logic of terror, as the prophet of a period of gloom and eclipse, the like of which has probably never taken place on earth before? . . . Even we, the born riddle-readers, who wait as it were on the mountains posted 'twixt to-day and to-morrow, and engirt by their contradiction, we, the firstlings and premature children of the coming century, into whose sight especially the shadows which must forthwith envelop Europe *should* already have come—how is it that even we, without genuine sympathy for this period of gloom, contemplate its advent without any *personal* solicitude or fear? Are we still, perhaps, too much under the *immediate effects* of the event—and are these effects, especially as regards *ourselves*, perhaps the reverse of what was to be expected—not at all sad and depressing, but rather like a new and indescribable variety of light, happiness, relief, enlivenment, encouragement, and dawning day? . . . In fact, we philosophers and "free spirits" feel ourselves irradiated as by a new dawn by the report that the "old God is dead"; our hearts overflow with gratitude, astonishment, presentiment and expectation. At last the horizon seems open once more, granting even that it is not bright; our ships can at last put out to sea in face of every danger; every hazard is again permitted to the discerner; the sea, *our* sea, again lies open before us; perhaps never before did such an "open sea" exist.—

What does your conscience say? "You should become him who you are."

Herd-Instinct.—Wherever we meet with a morality we find a valuation and order of rank of the human impulses and activities. These valuations and orders of rank are always the expression of the needs of a community or herd: that which is in the first place to *its* advantage—and in the second place and third place—is also the authoritative standard for the worth of every individual. By morality the individual is taught to become a function of the herd, and to ascribe to himself value only as a function. As the conditions for the maintenance of one community have been very different from those of another community, there have been very different moralities; and in respect to the future essential transformations of herds and communities, states and societies, one can prophesy that there will still be very divergent moralities. Morality is the herd-instinct in the individual.

The "Genius of the Species."—The problem of consciousness (or more correctly: of becoming conscious of oneself) meets us only when we begin to perceive in what measure we could dispense with it: and it is at the beginning of this perception that we are now placed by physiology and zoology (which have thus required two centuries to overtake the hint thrown out in advance by Leibnitz). For we could in fact think, feel, will and recollect, we could likewise "act" in every sense of the term, and nevertheless nothing of it all need necessarily "come into consciousness" (as one says metaphorically). The whole of life would be possible without its seeing itself as it were in a mirror: as in fact even at present the far greater part of our life still goes on without this mirroring,— and even our thinking, feeling, volitional life as well, however painful this statement may sound to an older philosopher. *What* then is *the purpose* of consciousness generally, when it is in the main *superfluous?*—Now it seems to me, if you will hear my answer and its perhaps extravagant supposition, that the subtlety and strength of consciousness are always in proportion to the *capacity for communication* of a man (or an animal), the capacity for communication in its turn being in proportion to the *necessity for communication*: the latter not to be understood as if precisely the individual himself who is master in the art of communicating and making known his necessities would at the same time have to be most dependent upon others for his necessities. It seems to me, however, to be so in relation to whole races and successions of generations: where necessity and need have long compelled men to communicate with their fellows and understand one another rapidly and subtly, a surplus of the power and art of communication is at last acquired, as if it were a fortune which had gradually accumulated, and now waited for an heir to squander it prodigally (the so-called artists are these heirs, in like manner the orators, preachers and authors: all of them men who come at the end of a long succession, "late-born" always, in the best sense of the word, and as has been said, *squanderers* by their very nature). Granted that this observation is correct, I may proceed further to the conjecture that *consciousness generally has only been developed under the pressure of the necessity for communication,*—that from the first it has been necessary and useful only between man and man (especially between those commanding and those obeying), and has only developed in proportion to its utility. Consciousness is properly only a connecting network between man and man, —it is only as such that it has had to develop; the recluse and wild-beast species of men would not have needed it. The very fact that our actions, thoughts, feelings and motions come within the range of our consciousness—at least a part of them—is the result of a terrible, prolonged "must" ruling man's destiny: as the most endangered animal he *needed* help and protection; he needed his fellows, he was obliged to express his distress, he had to know how to make himself understood —and for all this he needed "consciousness" first of all: he had to "know" himself what he lacked, to "know" how he felt, and to "know" what he thought. For, to repeat it once more, man, like every living creature, thinks unceasingly, but does not know it; the thinking which is becoming *conscious of itself* is only the smallest part thereof, we may say, the most superficial part, the worst part:—for this conscious thinking alone *is done in words, that is to say, in the symbols for communication,* by means of which the origin of consciousness is revealed. In short, the development of speech and the development of consciousness (not of reason, but of reason becoming self-conscious) go hand in hand. Let it be further accepted that it is not only speech that serves as a bridge between man and man, but also the looks, the pressure and the gestures; our becoming conscious of our sense impressions, our power of being able to fix them, and as it were to locate them outside of ourselves, has increased in proportion as the necessity has increased for communicating them to *others* by means of signs. The sign-inventing man is at the same time the man who is always more acutely self-conscious; it is only as a social animal that man has learned to become conscious of himself, —he is doing so still, and doing so more and more.—As is obvious, my idea is that consciousness does not properly belong to the individual existence of man, but rather to the social and gregarious nature in him; that, as follows therefrom, it is only in relation to communal and gregarious utility that it is finely developed; and that consequently each of us, in spite of the best intention of *understanding* himself as individually as possible, and of "knowing himself," will always just call into consciousness the non-individual in him, namely, his "averageness";—that our thought itself is continuously as it were *outvoted* by the character of consciousness—by the imperious "genius of the species" therein—and is translated back into the perspective of the herd. Fundamentally our actions are in an incomparable manner altogether personal, unique, and absolutely individual—there is no doubt about it; but as soon as we translate them into consciousness, they *do not appear so any longer. . . .* This is the proper phenomenalism and perspectivism as I understand it: the nature of *animal consciousness* involves the notion that the world of which we can become conscious is only a superficial and symbolic world, a generalised and vulgarised world;—that everything which becomes conscious *becomes* just thereby shallow, meagre, relatively stupid,—a generalisation, a symbol, a characteristic of the herd; that with the evolving of consciousness there is always combined a great, radical perversion, falsification, superficialisation and generalisation. Finally, the growing consciousness is a danger, and whoever lives among the most conscious Europeans knows even that it is a disease. As may be conjectured, it is not the antithesis of subject and object with which I am here concerned: I leave that distinction to the epistemologists who have remained entangled in the toils of grammar (popular metaphysics). It is still less the antithesis of "thing in itself" and phenomenon, for we do not "know" enough to be entitled even *to make such a distinction*. Indeed, we have not any organ at all for *knowing*, or for "truth": we "know" (or believe, or fancy) just as much as may be of *use* in the interest of the human herd, the species; and even what is here called "usefulness" is ultimately only a belief, a fancy, and perhaps precisely the most fatal stupidity by which we shall one day be ruined.

from
THUS SPOKE ZARATHUSTRA

When Zarathustra came into the next town, which lies on the edge of the forest, he found many people gathered together in the market place; for it had been promised that there would be a tightrope walker. And Zarathustra spoke thus to the people:

"*I teach you the overman.* Man is something that shall be overcome. What have you done to overcome him?

"All beings so far have created something beyond themselves; and do you want to be the ebb of this great flood and even go back to the beasts rather than overcome man? What is the ape to man? A laughingstock or a painful embarrassment. And man shall be just that for the overman: a laughingstock or a painful embarrassment. You have made your way from worm to man, and much in you is still worm. Once you were apes, and even now, too, man is more ape than any ape.

. . .

"Behold, I teach you the overman. The overman is the meaning of the earth. Let your will say: the overman *shall be* the meaning of the earth! I beseech you, my brothers, *remain faithful to the earth*, and do not believe those who speak to

From *The Portable Nietzsche*, edited and translated by Walter Kaufmann. Copyright 1954 by The Viking Press, Inc. Reprinted by permission of The Viking Press, Inc. (Ed. note: this acknowledgment also covers the excerpt from *Thus Spoke Zarathustra* on p. 74.)

you of otherworldly hopes! Poison-mixers are they, whether they know it or not. Despisers of life are they, decaying and poisoned themselves, of whom the earth is weary: so let them go.

"Once the sin against God was the greatest sin; but God died, and these sinners died with him. To sin against the earth is now the most dreadful thing, and to esteem the entrails of the unknowable higher than the meaning of the earth.

. . .

"What is the greatest experience you can have? It is the hour of the great contempt. The hour in which your happiness, too, arouses your disgust, and even your reason and your virtue.

"The hour when you say, 'What matters my happiness? It is poverty and filth and wretched contentment. But my happiness ought to justify existence itself.'"

. . .

Zarathustra, however, beheld the people and was amazed. Then he spoke thus:

"Man is a rope, tied between beast and overman—a rope over an abyss. A dangerous across, a dangerous on-the-way, a dangerous looking-back, a dangerous shuddering and stopping.

"What is great in man is that he is a bridge and not an end: what can be loved in man is that he is an *overture* and a *going under.*"

. . .

When Zarathustra had spoken these words he beheld the people again and was silent. "There they stand," he said to his heart; "there they laugh. They do not understand me; I am not the mouth for these ears. Must one smash their ears before they learn to listen with their eyes? Must one clatter like kettledrums and preachers of repentance? Or do they believe only the stammerer?

"They have something of which they are proud. What do they call that which makes them proud? Education they call it; it distinguishes them from goatherds. That is why they do not like to hear the word 'contempt' applied to them. Let me then address their pride. Let me speak to them of what is most contemptible: but that is the *last man.*"

And thus spoke Zarathustra to the people: "The time has come for man to set himself a goal. The time has come for man to plant the seed of his highest hope. His soil is still rich enough. But one day this soil will be poor and domesticated, and no tall tree will be able to grow in it. Alas, the time is coming when man will no longer shoot the arrow of his longing beyond man, and the string of his bow will have forgotten how to whir!

"I say unto you: one must still have chaos in oneself to be able to give birth to a dancing star. I say unto you: you still have chaos in yourselves.

"Alas, the time is coming when man will no longer give birth to a star. Alas, the time of the most despicable man is coming, he that is no longer able to despise himself. Behold, I show you the *last man*.

" 'What is love? What is creation? What is longing? What is a star?' thus asks the last man, and he blinks.

"The earth has become small, and on it hops the last man, who makes everything small. His race is as ineradicable as the flea-beetle; the last man lives longest.

" 'We have invented happiness,' say the last men, and they blink. They have left the regions where it was hard to live, for one needs warmth. One still loves one's neighbor and rubs against him, for one needs warmth.

"Becoming sick and harboring suspicion are sinful to them: one proceeds carefully. A fool, whoever still stumbles over stones or human beings! A little poison now and then: that makes for agreeable dreams. And much poison in the end, for an agreeable death.

"One still works, for work is a form of entertainment. But one is careful lest the entertainment be too harrowing. One no longer becomes poor or rich: both require too much exertion. Who still wants to rule? Who obey? Both require too much exertion.

"No shepherd and one herd! Everybody wants the same, everybody is the same: whoever feels different goes voluntarily into a madhouse.

" 'Formerly, all the world was mad,' say the most refined, and they blink.

"One is clever and knows everything that has ever happened: so there is no end of derision. One still quarrels, but one is soon reconciled—else it might spoil the digestion.

"One has one's little pleasure for the day and one's little pleasure for the night: but one has a regard for health.

" 'We have invented happiness,' say the last men, and they blink."

And here ended Zarathustra's first speech, which is also

called "the Prologue"; for at this point he was interrupted by
the clamor and delight of the crowd. "Give us this last man,
O Zarathustra," they shouted. "Turn us into these last men!
Then we shall make you a gift of the overman!" And all the
people jubilated and clucked with their tongues.

But Zarathustra became sad and said to his heart: "They
do not understand me: I am not the mouth for these ears. I
seem to have lived too long in the mountains . . ."

from
BEYOND GOOD AND EVIL

Gradually it has become clear to me what every great philosophy so far has been: namely, the personal confession of
its author and a kind of involuntary and unconscious memoir;
also that the moral (or immoral) intentions in every philosophy constituted the real germ of life from which the whole
plant had grown.

Indeed, if one would explain how the abstrusest metaphysical claims of a philosopher really came about, it is always well
(and wise) to ask first: at what morality does all this (does
he) aim? Accordingly, I do not believe that a "drive to knowledge" is the father of philosophy; but rather that another drive
has, here as elsewhere, employed understanding (and misunderstanding) as a mere instrument. But anyone who considers the basic drives of man to see to what extent they may
have been at play just here as *inspiring* spirits (or demons and
kobolds) will find that all of them have done philosophy at
some time—and that every single one of them would like only
too well to represent just *itself* as the ultimate purpose of existence and the legitimate *master* of all the other drives. For
every drive wants to be master—and it attempts to philosophize in *that spirit*.

To be sure: among scholars who are really scientific men,
things may be different—"better," if you like—there you may

From *Beyond Good and Evil* by Friedrich Nietzsche, translated by Walter
Kaufmann. Copyright © 1966 by Random House, Inc. Reprinted by permission of the publisher. (Ed. note: this acknowledgment also covers the
excerpt from *Beyond Good and Evil* on p. 74.)

really find something like a drive for knowledge, some small, independent clockwork that, once well wound, works on vigorously *without* any essential participation from all the other drives of the scholar. The real "interests" of the scholar therefore lie usually somewhere else—say, in his family, or in making money, or in politics. Indeed, it is almost a matter of total indifference whether his little machine is placed at this or that spot in science, and whether the "promising" young worker turns himself into a good philologist or an expert on fungi or a chemist: it does not *characterize* him that he becomes this or that. In the philosopher, conversely, there is nothing whatever that is impersonal; and above all, his morality bears decided and decisive witness to *who he is*—that is, in what order of rank the innermost drives of his nature stand in relation to each other.

Wandering through the many subtler and coarser moralities which have so far been prevalent on earth, or still are prevalent, I found that certain features recurred regularly together and were closely associated—until I finally discovered two basic types and one basic difference.

There are *master morality* and *slave morality*—I add immediately that in all the higher and more mixed cultures there also appear attempts at mediation between these two moralities, and yet more often the interpenetration and mutual misunderstanding of both, and at times they occur directly alongside each other—even in the same human being, within a *single* soul. The moral discrimination of values has originated either among a ruling group whose consciousness of its difference from the ruled group was accompanied by delight —or among the ruled, the slaves and dependents of every degree.

In the first case, when the ruling group determines what is "good," the exalted, proud states of the soul are experienced as conferring distinction and determining the order of rank. The noble human being separates from himself those in whom the opposite of such exalted, proud states finds expression: he despises them. It should be noted immediately that in this first type of morality the opposition of "good" and "*bad*" means approximately the same as "noble" and "contemptible." (The opposition of "good" and "*evil*" has a different origin.) One feels contempt for the cowardly, the anxious, the petty, those intent on narrow utility; also for the suspicious with their unfree glances, those who humble themselves, the doglike people who allow themselves to be maltreated, the begging flatterers, above all the liars: it is part of the fundamental faith of all aristocrats that the common people lie. "We truthful ones"—thus the nobility of ancient Greece referred to itself.

It is obvious that moral designations were everywhere first applied to *human beings* and only later, derivatively, to actions. Therefore it is a gross mistake when historians of morality start from such questions as: why was the compassionate act praised? The noble type of man experiences *itself* as determining values; it does not need approval; it judges, "what is harmful to me is harmful in itself"; it knows itself to be that which first accords honor to things; it is *value-creating*. Everything it knows as part of itself it honors: such a morality is self-glorification. In the foreground there is the feeling of fullness, of power that seeks to overflow, the happiness of high tension, the consciousness of wealth that would give and bestow: the noble human being, too, helps the unfortunate, but not, or almost not, from pity, but prompted more by an urge begotten by excess of power. The noble human being honors himself as one who is powerful, also as one who has power over himself, who knows how to speak and be silent, who delights in being severe and hard with himself and respects all severity and hardness. "A hard heart Wotan put into my breast," says an old Scandinavian saga: a fitting poetic expression, seeing that it comes from the soul of a proud Viking. Such a type of man is actually proud of the fact that he is *not* made for pity, and the hero of the saga therefore adds as a warning: "If the heart is not hard in youth it will never harden." Noble and courageous human beings who think that way are furthest removed from that morality which finds the distinction of morality precisely in pity, or in acting for others, or in *désintéressement*; faith in oneself, pride in oneself, a fundamental hostility and irony against "selflessness" belong just as definitely to noble morality as does a slight disdain and caution regarding compassionate feelings and a "warm heart."

It is the powerful who *understand* how to honor; this is their art, their realm of invention. The profound reverence for age and tradition—all law rests on this double reverence—the faith and prejudice in favor of ancestors and disfavor of those yet to come are typical of the morality of the powerful; and when the men of "modern ideas," conversely, believe almost instinctively in "progress" and "the future" and more and more lack respect for age, this in itself would sufficiently betray the ignoble origin of these "ideas."

A morality of the ruling group, however, is most alien and embarrassing to the present taste in the severity of its principle that one has duties only to one's peers; that against beings of a lower rank, against everything alien, one may behave as one pleases or "as the heart desires," and in any case "beyond good and evil"—here pity and like feelings may find their place. The capacity for, and the duty of, long gratitude and long revenge—both only among one's peers—refinement in repaying, the sophisticated concept of friendship, a certain necessity for having enemies (as it were, as drainage ditches for the affects of envy, quarrelsomeness, exuberance—at bottom, in order to be capable of being good *friends*): all these are typical characteristics of noble morality which, as suggested, is not the morality of "modern ideas" and therefore is hard to empathize with today, also hard to dig up and uncover.

· · ·

It is different with the second type of morality, *slave morality*. Suppose the violated, oppressed, suffering, unfree, who are uncertain of themselves and weary, moralize: what will their moral valuations have in common? Probably, a pessimistic suspicion about the whole condition of man will find expression, perhaps a condemnation of man along with his condition. The slave's eye is not favorable to the virtues of the powerful: he is skeptical and suspicious, *subtly* suspicious, of all the "good" that is honored there—he would like to persuade himself that even their happiness is not genuine. Conversely, those qualities are brought out and flooded with light which serve to ease existence for those who suffer: here pity, the complaisant and obliging hand, the warm heart, patience, industry, humility, and friendliness are honored—for here these are the most useful qualities and almost the only means for enduring the pressure of existence. Slave morality is essentially a morality of utility.

Here is the place for the origin of that famous opposition of "good" and "evil": into evil one's feelings project power and dangerousness, a certain terribleness, subtlety, and strength that does not permit contempt to develop. According to slave morality, those who are "evil" thus inspire fear; according to master morality it is precisely those who are "good" that inspire, and wish to inspire, fear, while the "bad" are felt to be contemptible.

The opposition reaches its climax when, as a logical consequence of slave morality, a touch of disdain is associated also with the "good" of this morality—this may be slight and benevolent—because the good human being has to be *undangerous* in the slave's way of thinking: he is good-natured, easy to deceive, a little stupid perhaps, *un bonhomme*. Wherever slave morality becomes preponderant, language tends to bring the words "good" and "stupid" closer together.

One last fundamental difference: the longing for *freedom*, the instinct for happiness and the subtleties of the feeling of freedom belong just as necessarily to slave morality and morals as artful and enthusiastic reverence and devotion are the regular symptoms of an aristocratic way of thinking and evaluating.

from
THE GENEALOGY OF MORALS

"Good and Evil,"
"Good and Bad"
. . .

Now it is plain to me, first of all, that in this theory [English utilitarianism] the source of the concept "good" has been sought and established in the wrong place: the judgment "good" did *not* originate with those to whom "goodness" was shown! Rather it was "the good" themselves, that is to say, the noble, powerful, high-stationed and high-minded, who felt and established themselves and their actions as good, that is, of the first rank, in contradistinction to all the low, low-minded, common and plebeian. It was out of this *pathos of distance* that they first seized the right to create values and to coin names for values: what had they to do with utility! The viewpoint of utility is as remote and inappropriate as it possibly could be in face of such a burning eruption of the highest rank-ordering, rank-defining value judgments: for here feeling has attained the

From *Basic Writings of Nietzsche* by Friedrich Nietzsche, translated by Walter Kaufmann. Copyright © 1966, 1967, 1968 by Random House, Inc. Reprinted by permission of the publisher. (Ed. note: this acknowledgment also covers the excerpt from *The Genealogy of Morals* on p. 78.)

antithesis of that low degree of warmth which any calculating prudence, any calculus of utility, presupposes—and not for once only, not for an exceptional hour, but for good. The pathos of nobility and distance, as aforesaid, the protracted and domineering fundamental total feeling on the part of a higher ruling order in relation to a lower order, to a "below" —*that* is the origin of the antithesis "good" and "bad." (The lordly right of giving names extends so far that one should allow oneself to conceive the origin of language itself as an expression of power on the part of the rulers: they say "this *is* this and this," they seal every thing and event with a sound and, as it were, take possession of it.) It follows from this origin that the word "good" was definitely *not* linked from the first and by necessity to "unegoistic" actions, as the superstition of these genealogists of morality would have it. Rather it was only when aristocratic value judgments *declined* that the whole antithesis "egoistic" "unegoistic" obtruded itself more and more on the human conscience—it is, to speak in my own language, the *herd instinct* that through this antithesis at last gets its word (and its *words*) in. And even then it was a long time before that instinct attained such dominion that moral evaluation was actually stuck and halted at this antithesis (as, for example, is the case in contemporary Europe: the prejudice that takes "moral," "unegoistic," "*désintéressé*" as concepts of equivalent value already rules today with the force of a "fixed idea" and brain-sickness).

• • •

The signpost to the *right* road was for me the question: what was the real etymological significance of the designations for "good" coined in the various languages? I found they all led back to the *same conceptual transformation*—that everywhere "noble," "aristocratic" in the social sense, is the basic concept from which "good" in the sense of "with aristocratic soul," "noble," "with a soul of a high order," "with a privileged soul" necessarily developed: a development which always runs parallel with that other in which "common," "plebeian," "low" are finally transformed into the concept "bad." The most convincing example of the latter is the German word *schlecht* [bad] itself: which is identical with *schlicht* [plain, simple]—compare *schlechtweg* [plainly], *schlechterdings* [simply]—and originally designated the plain, the common man, as yet with no inculpatory implication and simply in contradistinction to the nobility. About the time of

the Thirty Years' War, late enough therefore, this meaning
changed into the one now customary.

. . .

One will have divined already how easily the priestly mode
of valuation can branch off from the knightly-aristocratic and
then develop into its opposite; this is particularly likely when
the priestly caste and the warrior caste are in jealous opposition to one another and are unwilling to come to terms. The
knightly-aristocratic value judgments presupposed a powerful
physicality, a flourishing, abundant, even overflowing health,
together with that which serves to preserve it: war, adventure,
hunting, dancing, war games, and in general all that involves
vigorous, free, joyful activity. The priestly-noble mode of
valuation presupposes . . . other things: it is disadvantageous
for it when it comes to war! As is well known, the priests are
the *most evil enemies*—but why? Because they are the most
impotent. It is because of their impotence that in them hatred
grows to monstrous and uncanny proportions, to the most
spiritual and poisonous kind of hatred. The truly great haters
in world history have always been priests; likewise the most
ingenious haters: other kinds of spirit hardly come into consideration when compared with the spirit of priestly vengefulness. Human history would be altogether too stupid a thing
without the spirit that the impotent have introduced into it—
let us take at once the most notable example. All that has been
done on earth against "the noble," "the powerful," "the mas-
ters," "the rulers," fades into nothing compared with what the
Jews have done against them; the Jews, that priestly people,
who in opposing their enemies and conquerors were ultimately satisfied with nothing less than a radical revaluation of
their enemies' values, that is to say, an act of the *most spiritual revenge*. For this alone was appropriate to a priestly
people. the people embodying the most deeply repressed
priestly vengefulness. It was the Jews who, with awe-inspiring
consistency, dared to invert the aristocratic value-equation
(good = noble = powerful = beautiful = happy = beloved of
God) and to hang on to this inversion with their teeth, the
teeth of the most abysmal hatred (the hatred of impotence),
saying "the wretched alone are the good; the poor, impotent,
lowly alone are the good; the suffering, deprived, sick, ugly
alone are pious, alone are blessed by God, blessedness is for
them alone—and you, the powerful and noble, are on the contrary the evil, the cruel, the lustful, the insatiable, the godless

to all eternity; and you shall be in all eternity the unblessed, accursed, and damned!" . . . One knows *who* inherited this Jewish revaluation . . . In connection with the tremendous and immeasurably fateful initiative provided by the Jews through this most fundamental of all declarations of war, I recall the proposition I arrived at on a previous occasion (*Beyond Good and Evil*, section 195)—that with the Jews there begins *the slave revolt in morality*: that revolt which has a history of two thousand years behind it and which we no longer see because it—has been victorious.

. . .

The slave revolt in morality begins when *ressentiment* itself becomes creative and gives birth to values: the *ressentiment* of natures that are denied the true reaction, that of deeds, and compensate themselves with an imaginary revenge. While every noble morality develops from a triumphant affirmation of itself, slave morality from the outset says No to what is "outside," what is "different," what is "not itself"; and *this* No is its creative deed. This inversion of the value-positing eye— this *need* to direct one's view outward instead of back to one-self—is of the essence of *ressentiment*: in order to exist, slave morality always first needs a hostile external world; it needs, physiologically speaking, external stimuli in order to act at all —its action is fundamentally reaction.

The reverse is the case with the noble mode of valuation: it acts and grows spontaneously, it seeks its opposite only so as to affirm itself more gratefully and triumphantly—its negative concept "low," "common," "bad" is only a subsequently-invented pale, contrasting image in relation to its positive basic concept—filled with life and passion through and through—"we noble ones, we good, beautiful, happy ones!" When the noble mode of valuation blunders and sins against reality, it does so in respect to the sphere with which it is *not* sufficiently familiar, against a real knowledge of which it has indeed inflexibly guarded itself: in some circumstances it mis-understands the sphere it despises, that of the common man, of the lower orders; on the other hand, one should remember that, even supposing that the affect of contempt, of looking down from a superior height. *falsifies* the image of that which it despises, it will at any rate still be a much less serious falsi-fication than that perpetrated on its opponent—*in effigie* of course—by the submerged hatred. the vengefulness of the impotent. There is indeed too much carelessness, too much

taking lightly, too much looking away and impatience involved in contempt, even too much joyfulness, for it to be
able to transform its object into a real caricature and monster.

. . .

But let us return: the problem of the *other* origin of the
"good," of the good as conceived by the man of *ressentiment*,
demands its solution.

That lambs dislike great birds of prey does not seem strange:
only it gives no ground for reproaching these birds of prey
for bearing off little lambs. And if the lambs say among themselves: "these birds of prey are evil; and whoever is least like
a bird of prey, but rather its opposite, a lamb—would he not
be good?" there is no reason to find fault with this institution
of an ideal, except perhaps that the birds of prey might view
it a little ironically and say: "*we* don't dislike them at all,
these good little lambs; we even love them: nothing is more
tasty than a tender lamb."

To demand of strength that it should *not* express itself as
to throw down, a desire to become master, a thirst for enemies
and resistances and triumphs, is just as absurd as to demand
of weakness that it should express itself as strength. A quantum of force is equivalent to a quantum of drive, will, effect—
more, it is nothing other than precisely this very driving, willing, effecting, and only owing to the seduction of language
(and of the fundamental errors of reason that are petrified in
it) which conceives and misconceives all effects as conditioned
by something that causes effects, by a "subject," can it appear
otherwise. For just as the popular mind separates the lightning from its flash and takes the latter for an *action*, for the
operation of a subject called lightning, so popular morality
also separates strength from expressions of strength, as if there
were a neutral substratum behind the strong man, which was
strength, that it should *not* be a desire to overcome, a desire
free to express strength or not to do so. But there is no such
substratum; there is no "being" behind doing, effecting, becoming; "the doer" is merely a fiction added to the deed—the
deed is everything. The popular mind in fact doubles the
deed; when it sees the lightning flash, it is the deed of a deed:
it posits the same event first as cause and then a second time
as its effect. Scientists do no better when they say "force
moves," "force causes," and the like—all its coolness, its freedom from emotion notwithstanding, our entire science still
lies under the misleading influence of language and has not

disposed of that little changeling, the "subject" (the atom, for example, is such a changeling, as is the Kantian "thing-in-itself"); no wonder if the submerged, darkly glowering emotions of vengefulness and hatred exploit this belief for their own ends and in fact maintain no belief more ardently than the belief that *the strong man is free* to be weak and the bird of prey to be a lamb—for thus they gain the right to make the bird of prey *accountable* for being a bird of prey.

. . .

Let us conclude. The two *opposing* values "good and bad," "good and evil" have been engaged in a fearful struggle on earth for thousands of years; and though the latter value has certainly been on top for a long time, there are still places where the struggle is as yet undecided. One might even say that it has risen ever higher and thus become more and more profound and spiritual: so that today there is perhaps no more decisive mark of a *"higher nature,"* a more spiritual nature, than that of being divided in this sense and a genuine battle-ground of these opposed values.

The symbol of this struggle, inscribed in letters legible across all human history, is "Rome against Judea, Judea against Rome":—there has hitherto been no greater event than *this* struggle, *this* question, *this* deadly contradiction. Rome felt the Jew to be something like anti-nature itself, its antipodal monstrosity as it were: in Rome the Jew stood *"convicted* of hatred for the whole human race"; and rightly, provided one has a right to link the salvation and future of the human race with the unconditional dominance of aristocratic values, Roman values.

How, on the other hand, did the Jews feel about Rome? A thousand signs tell us; but it suffices to recall the Apocalypse of John, the most wanton of all literary outbursts that vengefulness has on its conscience. (One should not underestimate the profound consistency of the Christian instinct when it signed this book of hate with the name of the disciple of love, the same disciple to whom it attributed that amorous-enthusiastic Gospel: there is a piece of truth in this, however much literary counterfeiting might have been required to produce it.) For the Romans were the strong and noble, and nobody stronger and nobler has yet existed on earth or even been dreamed of: every remnant of them, every inscription gives delight, if only one divines *what* it was that was there at work. The Jews, on the contrary, were the priestly nation of

ressentiment par excellence, in whom there dwelt an unequaled popular-moral genius: one only has to compare similarly gifted nations—the Chinese or the Germans, for instance
—with the Jews, to sense which is of the first and which of the
fifth rank.

Which of them has won *for the present*, Rome or Judea?
But there can be no doubt: consider to whom one bows down
in Rome itself today, as if they were the epitome of all the
highest values—and not only in Rome but over almost half the
earth, everywhere that man has become tame or desires to
become tame: *three Jews*, as is known, and *one Jewess* (Jesus
of Nazareth, the fisherman Peter, the rug weaver Paul, and
the mother of the aforementioned Jesus, named Mary). This
is very remarkable: Rome has been defeated beyond all
doubt.

There was, to be sure, in the Renaissance an uncanny and
glittering reawakening of the classical ideal, of the noble
mode of evaluating all things; Rome itself, oppressed by the
new superimposed Judaized Rome that presented the aspect
of an ecumenical synagogue and was called the "church,"
stirred like one awakened from seeming death: but Judea
immediately triumphed again, thanks to that thoroughly
plebeian (German and English) *ressentiment* movement
called the Reformation, and to that which was bound to arise
from it, the restoration of the church—the restoration too of
the ancient sepulchral repose of classical Rome.

With the French Revolution, Judea once again triumphed
over the classical ideal, and this time in an even more profound and decisive sense: the last political noblesse in Europe,
that of the *French* seventeenth and eighteenth century, collapsed beneath the popular instincts of *ressentiment*—greater
rejoicing, more uproarious enthusiasm had never been heard
on earth! To be sure, in the midst of it there occurred the most
tremendous, the most unexpected thing: the ideal of antiquity
itself stepped *incarnate* and in unheard-of splendor before the
eyes and conscience of mankind—and once again, in opposition to the mendacious slogan of *ressentiment*, "supreme rights
of the majority," in opposition to the will to the lowering, the
abasement, the leveling and the decline and twilight of mankind, there sounded stronger, simpler, and more insistently
than ever the terrible and rapturous counterslogan "supreme
rights of the few"! Like a last signpost to the *other* path,
Napoleon appeared, the most isolated and late-born man there

has even been, and in him the problem of the *noble ideal as such* made flesh—one might well ponder *what* kind of problem it is: Napoleon, this synthesis of the *inhuman* and *superhuman*.

. . .

"Guilt," "Bad Conscience," and the Like

To breed an animal *with the right to make promises*—is not this the paradoxical task that nature has set itself in the case of man? is it not the real problem regarding man?

. . .

This precisely is the long story of how *responsibility* originated. The task of breeding an animal with the right to make promises evidently embraces and presupposes as a preparatory task that one first *makes* men to a certain degree necessary, uniform, like among like, regular, and consequently calculable. The tremendous labor of that which I have called "morality of mores" (*Dawn*, sections 9, 14, 16)—the labor performed by man upon himself during the greater part of the existence of the human race, his entire *prehistoric* labor, finds in this its meaning, its great justification, notwithstanding the severity, tyranny, stupidity, and idiocy involved in it: with the aid of the morality of mores and the social straitjacket, man was actually *made* calculable.

If we place ourselves at the end of this tremendous process, where the tree at last brings forth fruit, where society and the morality of custom at last reveal *what* they have simply been the means to: then we discover that the ripest fruit is the *sovereign individual,* like only to himself, liberated again from morality of custom, autonomous and supramoral (for "autonomous" and "moral" are mutually exclusive), in short, the man who has his own independent, protracted will and the *right to make promises*—and in him a proud consciousness, quivering in every muscle, of *what* has at length been achieved and become flesh in him. a consciousness of his own power and freedom, a sensation of mankind come to completion. This emancipated individual, with the actual *right* to make promises, this master of a *free* will, this sovereign man —how should he not be aware of his superiority over all those who lack the right to make promises and stand as their own guarantors, of how much trust, how much fear, how much reverence he arouses—he *"deserves"* all three—and of how this mastery over himself also necessarily gives him mastery over circumstances, over nature, and over all more short-willed and unreliable creatures? The "free" man, the possessor of a protracted and unbreakable will, also possesses his *measure of value*: looking out upon others from himself, he honors or he despises; and just as he is bound to honor his peers, the strong and reliable (those with the *right* to make promises)—that is, all those who promise like sovereigns, reluctantly, rarely, slowly, who are chary of trusting, whose trust is a mark of *distinction*, who give their word as something that can be relied on because they know themselves strong enough to maintain it in the face of accidents, even "in the face of fate"—he is bound to reserve a kick for the feeble windbags who promise without the right to do so, and a rod for the liar who breaks his word even at the moment he utters it. The proud awareness of the extraordinary privilege of *responsibility*, the consciousness of this rare freedom, this power over oneself and over fate, has in his case penetrated to the profoundest depths and become instinct, the dominating instinct. What will he call this dominating instinct, supposing he feels the need to give it a name? The answer is beyond doubt: this sovereign man calls it his *conscience*.

• • •

We Germans certainly do not regard ourselves as a particularly cruel and hardhearted people, still less as a particularly frivolous one, living only for the day; but one has only to look at our former codes of punishments to understand what effort it costs on this earth to breed a "nation of thinkers" (which is to say, *the* nation in Europe in which one still finds today the maximum of trust, seriousness, lack of taste, and matter-of-factness—and with these qualities one has the right to breed every kind of European mandarin). These Germans have employed fearful means to acquire a memory, so as to master their basic mob-instinct and its brutal coarseness. Consider the old German punishments; for example, stoning (the sagas already have millstones drop on the head of the guilty), breaking on the wheel (the most characteristic invention and speciality of the German genius in the realm of punishment!), piercing with stakes, tearing apart or trampling by horses ("quartering"), boiling of the criminal in oil or wine (still employed in the fourteenth and fifteenth centuries), the popular flaying alive ("cutting straps"), cutting flesh from the chest, and also the practice of smearing the wrongdoer with honey and leaving him in the blazing sun for the flies. With the aid of such images and procedures one finally remembers five or six "I will not's," in regard to which one had given one's *promise* so as to participate in the advantages of society —and it was indeed with the aid of this kind of memory that one at last came "to reason"! Ah, reason, seriousness, mastery over the affects, the whole somber thing called reflection, all these prerogatives and showpieces of man: how dearly they have been bought! how much blood and cruelty lie at the bottom of all "good things"!

· · ·

To return to our investigation: the feeling of guilt, of personal obligation, had its origin . . . in the oldest and most primitive personal relationship, that between buyer and seller, creditor and debtor: it was here that one person first encountered another person, that one person first *measured himself* against another. No grade of civilization, however low, has yet been discovered in which something of this relationship has not been noticeable. Setting prices, determining values, contriving equivalences, exchanging—these preoccupied the earliest thinking of man to so great an extent that in a certain sense they constitute thinking *as such*: here it was that the oldest kind of astuteness developed; here likewise, we may suppose, did human pride, the feeling of superiority in relation to other animals, have its first beginnings. Perhaps our word "man" (*manas*) still expresses something of precisely *this* feeling of self-satisfaction: man designated himself as the creature that measures values, evaluates and measures, as the "valuating animal as such."

Buying and selling, together with their psychological appurtenances, are older even than the beginnings of any kind of social forms of organization and alliances: it was rather out of the most rudimentary form of personal legal rights that the budding sense of exchange, contract, guilt, right, obligation, settlement, first *transferred* itself to the coarsest and most elementary social complexes (in their relations with other similar complexes), together with the custom of comparing, measuring, and calculating power against power. The eye was now focused on this perspective: and with that blunt consistency characteristic of the thinking of primitive mankind, which is hard to set in motion but then proceeds inexorably in the same direction, one forthwith arrived at the great generalization, "everything has its price; *all* things can be paid for"—the oldest and naïvest moral canon of *justice*, the beginning of all "good-naturedness," all "fairness," all "good will," all "objectivity" on earth. Justice on this elementary level is the good will among parties of approximately equal power to come to terms with one another, to reach an "understanding" by means of a settlement—and to *compel* parties of lesser power to reach a settlement among themselves.—

. . .

At this point I can no longer avoid giving a first, provisional statement of my own hypothesis concerning the origin of the "bad conscience": it may sound rather strange and needs to be pondered, lived with, and slept on for a long time. I regard the bad conscience as the serious illness that man was bound to contract under the stress of the most fundamental change he ever experienced—that change which occurred when he found himself finally enclosed within the walls of society and of peace. The situation that faced sea animals when they were compelled to become land animals or perish was the same as that which faced these semi-animals, well adapted to the wilderness, to war, to prowling, to adventure: suddenly all their instincts were disvalued and "suspended." From now on they had to walk on their feet and "bear themselves" whereas hitherto they had been borne by the water: a dreadful heaviness lay upon them. They felt unable to cope with the simplest undertakings; in this new world they no longer possessed their former guides, their regulating, unconscious and infallible drives: they were reduced to thinking, inferring, reckoning, co-ordinating cause and effect, these unfortunate creatures; they were reduced to their "consciousness," their weakest and most fallible organ! I believe there has never been such a feeling of misery on earth, such a leaden discomfort—and at the same time the old instincts had not suddenly ceased to make their usual demands! Only it was hardly or rarely possible to humor them: as a rule they had to seek new and, as it were, subterranean gratifications.

All instincts that do not discharge themselves outwardly *turn inward*—this is what I call the *internalization* of man: thus it was that man first developed what was later called his "soul." The entire inner world, originally as thin as if it were stretched between two membranes, expanded and extended itself, acquired depth, breadth, and height, in the same measure as outward discharge was *inhibited*. Those fearful bulwarks with which the political organization protected itself against the old instincts of freedom—punishments belong among these bulwarks—brought about that all those instincts of wild, free, prowling man turned backward *against man himself*. Hostility, cruelty, joy in persecuting, in attacking, in change, in destruction—all this turned against the possessors of such instincts: *that* is the origin of the "bad conscience."

The man who, from lack of external enemies and resistances and forcibly confined to the oppressive narrowness and punctiliousness of custom, impatiently lacerated, persecuted, gnawed at, assaulted, and maltreated himself; this animal that rubbed itself raw against the bars of its cage as one tried to "tame" it; this deprived creature, racked with homesickness for the wild, who had to turn himself into an adventure, a torture chamber, an uncertain and dangerous wilderness— this fool, this yearning and desperate prisoner became the inventor of the "bad conscience." But thus began the gravest and uncanniest illness, from which humanity has not yet recovered, man's suffering *of man, of himself*—the result of a forcible sundering from his animal past, as it were a leap and plunge into new surroundings and conditions of existence, a declaration of war against the old instincts upon which his strength, joy, and terribleness had rested hitherto.

Let us add at once that, on the other hand, the existence on earth of an animal soul turned against itself, taking sides against itself, was something so new, profound, unheard of, enigmatic, contradictory, *and pregnant with a future* that the aspect of the earth was essentially altered. Indeed, divine spectators were needed to do justice to the spectacle that thus began and the end of which is not yet in sight—a spectacle too subtle, too marvelous, too paradoxical to be played senselessly unobserved on some ludicrous planet! From now on, man is *included* among the most unexpected and exciting lucky throws in the dice game of Heraclitus' "great child," be he called Zeus or chance; he gives rise to an interest, a tension, a hope, almost a certainty, as if with him something were announcing and preparing itself, as if man were not a goal but only a way, an episode, a bridge, a great promise.—

• • •

The bad conscience is an illness, there is no doubt about that, but an illness as pregnancy is an illness.

• • •

What Is the Meaning of Ascetic Ideals?

. . .

But let us return to our problem. It will be immediately obvious that such a self-contradiction as the ascetic appears to represent, "life *against* life," is, physiologically considered and not merely psychologically, a simple absurdity. It can only be *apparent;* it must be a kind of provisional formulation, an interpretation and psychological misunderstanding of something whose real nature could not for a long time be understood or described *as it really was*—a mere word inserted into an old *gap* in human knowledge. Let us replace it with a brief formulation of the facts of the matter: *the ascetic ideal springs from the protective instinct of a degenerating life* which tries by all means to sustain itself and to fight for its existence; it indicates a partial physiological obstruction and exhaustion against which the deepest instincts of life, which have remained intact, continually struggle with new expedients and devices. The ascetic ideal is such an expedient; the case is therefore the opposite of what those who reverence this ideal believe: life wrestles in it and through it with death and *against* death; the ascetic ideal is an artifice for the *preservation* of life.

That this ideal acquired such power and ruled over men as imperiously as we find it in history, especially wherever the civilization and taming of man has been carried through, expresses a great fact: the *sickliness* of the type of man we have had hitherto, or at least of the tamed man, and the physiological struggle of man against death (more precisely: against disgust with life, against exhaustion, against the desire for the "end"). The ascetic priest is the incarnate desire to be different, to be in a different place, and indeed this desire at its greatest extreme, its distinctive fervor and passion; but precisely this power of his desire is the chain that holds him captive so that he becomes a tool for the creation of more favorable conditions for being here and being man—it is precisely this *power* that enables him to persuade to existence the whole herd of the ill-constituted, disgruntled, underprivileged, unfortunate, and all who suffer of themselves, by instinctively going before them as their shepherd. You will see my point: this ascetic priest, this apparent enemy of life, this *denier*—precisely he is among the greatest *conserving* and yes-creating forces of life.

Where does it come from, this sickliness? For man is more sick, uncertain, changeable, indeterminate than any other animal, there is no doubt of that—he is *the* sick animal: how has that come about? Certainly he has also dared more, done more new things, braved more and challenged fate more than all the other animals put together: he, the great experimenter with himself, discontented and insatiable, wrestling with animals, nature, and gods for ultimate dominion—he, still unvanquished, eternally directed toward the future, whose own restless energies never leave him in peace, so that his future digs like a spur into the flesh of every present—how should such a courageous and richly endowed animal not also be the most imperiled, the most chronically and profoundly sick of all sick animals?

Man has often had enough; there are actual epidemics of having had enough (as around 1348, at the time of the dance of death); but even this nausea, this weariness, this disgust with himself—all this bursts from him with such violence that it at once becomes a new fetter. The No he says to life brings to light, as if by magic, an abundance of tender Yeses; even when he *wounds* himself, this master of destruction, of self-destruction—the very wound itself afterward compels him *to live.*—

. . .

from TWILIGHT OF THE IDOLS

The Problem of Socrates

Concerning life, the wisest men of all ages have judged alike: *it is no good.* Always and everywhere one has heard the same sound from their mouths—a sound full of doubt, full of

From *The Portable Nietzsche*, edited and translated by Walter Kaufmann. Copyright 1954 by The Viking Press, Inc. Reprinted by permission of The Viking Press, Inc. (Ed. note: this acknowledgment also covers the excerpts from *Twilight of the Idols* on pp. 72, 73, and 78.)

melancholy, full of weariness of life, full of resistance to life.
Even Socrates said, as he died: "To live—that means to be
sick a long time: I owe Asclepius the Savior a rooster." Even
Socrates was tired of it. What does that evidence? What does
it evince? Formerly one would have said (—oh, it has been
said, and loud enough, and especially by our pessimists): "At
least something of all this must be true! The consensus of the
sages evidences the truth." Shall we still talk like that today?
May we? "At least something must be *sick* here," *we* retort.
These wisest men of all ages—they should first be scrutinized
closely. Were they all perhaps shaky on their legs? late? tot-
tery? decadents? Could it be that wisdom appears on earth as
a raven, inspired by a little whiff of carrion?

· · ·

When one finds it necessary to turn *reason* into a tyrant, as
Socrates did, the danger cannot be slight that something else
will play the tyrant. Rationality was then hit upon as the
savior; neither Socrates nor his "patients" had any choice
about being rational: it was *de rigeur*, it was their last resort.
The fanaticism with which all Greek reflection throws itself
upon rationality betrays a desperate situation; there was danger, there was but one choice: either to perish or—to be
absurdly rational. The moralism of the Greek philosophers
from Plato on is pathologically conditioned; so is their esteem
of dialectics. Reason-virtue-happiness, that means merely that
one must imitate Socrates and counter the dark appetites with
a permanent daylight—the daylight of reason. One must be
clever, clear, bright at any price: any concession to the instincts, to the unconscious, leads *downward*.

Morality
as Anti-Nature

All passions have a phase when they are merely disastrous,
when they drag down their victim with the weight of stupidity—and a later, very much later phase when they wed the
spirit, when they "spiritualize" themselves. Formerly, in view
of the element of stupidity in passion, war was declared on
passion itself, its destruction was plotted; all the old moral
monsters are agreed on this: *il faut tuer les passions*. The most
famous formula for this is to be found in the New Testament,
in that Sermon on the Mount, where, incidentally, things are

by no means looked at from a height. There it is said, for example, with particular reference to sexuality: "If thy eye offend thee, pluck it out." Fortunately, no Christian acts in accordance with this precept. *Destroying* the passions and cravings, merely as a preventive measure against their stupidity and the unpleasant consequences of this stupidity—today this itself strikes us as merely another acute form of stupidity. We no longer admire dentists who "pluck out" teeth so that they will not hurt any more.

* * *

Let us finally consider how naïve it is altogether to say: "Man *ought* to be such and such!" Reality shows us an enchanting wealth of types, the abundance of a lavish play and change of forms—and some wretched loafer of a moralist comments: "No! Man ought to be different." He even knows what man should be like, this wretched bigot and prig: he paints himself on the wall and comments, *"Ecce homo!"* But even when the moralist addresses himself only to the single human being and says to him, "You ought to be such and such!" he does not cease to make himself ridiculous. The single human being is a piece of *fatum* from the front and from the rear, one law more, one necessity more for all that is yet to come and to be. To say to him, "Change yourself!" is to demand that everything be changed, even retroactively. And indeed there have been consistent moralists who wanted man to be different, that is, virtuous—they wanted him remade in their own image, as a prig: to that end, they *negated* the world! No small madness! No modest kind of immodesty!

ON TRUTH

Sense for Truth.—Commend me to all skepticism where I am permitted to answer: "Let us put it to the test!" But I don't wish to hear anything more of things and questions which do not admit of being tested. That is the limit of my "sense for truth": for bravery has there lost its right.

(Joyful Wisdom)

Life no Argument.—We have arranged for ourselves a world in which we can live—by the postulating of bodies,

lines, surfaces, causes and effects, motion and rest, form and
content: without these articles of faith no one could manage
to live at present! But for all that they are still unproved. Life
is no argument; error might be among the conditions of life.
(Ibid)

Ultimate Scepticism.—But what after all are man's truths?
—They are his *irrefutable* errors.   *(Ibid)*

Truth is the kind of error without which a certain species of
life could not live. The value for *life* is ultimately decisive.
*(The Will to Power)**

The criterion of truth resides in the enhancement of the
feeling of power.   *(Ibid)*

What is truth?—Inertia; that hypothesis which gives rise to
contentment; smallest expenditure of spiritual force, etc. *(Ibid)*

There are many kinds of eyes. Even the sphinx has eyes—
and consequently there are many kinds of "truths," and consequently there is no truth.   *(Ibid)*

How the "True World"
Finally Became a Fable

The History of an Error

1. The true world—attainable for the sage, the pious, the
virtuous man; he lives in it, *he is it.*
(The oldest form of the idea, relatively sensible, simple, and
persuasive. A circumlocution for the sentence, "I, Plato, *am*
the truth.")
2. The true world—unattainable for now, but promised for
the sage, the pious, the virtuous man ("for the sinner who
repents").

*From *The Will to Power* by Friedrich Nietzsche, translated by Walter
Kaufmann and R.J. Hollingdale, edited by Walter Kaufmann. Copyright ©
1967 by Walter Kaufmann. Reprinted by permission of Random House, Inc.
(Ed. note: this acknowledgment also covers the excerpts from *The Will to
Power* on pp. 74, 75, 76, and 77.)

(Progress of the idea: it becomes more subtle, insidious, incomprehensible—*it becomes female*, it becomes Christian.)

3. The true world—unattainable, indemonstrable, unpromisable; but the very thought of it—a consolation, an obligation, an imperative.

(At bottom, the old sun, but seen through mist and skepticism. The idea has become elusive, pale, Nordic, Königsbergian [i.e., Kantian].)

4. The true world—unattainable? At any rate, unattained. And being unattained, also *unknown.* Consequently, not consoling, redeeming, or obligating: how could something unknown obligate us?

(Gray morning. The first yawn of reason. The cockcrow of positivism.)

5. The "true" world—an idea which is no longer good for anything, not even obligating—an idea which has become useless and superfluous—*consequently,* a refuted idea: let us abolish it!

(Bright day; breakfast; return of *bon sens* and cheerfulness; Plato's embarrassed blush; pandemonium of all free spirits.)

6. The true world—we have abolished. What world has remained? The apparent one perhaps? But no! *With the true world we have also abolished the apparent one.*

(Noon; moment of the briefest shadow; end of the longest error; high point of humanity; INCIPIT ZARATHUSTRA.)

(Twilight of the Idols)

ON THE WILL TO POWER

Suppose nothing else were "given" as real except our world of desires and passions, and we could not get down, or up, to any other "reality" besides the reality of our drives—for thinking is merely a relation of these drives to each other: is it not permitted to make the experiment and to ask the question whether this "given" would not be *sufficient* for also understanding on the basis of this kind of thing the so-called mechanistic (or "material") world? I mean, not as a deception, as "mere appearance," an "idea" (in the sense of Berkeley and Schopenhauer) but as holding the same rank of reality as our affect—as a more primitive form of the world of affects in which everything still lies contained in a powerful unity before it undergoes ramifications and developments in the organic process (and, as is only fair, also becomes tenderer and weaker)—as a kind of instinctive life in which all organic functions are still synthetically intertwined along with self-regulation, assimilation, nourishment, excretion, and metabolism—as a *pre-form* of life.

In the end not only is it permitted to make this experiment; the conscience of *method* demands it. Not to assume several kinds of causality until the experiment of making do with a single one has been pushed to its utmost limit (to the point of nonsense, if I may say so)—that is a moral of method which one may not shirk today—it follows "from its definition," as a mathematician would say. The question is in the end whether we really recognize the will as *efficient*, whether we believe in the causality of the will: if we do—and at bottom our faith in this is nothing less than our faith in causality itself—then we have to make the experiment of positing the causality of the will hypothetically as the only one. "Will," of course, can affect only "will"—and not "matter" (not "nerves," for example). In short, one has to risk the hypothesis whether will does not affect will wherever "effects" are recognized—and whether all mechanical occurrences are not, insofar as a force is active in them, will force, effects of will.

Suppose, finally, we succeeded in explaining our entire instinctive life as the development and ramification of *one* basic form of the will—namely, of the will to power, as *my* proposition has it; suppose all organic functions could be traced back to this will to power and one could also find in it the solution of the problem of procreation and nourishment—it is *one* problem—then one would have gained the right to determine *all* efficient force univocally as—*will to power*. The world viewed from inside, the world defined and determined according to its "intelligible character"—it would be "will to power" and nothing else.— *(Beyond Good and Evil)*

A tablet of the good hangs over every people. Behold, it is the tablet of their overcomings; behold, it is the voice of their will to power. *(Zarathustra)*

I understand by "morality" a system of evaluations that partially coincides with the conditions of a creature's life. *(Will to Power)*

My chief proposition: there are no moral phenomena, there is only a moral interpretation of these phenomena. This interpretation itself is of extra-moral origin. (Ibid)

Against positivism, which halts at phenomena—"There are only *facts*"—I would say: No, facts is precisely what there is not, only interpretations. We cannot establish any fact "in itself": perhaps it is folly to want to do such a thing.

"Everything is subjective," you say; but even this is interpretation. The "subject" is not something given, it is something added and invented and projected behind what there is.—Finally, is it necessary to posit an interpreter behind the interpretation? Even this is invention, hypothesis.

Insofar as the word "knowledge" has any meaning, the world is knowable; but it is *interpretable* otherwise, it has no meaning behind it, but countless meanings.—"Perspectivism."

It is our needs that interpret the world; our drives and their For and Against. Every drive is a kind of lust to rule; each one has its perspective that it would like to compel all the other drives to accept as a norm. (Ibid)

"Ends and means"
"Cause and effect"
"Subject and object"
"Acting and suffering"
"Thing-in-itself and appearance"
} as interpretations (not as facts) and to what extent perhaps *necessary* interpretations? (as required for "preservation")—all in the sense of a will to power. (Ibid)

What are our evaluations and moral tables really worth? What is the outcome of their rule? For whom? In relation to what?—Answer: for life. But *what is life?* Here we need a new, more definite formulation of the concept "life." My formula for it is: Life is will to power. (Ibid)

What is good? Everything that heightens the feeling of power in man, the will to power, power itself.

What is bad? Everything that is born of weakness.

What is happiness? The feeling that power is *growing*, that resistance is overcome.

Not contentedness but more power; not peace but war; not virtue but fitness (Renaissance virtue, *virtù*, virtue that is moraline-free).

The weak and the failures shall perish: first principle of *our* love of man. And they shall even be given every possible assistance.

What is more harmful than any vice? Active pity for all the failures and all the weak: Christianity.   *(The Antichrist)**

And do you know what "the world" is to me? Shall I show it to you in my mirror? This world: a monster of energy, without beginning, without end; a firm, iron magnitude of force that does not grow bigger or smaller, that does not expend itself but only transforms itself; as a whole, of unalterable size, a household without expenses or losses, but likewise without increase or income; enclosed by "nothingness" as by a boundary; not something blurry or wasted, not something endlessly extended, but set in a definite space as a definite force, and not a space that might be "empty" here or there, but rather as force throughout, as a play of forces and waves of forces, at the same time one and many, increasing here and at the same time decreasing there; a sea of forces flowing and rushing together, eternally changing, eternally flooding back, with tremendous years of recurrence, with an ebb and a flood of its forms; out of the simplest forms striving toward the most complex, out of the stillest, most rigid, coldest forms toward the hottest, most turbulent, most self-contradictory, and then again returning home to the simple out of this abundance, out of the play of contradictions back to the joy of concord, still affirming itself in this uniformity of its courses and its years, blessing itself as that which must return eternally, as a becoming that knows no satiety, no disgust, no weariness: this, my *Dionysian* world of the eternally self-creating. the eternally self-destroying, this mystery world of the twofold voluptuous delight. my "beyond good and evil," without goal, unless the joy of the circle is itself a goal; without will, unless a ring feels good will toward itself—do you want a *name* for this world? A *solution* for all its riddles? A *light* for you, too, you best-concealed, strongest, most intrepid, most midnightly men?—*This world is the will to power—and nothing besides!* And you yourselves are also this will to power —and nothing besides!   *(Will to Power)*

* From *The Portable Nietzsche*, edited and translated by Walter Kaufmann. Copyright 1954 by The Viking Press, Inc. Reprinted by permission of The Viking Press, Inc.

ON ETERNAL RECURRENCE

The greatest stress. How, if some day or night a demon were to sneak after you into your loneliest loneliness and say to you, "This life as you now live it and have lived it, you will have to live once more and innumerable times more; and there will be nothing new in it, but every pain and every joy and every thought and sigh and everything immeasurably small or great in your life must return to you—all in the same succession and sequence—even this spider and this moonlight between the trees, and even this moment and I myself. The eternal hourglass of existence is turned over and over, and you with it, a dust grain of dust." Would you not throw yourself down and gnash your teeth and curse the demon who spoke thus? Or did you once experience a tremendous moment when you would have answered him, "You are a god, and never have I heard anything more godly." If this thought were to gain possession of you, it would change you, as you are, or perhaps crush you. The question in each and every thing, "Do you want this once more and innumerable times more?" would weigh upon your actions as the greatest stress. Or how well disposed would you have to become to yourself and to life to *crave nothing more fervently* than this ultimate eternal confirmation and seal?   *(Joyful Wisdom)**

• • •

The two most extreme modes of thought—the mechanistic and the Platonic—are reconciled in the *eternal recurrence*: both as ideals.   *(Will to Power)*

The law of the conservation of energy demands *eternal recurrence.*   *(Ibid)*

If the world may be thought of as a certain definite quantity of force and as a certain definite number of centers of force—and every other representation remains indefinite and therefore useless—it follows that, in the great dice game of existence, it must pass through a calculable number of com-

* From *The Portable Nietzsche*, edited and translated by Walter Kaufmann. Copyright 1954 by The Viking Press, Inc. Reprinted by permission of The Viking Press, Inc.

binations. In infinite time, every possible combination would at some time or another be realized; more: it would be realized an infinite number of times. And since between every combination and its next recurrence all other possible combinations would have to take place, and each of these combinations conditions the entire sequence of combinations in the same series, a circular movement of absolutely identical series is thus demonstrated: the world as a circular movement that has already repeated itself infinitely often and plays its game *in infinitum.*   *(Ibid)*

. . . In its origin language belongs in the age of the most rudimentary form of psychology. We enter a realm of crude fetishism when we summon before consciousness the basic presuppositions of the metaphysics of language, in plain talk, the presuppositions of reason. . . .   *(Twilight of the Idols)*

. . . I am afraid we are not rid of God because we still have faith in grammar.   *(Ibid)*

The good four. Honest with ourselves and with whatever is friend to us; *courageous* toward the enemy; *generous* toward the vanquished; *polite*—always: that is how the four cardinal virtues want us.   *(Dawn)**

Here precisely is what has become a fatality for Europe— together with the fear of man we have also lost our love of him, our reverence for him, our hopes for him, even the will to him. The sight of man now makes us weary—what is nihilism today if it is not *that?*—We are weary *of man.*   *(Genealogy of Morals)*

One Thing is Needful.—To "give style" to one's character —that is a grand and a rare art! He who surveys all that his nature presents in its strength and in its weakness, and then fashions it into an ingenious plan, until everything appears artistic and rational, and even the weaknesses enchant the eye —exercises that admirable art. . . .   *(Joyful Wisdom)*

*From *The Portable Nietzsche,* edited and translated by Walter Kaufmann. Copyright 1954 by The Viking Press, Inc. Reprinted by permission of The Viking Press, Inc.

Hermann Hesse

(1877–1962) ————◆━◆———— GERMAN (SWISS)

Hesse is one of those rare writers who has mastered worlds of thought far removed from each other. He has captured the anguish of Kierkegaard and the frenzy of Nietzsche, the light rapture of the saint, the lust of the aesthete, the bliss of Eastern enlightenment. If it is ultimately the Nietzschean who emerges from his writings, it is not because the others have not been given a fair hearing. There are limits to freedom even in an imagination of genius, and Harry Haller and Emil Sinclair seem to emerge as far more convincing characters than Siddhartha. Haller, the Steppenwolf, *in particular, seems to be born of Nietzschean heritage. He is the obviously "superior" cultured man, pursuing his virtue against and in the midst of the bourgeoisie ("this fat brood of mediocrity"), seeking Goethe and "the Immortals." If he is not yet Nietzsche's* Übermensch *(for one thing, he cannot dance), he is, with Nietzsche, the bridge between man and* Übermensch. *Yet he is torn between his two selves, wolf and man (the reference is primarily from Goethe's* Faust: *"Two souls, alas, are dwelling in my breast. And one is striving to foresake its brother"). Haller suffers nostalgia for the very bourgeoisie he despises, and he is overwhelmed by uncreative suffering. So he numbers himself among "the suicides." Haller seems to be giving up his pursuit of "the Immortals" when he is mysteriously handed a pamphlet,* Treatise on the Steppenwolf (Not for Everybody). *This pamphlet is his introduction to a Zarathustra more Eastern than Nietzsche's and a concept of self more radical than Nietzsche's ("man is an onion . . ."). Ultimately, it is the discovery of laughter and his plenitude of selves that allows Haller to see—to begin to see—what it is to be more than human-all-too-human.*

from
STEPPENWOLF

And now that we come to these records of Haller's, these partly diseased, partly beautiful and thoughtful fantasies, I must confess that if they had fallen into my hands by chance and if I had not known their author, I should most certainly have thrown them away in disgust. But owing to my acquaintance with Haller I have been able, to some extent, to understand them, and even to appreciate them. I should hesitate to share them with others if I saw in them nothing but the pathological fancies of a single and isolated case of a diseased temperament. But I see something more in them. I see them as a document of the times, for Haller's sickness of the soul, as I now know, is not the eccentricity of a single individual, but the sickness of the times themselves, the neurosis of that generation to which Haller belongs, a sickness, it seems, that by no means attacks the weak and worthless only but, rather, precisely those who are strongest in spirit and richest in gifts.

These records, however much or however little of real life may lie at the back of them, are not an attempt to disguise or to palliate this widespread sickness of our times. They are an attempt to present the sickness itself in its actual manifestation. They mean, literally, a journey through hell, a sometimes fearful, sometimes courageous journey through the chaos of a world whose souls dwell in darkness, a journey undertaken with the determination to go through hell from one end to the other, to give battle to chaos, and to suffer torture to the full.

It was some remembered conversation with Haller that gave me the key to this interpretation. He said to me once when we were talking of the so-called horrors of the Middle Ages: "These horrors were really nonexistent. A man of the Middle Ages would detest the whole mode of our present-day life as something far more than horrible, far more than barbarous. Every age, every culture, every custom and tradition has its own character, its own weakness and its own strength, its beauties and ugliness; accepts certain sufferings as matters

From *Steppenwolf* by Hermann Hesse, translated by Basil Creighton. Copyright 1929 by Holt, Rinehart and Winston, Inc. Copyright renewed 1957 by Hermann Hesse. Reprinted by permission of Holt, Rinehart and Winston, Inc.

of course, puts up patiently with certain evils. Human life is reduced to real suffering, to hell, only when two ages, two cultures and religions overlap. A man of the Classical Age who had to live in medieval times would suffocate miserably just as a savage does in the midst of our civilization. Now there are times when a whole generation is caught in this way between two ages, two modes of life, with the consequence that it loses all power to understand itself and has no standard, no security, no simple acquiescence. Naturally, every one does not feel this equally strongly. A nature such as Nietzsche's had to suffer our present ills more than a generation in advance. What he had to go through alone and misunderstood, thousands suffer today."

I often had to think of these words while reading the records. Haller belongs to those who have been caught between two ages, who are outside of all security and simple acquiescence. He belongs to those whose fate it is to live the whole riddle of human destiny heightened to the pitch of a personal torture, a personal hell.

Treatise on the Steppenwolf

There was once a man, Harry, called the Steppenwolf. He went on two legs, wore clothes and was a human being, but nevertheless he was in reality a wolf of the Steppes. He had learned a good deal of all that people of a good intelligence can, and was a fairly clever fellow. What he had not learned, however, was this: to find contentment in himself and his own life. The cause of this apparently was that at the bottom of his heart he knew all the time (or thought he knew) that he was in reality not a man, but a wolf of the Steppes. Clever men might argue the point whether he truly was a wolf, whether, that is, he had been changed, before birth perhaps, from a wolf into a human being, or had been given the soul of a wolf, though born as a human being; or whether, on the other hand, this belief that he was a wolf was no more than a fancy or a disease of his. It might, for example, be possible that in his childhood he was a little wild and disobedient and disorderly and that those who brought him up had declared a war of extinction against the beast in him; and precisely this had given him the idea and the belief that he was in fact actually a beast with only a thin covering of the human. On this point one could speak at length and entertainingly, and indeed write a book about it. The Steppenwolf, however, would be none the better for it, since for him it was all one whether the wolf had been bewitched or beaten into him, or whether it was merely an idea of his own. What others chose to think about it or what he chose to think himself was no good to him at all. It left the wolf inside him just the same.

And so the Steppenwolf had two natures, a human and a wolfish one. This was his fate, and it may well be that it was not a very exceptional one. There must have been many men who have had a good deal of the dog or the fox, of the fish or the serpent in them without experiencing any extraordinary difficulties on that account. In such cases, the man and the fish lived on together and neither did the other any harm. The one even helped the other. Many a man indeed has carried this condition to such enviable lengths that he has owed his happiness more to the fox or the ape in him than to the man. So much for common knowledge. In the case of Harry, however, it was just the opposite. In him the man and the wolf did not go the same way together, but were in continual and deadly enmity. The one existed simply and solely to harm the other, and when there are two in one blood and in one soul who are at deadly enmity, then life fares ill. Well, to each his lot, and none is light.

Now with our Steppenwolf it was so that in his conscious life he lived now as a wolf, now as a man, as indeed the case is with all mixed beings. But, when he was a wolf, the man in him lay in ambush, ever on the watch to interfere and condemn, while at those times that he was man the wolf did just the same. For example, if Harry, as man, had a beautiful thought, felt a fine and noble emotion, or performed a so-called good act, then the wolf bared his teeth at him and laughed and showed him with bitter scorn how laughable this whole pantomime was in the eyes of a beast, of a wolf who knew well enough in his heart what suited him, namely, to trot alone over the Steppes and now and then to gorge himself with blood or to pursue a female wolf. Then, wolfishly seen, all human activities became horribly absurd and misplaced, stupid and vain. But it was exactly the same when Harry felt and behaved as a wolf and showed others his teeth and felt hatred and enmity against all human beings and their lying and degenerate manners and customs. For then the human part of him lay in ambush and watched the wolf, called him brute and beast, and spoiled and embittered for him all pleasure in his simple and healthy and wild wolf's being.

Thus it was then with the Steppenwolf, and one may well imagine that Harry did not have an exactly pleasant and happy life of it. This does not mean, however, that he was unhappy in any extraordinary degree (although it may have seemed so to himself all the same, inasmuch as every man takes the sufferings that fall to his share as the greatest). That cannot be said of any man. Even he who has no wolf in him, may be none the happier for that. And even the unhappiest life has its sunny moments and its little flowers of happiness between sand and stone. So it was, then, with the Steppenwolf too. It cannot be denied that he was generally very unhappy; and he could make others unhappy also, that is, when he loved them or they him. For all who got to love him saw always only the one side in him. Many loved him as a refined and clever and interesting man, and were horrified and disappointed when they had come upon the wolf in him. And they had to because Harry wished, as every sentient being does, to be loved as a whole and therefore it was just with those whose love he most valued that he could least of all conceal and belie the wolf. There were those, however, who loved precisely the wolf in him, the free, the savage, the untamable, the dangerous and strong, and these found it peculiarly disappointing and deplorable when suddenly the wild and wicked wolf was also a man, and had hankerings after goodness and refinement, and wanted to hear Mozart, to read poetry and to cherish human ideals. Usually these were the most disappointed and angry of all; and so it was that the Steppenwolf brought his own dual and divided nature into the destinies of others besides himself whenever he came into contact with them.

• • •

In this connection one thing more must be said. There are a good many people of the same kind as Harry. Many artists are of his kind. These persons all have two souls, two beings within them. There is God and the devil in them; the mother's blood and the father's; the capacity for happiness and the capacity for suffering; and in just such a state of enmity and entanglement toward and within each other as were the wolf and man in Harry. And these men, for whom life has no repose, live at times in their rare moments of happiness with such strength and indescribable beauty, the spray of their moment's happiness is flung so high and dazzlingly over the wide sea of suffering, that the light of it, spreading its radiance, touches others, too, with its enchantment. Thus, like a precious, fleeting foam over the sea of suffering arise all those works of art, in which a single individual lifts himself for an hour so high above his personal destiny that his happiness shines like a star and appears to all who see it as something eternal and as a happiness of their own. All these men, whatever their deeds and works may be, have really no life; that is to say, their lives are not their own and have no form. They are not heroes, artists or thinkers in the same way that other men are judges, doctors, shoemakers or schoolmasters. Their life consists of a perpetual tide, unhappy and torn with pain, terrible and meaningless, unless one is ready to see its meaning in just those rare experiences, acts, thoughts and works that shine out above the chaos of such a life. To such men the desperate and horrible thought has come that perhaps the whole of human life is but a bad joke, a violent and ill-fated abortion of the primal mother, a savage and dismal catastrophe of nature. To them, too, however, the other thought has come that man is perhaps not merely a half-rational animal but a child of the gods and destined to immortality.

Men of every kind have their characteristics, their features, their virtues and vices and their deadly sins. It was part of the sign manual of the Steppenwolf that he was a night prowler. The morning was a bad time of day for him. He feared it and it never brought him any good. On no morning of his life had he ever been in good spirits nor done any good before midday, nor ever had a happy idea, nor devised any pleasure for himself or others. By degrees during the afternoon he warmed and became alive, and only toward evening, on his good days, was he productive, active and, sometimes, aglow with joy. With this was bound up his need for loneliness and independence. There was never a man with a deeper and more passionate craving for independence than he. In his youth when he was poor and had difficulty in earning his bread, he preferred to go hungry and in torn clothes rather than endanger his narrow limit of independence. He never sold himself for money or an easy life or to women or to those in power, and had thrown away a hundred times what in the world's eyes was his advantage and happiness in order to safeguard his liberty. No prospect was more hateful and distasteful to him than that he should have to go to an office and conform to daily and yearly routine and obey others. He hated all kinds of offices, governmental or commercial, as he hated death, and his worst nightmare was confinement in barracks. He contrived, often at great sacrifice, to avoid all such predicaments. It was here that his strength and his virtue rested. On this point he could neither be bent nor bribed. Here his character was firm and indeflectable. Only, through this virtue, he was bound the closer to his destiny of suffering. It happened to him as it does to all; what he strove for with the deepest and stubbornest instinct of his being fell to his lot, but more than is good for men. In the beginning his dream and his happiness, in the end it was his bitter fate. The man of power is ruined by power, the man of money by money, the submissive man by subservience, the pleasure seeker by pleasure. He achieved his aim. He was ever more independent. He took orders from no man and ordered his ways to suit no man. Independently and alone, he decided what to do and to leave undone. For every strong man attains to that which a genuine impulse bids him seek. But in the midst of the freedom he had attained Harry suddenly became aware that his freedom was a death and that he stood alone. The world in an uncanny fashion left him in peace. Other men concerned him no longer. He was not even concerned about himself. He began to suffocate slowly in the more and more rarefied atmosphere of remoteness and solitude. For now it was his wish no longer, nor his aim, to be alone and independent, but rather his lot and his sentence. The magic wish had been fulfilled and could not be canceled, and it was no good now to open his arms with longing and good will to welcome the bonds of society. People left him alone now. It was not, however, that he was an object of hatred and repugnance. On the contrary, he had many friends. A great many people liked him. But it was no more than sympathy and friendliness. He received invitations, presents, pleasant letters; but no more. No one came near to him. There was no link left, and no one could have had any part in his life even had any one wished it. For the air of lonely men surrounded him now, a still atmosphere in which the world around him slipped away, leaving him incapable of relationship, an atmosphere against which neither will nor longing availed. This was one of the significant earmarks of his life.

Another was that he was numbered among the suicides. And here it must be said that to call suicides only those who actually destroy themselves is false. Among these, indeed, there are many who in a sense are suicides only by accident and in whose being suicide has no necessary place. Among the common run of men there are many of little personality and stamped with no deep impress of fate, who find their end in suicide without belonging on that account to the type of the suicide by inclination; while on the other hand, of those who are to be counted as suicides by the very nature of their beings are many, perhaps a majority, who never in fact lay hands on themselves. The "suicide," and Harry was one, need not necessarily live in a peculiarly close relationship to death. One may do this without being a suicide. What is peculiar to the suicide is that his ego, rightly or wrongly, is felt to be an extremely dangerous, dubious and doomed germ of nature; that he is always in his own eyes exposed to an extraordinary risk, as though he stood with the slightest foothold on the peak of a crag whence a slight push from without or an instant's weakness from within suffices to precipitate him into the void. The line of fate in the case of these men is marked by the belief they have that suicide is their most probable manner of death. It might be presumed that such temperaments, which usually manifest themselves in early youth and persist through life, show a singular defect of vital force. On the contrary, among the "suicides" are to be found unusually tenacious and eager and also hardy natures. But just as there are those who at the least indisposition develop a fever, so do those whom we call suicides, and who are always very emotional and sensitive, develop at the least shock the notion of suicide. Had we a science with the courage and authority to concern itself with mankind, instead of with the mechanism merely of vital phenomena, had we something of the nature of an anthropology, or a psychology, these matters of fact would be familiar to every one.

. . .

As every strength may become a weakness (and under some circumstances must) so, on the contrary, may the typical suicide find a strength and a support in his apparent weakness. Indeed, he does so more often than not. The case of Harry, the Steppenwolf, is one of these. As thousands of his like do, he found consolation and support, and not merely the melancholy play of youthful fancy, in the idea that the way to death was open to him at any moment. It is true that with him, as with all men of his kind, every shock, every pain, every untoward predicament at once called forth the wish to find an escape in death. By degrees, however, he fashioned for himself out of this tendency a philosophy that was actually serviceable to life. He gained strength through familiarity with the thought that the emergency exit stood always open, and became curious, too, to taste his suffering to the dregs. If it went too badly with him he could feel sometimes with a grim malicious pleasure: "I am curious to see all the same just how much a man can endure. If the limit of what is bearable is reached, I have only to open the door to escape." There are a great many suicides to whom this thought imparts an uncommon strength.

· · ·

. . . Humor alone, that magnificent discovery of those who are cut short in their calling to highest endeavor, those who falling short of tragedy are yet as rich in gifts as in affliction, humor alone (perhaps the most inborn and brilliant achievement of the spirit) attains to the impossible and brings every aspect of human existence within the rays of its prism. To live in the world as though it were not the world, to respect the law and yet to stand above it, to have possessions as though "one possessed nothing," to renounce as though it were no renunciation, all these favorite and often formulated propositions of an exalted worldly wisdom, it is in the power of humor alone to make efficacious.

And supposing the Steppenwolf were to succeed, and he has gifts and resources in plenty, in decocting this magic draft in the sultry mazes of his hell, his rescue would be assured. Yet there is much lacking. The possibility, the hope only are there. Whoever loves him and takes his part may wish him this rescue. It would, it is true, keep him forever tied to the bourgeois world, but his suffering would be bearable and productive. His relation to the bourgeois world would lose its sentimentality both in its love and its hatred, and his bondage to it would cease to cause him the continual torture of shame.

To attain to this, or, perhaps it may be, to be able at last to dare the leap into the unknown, a Steppenwolf must once have a good look at himself. He must look deeply into the chaos of his own soul and plumb its depths. The riddle of his existence would then be revealed to him at once in all its changelessness, and it would be impossible for him ever to escape first from the hell of the flesh to the comforts of a sentimental philosophy and then back to the blind orgy of his wolfishness. Man and wolf would then be compelled to recognize one another without the masks of false feeling and to look one another straight in the eye. Then they would either explode and separate forever, and there would be no more Steppenwolf, or else they would come to terms in the dawning light of humor.

It is possible that Harry will one day be led to this latter alternative. It is possible that he will learn one day to know himself. He may get hold of one of our little mirrors. He may encounter the Immortals. He may find in one of our magic theaters the very thing that is needed to free his neglected soul. A thousand such possibilities await him. His fate brings them on, leaving him no choice; for those outside of the bourgeoisie live in the atmosphere of these magic possibilities. A mere nothing suffices—and the lightning strikes.

And all this is very well known to the Steppenwolf, even though his eye may never fall on this fragment of his inner biography. He has a suspicion of his allotted place in the world, a suspicion of the Immortals, a suspicion that he may meet himself face to face; and he is aware of the existence of that mirror in which he has such bitter need to look and from which he shrinks in such deathly fear.

For the close of our study there is left one last fiction, a fundamental delusion to make clear. All interpretation, all psychology, all attempts to make things comprehensible, require the medium of theories, mythologies and lies; and a self-respecting author should not omit, at the close of an exposition, to dissipate these lies so far as may be in his power. If I say "above" or "below," that is already a statement that requires explanation, since an above and a below exist only in thought, only as abstractions. The world knows nothing of above or below.

So too, to come to the point, is the Steppenwolf a fiction. When Harry feels himself to be a werewolf, and chooses to consist of two hostile and opposed beings, he is merely availing himself of a mythological simplification. He is no werewolf at all, and if we appeared to accept without scrutiny this lie which he invented for himself and believes in, and tried to regard him literally as a twofold being and a Steppenwolf, and so designated him, it was merely in the hope of being more easily understood with the assistance of a delusion, which we must now endeavor to put in its true light.

The division into wolf and man, flesh and spirit, by means of which Harry tries to make his destiny more comprehensible to himself is a very great simplification. It is a forcing of the truth to suit a plausible, but erroneous, explanation of that contradiction which this man discovers in himself and which appears to himself to be the source of his by no means negligible sufferings. Harry finds in himself a "human being," that is to say, a world of thoughts and feelings, of culture and tamed or sublimated nature, and besides this he finds within himself also a "wolf," that is to say, a dark world of instinct, of savagery and cruelty, of unsublimated or raw nature. In spite of this apparently clear division of his being between two spheres, hostile to one another, he has known happy moments now and then when the man and the wolf for a short while were reconciled with one another. Suppose that Harry tried to ascertain in any single moment of his life, any single act, what part the man had in it and what part the wolf, he would find himself at once in a dilemma, and his whole beautiful wolf theory would go to pieces. For there is not a single human being, not even the primitive Negro, not even the idiot, who is so conveniently simple that his being can be explained as the sum of two or three principal elements; and to explain so complex a man as Harry by the artless division into wolf and man is a hopelessly childish attempt. Harry consists of a hundred or a thousand selves, not of two. His life oscillates, as everyone's does, not merely between two poles, such as the body and the spirit, the saint and the sinner, but between thousand and thousands.

We need not be surprised that even so intelligent and educated a man as Harry should take himself for a Steppenwolf and reduce the rich and complex organism of his life to a formula so simple, so rudimentary and primitive. Man is not capable of thought in any high degree, and even the most spiritual and highly cultivated of men habitually sees the world and himself through the lenses of delusive formulas and artless simplifications—and most of all himself. For it appears to be an inborn and imperative need of all men to regard the self as a unit. However often and however grievously this illusion is shattered, it always mends again. The judge who sits over the murderer and looks into his face, and at one moment recognizes all the emotions and potentialities and possibilities of the murderer in his own soul and hears the murderer's voice as his own, is at the next moment one and indivisible as the judge, and scuttles back into the shell of his cultivated self and does his duty and condemns the murderer to death. And if ever the suspicion of their manifold being dawns upon men of unusual powers and of unusually delicate perceptions, so that, as all genius must, they break through the illusion of the unity of the personality and perceive that the self is made up of a bundle of selves, they have only to say so and at once the majority puts them under lock and key, calls science to aid, establishes schizomania and protects humanity from the necessity of hearing the cry of truth from the lips of these unfortunate persons. Why then waste words, why utter a thing that every thinking man accepts as self-evident, when the mere utterance of it is a breach of taste? A man, therefore, who gets so far as making the supposed unity of the self twofold is already almost a genius, in any case a most exceptional and interesting person. In reality, however, every ego, so far from being a unity, is in the highest degree a manifold world, a constellated heaven, a chaos of forms, of states and stages, of inheritances and potentialities. It appears to be a necessity as imperative as eating and breathing for everyone to be forced to regard this chaos as a unity and to speak of his ego as though it were a onefold and clearly detached and fixed phenomenon. Even the best of us share the delusion.

The delusion rests simply upon a false analogy. As a body everyone is single, as a soul never. In literature, too, even in its ultimate achievement, we find this customary concern with apparently whole and single personalities. Of all literature up to our days the drama has been the most highly prized by writers and critics, and rightly, since it offers (or might offer) the greatest possibilities of representing the ego as a manifold entity, but for the optical illusion which makes us believe that the characters of the play are manifold entities by lodging each one in an undeniable body, singly, separately and once and for all. An artless aesthetic criticism, then, keeps its highest praise for this so-called character drama in which each character makes his appearance unmistakably as a separate and single entity. Only from afar and by degrees the suspicion dawns here and there that all this is perhaps a cheap and superficial aesthetic philosophy and that we make a mistake in attributing to our great dramatists those magnificent conceptions of beauty that come to us from antiquity. These conceptions are not native to us, but are merely picked up at second hand, and it is in them, with their common source in the visible body, that the origin of the fiction of an ego, an individual, is really to be found. There is no trace of such a notion in the poems of ancient India. The heroes of the epics of India are not individuals, but whole reels of individualities in a series of incarnations. And in modern times there are poems, in which, behind the veil of a concern with individuality and character that is scarcely, indeed, in the author's mind, the motive is to present a manifold activity of soul. Whoever wishes to recognize this must resolve once and for all not to regard the characters of such a poem as separate beings, but as the various facets and aspects of a higher unity, in my opinion, of the poet's soul. If "Faust" is treated in this way, Faust, Mephistopheles, Wagner and the rest form a unity and a supreme individuality; and it is in this higher unity alone, not in the several characters, that something of the true nature of the soul is revealed. When Faust, in a line immortalized among schoolmasters and greeted with a shudder of astonishment by the Philistine, says, "Two souls, alas, inhabit in my breast!" he has forgotten Mephisto and a whole crowd of other souls that he has in his breast likewise. The Steppenwolf, too, believes that he bears two souls (wolf and man) in his breast and even so finds his breast disagreeably cramped because of them. The breast and the body are indeed one, but the souls that dwell in it are not two, nor five, but countless in number. Man is an onion made up of a hundred integuments, a texture made up of many threads. The ancient Asiatics knew this well enough, and in the Buddhist Yoga an exact technique was devised for unmasking the illusion of the personality. The human merry-go-round sees many changes: The illusion that cost India the efforts of thousands of years to unmask is the same illusion that the West has labored just as hard to maintain and strengthen.

If we consider the Steppenwolf from this standpoint it will be clear to us why he suffered so much under his ludicrous dual personality. He believes, like Faust, that two souls are far too many for a single breast and must tear the breast asunder. They are on the contrary far too few, and Harry does shocking violence to his poor soul when he endeavors to apprehend it by means of so primitive an image. Although he is a most cultivated person, he proceeds like a savage that cannot count further than two. He calls himself part wolf, part man, and with that he thinks he has come to an end and exhausted the matter. With the "man" he packs in everything spiritual and sublimated or even cultivated to be found in himself, and with the wolf all that is instinctive, savage and chaotic. But things are not so simple in life as in our thoughts, nor so rough and ready as in our poor idiotic language; and Harry lies about himself twice over when he employs this niggardly wolf theory. He assigns, we fear, whole provinces of his soul to the "man" which are a long way from being human, and parts of his being to the wolf that long ago have left the wolf behind.

. . .

That man is not yet a finished creation but rather a challenge of the spirit; a distant possibility dreaded as much as it is desired; that the way toward it has only been covered for a very short distance and with terrible agonies and ecstasies even by those few for whom it is the scaffold today and the monument tomorrow—all this the Steppenwolf, too, suspected. What, however, he calls the "man" in himself, as opposed to the wolf, is to a great extent nothing else than this very same average man of the bourgeois convention.

. . .

Man designs for himself a garden with a hundred kinds of trees, a thousand kinds of flowers, a hundred kinds of fruit and vegetables. Suppose, then, that the gardener of this garden knew no other distinction than between edible and inedible, nine-tenths of this garden would be useless to him. He would pull up the most enchanting flowers and hew down the noblest trees and even regard them with a loathing and envious eye. This is what the Steppenwolf does with the thousand flowers of his soul. What does not stand classified as either man or wolf he does not see at all. And consider all that he imputes to "man"! All that is cowardly and apish, stupid and mean—while to the wolf, only because he has not succeeded in making himself its master, is set down all that is strong and noble.

Now we bid Harry good-by and leave him to go on his way alone. Were he already among the immortals—were he already there at the goal to which his difficult path seems to be taking him, with what amazement he would look back to all this coming and going, all this indecision and wild zigzag trail. With what a mixture of encouragement and blame, pity and joy, he would smile at this Steppenwolf.

Martin Heidegger

(b. 1889) ———◆◆◆——— GERMAN

The central problem of Heidegger's philosophy is the "problem of Being." In his early work the investigation of Being is inseparably tied to Edmund Husserl's phenomenology, though the differences between teacher and student were sufficient to cause uncomfortable friction between them. In his later work the problem of Being, although never openly theological, becomes increasingly tied to traditional religious themes. It is the earlier work, particularly Being and Time, *that influenced Sartre, Merleau-Ponty, and other existentialists. There, the investigation of Being begins with the study of "human Being" —"Dasein," or "Being-in-the-world." Unlike Sartre, Heidegger does not begin his investigation with human consciousness, and the hyphenated "Being-in-the-world" is intended to warn us against "detaching" Dasein from the world in which it finds itself. Neither does Heidegger have sympathy for the Cartesian Ego and the Cartesian separation of subject and object. The Ego, he argues, is "a merely formal indicator," and the dualism of subject-object wrongly supposes that our "commerce" with the world is first of all to know it rather than to live in it. Accordingly, the identity of each Dasein ("the 'who' of Dasein") is to be found in a collective "they" (das Man) engaged in joint endeavors in the world rather than in the solipsistic Cartesian cogito. Dasein consists of both its* facticity *(its being "thrown" into the world at this place at this time) and* Existenz *(possibilities for personal choice). Dasein can be authentic insofar as it breaks away from the "they" to seek its own possibilities, of which the most necessary is death. In inauthenticity, Dasein falls back to the "they," identifies itself with its facticity and ignores the possibility of its own death. In inauthenticity or fallenness, the search for authentic understanding becomes mere curiosity; philosophical discourse, mere idle talk; thinking, mere calculation. Heidegger often insists that authenticity and inauthenticity are not ethical no-*

tions. (They are "ontological" or "descriptive".) Yet Heidegger also insists that there is an intimate connection between how we describe ourselves (our ontology) and who we are (our ontic character). He says, for example, "Granted that we cannot do anything with philosophy, but might not philosophy . . . do something with us?" Heidegger has indeed avoided both ethical and political involvement, his apparent excursions into either as much a product of interpretation as intention.

from
BEING AND TIME

The Ontical Priority of the Question of Being

Science in general may be defined as the totality established through an interconnection of true propositions. This defininition is not complete, nor does it reach the meaning of science. As ways in which man behaves, sciences have the manner of Being which this entity—man himself—possesses. This entity we denote by the term "*Dasein*". Scientific research is not the only manner of Being which this entity can have, nor is it the one which lies closest. Moreover, Dasein itself has a special distinctiveness as compared with other entities, and it is worth our while to bring this to view in a provisional way. Here our discussion must anticipate later analyses, in which our results will be authentically exhibited for the first time.

Dasein is an entity which does not just occur among other entities. Rather it is ontically distinguished by the fact that, in its very Being, that Being is an *issue* for it. But in that case, this is a constitutive state of Dasein's Being, and this implies that Dasein, in its Being, has a relationship towards that Being—a relationship which itself is one of Being. And this means further that there is some way in which Dasein understands itself in its Being, and that to some degree it does so

From *Being and Time* by Martin Heidegger, translated by John Macquarrie and Edward Robinson. Copyright © 1962 by SCM Press Ltd. Reprinted by permission of Harper & Row, Inc., and Basil Blackwell & Mott Ltd.

explicitly. It is peculiar to this entity that with and through its Being, this Being is disclosed to it. *Understanding of Being is itself a definite characteristic of Dasein's Being.* Dasein is ontically distinctive in that it *is* ontological.

Here "Being-ontological" is not yet tantamount to "developing an ontology". So if we should reserve the term "ontology" for that theoretical inquiry which is explicitly devoted to the meaning of entities, then what we have had in mind in speaking of Dasein's "Being-ontological" is to be designated as something "pre-ontological". It does not signify simply "being-ontical", however, but rather "being in such a way that one has an understanding of Being".

That kind of Being towards which Dasein can comport itself in one way or another, and always does comport itself somehow, we call *"existence"* [*Existenz*]. And because we cannot define Dasein's essence by citing a "what" of the kind that pertains to a subject-matter and because its essence lies rather in the fact that in each case it has its Being to be, and has it as its own, we have chosen to designate this entity as "Dasein", a term which is purely an expression of its Being.

Dasein always understands itself in terms of its existence— in terms of a possibility of itself: to be itself or not itself. Dasein has either chosen these possibilities itself, or got itself into them, or grown up in them already. Only the particular Dasein decides its existence, whether it does so by taking hold or by neglecting. The question of existence never gets straightened out except through existing itself. The understanding of oneself which leads *along this way* we call *"existentiell"*. The question of existence is one of Daesein's ontical 'affairs'. This does not require that the ontological structure of existence should be theoretically transparent. The question about that structure aims at the analysis of what constitutes existence. The context of such structures we call *"existentiality"*. Its analytic has the character of an understanding which is not existentiell, but rather *existential*. The task of an existential analytic of Dasein has been delineated in advance, as regards both its possibility and its necessity, in Dasein's ontical constitution.

. . .

The Theme of
the Analytic of Dasein

We are ourselves the entities to be analysed. The Being of any such entity is *in each case mine*. These entities, in their Being, comport themselves towards their Being. As entities with such Being, they are delivered over to their own Being. *Being* is that which is an issue for every such entity. This way of characterizing Dasein has a double consequence:

1. The 'essence' ["*Wesen*"] of this entity lies in its "to be" [*Zu-sein*]. Its Being-what-it-is [*Was-sein*] (*essentia*) must, so far as we can speak of it at all, be conceived in terms of its Being (*existentia*). But here our ontological task is to show that when we choose to designate the Being of this entity as "existence" [*Existenz*], this term does not and cannot have the ontological signification of the traditional term "*existentia*"; ontologically, *existentia* is tantamount to *Being-present-at-hand*, a kind of Being which is essentially inappropriate to entities of Dasein's character. To avoid getting bewildered, we shall always use the Interpretative expression "*presence-at-hand*" for the term "*existentia*", while the term "existence", as a designation of Being, will be allotted solely to Dasein.

The essence of Dasein lies in its existence. Accordingly those characteristics which can be exhibited in this entity are not 'properties' present-at-hand of some entity which 'looks' so and so and is itself present-at-hand; they are in each case possible ways for it to be, and no more than that. All the Being-as-it-is [*So-sein*] which this entity possesses is primarily Being. So when we designate this entity with the term 'Dasein', we are expressing not its "what" (as if it were a table, house or tree) but its Being.

2. That Being which is an *issue* for this entity in its very Being, is in each case mine. Thus Dasein is never to be taken ontologically as an instance or special case of some genius of entities as things that are present-at-hand. To entities such as these, their Being is 'a matter of indifference'; or more precisely, they 'are' such that their Being can be neither a matter of indifference to them, nor the opposite. Because Dasein has *in each case mineness*, one must always use a *personal* pronoun when one addresses it: 'I am', 'you are'.

Furthermore, in each case Dasein is mine to be in one way or another. Dasein has always made some sort of decision as to the way in which it is in each case mine [je meines]. That entity which in its Being has this very Being as an issue, comports itself towards its Being as its ownmost possibility. In each case Dasein *is* its possibility, and it 'has' this possibility, but not just as a property, as something present-at-hand would. And because Dasein is in each case essentially its own possibility, it *can*, in its very Being, 'choose' itself and win itself; it can also lose itself and never win itself; or only 'seem' to do so. But only in so far as it is essentially something which can be *authentic*—that is, something of its own—can it have lost itself and not yet won itself. As modes of Being, *authenticity* and *inauthenticity* (these expressions have been chosen terminologically in a strict sense) are both grounded in the fact that any Dasein whatsoever is characterized by mineness. But the inauthenticity of Dasein does not signify any 'less' Being or any 'lower' degree of Being. Rather it is the case that even in its fullest concretion Dasein can be characterized by inauthenticity—when busy, when excited, when interested, when ready for enjoyment. . . .

. . . At the outset of our analysis it is particularly important that Dasein should not be Interpreted with the differentiated character of some definite way of existing, but that it should be uncovered [*aufgedeckt*] in the undifferentiated character which it has proximally and for the most part. . . . We call this everyday undifferentiated character of Dasein "*averageness.*" . . .

Dasein's average everydayness, however, is not to be taken as a mere 'aspect'. Here too, and even in the mode of inauthenticity, the structure of existentiality lies *a priori*. And here too Dasein's Being is an issue for it in a definite way; and Dasein comports itself towards it in the mode of average everydayness, even if this is only the mode of fleeing *in the face of it* and forgetfulness *thereof.*

• • •

The "Who" of Dasein

The answer to the question of who Dasein is, is one that was seemingly given in Section 9, where we indicated formally the basic characteristics of Dasein. Dasein is an entity which is in each case I myself; its Being is in each case mine. This definition *indicates* an *ontologically* constitutive state, but it does no more than indicate it. At the same time this tells us *ontically* (though in a rough and ready fashion) that in each case an "I"—not Others—is this entity. The question of the "who" answers itself in terms of the "I" itself, the 'subject', the 'Self'. The "who" is what maintains itself as something identical throughout changes in its Experiences and ways of behaviour, and which relates itself to this changing multiplicity in so doing. Ontologically we understand it as something which is in each case already constantly present-at-hand, both in and for a closed realm, and which lies at the basis, in a very special sense, as the *subjectum*. As something selfsame in manifold otherness, it has the character of the *Self*. Even if one rejects the "soul substance" and the Thinghood of consciousness, or denies that a person is an object, ontologically one is still positing something whose Being retains the meaning of present-at-hand, whether it does so explicitly or not. Substantiality is the ontological clue for determining which entity is to provide the answer to the question of the "who". Dasein is tacitly conceived in advance as something present-at-hand. This meaning of Being is always implicated in any case where the Being of Dasein has been left indefinite. Yet presence-at-hand is the kind of Being which belongs to entities whose character is not that of Dasein.

The assertion that it is I who in each case Dasein is, is ontically obvious; but this must not mislead us into supposing that the route for an ontological Interpretation of what is 'given' in this way has thus been unmistakably prescribed. Indeed it remains questionable whether even the mere ontical content of the above assertion does propr justice to the stock of phenomena belonging to everyday Dasein. It could be that the "who" of everyday Dasein just is *not* the "I myself".

. . .

. . . Perhaps when Dasein addresses itself in the way which is closest to itself, it always says "I am this entity", and in the long run says this loudest when it is 'not' this entity. Dasein is in each case mine, and this is its constitution; but what if this should be the very reason why, proximally and for the most part, Dasein *is not itself*? What if the aforementioned approach, starting with the givenness of the "I" to Dasein itself, and with a rather patent self-interpretation of Dasein, should lead the existential analytic, as it were, into a pitfall? If that which is accessible by mere "giving" can be determined, there is presumably an ontological horizon for determining it; but what if this horizon should remain in principle undetermined? It may well be that it is always ontically correct to say of this entity that 'I' am it. Yet the ontological analytic which makes use of such assertions must make certain reservations about them in principle. The word 'I' is to be understood only in the sense of a non-committal *formal indicator,* indicating something which may perhaps reveal itself as its 'opposite' in some particular phenomenal context of Being. In that case, the 'not-I' is by no means tantamount to an entity which essentially lacks 'I-hood' but is rather a definite kind of Being which the 'I' itself possesses, such as having lost itself.

Yet even the positive Interpretation of Dasein which we have so far given, already forbids us to start with the formal givenness of the "I", if our purpose is to answer the question of the "who" in a way which is phenomenally adequate. In clarifying Being-in-the-world we have shown that a bare subject without a world never 'is' proximally, nor is it ever given. And so in the end an isolated "I" without Others is just as far from being proximally given.

. . .

But if the Self is conceived 'only' as a way of Being of this entity, this seems tantamount to volatilizing the real 'core' of Dasein. Any apprehensiveness however which one may have about this gets its nourishment from the perverse assumption that the entity in question has at bottom the kind of Being which belongs to something present-at-hand, even if one is far from attributing to it the solidity of an occurrent corporeal Thing. Yet man's *'substance'* is not spirit as a synthesis of soul and body; it is rather *existence.*

. . .

Thus in characterizing the encountering of *Others,* one is again still oriented by that Dasein which is in each case one's *own.* But even in this characterization does one not start by marking out and isolating the 'I' so that one must then seek some way of getting over to the Others from this isolated subject? To avoid this misunderstanding we must notice in what sense we are talking about 'the Others'. By 'Others' we do not mean everyone else but me—those over against whom the "I" stands out. They are rather those from whom, for the most part, one does *not* distinguish oneself—those among whom one is too. This Being-there-too with them does not have the ontological character of a Being-present-at-hand-along-'with' them within a world. This 'with' is something of the character

of Dasein; the 'too' means a sameness of Being as circumspec-
tively concernful Being-in-the-world. 'With' and 'too' are to
be understood *existentially*, not categorically. By reason of this
with-like Being-in-the-world, the world is always the one that
I share with Others. The world of Dasein is a *with-world*
[*Mitwelt*]. Being-in is *Being-with* Others. Their Being-in-
themselves within-the-world is *Dasein-with* [*Mitdasein*].

· · ·

According to the analysis which we have now completed,
Being with Others belongs to the Being of Dasein, which is
an issue for Dasein in its very Being. Thus as Being-with,
Dasein 'is' essentially for the sake of Others. This must be
understood as an existential statement as to its essence. Even
if the particular factical Dasein does *not* turn to Others, and
supposes that it has no need of them or manages to get
along without them, it *is* in the way of Being-with. In Being-
with, as the existential "for-the-sake-of" of Others, these have
already been disclosed in their Dasein.

· · ·

One's own Dasein, like the Dasein-with of Others, is encountered proximally and for the most part in terms of the
with-world with which we are environmentally concerned.
When Dasein is absorbed in the world of its concern—that is,
at the same time, in its Being-with towards Others—it is not
itself. *Who* is it, then, who has taken over Being as everyday
Being-with-one-another?

Everyday Being-one's-Self
and the "They"

The *ontologically* relevant result of our analysis of Being-with
is the insight that the 'subject character' of one's own Dasein
and that of Others is to be defined existentially—that is, in
terms of certain ways in which one may be. In that with
which we concern ourselves environmentally the Others are
encountered as what they are; they *are* what they do [*sie sind
das, was sie betreiben*].

In one's concern with what one has taken hold of, whether
with, for, or against, the Others, there is constant care as to
the way one differs from them, whether that difference is

merely one that is to be evened out, whether one's own Dasein has lagged behind the Others and wants to catch up in relationship to them, or whether one's Dasein already has some priority over them and sets out to keep them suppressed. The care about this distance between them is disturbing to Being-with-one-another, though this disturbance is one that is hidden from it. If we may express this existentially, such Being-with-one-another has the character of *distantiality*. The more inconspicuous this kind of Being is to everyday Dasein itself, all the more stubbornly and primordially does it work itself out.

But this distantiality which belongs to Being-with, is such that Dasein, as everyday Being-with-one-another, stands in *subjection* to Others. It itself *is* not; its Being has been taken away by the Others. Dasein's everyday possibilities of Being are for the Others to dispose of as they please. These Others, moreover, are not *definite* Others. On the contrary, any Other can represent them. What is decisive is just that inconspicuous domination by Others which has already been taken over unawares from Dasein as Being-with. One belongs to the Others oneself and enhances their power. 'The Others' whom one thus designates in order to cover up the fact of one's belonging to them essentially oneself, are those who proximally and for the most part '*are there*' in everyday Being-with-one-another. The "who" is not this one, not that one, not oneself, not some people, and not the sum of them all. The 'who' is the neuter, *the "they"* [*das Man*].

We have shown earlier how in the environment which lies closest to us, the public 'environment' already is ready-to-hand and is also a matter of concern. In utilizing public means of transport and in making use of information services such as the newspaper, every Other is like the next. This Being-with-one-another dissolves one's own Dasein completely into the kind of Being of 'the Others', in such a way, indeed, that the Others, as distinguishable and explicit, vanish more and more. In this inconspicuousness and unascertainability, the real dictatorship of the "they" is unfolded. We take pleasure and enjoy ourselves as *they* [*man*] take pleasure; we read, see, and judge about literature and art as *they* see and judge; likewise we shrink back from the 'great mass' as *they* shrink back; we find 'shocking' what *they* find shocking. The "they", which is nothing definite, and which all are, though not as the sum, prescribes the kind of Being of everydayness.

The "they" has its own ways in which to be. That tendency of Being-with which we have called "distantiality" is grounded in the fact that Being-with-one-another concerns itself as such with *averageness*, which is an existential characteristic of the "they". The "they", in its Being, essentially makes an issue of this. Thus the "they" maintains itself factically in the averageness of that which belongs to it, of that which it regards as valid and that which it does not, and of that to which it grants success and that to which it denies it. In this averageness with which it prescribes what can and may be ventured, it keeps watch over everything exceptional that thrusts itself to the fore. Every kind of priority gets noiselessly suppressed. Overnight, everything that is primordial gets glossed over as something that has long been well known. Everything gained by a struggle becomes just something to be manipulated. Every secret loses its force. This care of averageness reveals in turn an essential tendency of Dasein which we call the "levelling down" of all possibilities of Being.

Distantiality, averageness, and levelling down, as ways of Being for the "they", constitute what we know as 'publicness'. Publicness proximally controls every way in which the world and Dasein get interpreted, and it is always right—not because there is some distinctive and primary relationship-of-Being in which it is related to 'Things', or because it avails itself of some transparency on the part of Dasein which it has explicitly appropriated, but because it is insensitive to every difference of level and of genuineness and thus never gets to the 'heart of the matter'. By publicness everything gets obscured, and what has thus been covered up gets passed off as something familiar and accessible to everyone.

The "they" is there alongside everywhere, but in such a manner that it has always stolen away whenever Dasein presses for a decision. Yet because the "they" presents every judgment and decision as its own, it deprives the particular Dasein of its answerability. The "they" can, as it were, manage to have 'them' constantly invoking it. It can be answerable for everything most easily, because it is not someone who needs to vouch for anything. It 'was' always the "they" who did it, and yet it can be said that it has been 'no one'. In Dasein's everydayness the agency through which most things come about is one of which we must say that "it was no one".

Thus the particular Dasein in its everydayness is *disburdened* by the "they". Not only that; by thus disburdening it of its Being, the "they" accommodates Dasein if Dasein has any tendency to take things easily and make them easy. And because the "they" constantly accommodates the particular Dasein by disburdening it of its Being, the "they" retains and enhances its stubborn dominion.

Everyone is the other, and no one is himself. The *"they"*, which supplies the answer to the question of the *"who"* of everyday Dasein, is the *"nobody"* to whom every Dasein has already surrendered itself in Being-among-one-other.

Furthermore, the "they" is not something like a 'universal subject' which a plurality of subjects have hovering above them. One can come to take it this way only if the Being of such 'subjects' is understood as having a character other than that of Dasein, and if these are regarded as cases of a genus of occurrents—cases which are factually present-at-hand. With this approach, the only possibility ontologically is that everything which is not a case of this sort is to be understood in the sense of genus and species. The "they" is not the genus to which the individual Dasein belongs, nor can we come across it in such entities as an abiding characteristic.

. . .

The Self of everyday Dasein is the *they-self*, which we distinguish from the *authentic Self*—that is, from the Self which has been taken hold of in its own way. As they-self, the particular Dasein has been *dispersed* into the "they", and must first find itself. This dispersal characterizes the 'subject' of that kind of Being which we know as concernful absorption in the world we encounter as closest to us. If Dasein is familiar with itself as they-self, this means at the same time that the "they" itself prescribes that way of interpreting the world and Being-in-the-world which lies closest. Dasein is for the sake of the "they" in an everyday manner, and the "they" itself Articulates the referential context of significance. When entities are encountered, Dasein's world frees them for a totality of involvements with which the "they" is familiar, and within the limits which have been established with the "they's" averageness. *Proximally*, factical Dasein is in the with-world, which is discovered in an average way. *Proximally*, it is not 'I', in the sense of my own Self, that 'am', but rather the Others, whose way is that of the "they". In terms of the "they", and as the "they", I am 'given' proximally to 'myself'. Proximally Dasein is "they", and for the most part it remains so. If Dasein discovers the world in its own way and brings it close, if it discloses to itself its own authentic Being, then this discovery of the 'world' and this disclosure of Dasein are always accomplished as a clearing-away of concealments and obscurities, as a breaking up of the disguises with which Dasein bars its own way.

• • •

[On Falling and Inauthenticity]

This term ["Falling"] does not express any negative evaluation, but is used to signify that Dasein is proximally and for the most part *alongside* the 'world' of its concern. This "absorption in . . ." has mostly the character of Being-lost in the publicness of the "they", Dasein has, in the first instance, fallen away from itself as an authentic potentiality for Being its Self, and has fallen into the 'world'. "Fallenness" into the 'world' means an absorption in Being-with-one-another, in so far as the latter is guided by idle talk, curiosity, and ambiguity. Through the Interpretation of falling, what we have called the "inauthenticity" of Dasein may now be defined more precisely. On no account, however, do the terms "inauthentic" and "non-authentic" signify 'really not'; as if in this mode of Being, Dasein were altogether to lose its Being. "Inauthenticity" does not mean anything like Being-no-longer-in-the-world, but amounts rather to a quite distinctive kind of Being-in-the-world—the kind which is completely fascinated by the 'world' and by the Dasein-with of Others in the "they". Not-Being-its-self functions as a *positive* possibility of that entity which, in its essential concern, is absorbed in a world. The kind of *not-Being* has to be conceived as that kind of Being which is closest to Dasein and in which Dasein maintains itself for the most part.

So neither must we take the fallenness of Dasein as a 'fall' from a purer and higher 'primal status'. Not only do we lack any experience of this ontically, but ontologically we lack any possibilities or clues for Interpreting it.

In falling, Dasein *itself* as factical Being-in-the-world, is something *from* which it has already fallen away. And it has not fallen into some entity which it comes upon for the first time in the course of its Being, or even one which it has not come upon at all; it has fallen into the *world*, which itself belongs to its Being. Falling is a definite existential characteristic of Dasein itself. It makes no assertion about Dasein as something present-at-hand, or about present-at-hand relations to entities from which Dasein 'is descended' or with which Dasein has subsequently wound up in some sort of *commercium.*

We would also misunderstand the ontologico-existential structure of falling if we were to ascribe to it the sense of a bad and deplorable ontical property of which, perhaps, more advanced stages of human culture might be able to rid themselves.

• • •

Idle talk discloses to Dasein a Being towards its world, towards Others, and towards itself—a Being in which these are understood, but in a mode of groundless floating. Curiosity discloses everything and anything, yet in such a way that Being-in is everywhere and nowhere. Ambiguity hides nothing from Dasein's understanding, but only in order that Being-in-the-world should be suppressed in this uprooted "everywhere and nowhere".

By elucidating ontologically the kind of Being belonging to everyday Being-in-the-world as it shows through in these phenomena, we first arrive at an existentially adequate determination of Dasein's basic state. Which is the structure that shows us the 'movement' of falling?

Idle talk and the way things have been publicly interpreted (which idle talk includes) constitute themselves in Being-with-one-another. Idle talk is not something present-at-hand for itself within the world, as a product detached from Being-with-one-another. And it is just as far from letting itself be volatilized to something 'universal' which, because it belongs essentially to nobody, is 'really' nothing and occurs as 'Real' only in the individual Dasein which speaks. Idle talk is the kind of Being that belongs to Being-with-one-another itself; it does not first arise through certain circumstances which have effects upon Dasein 'from outside'. But if Dasein itself. in idle talk and in the way things have been publicly interpreted, presents to itself the possibility of losing itself in the "they" and falling into groundlessness, this tells us that Dasein prepares for itself a constant temptation towards falling. Being-in-the-world is in itself *tempting. . . .*

Since the way in which things have been publicly interpreted has already become a temptation to itself in this manner, it holds Dasein fast in its fallenness. Idle talk and ambiguity, having seen everything, having understood everything, develop the supposition that Dasein's disclosedness, which is so available and so prevalent, can guarantee to Dasein that all the possibilities of its Being will be secure, genuine, and full. Through the self-certainty and decidedness of the "they", it gets spread abroad increasingly that there is no need of authentic understanding or the state-of-mind that goes with it. The supposition of the "they" that one is leading and sustaining a full and genuine 'life', brings Dasein a *tranquillity*, for which everything is 'in the best of order' and all doors are open. Falling Being-in-the-world, which tempts itself, is at the same time *tranquillizing*.

However, this tranquillity in inauthentic Being does not seduce one into stagnation and inactivity, but drives one into uninhibited 'hustle'. Being-fallen into the 'world' does not now somehow come to rest. The tempting tranquillization *aggravates* the falling. With special regard to the interpretation of Dasein, the opinion may now arise that understanding the most alien cultures and 'synthesizing' them with one's own may lead to Dasein's becoming for the first time thoroughly and genuinely enlightened about itself. Versatile curiosity and restlessly "knowing it all" masquerade as a universal understanding of Dasein. But at bottom it remains indefinite *what* is really to be understood, and the question has not even been asked. Nor has it been understood that understanding itself is a potentiality-for-Being which must be made free in one's *ownmost* Dasein alone. When Dasein, tranquillized, and 'understanding' everything, thus compares itself with everything, it drifts along towards an alienation [*Entfremdung*] in which its ownmost potentiality-for-Being is hidden from it. Falling Being-in-the-world is not only tempting and tranquillizing; it is at the same time *alienating*.

Yet this alienation cannot mean that Dasein gets factically torn away from itself. On the contrary, this alienation drives it into a kind of Being which borders on the most exaggerated 'self-dissection', tempting itself with all possibilities of explanation, so that the very 'characterologies' and 'typologies' which it has brought about are themselves already becoming something that cannot be surveyed at a glance. This alienation *closes off* from Dasein its authenticity and possibility, even if only the possibility of genuinely foundering. It does not, however, surrender Dasein to an entity which Dasein itself is not, but forces it into its inauthenticity—into a possible kind of Being *of itself*. The alienation of falling—at once tempting and tranquillizing—leads by its own movement, to Dasein's getting *entangled* in itself.

The phenomena we have pointed out—temptation, tranquillizing, alienation and self-entangling (entanglement)—characterize the specific kind of Being which belongs to falling. This 'movement' of Dasein in its own Being, we call its *"downward plunge"*. Dasein plunges out of itself into itself, into the groundlessness and nullity of inauthentic everydayness. But this plunge remains hidden from Dasein by the way things have been publicly interpreted, so much so, indeed, that it gets interpreted as a way of 'ascending' and 'living concretely'.

This downward plunge into and within the groundlessness of the inauthentic Being of the "they", has a kind of motion which constantly tears the understanding away from the projecting of authentic possibilities, and into the tranquillized supposition that it possesses everything, or that everything is within its reach. Since the understanding is thus constantly torn away from authenticity and into the "they" (though always with a sham of authenticity), the movement of falling is characterized by *turbulence*.

Falling is not only existentially determinative for Being-in-the world. At the same time turbulence makes manifest that the thrownness which can obtrude itself upon Dasein in its state-of-mind, has the character of throwing and of movement. Thrownness is neither a 'fact that is finished' nor a Fact that is settled. Dasein's facticity is such that *as long as* it is what it is, Dasein remains in the throw, and is sucked into the turbulence of the "they's" inauthenticity. Thrownness, in which facticity lets itself be seen phenomenally, belongs to Dasein, for which, in its Being, that very Being is an issue. Dasein exists factically.

But now that falling has been exhibited, have we not set forth a phenomenon which speaks directly *against* the definition we have used in indicating the formal idea of existence? Can Dasein be conceived as an entity for which, in its Being, its potentiality-for-Being is an *issue*, if this entity, in its very everydayness, *has lost itself*, and, in falling, 'lives' *away from itself*? But falling into the world would be phenomenal 'evidence' *against* the existentiality of Dasein only if Dasein were regarded as an isolated "I" or subject, as a self-point from which it moves away. In that case, the world would be an Object. Falling into the world would then have to be re-Interpreted ontologically as Being-present-at-hand in the manner of an entity within-the-world. If, however, we keep in mind that Dasein's Being is in the state of *Being-in-the-world*, as we have already pointed out, then it becomes manifest that falling, as a *kind of Being of this Being-in*, affords us rather the most elemental evidence *for* Dasein's existentiality. In falling, nothing other than our potentiality-for-Being-in-the-world is the issue, even if in the mode of inauthenticity. Dasein *can* fall only *because* Being-in-the-world understandingly with a state-of-mind is an issue for it. On the other hand, *authentic* existence is not something which floats above falling everydayness; existentially, it is only a modified way in which such everydayness is seized upon.

The phenomenon of falling does not give us something like a 'night view' of Dasein, a property which occurs ontically and may serve to round out the innocuous aspects of this entity. Falling reveals an *essential* ontological structure of Dasein itself. Far from determining its nocturnal side, it constitutes all Dasein's days in their everydayness.

It follows that our existential-ontological Interpretation makes no ontical assertion about the 'corruption of human Nature', not because the necessary evidence is lacking, but because the problematic of this Interpretation is *prior* to any assertion about corruption or incorruption. Falling is conceived ontologically as a kind of motion. Ontically, we have not decided whether man is 'drunk with sin' and in the *status corruptionis*, whether he walks in the *status integritatis*, or whether he finds himself in an intermediate stage, the *status gratiae*. But in so far as any faith or 'world view', makes any such assertions, and if it asserts anything about Dasein as Being-in-the-world, it must come back to the existential structures which we have set forth, provided that its assertions are to make a claim to *conceptual* understanding.

The leading question of this chapter has been about the Being of the "there". Our theme has been the ontological Constitution of the disclosedness which essentially belongs to Dasein. The Being of that disclosedness is constituted by states-of-mind, understanding, and discourse. Its everyday kind of Being is characterized by idle talk, curiosity, and ambiguity. These show us the movement of falling, with temptation, tranquillizing, alienation, and entanglement as its essential characteristics.

But with this analysis, the whole existential constitution of Dasein has been laid bare in its principal features, and we have obtained the phenomenal ground for a 'comprehensive' Interpretation of Dasein's Being as care.

[On Death and Authenticity]

When Dasein reaches its wholeness in death, it simultaneously loses the Being of its "there". By its transition to no-longer-Dasein, it gets lifted right out of the possibility of experiencing this transition and of understanding it as something experienced. Surely this sort of thing is denied to any particular Dasein in relation to itself. But this makes the death of Others more impressive. In this way a termination of Dasein becomes 'Objectively" accessible. Dasein can thus gain an experience of death, all the more so because Dasein is essentially Being with Others. In that case, the fact that death has been thus 'Objectively' given must make possible an ontological delimitation of Dasein's totality.

• • •

But if 'ending', as dying, is constitutive for Dasein's totality, then the Being of this wholeness itself must be conceived as an existential phenomenon of a Dasein which is in each case one's own. In 'ending', and in Dasein's Being-a-whole, for which such ending is constitutive, there is, by its very essence, no representing. These are the facts of the case existentially; one fails to recognize this when one interposes the expedient of making the dying of Others a substitute theme for the analysis of totality.

• • •

We may formulate in three theses the discussion of death up to this point: 1. there belongs to Dasein, as long as it is, a "not-yet" which it will be—that which is constantly still outstanding; 2. the coming-to-its-end of what-is-not-yet-at-an-end (in which what is still outstanding is liquidated as regards its Being) has the character of no-longer-Dasein; 3. coming-to-an-end implies a mode of Being in which the particular Dasein simply cannot be represented by someone else.

. . .

From our considerations of totality, end, and that which is still outstanding, there has emerged the necessity of Interpreting the phenomenon of death as Being-towards-the-end, and of doing so in terms of Dasein's basic state. Only so can it be made plain to what extent Being-a-whole, as constituted by Being-towards-the-end, is possible in Dasein itself in conformity with the structure of its Being. We have seen that care is the basic state of Dasein. The ontological signification of the expression "care" has been expressed in the 'definition'; "ahead-of-itself-Being-already-in (the world) as Being-alongside entities which we encounter (within-the-world)". In this are expressed the fundamental characteristics of Dasein's Being; existence, in the "ahead-of-itself"; facticity, in the "Being-already-in"; falling, in the "Being-alongside". If indeed death belongs in a distinctive sense to the Being of Dasein, then death (or Being-towards-the-end) must be defined in terms of these characteristics.

. . .

But if Being-towards-death belongs primordially and essentially to Dasein's Being, then it must also be exhibitable in everydayness, even if proximally in a way which is inauthentic. And if Being-towards-the-end should afford the existential possibility of an existentiell Being-a-whole for Dasein, then this would give phenomenal confirmation for the thesis that "care" is the ontological term for the totality of Dasein's structural whole. . . .

Being-towards-death and the Everydayness of Dasein

In setting forth average everyday Being-towards-death, we must take our orientation from those structures of everydayness at which we have earlier arrived. In Being-towards-death, Dasein comports itself *towards itself* as a distinctive potentiality-for-Being. But the Self of everydayness is the "they". The "they" is constituted by the way things have been publicly interpreted, which expresses itself in idle talk. Idle talk must accordingly make manifest the way in which everyday Dasein interprets for itself its Being-towards-death. The foundation of any interpretation is an act of understanding, which is always accompanied by a state-of-mind, or, in other words, which has a mood. So we must ask how Being-towards-death is disclosed by the kind of understanding which, with its state-of-mind, lurks in the idle talk of the "they". How does the "they" comport itself understandingly towards that ownmost possibility of Dasein, which is non-relational and is not to be outstripped? What state-of-mind discloses to the "they" that it has been delivered over to death, and in what way?

In the publicness with which we are with one another in our everyday manner, death is 'known' as a mishap which is constantly occurring—as a 'case of death'. Someone or other 'dies', be he neighbour or stranger. . . . People who are no acquaintances of ours are 'dying' daily and hourly. 'Death' is encountered as a well-known event occurring within-the-world. As such it remains in the inconspicuousness characteristic of what is encountered in an everyday fashion. The "they" has already stowed away an interpretation for this event. It talks of it in a 'fugitive' manner, either expressly or else in a way which is mostly inhibited, as if to say, "One of these days one will die too, in the end; but right now it has nothing to do with us."

The analysis of the phrase 'one dies' reveals unambiguously the kind of Being which belongs to everyday Being-towards-death. In such a way of talking, death is understood as an indefinite something which, above all, must duly arrive from somewhere or other, but which is proximally *not yet present-at-hand* for oneself, and is therefore no threat. The expression 'one dies' spreads abroad the opinion that what gets reached, as it were, by death, is the "they". In Dasein's public way of interpreting, it is said that 'one dies', because everyone else and oneself can talk himself into saying that "in no case is it I myself", for this "one" is *the "nobody"*. 'Dying' is levelled off to an occurrence which reaches Dasein, to be sure, but belongs to nobody in particular. If idle talk is always ambiguous, so is this manner of talking about death. Dying, which is essentially mine in such a way that no one can be my representative, is perverted into an event of public occurrence which the "they" encounters. In the way of talking which we have characterized, death is spoken of as a 'case' which is constantly occurring. Death gets passed off as always something 'actual'; its character as a possibility gets concealed, and so are the other two items that belong to it—the fact that it is non-relational and that it is not to be outstripped. By such ambiguity, Dasein puts itself in the position of losing itself in the "they" as regards a distinctive potentiality-for-Being which belongs to Dasein's ownmost Self. The "they" gives its approval, and aggravates the *temptation* to cover up from oneself one's ownmost Being-towards-death. This evasive concealment in the face of death dominates everydayness so stubbornly that, in Being with one another, the 'neighbours' often still keep talking the 'dying person' into the belief that he will escape death and soon return to the tranquillized everydayness of the world of his concern. Such 'solicitude' is meant to 'console' him. It insists upon bringing him back into Dasein, while in addition it helps him to keep his ownmost non-relational possibility-of-Being completely concealed. In this manner the "they" provides a *constant tranquillization about death*. At bottom, however, this is a tranquillization not only for him who is 'dying' but just as much for those who 'console' him. And even in the case of a demise, the public is still not to have its own tranquillity upset by such an event, or be disturbed in the carefreeness with which it concerns itself. Indeed the dying of Others is seen often enough as a social inconvenience, if not even a downright tactlessness, against which the public is to be guarded.

But along with this tranquillization, which forces Dasein away from its death, the "they" at the same time puts itself in the right and makes itself respectable by tacitly regulating the way in which *one* has to comport oneself towards death. It is already a matter of public acceptance that 'thinking about death' is a cowardly fear, a sign of insecurity on the part of Dasein, and a sombre way of fleeing from the world. *The "they" does not permit us the courage for anxiety in the face of death.* The dominance of the manner in which things have been publicly interpreted by the "they", has already decided what state-of-mind is to determine our attitude towards death. In anxiety in the face of death, Dasein is brought face to face with itself as delivered over to that possibility which is not to be outstripped. The "they" concerns itself with transforming this anxiety into fear in the face of an oncoming event. In addition, the anxiety which has been made ambiguous as fear, is passed off as a weakness with which no self-assured Dasein may have any acquaintance.

What is 'fitting' according to the unuttered decree of the "they", is indifferent tranquillity as to the 'fact' that one dies. The cultivation of such a 'superior' indifference *alienates* Dasein from its ownmost non-relational potentiality-for-Being.

But temptation, tranquillization, and alienation are distinguishing marks of the kind of Being called "*falling*". As falling, everyday Being-towards-death is a constant *fleeing in the face of death*. Being-*towards*-the-end has the mode of *evasion in the face of it*—giving new explanations for it, understanding it inauthentically, and concealing it. Factically one's own Dasein is always dying already; that is to say, it is in a Being-towards-its-end. And it hides this Fact from itself by recoining "death" as just a "case of death" in Others —an everyday occurrence which, it need be, gives us the assurance still more plainly that 'oneself' is still 'living'. But in thus falling and fleeing *in the face of* death, Dasein's everydayness attests that the very "they" itself already has the definite character of *Being-towards-death*, even when it is not explicitly engaged in 'thinking about death'. *Even in average everydayness, this ownmost potentiality-for-Being, which is non-relational and not to be outstripped, is constantly an issue for Dasein. This is the case when its concern is merely in the mode of an untroubled indifference* towards *the uttermost possibility of existence.*

• • •

Dasein is constituted by disclosedness—that is, by an understanding with a state-of-mind. *Authentic* Being-towards-death can *not evade* its ownmost non-relational possibility, or *cover up* this possibility by thus fleeing from it, or *give a new explanation* for it to accord with the common sense of the "they". In our existential projection of an authentic Being-towards-death, therefore, we must set forth those items in such a Being which are constitutive for it as an understanding of death—and as such an understanding in the sense of Being towards this possibility without either fleeing it or covering it up.

• • •

Manifestly Being-towards-death, which is now in question, cannot have the character of concernfully Being out to get itself actualized. For one thing, death as possible is not something possible which is ready-to-hand or present-at-hand, but a possibility of *Dasein's* Being. So to concern oneself with actualizing what is thus possible would have to signify, "bringing about one's demise". But if this were done, Dasein would deprive itself of the very ground for an existing Being-towards-death.

Thus, if by "Being-towards-death" we do not have in view an 'actualizing' of death, neither can we mean "dwelling upon the end in its possibility". This is the way one comports oneself when one 'thinks about death', pondering over when and how this possibility may perhaps be actualized. Of course such brooding over death does not fully take away from it its character as a possibility: Indeed, it always gets brooded over as something that is coming; but in such brooding we weaken it by calculating how we are to have it at our disposal. As something possible, it is to show as little as possible of its possibility. On the other hand, if Being-towards-death has to disclose understandingly the possibility which we have characterized, and if it is to disclose it *as a possibility*, then in such Being-towards-death this possibility must not be weakened: it must be understood *as a possibility*, it must be cultivated *as a possibility*, and we must *put up with* it *as a possibility*, in the way we comport ourselves towards it.

However, Dasein comports itself towards something possible in its possibility by *expecting* it. Anyone who is intent on something possible, may encounter it unimpeded and undiminished in its 'whether it comes or does not, or whether it comes after all'. But with this phenomenon of expecting, has not our analysis reached the same kind of Being towards the possible to which we have already called attention in our description of "Being out for something" concernfully? to expect something possible is always to understand it and to 'have' it with regard to whether and when and how it will be actually present-at-hand. Expecting is not just an occasional looking-away from the possible to its possible actualization, but is essentially a *waiting for that actualization*. Even in expecting. one leaps away from the possible and gets a foothold in the actual. It is for its actuality that what is expected is expected. By the very nature of expecting, the possible is drawn into the actual, arising out of the actual and returning to it.

. . .

Being-towards-death is the anticipation of a potentiality-for-Being of that entity whose kind of Being is anticipation itself. In the anticipatory revealing of this potentiality-for-

Being, Dasein discloses itself to itself as regards its uttermost possibility. But to project itself on its ownmost potentiality-for-Being means to be able to understand itself in the Being of the entity so revealed—namely, to exist. Anticipation turns out to be the possibility of understanding one's *ownmost* and uttermost potentiality-for-Being—that is to say, the possibility of *authentic existence*. The ontological constitution of such existence must be made visible by setting forth the concrete structure of anticipation of death. How are we to delimit this structure phenomenally? Manifestly, we must do so by determining those characteristics which must belong to an anticipatory disclosure so that it can become the pure understanding of that ownmost possibility which is non-relational and not to be outstripped—which is certain and, as such, indefinite. It must be noted that understanding does not primarily mean just gazing at a meaning, but rather understanding oneself in that potentiality-for-Being which reveals itself in projection.

Death is Dasein's *ownmost possibility*. Being towards this possibility discloses to Dasein its *ownmost* potentiality-for-Being, in which its very Being is the issue. Here it can become manifest to Dasein that in this distinctive possibility of its own self, it has been wrenched away from the "they". This means that in anticipation any Dasein can have wrenched itself away from the "they" already. But when one understands that this is something which Dasein 'can' have done, this only reveals its factical lostness in the everydayness of the they-self.

. . .

. . . In anticipating the indefinite certainty of death, Dasein opens itself to a constant *threat* arising out of its own "there". In this very threat Being-towards-the-end must maintain itself. So little can it tone this down that it must rather cultivate the indefiniteness of the certainty. How is it existentially possible for this constant threat to be genuinely disclosed? All understanding is accompanied by a state-of-mind. Dasein's mood brings it face to face with the thrownness of its 'that it is there'. *But the state-of-mind which can hold open the utter and constant threat to itself arising from Dasein's ownmost individualized Being, is anxiety*. In this state-of-mind, Dasein finds itself *face to face* with the "nothing" of the possible impossibility of its existence. Anxiety is anxious *about* the potentiality-for-Being of the entity so destined, and in this way it discloses the uttermost possibility. Anticipation utterly individualizes Dasein, and allows it, in this individualization of itself, to become certain of the totality of its potentiality-for-Being. For this reason, anxiety as a basic state-of-mind belongs to such a self-understanding of Dasein on the basis of Dasein itself. Being-towards-death is essentially anxiety. This is attested unmistakably, though 'only' indirectly, by Being-towards-death as we have described it, when it perverts anxiety into cowardly fear and, in surmounting this fear, only makes known its own cowardliness in the face of anxiety.

We may now summarize our characterization of authentic Being-towards-death as we have projected it existentially: *anticipation reveals to Dasein its lostness in the they-self, and brings it face to face with the possibility of being itself, primarily unsupported by concernful solicitude, but of being itself, rather, in an impassioned* freedom *towards death—a freedom which has been released from the Illusions of the "they", and which is factical, certain of itself, and anxious.*

THE FUNDAMENTAL QUESTION
OF METAPHYSICS

Why are there essents* rather than nothing? That is the question. Clearly it is no ordinary question. "Why are there essents, why is there anything at all, rather than nothing?"— obviously this is the first of all questions, though not in a chronological sense. Individuals and peoples ask a good many questions in the course of their historical passage through time. They examine, explore, and test a good many things before they run into the question "Why are there essents rather than nothing?" Many men never encounter this question, if by encounter we mean not merely to hear and read

From *An Introduction to Metaphysics* by Martin Heidegger, translated by Ralph Manheim. Copyright © 1959 by Yale University Press. Reprinted by permission of Yale University Press.
* *Entities, things that exist. (Editor's note.)*

about it as an interrogative formulation but to ask the question, that is, to bring it about, to raise it, to feel its inevitability.

And yet each of us is grazed at least once, perhaps more than once, by the hidden power of this question, even if he is not aware of what is happening to him. The question looms in moments of great despair, when things tend to lose all their weight and all meaning becomes obscured. Perhaps it will strike but once like a muffled bell that rings into our life and gradually dies away. It is present in moments of rejoicing, when all the things around us are transfigured and seem to be there for the first time, as if it might be easier to think they are not than to understand that they are and are as they are. The question is upon us in boredom, when we are equally removed from despair and joy, and everything about us seems so hopelessly commonplace that we no longer care whether anything is or is not—and with this the question "Why are there essents rather than nothing?" is evoked in a particular form.

But this question may be asked expressly, or, unrecognized as a question, it may merely pass through our lives like a brief gust of wind; it may press hard upon us, or, under one pretext or another, we may thrust it away from us and silence it. In any case it is never the question that we ask first in point of time.

But it is the first question in another sense—in regard to rank. This may be clarified in three ways. The question "Why are there essents rather than nothing?" is first in rank for us first because it is the most far reaching, second because it is the deepest, and finally because it is the most fundamental of all questions.

• • •

All essential philosophical questioning is necessarily untimely. This is so because philosophy is always projected far in advance of its time, or because it connects the present with its antecedent, with what *initially* was. Philosophy always remains a knowledge which not only cannot be adjusted to a given epoch but on the contrary imposes its measure upon its epoch.

Philosophy is essentially untimely because it is one of these few things that can never find an immediate echo in the present. When such an echo seems to occur, when a philosophy becomes fashionable, either it is no real philosophy or it has been misinterpreted and misused for ephemeral and extraneous purposes.

Accordingly, philosophy cannot be directly learned like manual and technical skills; it cannot be directly applied, or judged by its usefulness in the manner of economic or other professional knowledge.

But what is useless can still be a force, perhaps the only real force. What has no immediate echo in everyday life can be intimately bound up with a nation's profound historical development, and can even anticipate it. What is untimely will have its own times. This is true of philosophy. Consequently there is no way of determining once and for all what the task of philosophy is, and accordingly what must be expected of it. Every stage and every beginning of its development bears within it its own law. All that can be said is what philosophy cannot be and cannot accomplish.

• • •

Every essential form of spiritual life is marked by ambiguity. The less commensurate it is with other forms, the more it is misinterpreted.

Philosophy is one of the few autonomous creative possibilities and at times necessities of man's historical being-there [Dasein]. The current misinterpretations of philosophy, all of which have some truth about them, are legion. Here we shall mention only two, which are important because of the light they throw on the present and future situation of philosophy. The first misinterpretation asks too much of philosophy. The second distorts its function.

Roughly speaking, philosophy always aims at the first and last grounds of the essent, with particular emphasis on man himself and on the meaning and goals of human being-there. This might suggest that philosophy can and must provide a foundation on which a nation will build its historical life and culture. But this is beyond the power of philosophy. As a rule such excessive demands take the form of a belittling of philosophy It is said, for example: Because metaphysics did nothing to pave the way for the revolution it should be rejected. This is no cleverer than saying that because the carpenter's bench is useless for flying it should be abolished. Philosophy can never *directly* supply the energies and create the opportunities and methods that bring about a historical change; for one thing, because philosophy is always the concern of the few. Which few? The creators, those who initiate profound transformation. It spreads only indirectly, by devious paths that can never be laid out in advance, until at last, at some future date, it sinks to the level of a commonplace; but by then it has long been forgotten as original philosophy.

What philosophy essentially can and must be is this: a thinking that breaks the paths and opens the perspectives of the knowledge that sets the norms and hierarchies, of the knowledge in which and by which a people fulfills itself historically and culturally, the knowledge that kindles and necessitates all inquiries and thereby threatens all values.

The second misinterpretation involves a distortion of the function of philosophy. Even if philosophy can provide no foundation for a culture, the argument goes, it is nevertheless a cultural force, whether because it gives us an overall, systematic view of what is, supplying a useful chart by which we may find our way amid the various possible things and realms of things, or because it relieves the sciences of their work by reflecting on their premises, basic concepts, and principles. Philosophy is expected to promote and even to accelerate—to make easier as it were—the practical and technical business of culture.

But—it is in the very nature of philosophy never to make things easier but only more difficult. And this not merely because its language strikes the everyday understanding as strange if not insane. Rather, it is the authentic function of philosophy to challenge historical being-there and hence, in the last analysis, being pure and simple. It restores to things, to the essents, their weight (being). How so? Because the challenge is one of the essential prerequisites for the birth of all greatness, and in speaking of greatness we are referring primarily to the works and destinies of nations. We can speak of historical destiny only where an authentic knowledge of things dominates man's being-there. And it is philosophy that opens up the paths and perspectives of such knowledge.

The misinterpretations with which philosophy is perpetually beset are promoted most of all by people of our kind, that is, by professors of philosophy. It is our customary business—which may be said to be justified and even useful—to transmit a certain knowledge of the philosophy of the past, as part of a general education. Many people suppose that this is philosophy itself, whereas at best it is the technique of philosophy.

In correcting these two misinterpretations I cannot hope to give you at one stroke a clear conception of philosophy. But I do hope that you will be on your guard when the most current judgments and even supposed observations assail you unawares. Such judgments are often disarming, precisely because they seem so natural. You hear remarks such as "Philosophy leads to nothing," "You can't do anything with philosophy," and readily imagine that they confirm an expression of your own. There is no denying the soundness of these two phrases, particularly common among scientists and teachers of science. Any attempt to refute them by proving that after all it does "lead to something" merely strengthens the prevailing misinterpretation to the effect that the everyday standards by which we judge bicycles or sulphur baths are applicable to philosophy.

It is absolutely correct and proper to say that "You can't do anything with philosophy." It is only wrong to suppose that this is the last word on philosophy. For the rejoinder imposes itself; granted that *we* cannot do anything with philosophy, might not philosophy, if we concern ourselves with it, do something *with us*? So much for what philosophy is not.

At the outset we stated a question: "Why are there essents rather than nothing?" We have maintained that to ask this question is to philosophize. When in our thinking we open our minds to this question, we first of all cease to dwell in any of the familiar realms. We set aside everything that is on the order of the day. Our question goes beyond the familiar and the things that have their place in everyday life. Nietzsche once said (*Werke*, 7, 269): "A philosopher is a man who never ceases to experience, see, hear, suspect, hope, and dream extraordinary things . . ."

To philosophize is to inquire into the *extra*-ordinary. But because, as we have just suggested, this questioning recoils upon itself, not only what is asked after is extra-ordinary but also the asking itself. In other words: this questioning does not lie along the way so that we bump into it one day unexpectedly. Nor is it part of everyday life: there is no requirement or regulation that forces us into it; it gratifies no urgent or prevailing need. The questioning itself is "out of order." It is entirely voluntary, based wholly and uniquely on the mystery of freedom, on what we have called the leap. The same Nietzsche said: "Philosophy . . . is a voluntary living amid ice and mountain heights (*Werke*, 15, 2). To philosophize, we may now say, is an extra-ordinary inquiry into the extra-ordinary.

from
DISCOURSE ON THINKING

Let us not fool ourselves. All of us, including those who think professionally, as it were, are often enough thought-poor; we all are far too easily thought-less. Thoughtlessness is an uncanny visitor who comes and goes everywhere in today's world. For nowadays we take in everything in the quickest and cheapest way, only to forget it just as quickly, instantly. Thus one gathering follows on the heels of another. Commemorative celebrations grow poorer and poorer in thought. Commemoration and thoughtlessness are found side by side.

But even while we are thoughtless, we do not give up our capacity to think. We rather use this capacity implicitly, though strangely: that is, in thoughtlessness we let it lie fallow. Still only that can lie fallow which in itself is a ground for growth, such as a field. An expressway, where nothing grows, cannot be a fallow field. Just as we can grow deaf only because we hear, just as we can grow old only because we were young; so we can grow thought-poor or even thought-less only because man at the core of his being has the capacity to think; has "spirit and reason" and is destined to think. We can only lose or, as the phrase goes, get loose from that which we knowingly or unknowingly possess.

The growing thoughtlessness must, therefore, spring from some process that gnaws at the very marrow of man today: man today is in *flight from thinking*. This flight-from-thought

From *Discourse on Thinking*, by Martin Heidegger, translated by John M. Anderson and E. Hans Freund. Originally published under the title *Gelassenheit*. Copyright © 1959 by Verlage Gunther Neske. Copyright © 1966 in the English translation by Harper & Row, Publishers, Inc. Reprinted by permission of Harper & Row, Publishers, Inc.

is the ground of thoughtlessness. But part of this flight is that man will neither see nor admit it. Man today will even flatly deny this flight from thinking. He will assert the opposite. He will say—and quite rightly—that there were at no time such far-reaching plans, so many inquiries in so many areas, research carried on as passionately as today. Of course. And this display of ingenuity and deliberation has its own great usefulness. Such thought remains indispensable. But—it also remains true that it is thinking of a special kind.

Its peculiarity consists in the fact that whenever we plan, research, and organize, we always reckon with conditions that are given. We take them into account with the calculated intention of their serving specific purposes. Thus we can count on definite results. This calculation is the mark of all thinking that plans and investigates. Such thinking remains calculation even if it neither works with numbers nor uses an adding machine or computer. Calculative thinking computes. It computes ever new, ever more promising and at the same time more economical possibilities. Calculative thinking races from one prospect to the next. Calculative thinking never stops, never collects itself. Calculative thinking is not meditative thinking, not thinking which contemplates the meaning which reigns in everything that is.

There are, then, two kinds of thinking, each justified and needed in its own way: calculative thinking and meditative thinking.

This meditative thinking is what we have in mind when we say that contemporary man is in flight from thinking. Yet you may protest: mere meditative thinking finds itself floating unaware above reality. It loses touch. It is worthless for dealing with current business. It profits nothing in carrying out practical affairs.

And you may say, finally, that mere meditative thinking, persevering meditations, is "above" the reach of ordinary understanding. In this excuse only this much is true, meditative thinking does not just happen by itself any more than does calculative thinking. At times it requires a greater effort. It demands more practice. It is in need of even more delicate care than any other genuine craft. But it must also be able to bide its time, to await as does the farmer, whether the seed will come up and ripen.

Yet anyone can follow the path of meditative thinking in his own manner and within his own limits. Why? Because man is a *thinking*, that is, a *meditating* being. Thus meditative thinking need by no means be "high-flown." It is enough if we dwell on what lies close and meditate on what is closest; upon that which concerns us, each one of us, here and now; here, on this patch of home ground; now, in the present hour of history.

Gabriel Marcel

(1889-1973)   FRENCH

Marcel is frequently referred to by Sartre as the contemporary proponent of "theistic existentialism." Marcel, less than charmed by his association with Sartre's atheistic existentialism, prefers to call his work "Neo-Socratic." After a series of horrible experiences during World War I, Marcel found himself incapable of abstract philosophical thinking: he insisted upon a "philosophy of the concrete." In his development of this philosophy he independently formulated many of the central insights of Husserl's phenomenology, Heidegger's ontology, Sartre's notion of freedom, and Merleau-Ponty's theories of intersubjectivity and the role of the body in perception. His philosophy shares many similarities with Kierkegaard's, notably the conception of God as an absolute presence. But unlike Kierkegaard, Marcel does not argue that belief in God requires an irrational leap of faith, nor does he share Kierkegaard's insistence that each of us face God alone. His religious concept of Being is defended more in a Heideggerian way—as the presupposition of Existenz—rather than as one possibility of irrational choice. But Marcel's concerns remain centered upon the notions of freedom and the individual, and his insistence upon the immediacy of our life with others is not to be taken as a return to the warmth of Kierkegaard's despised "public," as the following selection from Man Against Mass Society *will show.*

WHAT IS A FREE MAN?

A problem such as the one we are dealing with in this chapter, 'What is a free man?' cannot, or so it seems to me, be usefully discussed in the abstract. It cannot be discussed,

From *Man Against Mass Society* (Gateway ed.) by Gabriel Marcel. Reprinted by permission of Henry Regnery Company.

that is, out of the context of historical situations, considered in their concrete fullness; it is, for that matter, of the very essence of the human lot that man always is in a situation of some sort or other, and that is what a too abstract kind of humanism always runs the risk of forgetting. We are not therefore here asking ourselves what a free man is *in se*, what the essential notion of a free man is; for that question very possibly has no meaning at all. But we are asking ourselves how in an historical situation which is *our* situation, which we have to face here and now, man's freedom can be conceived, and how we can bear witness to it.

About seventy-five years ago, Nietzsche asserted: 'God is dead'. To-day, we can hear, not so much boldly asserted as muttered in anguish, a statement that seems to echo that of Nietzsche: 'Man is in his death-throes'. Let us make ourselves clear; this statement, by those who make it sincerely, is not intended to have the force of prophecy; at the level of reflective awareness (and it is at this level that the statement is made) we canot make any sort of pronouncement at all on coming events, we are in fact even forced to acknowledge our ignorance of the future. And there is a sense in which we ought even to rejoice in that ignorance, for it is that ignorance alone which makes possible that perpetual hopeful betting on the future without which human activity, as such, would find itself radically inhibited. To say that man is in his death-throes is only to say that man to-day finds himself facing, not some external event, such as the annihilation of our planet, for instance, which might be the consequence of some catastrophe in the heavens, but rather possibilities of complete self-destruction inherent in himself. These possibilities, always latent, become patent from the moment in which man makes a bad use, or rather an impious use, of the powers that constitute his nature. I am thinking here both of the atomic bomb and of techniques of human degradation, as these have been put into effect in all totalitarian states without exception. Between the physical destruction wrought by the atomic bomb, and the spiritual destruction wrought by techniques of human degradation there exists, quite certainly, a secret bond; it is precisely the duty of reflective thinking to lay bare that secret.

The relationship which can exist between the two statements, 'God is dead', 'Man is in his death-throes', is not only a complex relationship, but an ambiguous one. We can ask ourselves, for instance, whether Nietzsche's cry of exultation or pain did not, just like the modern cry of mere pain, pre-suppose a concrete historical situation; linked itself, like our situation, to a preliminary misuse of human powers, of which men at that time had been guilty. No doubt we ought to recognize that the relationship between the two statements, 'God is dead', and 'Man is in his death-throes', is concrete and existential, not logical: it is quite impossible to extract from Nietzsche's statement about God by any method of analysis the other statement about man, though Nietzsche perhaps would have accepted the statement about man, at least during the ultimate or penultimate period of his work-ing life. Even if he had accepted it, however, he would probably not have perceived all the overtones in the state-ment, 'Man is in his death-throes', which we can perceive to-day. Also (this is a strange reflection, but a true one) it is perhaps by starting from the statement, 'Man is in his death-throes', that we may be able to question once more the statement, 'God is dead', and to discover that God is living after all. It is, as the reader will soon discover, towards the latter conclusion that the whole of my subsequent argument tends.

But what we have to ask ourselves first is the following question: what becomes of freedom in a world in which man, or at least man at a certain level of self-awareness, is forced to recognize that he has entered into his death-throes?

At this point, however, we may be faced with a preliminary objection. It is one which presents itself readily to the mind. Might it not be convenient to say that the question, 'What is a free man?' can only receive a positive answer in a country which has itself remained a free country?

However, the very notion of a free country or a free peo-ple, on a little analysis, appears to be a much less distinct notion than we should be tempted to think it at first. I shall take two examples: Switzerland, as the sequel to a process of political blackmail, found itself under the necessity of putting its factories to work for the benefit of Nazi Germany —was Switzerland still a free country? Sweden, at the end of the war, was obliged to conclude with Soviet Russia a very burdensome trade treaty, which had the effect of throttling her economic life. Ought not Sweden to have admitted to herself that—at the level of facts, if not at the level of words—she was no longer a free country? If the freedom of a people or a country be defined as *absolute independence,* is it not obvious that in a world like ours freedom cannot exist, not only because of inevitable economic interdependence, but because of the part played by pressure, or, less politely, by blackmail, at all levels of international intercourse?

Following out this line of thought, we should be led to acknowledge that the individual himself, in any country whatsoever, not only finds himself dependent but finds himself, in a great many cases, obliged to carry out actions which his conscience disapproves. (We have only to think, for instance, of military conscription and its consequences to become aware of this fact.) All that we can say is that in countries where there is still a recognition of what we can call in a very general fashion the rights of the human person, a certain number of guarantees of freedom survive: but we ought immediately to add that such guarantees are becoming less and less numerous and that, failing a very improbable reversal of the present general tendency of things, there will be a continuing demand for their further reduction. It would be contrary to the facts of the case to assert that men, in what we broadly call 'the free countries', enjoy absolute independence. That does not matter so much, for, except to a pedantic type of anarchist, such absolute independence is inconceivable. But it would also be contrary to the facts to assert that men in free countries to-day generally possess the power to square their conduct with their consciences.

This is the point at which we ought to pass to the extreme case and ask ourselves what becomes of the freedom of the individual, even of what we call his inner freedom, in a totalitarian country. Here, I believe, we shall find ourselves forced to recognize an exceptionally important fact: Stoicism (and I am thinking less of an abstract philosophical doctrine than of a spiritual attitude) has been to-day, I shall not say refuted by the facts, but uprooted by them from the soil which used to nourish it. This ancient and respectable attitude rested on the distinction made so forcibly and severely by such writers as Epictetus, Seneca, and Marcus Aurelius: the distinction between what depends on my will, and what does not depend on it. Stoic thought, in so far as it was not merely formulated in abstract terms but adopted with dauntless courage as a way of life, implied a belief in the inner tribunal of conscience: a tribunal unviolated, and indeed inviolable, by any intrusion of external power. There can be no Stoicism without a belief in an inalienable inner sovereignty, an absolute possession of the self by the self.

However, the very essence of those modern techniques of degradation, to which I made an earlier allusion, consists precisely in putting the individual into a situation in which he loses touch with himself, in which he is literally beside himself, even to the point of being able sincerely to disavow acts into which nevertheless he had put sincerely his whole heart, or on the other hand of being able to confess to acts which he had not committed. I shall not attempt at this point to define the *kind* of sincerity, obviously a factitious and artificial kind, that we are talking of. I shall note merely that, though in recent years such techniques of degradation have been brought to an almost unimaginable degree of refinement, they were already in use in periods much earlier than ours. I was told recently that during the trial of the Knights Templars under Philip the Fair confessions were obtained by processes which cannot have consisted merely of physical torture; since later on, during a second and last retraction of their original confessions, the accused, once more in possession of their faculties, declared that they had originally *sincerely* accused themselves of acts which they *had not committed*. Physical torture by itself seems incapable of producing such sincerity; it can be evoked only by those abominable methods of *psychological* manipulation to which so many countries, in such various latitudes, have in recent years had recourse.

Given these conditions, the situation that each one of us must face to-day is as follows: (I say *each one of us*, supposing that we do not want to lie to ourselves or to commit the sin of unwarranted presumption; given that supposition, we must admit that there are real and practical methods that can be applied to any of us to-morrow with the effect of depriving us of self-sovereignty or, less grandiosely, of self-control: even though in another age we should have had sound reasons for regarding that self-sovereignty as infrangible and inviolable). Our situation, then, is this: we ought not even to say, as the Stoics said, that even at the very worst there remains for us the possibility of suicide, as a happy way out. That is no longer a true statement of the case. A man to-day can be put into a situation in which he *will no longer want to kill himself*; in which suicide will appear to him as an *illicit* or *unfair* way out; in which he will think of himself as under an obligation not merely to suffer, but to wish for, the punishment appropriate to crimes which he will impute to himself *without having committed them*.

It may be objected here that the mere mention of such horrible possibilities is itself dangerous, almost criminal. Certainly, if I were addressing myself to a class of schoolboys or students, it might be proper to leave this aspect of my subject in the shadow. But I am addressing myself to mature minds, minds I assume already capable of higher reflection; and on such minds, just because of their maturity, a real responsibility rests.

What we have to recognize is this. Thanks to the techniques of degradation it is creating and perfecting, a materialistic mode of thought, in our time, is showing itself capable of bringing into being a world which more and more *tends to verify its own materialistic postulates*. I mean that a human being who has undergone a certain type of psychological manipulation tends progressively to be reduced to the status of a mere *thing*; a psychic thing, of course, but nevertheless a thing which falls quite tidily within the province of the theories elaborated by an essentially materialistic psychology. This assertion of mine is, of course, obviously ambiguous; it does not mean that this materialistic psychology, with however startling powers of reductive transformation it may become endowed, will ever be of a nature to grasp and reveal to us reality as it is in itself. Rather, my assertion emphasizes the fact that there is nothing surprising for a philosophy like my own, a philosophy of man as a being in a situation, in the fact that man depends, to a very great degree, on the idea he has of himself and that this idea cannot be degraded without at the same time degrading man. This is one more reason, and on the face of things the most serious and imperative reason for condemning materialistic thinking, root and branch. And it is relevant to note here that in our day the materialistic attitude has acquired a virulence and a cohesion which it was far from possessing in the last century. It was a common spectacle then to see thinkers who regarded themselves as thoroughly imbued with materialistic principles showing in their personal lives all the scrupulosity of Kantian rigorists.

It may seem that I am rather straying here from the question which I set out to answer at the beginning of this chapter, 'What is a free man?' But this is not in fact by any means the case, for it is very important for us to recognize, whatever fancies certain thinkers incapable of the least coherence may have had about this question, that a materialistic conception of the universe is radically incompatible with the idea of a free man: more precisely, that, in a society ruled by materialistic principles, freedom is transmuted into its opposite, or becomes merely the most treacherous and deceptive of empty slogans.

Theoretically, of course, we can imagine the possibility of man's preserving a minimum of independence even in a society ruled on materialistic principles; but, as we ought to be immediately aware, this possibility is an evanescent one, implying contradictions: for freedom in such a society would consist, if I may put it so, in rendering oneself sufficiently insignificant to escape the attention of the men in power. But is it not fairly obvious that this wish for insignificance, supposing even that it is a wish that can be put into effect, is already in a sense a suicidal wish? In such a society, the mere keeping, for instance, of an intimate diary might be a capital crime, and one does not see why, by the use of tape recorders and tapped telephones, as well as by various quite conceivable extensions of the use of radio, it should not be quite possible to keep the police well informed about the thoughts and the feelings of any individual whatsoever.[1] From the point of view of the individual in such a society, there is no conceivable way out at all: private life, as such, does not exist any more.

But let us imagine, then, the situation of our country immediately after a *putsch* or a *coup d'état*: if rebellion is futile, and a retreat into insignificance impracticable, what, supposing that we are fully aware of our situation, does there remain for us to do? At the risk of discontenting and even of shocking those who still tend to think of solutions for political problems in terms of positive action, I shall say that in that region all the ways of escape seem to me to be barred. Our own recourse can be to the Transcendent: but what does that mean? 'The transcendent', 'transcendence', these are words which among philosophers and intellectuals, for a good

---

[1] *See George Orwell's* 1984.

many years past, have been strangely misused. When I myself speak here of a recourse to the transcendent, I mean, as concretely as possible, that our only chance in the sort of horrible situation I have imagined is to appeal, I should perhaps *not* say to a power, but rather to a level of being, an order of the spirit, which is also the level and order of grace, of mercy, of charity; and to proclaim, while there is still time, that is to say before the state's psychological manipulations have produced in us the alienation from our true selves that we fear, that we repudiate *in advance* the deeds and the acts that may be obtained from us by any sort of constraint whatsoever. We solemnly affirm, by this appeal to the transcendent, that the reality of our selves lies *beyond* any such acts and any such words. It will be said, no doubt, that by this gesture we are giving ourselves a very ideal, a very unreal, sort of satisfaction; but to say so is to fail to recognize the real nature of the thought which I am groping to put into shape. What we have to do is to proclaim that we do *not* belong entirely to the world of objects to which men are seeking to assimilate us, in which they are straining to imprison us. To put it very concretely indeed, we have to proclaim that this life of ours, which it has now become technically possible to make into a hideous and grimacing parody of all our dreams, may in reality be only the most insignificant aspect of a grand process unfolding itself far beyond the boundaries of the visible world. In other words, this amounts to saying that *all philosophies of immanence have had their day*, that in our own day they have revealed their basic unreality or, what is infinitely more serious, their complicity with those modern idolatries which it is our duty to denounce without pity: the idolatry of race, the idolatry of class. I should add here that even the authentic religions may become similarly degraded in their very principle of being. They too can degenerate into idolatries; especially where the will to power is waiting to corrupt them; and this, alas, is almost invariably the case when the Church becomes endowed with temporal authority.

But we are now on the road towards a number of pretty positive conclusions. I should formulate them as follows: a man cannot be free or remain free, except in the degree to which he remains linked with that which transcends him, whatever the particular form of that link may be: for it is pretty obvious that the form of the link need not reduce itself to official and canonical prayers. I should say that in the case particularly of the true artist in paint, or stone, or music, or words, this relationship to the transcendent is something that is experienced in the most authentic and profound way. I am supposing, of course, that he does not yield to the innumerable temptations to which the artist is exposed to-day: the temptation to startle, to innovate at all costs, to shut oneself up in a private world leaving as few channels as possible open for communication with the world of eternal forms: and so on. But nothing could be falser and more dangerous than to base on these observations of mine some sort of neo-aestheticism. We have to recognize that there are modes of creation which do not belong to the aesthetic order, and which are within the reach of everybody; and it is in so far as he is a creator, at however humble a level, that any man at all can recognize his own freedom. It would be necessary, moreover, to show that the idea of being creative, taken in this quite general sense, always implies the idea of being open towards others: that openness I have called in my Gifford Lectures, intersubjectivity, whether that is conceived as *agape* (charity) or *philia* (attachment): these two notions, in any case, I think, tend ultimately to converge. But what must be stated as forcibly as possible is that societies built on a materialistic basis, whatever place they tactfully leave for a collective and at bottom purely animal exaltation, sin radically against intersubjectivity; they exclude it in principle; and it is because they exclude it, that they grub up every possible freedom by its roots.

It is quite conceivable—and I put this idea forward not as an abstract hypothesis but as a familiar fact—that in a country enslaved by a totalitarian power, a man might find himself constrained, not merely in order to live but in order to draw his dependents from a state of absolute wretchedness, to accept, for instance, a job with the security police: a job which might compel him to carry out acts absolutely repugnant to his conscience. Is mere refusal to carry out such acts a solution to his problem? We may doubt this, for the very reason that such a refusal might entail direful consequences not only for the man himself but for his innocent dependents. But it could happen that the man who accepted such a job might make a religious vow to use the share of power which he has been given so much as possible to help the very people of whom he was officially the persecutor. Such a vow, with the creative power that it re-bestows on him who makes it, is a concrete example of that recourse to the transcendent of which I spoke earlier on. But it is obvious that there is nothing in such an extremely particular case out of which any general rule can be framed. A rigoristic moral formalism, an attempt to bring all human acts under very general rules, ceases almost entirely to be acceptable as soon as one becomes aware of that element of the unique and the incommensurable which is the portion of every concrete being, confronted with a concrete situation. No two beings, and no two situations, are really commensurable with each other. To become aware of this fact is to undergo a sort of crisis. But it is with the crisis in our moral awareness as a starting-point, that there becomes possible that cry from us towards the creative principle, and that demand by it on us, which each must answer in his own way, if he does not wish to become an accomplice of what Simone Weil called 'the gross beast'. In our world as it is to-day there can be hardly any set of circumstances in which we may not be forced to ask ourselves whether, through our free choice, through our particular decisions, we are not going to make ourselves guilty of just such a complicity.

Karl Jaspers

(1883–1969) ———————— GERMAN (SWISS)

Jaspers entered philosophy from a medical career in psychiatry. Accordingly, his philosophy displays a fascinating combination of scientific knowledge and antiscientific humanism. Jaspers, perhaps the most systematic of the existentialists, is heavily influenced by Kant, Kierkegaard, and Nietzsche. Like Kant, he is interested in the limits of experience, the limitations of science. Like Kierkegaard and Nietzsche, he is interested in the individual, in "philosophizing as an exception." Philosophy for him is an activity, one developing out of the *need to communicate to others one's own* Existenz. Existenz *is a notion Jaspers takes directly from Kierkegaard to refer to the authentic self.* Existenz *is, still following Kierkegaard, lived and not merely an object of knowledge. It is an experience of subjective freedom within certain boundary situations, exemplified by death and guilt. Authentic* Existenz *is the human attempt to push past these boundaries and reach the Encompassing ("transcendence"). This "will to infinity" is also called faith, the ideal attempt to go beyond the limits of experience. Again, one is very much reminded of Kant's philosophy—the separation of the world of our experience and world-in-itself, the world of knowledge and the world of faith. But this is Kant with a Kierkegaardian twist: for Jaspers there is no rationality to faith as there always is for Kant.*

The selections here are taken from Jaspers' Philosophy, *vol. II, his most systematic exposition of these themes, and* The Question of German Guilt, *his elegant personal response to the most severe moral challenge of this century.*

EXISTENZ

Mundane Existence and Existenz

If by "world" I mean the sum of all that cognitive orientation can reveal to me as cogently knowable for everyone, the question arises whether the being of the world is all there is. Does cognitive thinking stop with world orientation? What we refer to in mythical terms as the soul and God, and in philosophical language as Existenz and transcendence, is not of this world. Neither one is knowable, in the sense of things in the world. Yet both might have another kind of being. They need not be nothing, even though they are not known. They could be objects of thought, if not of cognition.

What is there, as against all mundane being? In the answer to this question lies the basic decision of philosophy.

We answer: there is the being which in the phenomenality of existence *is not* but *can be, ought to be*, and therefore decides in time whether it is in eternity.

This being is myself as *Existenz*. I am Existenz if I do not become an object for myself. In Existenz I know, without being able to see it, that what I call my "self" is independent. The possibility of Existenz is what I live by; it is only in its realization that I am myself. Attempts to comprehend it make it vanish, for it is not a psychological subject. I feel more deeply rooted in its possibility than in my self-objectifying grasp of my nature and my character. Existenz appears to itself as existence, in the polarity of subjectivity and objectivity; but it is not the appearance of an object given anywhere, or uncoverable as underlying any reflection. It is phenomenal only for itself and for other Existenz.

It is thus not my existence that is Existenz; but, *being human*, I am possible Existenz *in existence*. I exist or I do not exist, but my Existenz, as a possibility, takes a step toward being or away from being, toward nothingness, in every choice or decision I make. My existence differs from other existence in scope; my world can be broad or narrow. But

From *Philosophy*, Vol. 2, by Karl Jaspers, translated by E. B. Ashton. Reprinted by permission of E. B. Ashton and The University of Chicago Press.

Existenz differs from other Existenz in essence, because of its freedom. As existence I live and die; my Existenz is unaware of death but soars or declines in relation to its being. Existence exists empirically. Existenz as freedom only. Existence is wholly temporal, while Existenz, in time, is more than time. My existence is finite, since it is not all existence, and yet, for me, it is concluded within itself. Existenz is not everything and not for itself alone either, for its being depends on its relation to other Existenz and to transcendence—the wholly Other that makes it aware of being not by itself alone—but while existence may be termed infinite as relatively rounded endlessness, the infinity of Existenz is unrounded, an open possibility. Action on the ground of possible Existenz disconcerts me in existence; as existence, concerned with enduring in time, I cannot but turn against the doubtful path of unconditionality that may be costly, even ruinous, in existence. My concern with existence tends to make existential actions conditional upon the preservation of my existence; but to possible Existenz, the unqualified enjoyment of existence is already apostasy; to Existenz, the condition of its reality in existence is that it comprehends itself as unconditional. If I merely want to exist, without qualifications, I am bound to despair when I see that the reality of my existence lies in total foundering.

Existence is fulfilled in *mundane being*; to possible Existenz, the world is the field of its phenomenality.

The *known* world is the alien world. I am *detached* from it. What my intellect can know and what I can experience empirically repulses me as such, and I am irrelevant to it. Subject to overpowering causality in the realm of reality and to logical compulsion in the realm of validity, I am not sheltered in either. I hear no kindred language, and the more determined I am to comprehend the world, the more homeless will it make me feel; as the Other, as nothing but the world, it holds no comfort. Unfeeling, neither merciful nor unmerciful, subject to laws or foundering in coincidence, it is unaware of itself. I cannot grasp it, for it faces me impersonally, explicable in particulars but never intelligible as a whole.

And yet *there is another way in which I know the world*. It is akin to me then; I am at home in it and even sheltered in it. Its laws are the laws of my own reason. I find peace as I adjust to it, as I make my tools and expand my cognition of the world. It will speak to me now; it breathes a life that I share. I give myself up to it, and when I am in it I am with myself. It is familiar in small, present things, and thrilling in its grandeur; it will make me unwary in proximity or tend to sweep me along to its far reaches. Its ways are not the ways I expect, but though it may startle me with undreamed of fulfillments and incomprehensible failures, I shall trust it even as I perish.

This is no longer the world I know about in purely cognitive orientation. But my contentment in dealing with it is ambiguous. I may *crave* the world as the font of my joy of living, may be drawn to it and deceived about it by my blind will to live. I can indeed not exist without this craving, but as an absolute impulse it becomes self-destructive; it is against this impulse that my possible Existenz warns me to detach myself from the world lest I become its prey. Or, *in the world* that is so close to me, so much my kin, I may set out to *transcend* the world. Whether seeing it, thinking about it, acting and loving, producing and developing in it—in all that, then, I deal with something else at the same time, with a phenomenon of the transcendence that speaks to me. This is not a world I know but one that seems to have lost its continuity. It will change according to times and persons, and depending on my inner attitudes; it does not say the same things to all men, and not the same things at all times. I must be ready for it if I want to hear it. If I withhold myself, the very thing I might transcend to will withdraw. For it is only for freedom and by freedom, and there is nothing cogent about it at all.

Possible Existenz thus *sets itself off* from the world in order to find the right way into the world. It cuts loose from the world so that its grasp of the world will give it more than the world can be. The world attracts Existenz as the medium of its realization, and repels it as its possible decay to mere existence. There is a tension between the world and Existenz. They cannot become one, and they cannot separate either.

In philosophizing on the ground of possible Existenz we presuppose this tension. The world, as *what can be known,* and Existenz, as *what must be elucidated,* are dialectically distinguished and then reconsidered as one.

Mundane being, the being we know, is *general* because it is generally valid for everyone. It is the common property of all rational creatures who can agree on its being the same thing they mean. Its validity applies, in the endlessness of real things, to the definable particular.

Existenz is *never general*, and thus not a case that might be subsumed as particular under a universal. Objectified as a phenomenon, however, Existenz is also the individuality of the historic particular. We still comprehend this under general categories, limited only by the endlessness of individual factuality, which makes the individual inexhaustible and thus ineffable. But individuality as such is not Existenz. All that it is, to begin with, is the visible profusion of mundane existence —a profusion whose existential originality can be examined by the questioner's self-being, but not by any knowledge.

The union of Existenz and the world is the incalculable process of which no one who is a part of it can be sure.

Possible Existenz
Unsatisfied in Existence

1. Doubts of the Being of Existenz

Once we divorce Existenz from existence, from the world, and from a general character, there seems to be nothing left. Unless Existenz becomes an object, it seems a vain hope to think of it; such thinking cannot last or produce results, so the attempted conception of Existenz seems bound to destroy itself. We can doubt the being of Existenz in every respect and let common sense tell us to stick to objectivity as both real and true. Was the attempt the outgrowth of a chimera?

There is no way to remove our doubts about Existenz. It is neither knowable as existence nor extant as validity. We can deny Existenz as we can deny the content of any philosophical thought—as opposed to particular objective cognition, whose object is demonstrable. I can never say of myself what I am, as if I were demonstrably extant. Whatever can be said of me by way of objectification applies to my empirical individuality, and as this can be the phenomenon of my Existenz, it is not subject to any definitive psychological analysis either —a limit of my self-knowledge which indirectly points to something else, without ever being able to compel that something to become apparent. Hence the elucidation of Existenz is a deliverance but not a fulfillment, as knowledge would be;

it widens my scope, but it does not create substance by demonstrating any being that I might objectively comprehend.

Since Existenz is thus inaccessible to one who asks about it in terms of the purely objective intellect, it remains subject to lasting doubt. Yet though no proof can force me to admit its being, my thinking is still not an end: it gets beyond the bounds of objective knowability in a *leap* that exceeds the capacity of rational insight. Philosophizing begins and ends at a point to which that leap takes me. Existenz is the *origin* of existential philosophizing, not its goal. Nor is its origin the same as its beginning, beyond which I would go on asking for an earlier beginning; it is not my license either, which would drive me to despair, and it is not a will resulting from the endlessness of questionable motivations. The origin is free being. This is what I transcend to as *philosophizing, not knowing, brings me to myself.* The helplessness to which philosophizing reduces me when I doubt its origin is an expression of the helplessness of my self-being, and the reality of philosophizing is the incipient upsurge of that self-being. The premise of philosophizing, therefore, is to *take hold* of Existenz—which begins as no more than a dark striving for sense and support, turns into doubt and despair as reminders of its derivation from the realm of possibility, and then appears as the incomprehensible certainty that is elucidated in philosophizing.

2. Being Unsatisfied as an Expression of Possible Existenz

If I reduce all things to mundane existence, either in theory or in practice, I feel unsatisfied. This feeling is a negative origin; in separating Existenz from mundane existence it makes me sense the truth of that separation. As there is no knowledge for which the world is conclusive, no "right" order of existence that could possibly be definitive, and no absolute final goal that all might see as one, I cannot help getting more unsatisfied the clearer I am in my mind about what I know, and the more honest I am about the sense of what I am doing.

No reasons will sufficiently explain this feeling. It expresses the being of possible Existenz, which understands itself, not something else, when it declares itself unsatisfied. What I feel then is not the impotence of knowledge. It is not the emptiness at the end of all my achievements in a world in which I face the brink of nothingness. Instead, I feel a discontent that eggs me on.

An inexplicable discontent is a step out of mere existence, the step into the *solitude of possibility* where all mundane existence disappears. This solitude is not the resignation of the scientist who buries his hopes for a cognition of intrinsic being. It is not the irritation of the man of action who has come to doubt the point of all action. Nor is it the grief of a man in flight from himself and loath to be alone. Instead, after all these disillusionments, it is my dissatisfaction with existence at large, *my need to have my own origin.* To be unsatisfied is a condition inadequate to existence, and when this condition has opposed me to the world, it is my freedom that conquers all disenchantment and returns me to the world, to my fellow man with whom I ascertain the origin. I do not, however, comprehend all this in thoughtful reflection —which is indeed what fails me—but in the reality of my actions and in total foundering.

This possible conquest alone lends substance and significance to the otherwise irremovable relativity of theoretical *knowledge* and practical *action*.

I may well derive a peculiar and profound satisfaction from a theoretical knowledge of things in general, from surveying world images, from contemplating forms and existence, and from expanding all of this farther and farther, under ideas. But it is my dissatisfaction that makes me feel that this whole world, for all its universality and validity, is not all of being. My attitude in it is not one of curiosity about every particular, shared with a fellow scientist who might be interchangeable according to his function; it is an attitude of original curiosity about being itself, shared with a friend. What grips me is a communion in asking and answering questions, and a communication which within objective validity goes indirectly beyond it.

When I face objective tasks in *practical* life, when I deal with them and ask about their meaning, no meaning that I can grasp in the world will satisfy me. My sense of possible Existenz will not rest even if my conscious comprehension feeds on the idea of a whole in which I have my place and do my job. The thought of fulfillment in an entirety will come to be merely relative, like a temptation to conceal the boundary situations which break up any entirety. Though each idea of the whole is also a step beyond the fission into sheer coincidence, I am never able to survey the whole; eventually it will be back at the mercy of the accidents of mundane existence. A place within the whole, a place that would lend importance to the individual as a member of the body of this kind of being, is always questionable. But what remains to me as an individual is what never fits into a whole: the choice of my tasks and my striving for accomplishment are simultaneous manifestations of *another* origin, unless the annihilating thought that all I do might be senseless makes me shut my eyes. While I devote my empirical individuality to my finite tasks, my possible Existenz is more than that empirical individuality, and more than the objective, realistic impersonality of my political, scientific, or economic achievements. Although its essence is realized solely by this participation in the historic process of mundane existence, Existenz is at war with the lower depths of the encompassing world in which it finds itself. It is against those depths that, failing in the world, it seeks to hold its own in the eternity of intrinsic being.

Not unless it is indeed unsatisfied—both theoretically, with the mere knowledge and contemplation of all things in the world, and practically, with the mere performance of a task in an ideal entirety—can possible Existenz *utter* and understand this dissatisfaction. It is never *motivated* by generally valid reasons; those rather tend to induce contentment and tranquillity in the totality of a mundane existence permeated by the idea and thus spiritualized. The discontent of possible self-being has broken through mundane existence and cast the individual back upon himself, back to the origin that lets him deal with his world and, with his fellow, realize his Existenz.

3. The Breakthrough Ascertained in Existential Elucidation

If I am unsatisfied and want to clarify this not just by setting myself apart but by positive thoughts on what this is all about, I come to existential elucidation.

As Existenz results from the real act of breaking through mundane existence, existential elucidation is the *thinking ascertainment* of that act. The breakthrough goes from possible Existenz to its realization, without being able to leave the borderline of possibility. To have its reality—although it is not objectively demonstrable—in action itself is the peculiar quality of Existenz. In its philosophical elucidation we pursue each thought that leads to the breakthrough, no matter from what side.

a. The breakthrough occurs at the *limits* of mundane existence. Philosophical thinking leads up to such limits and puts us in mind of the experiences they involve and of the appeal they issue. From the situations in the world, it leads to "boundary situations"; from empirical consciousness, to "absolute consciousness"; from actions qualified by their purposes, to "unconditional actions."

b. But the breakthrough still does not lead us out of the world. It occurs in the world, and so philosophical thought follows the appearance of Existenz in the world, in "historic consciousness" and in the "tension of subjectivity and objectivity" in its existence.

c. The breakthrough is *original*. Events happen in the world, but in the breakthrough something is settled by me. Existenz is certain that no part of intrinsic being can stay unsettled for it as a phenomenon in temporal existence. For either I allow the course of things to decide *about* me—vanishing as myself, since there is no real decision when everything just *happens*—or I deal with being originally, as myself, with the feeling that there must be a decision. My thought, aimed at the origin, seeks to elucidate "freedom."

d. Nothing I know in the world can give me any reasons for my decision; but what I am to decide can be grasped in the medium of that knowledge. Existential elucidation pervades my existence in the world, not in the sense that what matters were now known, but so I can sense possibilities that may give me a grasp on truth—on what is true as I *become* true. "I myself" and "communication" as the premise of self-being are the things we try to cover in the fundamental thoughts of all existential elucidation.

Elucidating Existential Communication

Against the inclination to be self-sufficient, against contentment with the knowledge of consciousness at large, against individual self-will, against the craving for an all-inclusive

life, against surrender to the habitual living patterns of existing tradition—against all these we want our philosophizing
to illuminate the free, original, communicative grasp on being
that will let us meet the constant threat of solipsism or universalism in existence. This philosophizing is my own appeal
to myself for an open mind, and then, once the bond of communication has been established, for an unconditional acceptance of that bond. It is an effort to *preserve the possibility*
which in solipsism, and in the universalism of consciousness
at large, is disconsolately denied.

1. Solitude and Union

When I come to myself there are two things that lie in this
communication: my being I, and my being with another. If I
am not independently myself as well, standing on my own,
I shall be completely lost in the other; our communication
will void me and itself at the same time. Conversely, when I
begin to isolate myself, I impoverish and empty my communication. In the extreme case of its absolute rupture I stop
being myself, having evaporated into point-like emptiness.

Solitude is not the same as social isolation. If a primitive
lacking a self-consciousness of his own is cast out of his community, for instance, he will either go on living in it inwardly
or he will have a dark, desperate sense of not being. Neither
sheltered in community nor as an outcast will he be lonely,
because he is not an I for himself.

Only in the lucid consciousness of higher development can
it be called a rule that self-being means loneliness, but a
loneliness in which I am not yet myself; for loneliness is the
sense of readiness in possible Existenz—which becomes real
Existenz only in communication.

Communication always takes place between two people
who join but remain two, who come to each other out of
solitude and yet know solitude only because they are communicating. I cannot come to myself without entering into communication, and I cannot enter into communication without
being lonely. Every communicative conquest of solitude gives
rise to a new solitude that cannot disappear unless I myself
cease to be a condition of my communication. I must have
the will to be lonely if I dare to be on my own and thus to
enter into the deepest communication. I can, of course, give
myself up, let distance go by the boards, and dissolve in the

other; but just as undammed water trickles feebly in thin
rivulets, so does the I which no longer wants the rigor of
self-being and keeping its distance.

In existence the polarity of enthusiastic abandon and rigid,
solitary self-discipline is existentially irremovable. In existence, possible Existenz moves only between these two poles,
on a course whose starting point and goal remain obscure. If
I will not put up with my solitude, if I will not overcome it
again and again, I choose either a chaotic ego dissolution or a
fixation in forms and tracks without selfhood. If I will not
risk abandoning myself, I perish as an empty, petrified I.

Thus there remains in the existence of the self an element
of unrest that will be still for moments, only to rise promptly
in a new form. And yet, this motion is no endless, hopelessly
driven occurrence. Possible Existenz will draw upon it, rather,
for a direction and surge whose aim and basis, though non-
existent for insight, can then be elucidated in existential
transcending.

This communication of solitude is opposed by those whose
basic posture differs in its very origin. In their eyes such
communication is just a hopeless effort on the part of a community of the lonely, expressing nothing but a self-willed
self-being shut off from the truth. The truth, they maintain,
lies in genuine community. The culpably lonely are held to be
making a philosophizing for themselves that will give them
the illusion of having companions in loneliness. Asked what a
genuine community is, these men will answer: "What can
unite all men." They see it either in revealed truth, to be
obediently followed by the community of the faithful, or in
ideas such as a correct world order, an exclusive massing of
all forces of the nation-state into a power steered by a single
will, a conquest and reshaping of the world as the way to
universal happiness, and so forth. Man has to renounce himself, they tell us; in serving the whole, I belong to the true
community. Self-being means being selfless.

In both cases, in the philosophical approach to communication and in the opposition to it, I am convinced of the same
thesis: truth is what unites. Another point on which religion
and philosophy agree is that mere intelligibility makes for
pseudo-unions in objective knowledge only. In fact, the intelligible is the medium of union in the unintelligible, which
it brings into an infinite process of clarification. Once something merely intelligible is known, it is detached from self-

being and is thus no longer connective; when it becomes the main point, it weakens the communal bond. In a limpid rationalization of all things, communication as community would have vanished.

The division begins in regard to the where and whence of the unintelligible that establishes community. For a philosophizing existence it lies in the real self-being of men who meet in fact; for an obedient existence it lies in objectively fixed divine revelation or in the authoritatively laid down rightness of a world image—of Marxism, for instance. Either the historic reality of my communication with men of flesh and blood, men to whose self-being I owe my own, means more to me than audible objective truth, or I submerge my possible communication with human beings in a general neighborly love of all mankind, a love sustained by my wordless love of the deity or by a rationalistic and nonetheless unintelligibly obscure sense of mankind's destiny. Either I keep risking loneliness over and over, to win my self-being in communication, or I have definitively voided my own self in another being.

The division is deepened in the attitude toward a possible community of all. In an empirical view, to be sure, we are struck again and again by the truth of the proposition that the more people understand a thing, the less its substance. But since the truly philosophical approach is to regard all men as possible partners with whom we ought to communicate, we cannot avoid the challenge implied in the contrary proposition: that the most profound truth is that which all men might understand so as to form one community. In this dilemma, two fundamental mentalities part company. One would compel unity by force and content itself with the most superficial comprehension, indeed with uncomprehending obedience, while the other, for the sake of truth, would eschew any deceptive anticipation. It will acknowledge, therefore, what exists in fact and can only be overcome by an incalculable process of truthful communication. The community whose order assures that we can exist, of course, requires purposes which everyone understands; but this is precisely not the community in which I come to a sense of intrinsic being. It is the order of the world of men, rather, in which even those who do not come to understand each other can respect one another—the world in which their task remains to come ever closer to each other in expanding communication.

2. Manifestation and Realization

In communication I am revealed to myself, along with the other. This manifestation, however, is at the same time the realization of an I as a self. To think, for instance, that it is my inborn character that comes to light in communicative manifestation would be a departure from the possibility of Existenz, for which the process of becoming manifest is one of self-creation by self-elucidation. For objective thinking, of course, what becomes manifest has first to be in being. A manifestation that causes me not only to become but to be is like an emergence from nothing—and so, in the sense of mere existence, there can be no such thing. If I take the view that I am the way I was born, that in life I can come to know my disposition but remain what I am, I proceed as a psychological observer and assume that a perfected empirical knowledge might inform me at an early stage about what I am. This is quite true as far as traits and propensities are concerned; and without knowing those, I cannot get my bearings in my situation. But as possible Existenz I use these data to make conscious decisions; seeking to clarify the data is just a premise of the existential manifestation which brings to light in the world not only what I am as empirical existence but what I am myself. For this sort of manifestation the acknowledgment of real limits in my given situation means that they can provide me only with material for another realization; since nothing we know is final, any such recognition of data will include the possibility—unlikely for the empirical way of looking at things—that every limit can be passed. The existential will to be manifest includes seeming opposites: relentless clarity about everything empirical, and the chance of thus coming to be what I eternally am; the shackles of inescapable empirical reality, and the freedom to change that reality by taking hold of it; recognition of "the way I am," and a denial of being anything definitive.

If I want to be manifest, I will risk myself completely in communication, which is my only way of self-realization. I will put "the way I am" completely at stake, because I know that in it my own Existenz has yet to come to itself. But if I want seclusion, if I want masks and protective facades, I only seem to enter into communication; I will not risk myself, then, because I confuse the way I am with what I eternally am, and the way I am is what I want to save. I feel, then, that manifestation would destroy me. To my self-being, on the other hand, to be manifest means to have a grip on empirical reality and to conquer that reality for the sake of possible Existenz. For in manifestation I lose my stable empirical existence in order to gain my possible Existenz, whereas in seclusion I maintain my empirical stability at the cost of losing my possible Existenz. The relation of manifestness and existential reality is that they mutually seem to emerge from nothing and to be sustaining themselves.

This process of realization as manifestation does not occur in isolated Existenz. It occurs only with another. To myself as an individual I am neither manifest nor real. The process of manifestation in communication is a unique struggle, combative and loving at once.

3. Loving Struggle

The love in this communication is not blind love regardless of its object. It is the fighting, clear-sighted love of possible Existenz tackling another possible Existenz, questioning it, challenging it, making things hard for it.

The struggle in this communication is the individual's fight for Existenz, both for his own and for the other's. It is unlike the struggle for existence in which all weapons are brought into play and trickery and fraud become inevitable, in which my fellow man is treated as an enemy, as simply part of the "other than I," like resistant nature. The struggle for Existenz has to do with infinitely different things: with utter candor, with the elimination of all kinds of power and superiority, with the other's self-being as well as with my own. It is a struggle in which both combatants dare to show themselves without reserve and to allow themselves to be thrown into question. If Existenz is possible, it will appear as this self-attainment—which is never objectified—by means of a fighting self-abandonment that is objectified in part but beyond comprehension by any motives from the realm of existence.

An incomparable solidarity prevails in the communicative struggle. The utmost questioning would not be possible without this solidarity; it sustains the venture, turns it into a joint one, and shares the liability for the result. It confines the fight to existential communication, which is always the secret of two, so that the most intimate friends in the eyes of the public may be the ones locked in the fiercest battle for Existenz, in a match in which both jointly win or lose.

We might draw up rules for this battle over manifestation.

It never aims at superiority and victory; if these are gained, they will be felt as disturbing, indeed as culpable, and will be fought in turn. All cards are put on the table; there is no calculating reserve whatever. Mutual transparency is sought not only in the matters at issue, but in the means of questioning and of contention. Each combatant penetrates himself along with the other. The fight is not waged by Existenz against Existenz; it is a joint fight against oneself and the other, but solely for truth. It can only be waged on a level of complete equality. If the technical arsenal of the combatants differs, if one is more knowledgeable or more intelligent than the other, has a better memory or is less prone to fatigue, both will equalize the level by handicapping themselves. But this equalization requires each to be existentially as tough as possible on himself, and on the other. Chivalry and all kinds of disembarrassment have a place here—with the approval of both sides—only as transient safeguards against the vicissitudes that occur for limited times in the phenomenality of our existence. If they last, communication is at an end. On the other hand, the need for toughness applies only to the most essential grounds of substantial decision; where the stronger psychological equipment carries the day, not to mention the possibility of sophistry, communication also ceases. In existentially embattled communication each will put everything at the other's disposal.

In this communication nothing that strikes me as relevant may stay unanswered. If as Existenz I hear a nuance in a figure of speech, I am going to take it seriously and react to it —whether the other asks and demands an answer consciously, though indirectly, or whether his instinctive desire was really to keep silent and not to elicit the answer he now has to hear. What I say is intended as a question; I want to hear answers, never just to persuade or to compel. Unlimited response is essential to true communication. When the answer is not promptly forthcoming, it will remain an unforgotten challenge.

Since it takes place on the same level, the fight as such implies mutual recognition, and the questioning as such, mutual affirmation. This is why the solidarity in existential communication will show in the very heat of battle. This struggle, instead of separating Existenz from Existenz, is the way of their true conjunction. Hence the rule of this solidarity that the individuals it links will trust each other absolutely, and that their fight is not an objective one which others might see and take sides in. It is a fight for the truth of Existenz, not for general validity.

Finally, truthfulness in combative communication is not to be gained, nor is freedom between Existenz and Existenz to be secured, unless the reality of those private codes of the mind and psychological drives which isolate the self and focus it upon themselves is recognized at the same time. These forces are disturbing and confining; they block the free activity of communication, which they would limit or qualify. Without knowing and uncovering them man cannot control these forces. He may be free of them at high points of his Existenz, but he will relapse without knowing how.

FREEDOM

Why do I ask about freedom? Not because it occurs to me as a concept whose object I want to know; pursued by means of objective research, the question whether there is freedom at all would lead me to deny it, rather. What makes freedom possible for me is that I myself do not become an object. The question of its being originates in me. I *will* its being.

In every kind of questioning there is some sense in which the way to ask and the mode of the objective answer depend upon the subject; but when I ask about freedom my potential self-being is both what asks and what answers. Hence my question whether there is freedom becomes my action at the same time. I am asking whether and how I take hold of myself or let myself go; I am not looking about me to see whether freedom might occur, perhaps, somewhere in the world. This is why the question of its being becomes meaningless if raised in consciousness at large. It does not carry an invariable weight, only one that grows along with true self-being. I do not ask abstractly; I ask insofar as I myself am involved.

Whoever believes that a mere conceptuality can truly answer the question of freedom will simply call it philosophy's *basic concept*. But for a man who does not "know" anything

From *Philosophy*, Vol. 2, by Karl Jaspers, translated by E. B. Ashton. Reprinted by permission of E. B. Ashton and The University of Chicago Press.

here and accordingly does not expect a result at all, for the man who wants clarity because he wants to come to himself on his historic road, freedom will turn into the specific *sign* of existential elucidation.

When I look around and review all the things we *call* freedom, I get into a variety of facts and definitions without an objective sense consciousness to let me choose what and where freedom is and is not. Not unless a real *interest* in freedom guides me do I perceive in this variety what speaks to me as freedom—speaks to me because potentially I am already free. Without this possibility of being free myself I cannot ask about freedom. Hence there is either no freedom at all or it *is* in asking about it. But what makes me ask is an original will to be free, so that my freedom is anticipated in the fact of asking. I cannot prove it first, and then will it. I will it because I am already conscious of its possibility.

Philosophizing on the basis that we *might* be free leads us to want to make sure of freedom—of the fact that it exists— by way of argument. We might say that these argumentations were born with freedom itself; to the philosopher they are indispensable as something to rebound from, to freedom proper. Their elucidation has a negative meaning: not to want to prove that there is such a thing as freedom. Freedom is proved by my actions, not by my insight. My concern with its being includes the activity I realize it in.

Yet to say that I might be free is to say that I might also be unfree. The agonizing fact that this might be the case is the *negative impulse* of freedom. As self-being I cannot bear the possibility of being unfree. That I cannot bear it makes me aware of myself: because I exist as myself, because things that depend on me can be to me of absolute importance, I must be able to be free. This is not a conclusion I draw from a fact on its condition; it is the expression of my very self-being, of my awareness of my own potential, of being still in a position to decide about myself. I demand my selfhood by making demands on myself. To be myself, I must be able to meet my demands.

Freedom is the alpha and omega of existential elucidation. It speaks there and there alone—not in world orientation, and not in transcendence. In world orientation, being is extant, objective, valid; as far as cognition goes there is no freedom yet. In transcendence there is no freedom any more. To absolutize it into transcendent being would be a fallacy;

nothing but Existenz in temporal existence can be free. Freedom does have a tendency to render itself superfluous— as the ultimate phenomenon of temporally existing Existenz it seeks to void itself in transcendence—but it can always be only a being of Existenz, not one of transcendence. It is the lever by which transcendence acts on Existenz, but only as that Existenz is its independent self.

Elucidating Existential Freedom

1. Freedom as Knowledge, as Arbitrary Act, as Law

Whatever merely exists or occurs is unfree. I find myself in this existence as though a leap had put me there. I am not just a sequence of events; I know that I am. I do something and know what I am doing. I have to die like everything that lives, but I know I have to die. My knowledge of what is passively and necessarily happening does not free me from any necessity, but it lifts my knowing ego beyond mere necessity; to be involved myself, to understand the things I must do, is a moment of freedom. Knowledge does not make me free as yet, but *without knowledge there is no freedom.*

Knowing, I see a realm of my possibilities. I can choose among the several I know. Where several things are possible for me, the cause of what will occur is my arbitrary act. I can, of course, try in objective contemplation to understand this act as a necessary occurrence: my choice depends upon my mode of knowing, and I can trace the way this came about. I choose the object of my supposed knowledge only *as* I know it; but since—measured by the existing reality which I do not know as yet—my knowledge is always in error, too, my experience will be that what happens differs from my expectation. My choice depends, moreover, on observable psychological driving forces among which the psychologically strong motive decides. And yet, despite these two dependencies, the arbitrary act remains one that is presupposed rather than comprehended in any cognition. I can neither deduce its being nor, with the rigor of causal insight, prove or predict any factual decision as necessary in a particular case. Even if I turn my decision into what is to me a mere accident—by flipping a coin or rolling dice, for example—the arbitrary element remains because I voluntarily put myself into a state of passive submission to objective chance. The last instance clearly shows the peculiarity of the arbitrary act in general: my objectively random procedure will seem haphazard—in other words, even subjectively I seem to be acting at random. This, however, is an impossible thought; what is at work in all arbitrary decisions, rather, is a spontaneity coincident with my being I. Lacking substance, arbitrariness does not amount to freedom; but *without an arbitrary act there is no freedom*.

But suppose I do not knowingly make an arbitrary decision. Suppose I decide not at random but in accord with a *law* I recognize as binding. I am free, then, since I am bowing to an imperative I found within myself, an imperative I might as well not bow to. A law is not an inescapable natural necessity to which I am subject; it is the necessity of norms of action and motivation with which I can either comply or not comply. To me such norms are manifestly binding, and in recognizing and obeying them I am aware of my free self, realizing things which are necessarily valid, though not necessary in themselves. I have no authority to tell me which norms apply; if I had such an authority I would be arbitrarily submitting to something alien—either facing it trustfully, following it without insight and yet remaining myself, or slowly turning into it, so to speak, as I abandon myself. Because the norms are identical with my own self, I feel they are self-evidently valid. Although the form of these validities is general, the substance of particular ones will be specified down to the utmost concretion, and its discovery in each case takes a fully present self. This *transcendental freedom*, in which I freely find myself by obeying valid norms, is active as opposed to mere passive knowledge, and it is borne by a necessity as against the random relativity of arbitrary acts. It includes the freedom of knowledge and that of the arbitrary act. There could be no proper freedom without those two, and there is *no freedom without law*.

Thus transcendental freedom assures me of myself in obeying a law which I recognize as mine on my own evidence. And yet, I cannot stop there as if I had the true explication of freedom. If I state the imperative of the law, I reduce it to the level of a rule that can be definitively formulated, and I reduce the self to the level of a case in which the rule is applied. Such a generalization of the law, and of the self into a self at large, cannot adequately elucidate my concrete sense of freedom. A rationally unequivocal formula cannot but become rigid. The consequences are inevitably straight-lined and mechanical.

The *substance* of legality in the particular, in approaching the historic self in a distinct temporal situation, is not determined by the law of transcendental freedom. That substance springs from the polarity between the total guiding idea and the historically singular self-being that makes the choice.

2. Freedom as Idea

I become free by incessantly broadening my world orientation, by limitlessly visualizing premises and possibilities of action, and by allowing all motives to speak to me and to work within me. But this accumulative aggregate will bring forth freedom only insofar as I really, inwardly relate to the world in which I am active—only insofar as everything will not just factually tie in with everything else but will do so for my consciousness as the eye of possible Existenz. An interrelation of this kind will not become solidly rounded; it will remain in that infinite whole that has no being, only the becoming of an idea. Out of the endless diversity of accumulated motives and elements of orientation, the idea I have in mind creates order and a structure without coming to be an object otherwise than by substitution, in mere schemata. To move in a medium of infinite objective relations and in infinite reflection within myself, so as there to integrate them in a present freedom—this is the opposite of my confinement in the situation, of the one-sided determinacy of a law, of the isolating effect of particular knowledge. The more the totality, without forgetting a thing, determines my visions and decisions, my feelings and actions, the freer I know I am.

3. Freedom as Choice (Resolution)

And yet, wherever I decide and act, I *am* not a totality but an ego in distinct, given circumstances, in a situation that is objectively particular. My actions do not simply result from my boundless orientation in the world and from the expansion of my possible self-being in infinite reflection. I am not the stage of a general idea from which the temporal events of my existence would necessarily flow. Instead, my first experience is that while totality is never complete, while the expansion of my possible self-being remains unfinished, *time is pressing*. I could never act at all if I wanted to wait for the idea to evolve as I visualize all premises and possibilities. The first consequence of this friction between the unfinished totality and the need to live, to choose, to decide at a certain time, now or never, is a specific sense of unfreedom in being tied to time and place, in having my possible ideal tests and safeguards narrowed down. But then I experience this temporally definite choice as not just an inevitably negative and unfree thing I must needs do without completing the idea: it is this choice, in fact, that makes me aware of my *original freedom*, because only there do I know myself as my true self. From this point of view all other elements of freedom seem like mere premises of the manifestation of the deepest, existential freedom beyond all objectification and generalization. Now, having recognized and adopted the earlier elements, I see the limit that gives me either a desperate sense of not being at all or an awareness of a more original being. It is in this choice that one who is historically, singularly himself will be revealed to himself and to other Existenz.

An existential choice does not result from a struggle of motives, which would be an objective occurrence. It is not a decision in which I merely seem to decide after performing a calculation, so to speak, that has yielded the correct result—this would be cogent, and I could do nothing but admit its evidence and act accordingly. Nor is it obedience to an objectively phrased imperative, for such obedience is either a preliminary form or a decline of freedom. Instead, the crux of the choice is that *I* choose. Pervading the realm of determinacy and particularity, the historic, objectively unsurveyable substance comes to exist—not only with a sense of being accidental, as if it might just as well be different, but so that I feel it as the original necessity of my intrinsic self.

In this choice I *resolve* to be myself in existence. Resolution as such is not yet the rational will that makes me take some finite action "resolutely" despite everything. Nor does it lie in a heedlessly, blindly courageous existence. Resolution is what comes to my will as the gift that in willing I can really be—it is what I can will *out of*, without being able to will *it*. In resolution I plunge into freedom, hoping at the bottom of it to meet myself, because I can will. But what manifests my resolution is my concrete choice.

This choice is thoroughly indirect. Considering all objectivities in the realm of the possible and tested in the infinite reflection of the subject, it expresses the absolute decision of Existenz. It is not the result of those deliberations, however. It has gone through them and thus does not happen without them, but the resolution as such comes in a leap. On the basis of deliberations I would never get to more than probabilities. And if probability alone determined my actions, I would not come to any existential resolution; for resolution is unconditional. Moreover, if I calculate the chances and let success alone decide my actions, resolution has entirely disappeared—for the ultimate criterion of truth in resolution is not success but what remains true in failure. Even less, finally, is resolution the immediate arbitrary act as opposed to insight. It is, rather, to *know my own will* in the historic concreteness of my existence. If I have not considered everything, if I have not weighed the possibilities, if I have not lost myself in infinite reflection, I am acting on blind intuition rather than arriving at a resolution.

And yet, resolution is also quite direct, though its immediacy is not that of existence. It is the immediacy of intrinsic self-being. Resolution and self-being are one. Irresolution as such is a lack of self-being; irresolution at a particular moment indicates only that I have not found myself as yet. But choice and resolution coincide, as do lucidity and origin. If my resolution looks arbitrary, there is indeed no objective distinguishing criterion, but what I subjectively come to in a resolution is the very opposite pole of arbitrariness. What seems like arbitrariness is the freedom of one who must do this because he is himself.

In regard to time, the import of resolution is that once I have made a choice I will unconditionally *stick to it*. I cannot give it up again; there is no other I behind what I am as myself. If I do give it up just the same, canceling what I was in it, I destroy myself at the same time. The existence on which I have entered in my original resolution is the font I live by, the font that animates everything new. My resolution starts the *movement* that can give my life a self-based continuity in the diffusion of existence.

This freedom of choice is not the kind that consists only in the absence of outward restraints on calm choosing. Objectively it is incomprehensible, but I myself am aware of it as a free origin, as the flatly incomparable and intrinsic point of everything. For in this freedom I hold myself squarely responsible for myself, while from outside I am held responsible only for my actions in their factuality. What the word "choice" expresses is that in my free decision I am not only conscious of acting in the world but of creating my own being in historic continuity. I know that I not only exist, that I not only am the way I am and therefore act in that way, but that as I act and decide I originate both my actions and the way I am. My resolution makes me feel the freedom in which I no longer merely decide about things but about myself, the freedom in which I can no longer separate the choice and me because *I am this free choice.* Choice alone appears as a choice between objectivities; freedom is the choice of my own self. This is why I cannot step out once again to choose between being myself and not being myself, as if freedom were nothing but a tool of mine. I am by choosing, rather; if I am not, I choose not. What I am myself is left open, of course, because of decisions still unmade; to that extent I am not yet. But this not-being, in the sense of not-being-definitive in phenomenal existence, is illuminated by the existential certainty of my being where I choose and thus originate in resolution.

This resolution in choice is originally *communicative.* I choose myself as I choose another. But my choice of the other is not one in which I, as a previously extant being, might set myself absolute and outside humankind from which I then choose the few I want to associate with. I cannot make such a comparative appraisal as if I could be without the other. The real choice is not a process of selection; it is my original resolution to communicate unconditionally with the person with whom I come to myself. I do not find myself by looking around and searching, but by being ready to resolve upon unconditional historic communication. It is then that not my outward fate alone but my very being will entwine with the other. A choice born of resolution knows no question and no alternative. Not until I am sure of this origin can I decide alternatives and answer questions.

4. Flight from Freedom

Once a man has tasted the original freedom that made him the fundament of his own self, nothing else will seem to him like real being. If possible, he would like nothing in himself to remain merely given; he would like to turn himself wholly into his own choice, his own responsibility. His attitude toward given things will be one of taking responsibility for them: rather than resign himself to what is given, he will "assume" it as his own to the extent of his original freedom. He knows he has relinquished his self-being when he denies his identity with his historic existence. In this self-identification lies resolution, and so does unconditional commitment. To realize myself, I leave the possibilities behind. From the emptiness of the rich world that might be, I step into the abundance of a world that is poor compared with the other; but that becomes real and is sustained by self-being.

I promptly shrink from this commitment, however. I do not want to become real; I want to stay possible. My deliberations and drafts do not result in any compelling decision. Not my factual insight alone—which is always inadequate—but even an ideally perfected insight fails to provide me with sufficient reasons for a resolution. As long as it has not been made, any choice has something uncertain and thus disquieting about it. It requires an incomparable assurance. While this is lacking, I recoil from the irrevocable decision that covers my kind of self; for *watching* will not tell me when my being hangs in the balance.

Preceding the assurance, therefore, is the *crisis of not knowing:* the fear, the moment of flinching, when I cannot tell whether it is a last try to keep from straying or a last deep breath before the decision. This fear in the liberating process is not a thing I can share with another, although without him I cannot really come to be. As a result, there may be utter loneliness in the crisis and profound communication in the decision. Because decision is my lucid, thoughtful grasp of my own being, a default of original freedom lets me tumble wildly into decisions made in a vacuum, without knowledge or choice. I give myself up, then, reemerging with a purely social rather than existential self-consciousness determined from outside. I play a role that no longer contains any self.

I feel this nonbeing of myself when I do not know my duty; when no calculation, no law, no unfolding idea tells me what to do, in generally valid terms; when amidst all this, instead of knowing the truth—that in this way I try to flee from freedom—I finally let chance decide about me rather than decide myself. Then I have indeed turned into a mere stage; and as I see my own being dissolve, I may utter the ambiguous words, "I don't count at all." Here lies the deepest root in which Existenz will loose or bind itself to Existenz in communication. A man who shows his nonbeing at this point has slipped through the net, as it were.

But it is the essence of phenomenal Existenz in temporal existence that there must be a decision. Either I decide as Existenz, or a decision will be made about me, turning me into material for someone else and stripping me of Existenz. Nothing remains unsettled. There is but a limited margin of temporal possibility beyond which I cannot postpone a decision without having it made about me rather than by me.

The freedom that is possible in knowledge, arbitrary action, law, and idea leaves a kind of unfilled space. Once the question of "freedom from what" has been answered by shattering all objectivities, the question of "freedom for what" seems all the more urgent. If I do not know what I want, I am helpless in the face of endless possibilities. I feel I am nothing. Instead of being afraid in my freedom, I am afraid of my freedom.

It is in many small acts—acts unnoticeable in detail and yet on the whole determining my being—that I take the steps in which I win or lose myself. I may resist decision, shut my eyes because I do not want to will; horrified by my freedom to bind myself, to decide something for all time, I would like to shift the responsibility and let things happen. Or, without any violence, I may calmly and just as unnoticeably go my way in small inner and outer actions, ripening to stay myself in real decisions. To welcome freedom or to shun it— whichever I choose over any length of time is the phenomenon of what I am.

5. The Conception of Existential Freedom

Formal freedom, we have seen, was knowledge and arbitrary action; transcendental freedom was self-assured obedience to an evident law; freedom as an idea was life in a whole; existential freedom was my self assurance in decision as a historic origin. Existential freedom is downright incomprehensible— that is to say, it will not fit any concept—and there alone is the sense of freedom *fulfilled*. I cannot realize this freedom without knowledge, nor without being aware of the possibility of arbitrariness; in the phenomenon of legal order the arbitrariness is deepened, first, into a free choice of duty and attentiveness to the idea, and ultimately encompassed by the absolutely singular origin which these premises elucidate.

The proximity of self-being to other self-being creates a certainty of what will no longer be clearly true in the distant form of a law—of what need not violate a law but can violate it, invalidating it as a law. The origin of existential freedom pits it against the superficiality of chance; existential necessity pits it against the arbitrary volition of the moment; fidelity and continuity pit it against obliviousness and dissipation.

What the elucidation of freedom begins and ends with, however, is that freedom *cannot be known*, that there is no way in which it might be objectively conceived. I am sure of it *for myself*, not in thought but as Existenz, not in musing and asking about it, but in action. Whatever I say about freedom is a means of communication, invariably open to misunderstanding and only indirectly indicative.

Freedom is not absolute; it is always bound at the same time. I do not have it; I gain it. Like freedom itself, the conception of freedom is pure *motion*. No single expression can characterize the sense of freedom; only the movement from one expression to the other will reveal a meaning that is not visible in any one expression by itself. If I say "I choose" and my sense of decision covers freedom proper, it still does not lie in arbitrary choice but in the necessity I mean when I say "I will," in the sense of "I must." Both terms assure Existenz of its original being as distinct from empirical existence; both would allow it to say, at that moment, "I am," and to mean free being. Only *together* can all these expressions—I am, I must, I will, I choose—be taken to express freedom. By itself, without interpretation by the others, each of them would mean either empirical existence or impulsive necessity or arbitrary psychological action. In the sense of freedom all elements are so entwined as to make one source from the depths of which those single elements spring as phenomenal forms: there is no choice without decision, no decision without a will, no will without necessity, no necessity without being.

Directly understood, each formula means mere existence; it is only in a transcending elucidation that they cover possible Existenz. If I look for freedom and say "I become," the phrase expresses unfreedom if I mean only my growth, my passive unfoldment in time; but it expresses freedom if I mean the historic continuity of substantial volition.

The words "I can" or "I cannot," whether right or wrong in a particular case, refer initially to the physical and psychological energies of the empirical individual and to his domain in a situation, not to Existenz. I identify myself with empirical existence, turn myself into an object, and give up on my Existenz. But then it is possible to say, in the sense of transcendental freedom, "I can because I ought to," and in the sense of existential freedom, "I can because I must." This "can" no longer refers to the factual realization of a mundane goal; it refers to my inner and outer action, even though empirically I should fail in it. In the sense of original freedom there are no bounds to what I unconditionally can.

MORAL GUILT

Every German asks himself: how am I guilty?

The question of the guilt of the individual analyzing himself is what we call the moral one. Here we Germans are divided by the greatest differences.

While the decision in self-judgment is up to the individual alone, we are free to talk with one another, insofar as we are in communication, and morally to help each other achieve clarity. The moral sentence on the other is suspended, however—neither the criminal nor the political one.

There is a line at which even the possibility of moral judgment ceases. It can be drawn where we feel the other not even trying for a moral self-analysis—where we perceive mere sophistry in his argument, where he seems not to hear at all. Hitler and his accomplices, that small minority of tens of thousands, are beyond moral guilt for as long as they do not feel it. They seem incapable of repentance and change. They are what they are. Force alone can deal with such men who live by force alone.

But the moral guilt exists for all those who give room to conscience and repentance. The morally guilty are those who are capable of penance, the ones who knew, or could know, and yet walked in ways which self-analysis reveals to them as culpable error—whether conveniently closing their eyes to events, or permitting themselves to be intoxicated, seduced or

From *The Question of German Guilt* by Karl Jaspers. Copyright 1947 by The Dial Press, Inc. Reprinted by permission of the publisher.

bought with personal advantages, or obeying from fear. Let us look at some of these possibilities.

1. By *living in disguise*—unavoidable for anyone who wanted to survive—moral guilt was incurred. Mendacious avowals of loyalty to threatening bodies like the Gestapo, gestures like the Hitler salute, attendance at meetings, and many other things causing a semblance of participation—who among us in Germany was not guilty of that, at one time or another? Only the forgetful can deceive themselves about it, since they want to deceive themselves. Camouflage had become a basic trait of our existence. It weighs on our moral conscience.

2. More deeply stirring at the instant of cognition is guilt incurred by a *false conscience*. Many a young man or woman nowadays awakens with a horrible feeling: my conscience has betrayed me. I thought I was living in idealism and self-sacrifice for the noblest goal, with the best intentions—what can I still rely on? Everyone awakening like this will ask himself how he became guilty, by haziness, by unwillingness to see, by conscious seclusion, isolation of his own life in a "decent" sphere.

Here we first have to distinguish between military honor and political sense. For whatever is said about guilt cannot affect the consciousness of military honor. If a soldier kept faith with his comrades, did not flinch in danger and proved himself calm and courageous, he may preserve something inviolate in his self-respect. These purely soldierly, and at the same time human, values are common to all peoples. No guilt is incurred by having stood this test; in fact, if probation here was real, unstained by evil acts or execution of patently evil commands, it is a foundation of the sense of life.

But a soldier's probation must not be identified with the cause he fought for. To have been a good soldier does not absolve from all other guilt.

The unconditional identification of the actual state with the German nation and army constitutes guilt incurred through false conscience. A first-class soldier may have succumbed to the falsification of his conscience which enabled him to do and permit obviously evil things because of patriotism. Hence the good conscience in evil deeds.

Yet our duty to the fatherland goes far beneath blind obedience to its rulers of the day. The fatherland ceases to be a fatherland when its soul is destroyed. The power of the state is not an end in itself; rather, it is pernicious if this state destroys the German character. Therefore, duty to the fatherland did not by any means lead consistently to obedience to Hitler and to the assumption that even as a Hitler state Germany must, of course, win the war at all costs. Herein lies the false conscience. It is no simple guilt. It is at the same time a tragic confusion, notably of a large part of our unwitting youth. To do one's duty to the fatherland means to commit one's whole person to the highest demands made on us by the best of our ancestors, not by the idols of a false tradition.

It was amazing to see the complete self-identification with army and state, in spite of all evil. For this unconditionality of a blind nationalism—only conceivable as the last crumbling ground in a world about to lose all faith—was moral guilt.

It was made possible, furthermore, by a misinterpretation of the Biblical warning: "Let every soul be subject unto the higher powers"—a warning completely perverted by the curious sanctity appertaining to orders in military tradition. "This is an order"—in the ears of many these words had and still have a ring of pathos as if voicing the highest duty. But simultaneously, by shrugging off stupidity and evil as inevitable, they furnished an excuse. What finally turned this conduct into full-fledged moral guilt was the eagerness to obey—that compulsive conduct, feeling itself conscientious and, in fact, forsaking all conscience.

Many a youth nauseated by Nazi rule in the years after 1933 chose the military career because it seemed to offer the only decent atmosphere uninfluenced by the Party. The army, mentally against the Party, seemed to exist outside and without the Party as though it were a power of its own. It was another error of conscience; eventually, with all the independent generals in the old tradition eliminated, the consequences appeared as moral decay of the German officer in all positions of leadership—notwithstanding the many likable and even noble soldierly personalities who had sought salvation in vain, misled by a betraying conscience.

The very fact that honest consciousness and good-will were our initial guides is bound to deepen our later disillusionment and disappointment in ourselves. It leads us to question even our best faith; for we are responsible for our delusions—for every delusion to which we succumb.

Awakening and self-analysis of this delusion are indispensable. They turn idealistic youths into upright, morally reliable, politically lucid German men acquiescing in their lot as now cast.

3. By partial approval of National-Socialism, by *straddling* and occasional *inner assimilation* and accommodation, moral guilt was incurred without any of the tragic aspects of the previous types.

The argument that there was some good to it, after all—this readiness to a supposedly unbiased appraisal—was widespread among us. Yet the truth could be only a radical "either-or": if I recognize the principle as evil, everything is evil and any seemingly good consequences are not what they seem to be. It was this erring objectiveness, ready to grant something good in National-Socialism, which estranged close friends so they could no longer talk frankly. The same man who had just lamented the failure of a martyr to appear and sacrifice himself for the old freedom and against injustice was apt to praise the abolition of unemployment (by means of armament and fraudulent financial policies), apt to hail the absorption of Austria in 1938 as the fulfillment of the old ideal of a united Reich, apt to cast doubts on Dutch neutrality in 1940 and to justify Hitler's attack, and apt, above all, to rejoice in the victories.

4. Many engaged in convenient *self-deception*. In due time they were going to change this evil government. The Party would disappear again—with the Fuehrer's death at the latest. For the present one had to belong, to right things from within. The following conversations were typical:

An officer speaks: "After the war we'll finish National-Socialism on the very basis of our victory; but now we must stick together and lead Germany to that victory—when the house burns down you pour water and don't stop to ask what caused the fire."—Answer: "After victory you'll be discharged and glad to go home. The SS alone will stay armed, and the reign of terror will grow into a slave state. No individual human life will be possible; pyramids will rise; highways and towns will be built and changed at the Fuehrer's whim. A giant arms machine will be developed for the final conquest of the world."

A professor speaks: "We are the Fronde within the Party. We dare frank discussion. We achieve spiritual realizations. We shall slowly turn all of it back into the old German spirituality."—Answer: "You are deceiving yourselves. Allowed a fool's freedom, on condition of instant obedience, you shut up and give in. Your fight is a mirage, desired by the leaders. You only help to entomb the German spirit."

Many intellectuals went along in 1933, sought leading positions and publicly upheld the ideology of the new power, only to become resentful later when they personally were shunted aside. These—although mostly continuing positive until about 1942, when the course of the war made an unfavorable outcome certain and sent them into the oppositionist ranks—now feel that they suffered under the Nazis and are therefore called for what follows. They regard themselves as anti-Nazis. In all these years, according to their self-proclaimed ideology, these intellectual Nazis were frankly speaking truth in spiritual matters, guarding the tradition of the German spirit, preventing destructions, doing good in individual cases.

Many of these may be guilty of persisting in a mentality which, while not identical with Party tenets and even disguised as metamorphosis and opposition, still clings in fact to the mental attitude of National-Socialism and fails to clear itself. Through this mentality they may be actually akin to National-Socialism's inhuman, dictatorial, unexistentially nihilistic essence. If a mature person in 1933 had the certainty of inner conviction—due not merely to political error but to a sense of existence heightened by National-Socialism—he will be purified only by a transmutation which may have to be more thorough than any other. Whoever behaved like that in 1933 would remain inwardly brittle otherwise, and inclined to further fanaticism. Whoever took part in the race mania, whoever had delusions of a revival based on fraud, whoever winked at the crimes then already committed is not merely liable but must renew himself morally. Whether and how he can do it is up to him alone, and scarcely open to any outside scrutiny.

5. There is a difference between *activity* and *passivity*. The political performers and executors, the leaders and the propagandists are guilty. If they did not become criminals, they still have, by their activity, incurred a positively determinable guilt.

But each one of us is guilty insofar as he remained inactive. The guilt of passivity is different. Impotence excuses; no normal law demands a spectacular death. Plato already deemed it a matter of course to go into hiding in desperate times of calamity, and to survive. But passivity knows itself morally guilty of every failure, every neglect to act whenever possible, to shield the imperiled, to relieve wrong, to countervail. Impotent submission always left a margin of activity which, though not without risk, could still be cautiously effective. Its anxious omission weighs upon the individual as moral guilt. Blindness for the misfortune of others, lack of imagination of the heart, inner indifference toward the witnessed evil—that is moral guilt.

Franz Kafka

(1883–1924) ━━━━━◆━◆◆━━━━━ GERMAN-CZECH

It is now standard to link Kafka with Camus as a prophet of the absurd, but this view ignores the ultimate despair of Kafka that Camus rejects. In The Trial, *for example, Kafka presents us with a terrifyingly concrete representation of Kierkegaardian sin and guilt, secularized in a bizarre indictment without a charge, by a court that is as comical as it is absurd. Joseph K is arrested without reason, and his protests of his "rights" never seem to make contact with the Power of the mysterious court itself. In Kafka's short story "Metamorphosis" Gregor Samsa, a young executive type, awakens to find himself turned into a giant cockroach. Samsa's attempts to hold onto his bourgeois self-identity become more horrifying than the metamorphosis itself. For Kafka, the absurdity of sin and guilt lies not in the indifferent world but rather in the very indistinguishability of the subjective and the objective: What first appears as an accusation from the senseless legal system becomes more and more K's own consciousness of guilt; and the absurdity of Samsa's metamorphosis lies, not in the change itself, but in Samsa's unchanged self-consciousness. One might say that the basic difference between Camus and Kafka is that Camus attempts to provide an answer for the problem Kafka sees as inescapable.*

The first selection here is a brilliant Kafkaesque gem, reflecting in a short matter-of-fact parable all the horror and absurdity of the life of the middle-class so bitterly rejected by Kierkegaard, Nietzsche, and Hesse. The second selection is an early parable, later expanded and incorporated into the heart of The Trial.

COURIERS

They were offered the choice between becoming kings or the couriers of kings. The way children would, they all wanted to be couriers. Therefore there are only couriers who hurry about the world, shouting to each other—since there are no kings—messages that have become meaningless. They would like to put an end to this miserable life of theirs but they dare not because of their oaths of service.

BEFORE THE LAW

Before the Law stands a doorkeeper. To this doorkeeper there comes a man from the country and prays for admittance to the Law. But the doorkeeper says that he cannot grant admittance at the moment. The man thinks it over and then asks if he will be allowed in later. "It is possible," says the doorkeeper, "but not at the moment." Since the gate stands open, as usual, and the doorkeeper steps to one side, the man stoops to peer through the gateway into the interior. Observing that, the doorkeeper laughs and says: "If you are so drawn to it, just try to go in despite my veto. But take note: I am powerful. And I am only the least of the doorkeepers. From hall to hall there is one doorkeeper after another, each more powerful than the last. The third doorkeeper is already so terrible that even I cannot bear to look at him." These are difficulties the man from the country has not expected; the Law, he thinks, should surely be accessible at all times and to everyone, but as he now takes a closer look at the doorkeeper in his fur coat, with his big sharp nose and long, thin, black Tartar beard, he decides that it is better to wait until he gets permission to enter. The doorkeeper gives him a stool and lets him sit down at one side of the door. There he sits for

From *Parables and Paradoxes* by Franz Kafka. Copyright 1946, 1948, © 1958 by Schocken Books Inc. Reprinted by permission of Schocken Books Inc.
From *The Penal Colony* by Franz Kafka. Copyright by Schocken Books Inc. Reprinted by permission of Schocken Books Inc.

days and years. He makes many attempts to be admitted, and
wearies the doorkeeper by his importunity. The doorkeeper
frequently has little interviews with him, asking him questions about his home and many other things; but the questions are put indifferently, as great lords put them, and
always finish with the statement that he cannot be let in yet.
The man, who has furnished himself with many things for
his journey, sacrifices all he has, however valuable, to bribe
the doorkeeper. The doorkeeper accepts everything, but always
with the remark: "I am only taking it to keep you from thinking you have omitted anything." During these many years
the man fixes his attention almost continuously on the doorkeeper. He forgets the other doorkeepers, and this first one
seems to him the sole obstacle preventing access to the Law.
He curses his bad luck, in his early years boldly and loudly,
later, as he grows old, he only grumbles to himself. He becomes childish, and since in his yearlong contemplation of
the doorkeeper he has come to know even the fleas in his fur
collar, he begs the fleas as well to help him and to change the
doorkeeper's mind. At length his eyesight begins to fail, and
he does not know whether the world is really darker or
whether his eyes are only deceiving him. Yet in his darkness
he is now aware of a radiance that streams inextinguishably
from the gateway of the Law. Now he has not very long to
live. Before he dies, all his experiences in these long years
gather themselves in his head to one point, a question he has
not yet asked the doorkeeper. He waves him nearer, since he
can no longer raise his stiffening body. The doorkeeper has
to bend low towards him, for the difference in height between them has altered much to the man's disadvantage.
"What do you want to know now?" asks the doorkeeper; "you
are insatiable." "Everyone strives to reach the Law," says
the man, "so how does it happen that for all these many
years no one but myself has ever begged for admittance?"
The doorkeeper recognizes that the man has reached his end,
and to let his failing senses catch the words roars in his ear:
"No one else could ever be admitted here, since this gate was
made only for you. I am now going to shut it."

André Gide

(1869–1951)　　━━━◆━◆━◆━━━　　FRENCH

Though perhaps not an existentialist himself, André Gide has contributed some of the finest literary expressions of the existential attitude. Of particular interest are his novels The Immoralist *and* The Counterfeiters. *A portion of the latter is included here. The problem is* sincerity, *the same problem that occupies Sartre throughout* Being and Nothingness.

EDOUARD'S JOURNAL

Oct. 18th.—Laura does not seem to suspect her power; but I, who can unravel the secrets of my own heart, know well enough that up till now I have never written a line that has not been indirectly inspired by her. I feel her still a child beside me, and all the skill of my discourse is due only to my constant desire to instruct, to convince, to captivate her. I see nothing—I hear nothing without asking myself what she would think of it. I forsake my own emotion to feel only hers. And I think that if she were not there to give definition to my personality, it would vanish in the excessive vagueness of its contours. It is only round her that I concentrate and define myself. By what illusion have I hitherto believed that I was fashioning her to my likeness, when, on the contrary, I was bending myself to hers? And I never noticed it! Or rather—the influence of love, by a curious action of give and take, made us both reciprocally alter our natures. Involuntarily—unconsciously—each one of a pair of lovers fashions himself to meet the other's requirements—endeavours by a con-

From *The Counterfeiters* by André Gide, translated by Dorothy Bussy. Copyright 1927 and renewed 1955 by Alfred A. Knopf, Inc. Reprinted by permission of Alfred A. Knopf, Inc.

tinual effort to resemble that idol of himself which he beholds in the other's heart. . . . Whoever really loves abandons all sincerity.

This was the way in which she deluded me. Her thought everywhere companioned mine. I admired her taste, her curiosity, her culture, and did not realize that it was her love for me which made her take so passionate an interest in everything that I cared for. For she never discovered anything herself. Each one of her admirations—I see it now—was merely a couch on which she could lay her thought alongside of mine; there was nothing in all this that responded to any profound need of her nature. "It was only for you that I adorned and decked myself," she will say. Yes! But I could have wished that it had been only for *her* and that she had yielded in doing so to an intimate and personal necessity. But of all these things that she has added to herself for my sake, nothing will remain—not even a regret—not even a sense of something missing. A day comes when the true self, which time has slowly stripped of all its borrowed raiment, reappears, and then, if it was of these ornaments that the other was enamoured, he finds that he is pressing to his heart nothing but an empty dress—nothing but a memory—nothing but grief and despair.

Ah! with what virtues, with what perfections I had adorned her!

How vexing this question of sincerity is! *Sincerity!* When I say the word I think only of her. If it is myself that I consider, I cease to understand its meaning. I am never anything but what I think myself—and this varies so incessantly, that often, if I were not there to make them acquainted, my morning's self would not recognize my evening's. Nothing could be more different from me than myself. It is only sometimes when I am alone that the substratum emerges and that I attain a certain fundamental continuity; but at such times I feel that my life is slowing down, stopping, and that I am on the very verge of ceasing to exist. My heart beats only out of sympathy; I live only through others—by procuration, so to speak, and by espousals; and I never feel myself living so intensely as when I escape from myself to become no matter who.

This anti-egoistical force of decentralization is so great in me, that it disintegrates my sense of property—and, as a consequence, of responsibility. Such a being is not of the kind that one can marry. How can I make Laura understand this?

Oct. 26th.—The only existence that anything (including myself) has for me, is poetical—I restore this word its full signification. It seems to me sometimes that I do not really exist, but that I merely imagine I exist. The thing that I have the greatest difficulty in believing in, is my own reality. I am constantly getting outside myself, and as I watch myself act I cannot understand how a person who acts is the same as the person who is watching him act. and who wonders in astonishment and doubt how he can be actor and watcher at the same moment.

Psychological analysis lost all interest for me from the moment that I became aware that men feel what they imagine they feel. From that to thinking that they imagine they feel what they feel was a very short step . . . ! I see it clearly in the case of my love for Laura: between loving her and imagining I love her—between imagining I love her less and loving her less—what God could tell the difference? In the domain of feeling, what is real is indistinguishable from what is imaginary. And if it is sufficient to imagine one loves, in order to love, so it is sufficient to say to oneself that when one loves one imagines one loves, in order to love a little less and even in order to detach oneself a little from one's love, or at any rate to detach some of the crystals from one's love. But if one is able to say such a thing to oneself, must one not already love a little less?

It is by such reasoning as this, that X. in my book tries to detach himself from Z.—and, still more, tries to detach her from himself.

Oct. 28th.—People are always talking of the sudden crystallization of love. Its slow *decrystallization*, which I never hear talked of, is a psychological phenomenon which interests me far more. I consider that it can be observed, after a longer or shorter period, in all love marriages. There will be no reason to fear this, indeed, in Laura's case (and so much the better) if she marries Felix Douviers, as reason, and her family, and I myself advise her to do. Douviers is a thoroughly estimable professor, with many excellent points, and very capable in his own line (I hear that he is greatly appreciated by his pupils). In process of time and in the wear of daily life, Laura is sure to discover in him all the more virtues for having had fewer illusions to begin with; when she praises him, indeed, she seems to me really not to give him his due. Douviers is worth more than she thinks.

What an admirable subject for a novel—the progressive and reciprocal decrystallization of a husband and wife after fifteen or twenty years of married life. So long as he loves and desires to be loved, the lover cannot show himself as he really is, and moreover he does not see the beloved—but instead, an idol whom he decks out, a divinity whom he creates.

So I have warned Laura to be on her guard against both herself and me. I have tried to persuade her that our love could not bring either of us any lasting happiness. I hope I have more or less convinced her.

Albert Camus

(1913–1960) ━━━━◆◆◆◆◆━━━━ ALGERIAN-FRENCH

Camus is described by Sartre, in the obituary he wrote at the tragic end of a long and sometimes bitter feud between them, as the "Cartesian of the absurd," the "stubborn humanist." Whereas ambiguity, alienation, anxiety, Existenz, the polarity of for-itself/in-itself, are central in other authors, the key concept in Camus's philosophy is the "absurd," the confrontation between "rational man and the indifferent universe." Against the absurd there is rebellion, the scorn of Sisyphus, the "revolt of the flesh," the "I rebel, therefore we exist." For Camus there is no Kierkegaardian leap, which he degrades as "philosophical suicide"; there is no appeal to transcendence, which he dismisses as pointless hope; nor is there any role in Camus's philosophy for Sartre's notion of existential commitment. Rather, the point is to "keep the absurd alive." Politically, Camus's philosophical neglect of commitment manifests itself in his painful debates with Sartre and Merleau-Ponty. Always the moralist, the pacifist, Camus is hesitant about taking sides in the Algerian war, finding himself, like Meursault in The Stranger *and like Clamence in* The Fall, *often feeling for both sides at once. He sympathizes with Sartre's and Merleau-Ponty's efforts to inaugurate a new Left, but he continuously moves away as they find themselves increasingly in alliance with the Communist party. Camus objects to their Marxism, their lack of humanism, their violence, and their belief that ends justify means (a topic that ruptured Camus's friendships with both Sartre and Merleau-Ponty). Central to Camus's works is a resolute moralistic concern with good and evil, the source of the absurd in* The Myth Of Sisyphus, *the source of guilt in* The Fall. *In* The Stranger, *Camus creates an innocent young man whom he describes elsewhere as "totally honest," but honest in a peculiar way. He never reflects and thus never sees the significance of his actions. After committing a bizarre murder, neither intentional nor unintentional, Meursault (in the fol-*

*lowing selection) comes, while facing death, to the hesitant
recognition of the absurd. In* The Fall *Clamence (a pseudonym) relates in restrospect his lucidity regarding the absurdity of his previous self-esteem as a successful defender of good
causes and his "fall" into the role of Judge-Penitent, now
resentfully "happy" as Sisyphus is "happy," in scorn and in
constant recognition of his avoidance of judgment ("Judge that
ye not be judged").*

from
THE STRANGER

Then all day there was my appeal to think about. I made the
most of this idea, studying my effects so as to squeeze out the
maximum of consolation. Thus, I always began by assuming
the worst; my appeal was dismissed. That meant, of course, I
was to die. Sooner than others, obviously. "But," I reminded
myself, "it's common knowledge that life isn't worth living,
anyhow." And, on a wide view, I could see that it makes
little difference whether one dies at the age of thirty or three-
score and ten—since, in either case, other men and women
will continue living, the world will go on as before. Also,
whether I died now or forty years hence, this business of
dying had to be got through, inevitably. Still, somehow this
line of thought wasn't as consoling as it should have been;
the idea of all those years of life in hand was a galling re-
minder! However, I could argue myself out of it, by picturing
what would have been my feelings when my term was up,
and death had cornered me. Once you're up against it, the
precise manner of your death has obviously small importance.
Therefore—but it was hard not to lose the thread of the argument leading up to that "therefore"—I should be prepared to
face the dismissal of my appeal.

• • •

The chaplain gazed at me with a sort of sadness. I now
had my back to the wall and light was flowing over my fore-
head. He muttered some words I didn't catch; then abruptly

From *The Stranger,* by Albert Camus, translated by Stuart Gilbert. Copyright
1946 by Alfred A. Knopf, Inc. Reprinted by permission of Alfred A. Knopf,
Inc. and Hamish Hamilton, Ltd.

asked if he might kiss me. I said, "No." Then he turned, came up to the wall, and slowly drew his hand along it.

"Do you really love these earthly things so very much?" he asked in a low voice.

I made no reply.

For quite a while he kept his eyes averted. His presence was getting more and more irksome, and I was on the point of telling him to go, and leave me in peace, when all of a sudden he swung around on me, and burst out passionately:

"No! No! I refuse to believe it. I'm sure you've often wished there was an afterlife."

Of course I had, I told him. Everybody has that wish at times. But that had no more importance than wishing to be rich, or to swim very fast, or to have a better-shaped mouth. It was in the same order of things. I was going on in the same vein, when he cut in with a question. How did I picture the life after the grave?

I fairly bawled out at him: "A life in which I can remember this life on earth. That's all I want of it." And in the same breath I told him I'd had enough of his company.

But, apparently, he had more to say on the subject of God. I went close up to him and made a last attempt to explain that I'd very little time left, and I wasn't going to waste it on God.

Then he tried to change the subject by asking me why I hadn't once addressed him as "Father," seeing that he was a priest. That irritated me still more, and I told him he wasn't my father; quite the contrary, he was on the others' side.

"No, no, my son," he said, laying his hand on my shoulder. "I'm on *your* side, though you don't realize it—because your heart is hardened. But I shall pray for you."

Then, I don't know how it was, but something seemed to break inside me, and I started yelling at the top of my voice. I hurled insults at him, I told him not to waste his rotten prayers on me; it was better to burn than to disappear. I'd taken him by the neckband of his cassock, and, in a sort of ecstasy of joy and rage, I poured out on him all the thoughts that had been simmering in my brain. He seemed so cocksure, you see. And yet none of his certainties was worth one strand of a woman's hair. Living as he did, like a corpse, he couldn't even be sure of being alive. It might look as if my hands were empty. Actually, I was sure of myself, sure about everything, far surer than he; sure of my present life and of the death that was coming. That, no doubt, was all I had;

but at least that certainty was something I could get my teeth into—just as it had got its teeth into me. I'd been right, I was still right, I was always right. I'd passed my life in a certain way, and I might have passed it in a different way, if I'd felt like it. I'd acted thus, and I hadn't acted otherwise; I hadn't done x, whereas I had done y or z. And what did that mean? That, all the time, I'd been waiting for this present moment, for that dawn, tomorrow's or another day's, which was to justify me. Nothing, nothing had the least importance, and I knew quite well why. He, too, knew why. From the dark horizon of my future a sort of slow, persistent breeze had been blowing toward me, all my life long, from the years that were to come. And on its way that breeze had leveled out all the ideas that people tried to foist on me in the equally unreal years I then was living through. What difference could they make to me, the deaths of others, or a mother's love, or his God; or the way a man decides to live, the fate he thinks he chooses, since one and the same fate was bound to "choose" not only me but thousands of millions of privileged people who, like him, called themselves my brothers. Surely, surely he must see that? Every man alive was privileged; there was only one class of men, the privileged class. All alike would be condemned to die one day; his turn, too, would come like the others'. And what difference could it make if, after being charged with murder, he were executed because he didn't weep at his mother's funeral, since it all came to the same thing in the end? The same thing for Salamano's wife and for Salamano's dog. That little robot woman was as "guilty" as the girl from Paris who had married Masson, or as Marie, who wanted me to marry her. What did it matter if Raymond was as much my pal as Céleste, who was a far worthier man? What did it matter if at this very moment Marie was kissing a new boy friend? As a condemned man himself, couldn't he grasp what I meant by that dark wind blowing from my future? . . .

I had been shouting so much that I'd lost my breath, and just then the jailers rushed in and started trying to release the chaplain from my grip. One of them made as if to strike me. The chaplain quietened them down, then gazed at me for a moment without speaking. I could see tears in his eyes. Then he turned and left the cell.

Once he'd gone, I felt calm again. But all this excitement had exhausted me and I dropped heavily on to my sleeping plank. I must have had a longish sleep, for, when I woke, the stars were shining down on my face. Sounds of the countryside came faintly in, and the cool night air, veined with smells of earth and salt, fanned my cheeks. The marvelous peace of the sleepbound summer night flooded through me like a tide. Then, just on the edge of daybreak, I heard a steamer's siren. People were starting on a voyage to a world which had ceased to concern me forever. Almost for the first time in many months I thought of my mother. And now, it seemed to me, I understood why at her life's end she had taken on a "fiancé"; why she'd played at making a fresh start. There, too, in that Home where lives were flickering out, the dusk came as a mournful solace. With death so near, Mother must have felt like someone on the brink of freedom, ready to start life all over again. No one, no one in the world had any right to weep for her. And I, too, felt ready to start life all over again. It was as if that great rush of anger had washed me clean, emptied me of hope, and, gazing up at the dark sky spangled with its signs and stars, for the first time, the first, I laid my heart open to the benign indifference of the universe. To feel it so like myself, indeed, so brotherly, made me realize that I'd been happy, and that I was happy still. For all to be accomplished, for me to feel less lonely, all that remained to hope was that on the day of my execution there should be a huge crowd of spectators and that they should greet me with howls of execration.

from
THE MYTH OF SISYPHUS

An Absurd
Reasoning

There is but one truly serious philosophical problem, and that is suicide. Judging whether life is or is not worth living amounts to answering the fundamental question of philoso-

From *The Myth of Sisyphus* by Albert Camus, translated by Justin O'Brien. Copyright © 1955 by Alfred A. Knopf, Inc. Reprinted by permission of Alfred A. Knopf, Inc.

phy. All the rest—whether or not the world has three dimensions, whether the mind has nine or twelve categories—comes
afterwards. These are games; one must first answer. And if it
is true, as Nietzsche claims, that a philosopher, to deserve our
respect, must preach by example, you can appreciate the
importance of that reply, for it will precede the definitive act.
These are facts the heart can feel; yet they call for careful
study before they become clear to the intellect.

If I ask myself how to judge that this question is more
urgent than that, I reply that one judges by the actions it
entails. I have never seen anyone die for the ontological argument. Galileo, who held a scientific truth of great importance,
abjured it with the greatest ease as soon as it endangered his
life. In a certain sense, he did right.[1] That truth was not
worth the stake. Whether the earth or the sun revolves around
the other is a matter of profound indifference. To tell the
truth, it is a futile question. On the other hand, I see many
people die because they judge that life is not worth living. I
see others paradoxically getting killed for the ideas or illusions that give them a reason for living (what is called a
reason for living is also an excellent reason for dying). I
therefore conclude that the meaning of life is the most urgent
of questions. How to answer it? On all essential problems (I
mean thereby those that run the risk of leading to death or
those that intensify the passion of living) there are probably
but two methods of thought: the method of La Palisse and
the method of Don Quixote. Solely the balance between evidence and lyricism can allow us to achieve simultaneously
emotion and lucidity. In a subject at once so humble and so
heavy with emotion, the learned and classical dialectic must
yield, one can see, to a more modest attitude of mind deriv-
ing at once and the same time from common sense and
understanding.

Suicide has never been dealt with except as a social phenomenon. On the contrary, we are concerned here, at the
outset, with the relationship between individual thought and
suicide. An act like this is prepared within the silence of the
heart, as is a great work of art. The man himself is ignorant
of it. One evening he pulls the trigger or jumps. Of an

---

[1] *From the point of view of the relative value of truth. On the other hand,
from the point of view of virile behavior, this scholar's fragility may well
make us smile.*

apartment-building manager who had killed himself I was told that he had lost his daughter five years before, that he had changed greatly since, and that that experience had "undermined" him. A more exact word cannot be imagined. Beginning to think is beginning to be undermined. Society has but little connection with such beginnings. The worm is in man's heart. That is where it must be sought. One must follow and understand this fatal game that leads from lucidity in the face of existence to flight from light.

There are many causes for a suicide, and generally the most obvious ones were not the most powerful. Rarely is suicide committed (yet the hypothesis is not excluded) through reflection. What sets off the crisis is almost always unverifiable. Newspapers often speak of "personal sorrows" or of "incurable illness." These explanations are plausible. But one would have to know whether a friend of the desperate man had not that very day addressed him indifferently. He is the guilty one. For that is enough to precipitate all the rancors and all the boredom still in suspension.[2]

But if it is hard to fix the precise instant, the subtle step when the mind opted for death, it is easier to deduce from the act itself the consequences it implies. In a sense, and as in melodrama, killing yourself amounts to confessing. It is confessing that life is too much for you or that you do not understand it. Let's not go too far in such analogies, however, but rather return to everyday words. It is merely confessing that that "is not worth the trouble." Living, naturally, is never easy. You continue making the gestures commanded by existence for many reasons, the first of which is habit. Dying voluntarily implies that you have recognized, even instinctively, the ridiculous character of that habit, the absence of any profound reason for living, the insane character of that daily agitation, and the uselessness of suffering.

What, then, is that incalculable feeling that deprives the mind of the sleep necessary to life? A world that can be explained even with bad reasons is a familiar world. But, on the other hand, in a universe suddenly divested of illusions and lights, man feels an alien, a stranger. His exile is without

---

[2] *Let us not miss this opportunity to point out the relative character of this essay. Suicide may indeed be related to much more honorable considerations—for example, the political suicides of protest, as they were called, during the Chinese revolution.*

remedy since he is deprived of the memory of a lost home or the hope of a promised land. This divorce between man and his life, the actor and his setting, is properly the feeling of absurdity. All healthy men having thought of their own suicide, it can be seen, without further explanation, that there is a direct connection between this feeling and the longing for death.

. . .

Like great works, deep feelings always mean more than they are conscious of saying. The regularity of an impulse or a repulsion in a soul is encountered again in habits of doing or thinking, is reproduced in consequences of which the soul itself knows nothing. Great feelings take with them their own universe, splendid or abject. They light up with their passion an exclusive world in which they recognize their climate. There is a universe of jealousy, of ambition, of selfishness, or of generosity. A universe—in other words, a metaphysic and an attitude of mind. What is true of already specialized feelings will be even more so of emotions basically as indeterminate, simultaneously as vague and as "definite," as remote and as "present" as those furnished us by beauty or aroused by absurdity.

At any streetcorner the feeling of absurdity can strike any man in the face. As it is, in its distressing nudity, in its light without effulgence, it is elusive. But that very difficulty deserves reflection. It is probably true that a man remains forever unknown to us and that there is in him something irreducible that escapes us. But *practically* I know men and recognize them by their behavior, by the totality of their deeds, by the consequences caused in life by their presence. Likewise, all those irrational feelings which offer no purchase to analysis. I can define them *practically*, appreciate them *practically*, by gathering together the sum of their consequences in the domain of the intelligence, by seizing and noting all their aspects, by outlining their universe. It is certain that apparently, though I have seen the same actor a hundred times, I shall not for that reason know him any better personally. Yet if I add up the heroes he has personified and if I say that I know him a little better at the hundredth character counted off, this will be felt to contain an element of truth. For this apparent paradox is also an apologue. There is a moral to it. It teaches that a man defines himself by his make-believe as well as by his sincere impulses. There is thus a lower key of feelings, inaccessible in the heart but partially disclosed by the acts they imply and the attitudes of mind they assume. It is clear that in this way I am defining a method. But it is also evident that that method is one of analysis and not of knowledge. For methods imply metaphysics; unconsciously they disclose conclusions that they often claim not to know yet. Similarly, the last pages of a book are already contained in the first pages. Such a link is inevitable. The method defined here acknowledges the feeling that all true knowledge is impossible. Solely appearances can be enumerated and the climate make itself felt.

Perhaps we shall be able to overtake that elusive feeling of absurdity in the different but closely related worlds of intelligence, of the art of living, or of art itself. The climate of absurdity is in the beginning. The end is the absurd universe and that attitude of mind which lights the world with its true colors to bring out the privileged and implacable visage which that attitude has discerned in it.

All great deeds and all great thoughts have a ridiculous beginning. Great works are often born on a streetcorner or in a restaurant's revolving door. So it is with absurdity. The absurd world more than others derives its nobility from that abject birth. In certain situations, replying "nothing" when asked what one is thinking about may be pretense in a man. Those who are loved are well aware of this. But if that reply is sincere, if it symbolizes that odd state of soul in which the void becomes eloquent, in which the chain of daily gestures is broken, in which the heart vainly seeks the link that will connect it again, then it is as it were the first sign of absurdity.

It happens that the stage sets collapse. Rising, streetcar, four hours in the office or the factory, meal, streetcar, four hours of work, meal, sleep, and Monday Tuesday Wednesday Thursday Friday and Saturday according to the same rhythm —this path is easily followed most of the time. But one day the "why" arises and everything begins in that weariness tinged with amazement. "Begins"—this is important. Weariness comes at the end of the acts of a mechanical life, but at the same time it inaugurates the impulse of consciousness. It awakens consciousness and provokes what follows. What follows is the gradual return into the chain or it is the definitive awakening. At the end of the awakening comes, in time, the consequence: suicide or recovery. In itself weariness has something sickening about it. Here, I must conclude that it is good. For everything begins with consciousness and nothing is worth anything except through it. There is nothing original about these remarks. But they are obvious; that is enough for a while, during a sketchy reconnaissance in the origins of the absurd. Mere "anxiety," as Heidegger says, is at the source of everything.

Likewise and during every day of an unillustrious life, time carries us. But a moment always comes when we have to carry it. We live on the future: "tomorrow," "later on," "when you have made your way," "you will understand when you are old enough." Such irrelevancies are wonderful, for, after all, it's a matter of dying. Yet a day comes when a man notices or says that he is thirty. Thus he asserts his youth. But simultaneously he situates himself in relation to time. He takes his place in it. He admits that he stands at a certain point on a curve that he acknowledges having to travel to its end. He belongs to time, and by the horror that seizes him, he recognizes his worst enemy. Tomorrow, he was longing for tomorrow, whereas everything in him ought to reject it. That revolt of the flesh is the absurd.[3]

A step lower and strangeness creeps in: perceiving that the world is "dense," sensing to what a degree a stone is foreign and irreducible to us, with what intensity nature or a landscape can negate us. At the heart of all beauty lies something inhuman, and these hills, the softness of the sky, the outline of these trees at this very minutes lose the illusory meaning with which we had clothed them, henceforth more remote than a lost paradise. The primitive hostility of the world rises up to face us across millennia. For a second we cease to understand it because for centuries we have understood in it solely the images and designs that we had attributed to it beforehand, because henceforth we lack the power to make use of that artifice. The world evades us because it becomes itself again. That stage scenery masked by habit becomes again what it is. It withdraws at a distance from us. Just as there are days when under the familiar face of a woman, we see as a stranger her we had loved months or years ago, perhaps we shall come even to desire what suddenly leaves us so

---

[3] *But not in the proper sense. This is not a definition, but rather an enumeration of the feelings that may admit of the absurd. Still, the enumeration finished, the absurd has nevertheless not been exhausted.*

alone. But the time has not yet come. Just one thing: that denseness and that strangeness of the world is the absurd.

Men, too, secrete the inhuman. At certain moments of lucidity, the mechanical aspect of their gestures, their meaningless pantomime makes silly everything that surrounds them. A man is talking on the telephone behind a glass partition; you cannot hear him, but you see his incomprehensible dumb show: you wonder why he is alive. This discomfort in the face of man's own inhumanity, this incalculable tumble before the image of what we are, this "nausea," as a writer of today calls it, is also the absurd. Likewise the stranger who at certain seconds comes to meet us in a mirror, the familiar and yet alarming brother we encounter in our own photographs is also the absurd.

. . .

Now I can broach the notion of suicide. It has already been felt what solution might be given. At this point the problem is reversed. It was previously a question of finding out whether or not life had to have a meaning to be lived. It now becomes clear, on the contrary, that it will be lived all the better if it has no meaning. Living an experience, a particular fate, is accepting it fully. Now, no one will live this fate, knowing it to be absurd, unless he does everything to keep before him that absurd brought to light by consciousness. Negating one of the terms of the opposition on which he lives amounts to escaping it. To abolish conscious revolt is to elude the problem. The theme of permanent revolution is thus carried into individual experience. Living is keeping the absurd alive. Keeping it alive is, above all, contemplating it. Unlike Eurydice, the absurd dies only when we turn away from it. One of the only coherent philosophical positions is thus revolt. It is a constant confrontation between man and his own obscurity. It is an insistence upon an impossible transparency. It challenges the world anew every second. Just as danger provided man the unique opportunity of seizing awareness, so metaphysical revolt extends awareness to the whole of experience. It is that constant presence of man in his own eyes. It is not aspiration, for it is devoid of hope. That revolt is the certainty of a crushing fate, without the resignation that ought to accompany it.

This is where it is seen to what a degree absurd experience is remote from suicide. It may be thought that suicide follows revolt—but wrongly. For it does not represent the logical

outcome of revolt. It is just the contrary by the consent it presupposes. Suicide, like the leap, is acceptance at its extreme.
Everything is over and man returns to his essential history.
His future, his unique and dreadful future—he sees and
rushes toward it. In its way, suicide settles the absurd. It
engulfs the absurd in the same death. But I know that in
order to keep alive, the absurd cannot be settled. It escapes
suicide to the extent that it is simultaneously awareness and
rejection of death. It is, at the extreme limit of the condemned
man's last thought, that shoelace that despite everything he
sees a few yards away, on the very brink of his dizzying fall.
The contrary of suicide, in fact, is the man condemned to
death.

That revolt gives life its value. Spread out over the whole
length of a life, it restores its majesty to that life. To a man
devoid of blinders, there is no finer sight than that of the
intelligence at grips with a reality that transcends it. The
sight of human pride is unequaled. No disparagement is of
any use. That discipline that the mind imposes on itself, that
will conjured up out of nothing, that face-to-face struggle
have something exceptional about them. To impoverish that
reality whose inhumanity constitutes man's majesty is tantamount to impoverishing him himself. I understand then why
the doctrines that explain everything to me also debilitate me
at the same time. They relieve me of the weight of my own
life, and yet I must carry it alone. At this juncture, I cannot
conceive that a skeptical metaphysics can be joined to an
ethics of renunciation.

Consciousness and revolt, these rejections are the contrary
of renunciation. Everything that is indomitable and passionate in a human heart quickens them, on the contrary, with
its own life. It is essential to die unreconciled and not of one's
own free will. Suicide is a repudiation. The absurd man can
only drain everything to the bitter end, and deplete himself.
The absurd is his extreme tension, which he maintains constantly by solitary effort, for he knows that in that consciousness and in that day-to-day revolt he gives proof of his only
truth, which is defiance. This is a first consequence.

• • •

But what does life mean in such a universe? Nothing else
for the moment but indifference to the future and a desire to
use up everything that is given. Belief in the meaning of life
always implies a scale of values, a choice, our preferences.

Belief in the absurd, according to our definitions, teaches the contrary. But this is worth examining.

Knowing whether or not one can live *without appeal* is all that interests me. I do not want to get out of my depth. This aspect of life being given me, can I adapt myself to it? Now, faced with this particular concern, belief in the absurd is tantamount to substituting the quantity of experiences for the quality. If I convince myself that this life has no other aspect than that of the absurd, if I feel that its whole equilibrium depends on that perpetual opposition between my conscious revolt and the darkness in which it struggles, if I admit that my freedom has no meaning except in relation to its limited fate, then I must say that what counts is not the best living but the most living. It is not up to me to wonder if this is vulgar or revolting, elegant or deplorable. Once and for all, value judgments are discarded here in favor of factual judgments. I have merely to draw the conclusions from what I can see and to risk nothing that is hypothetical. Supposing that living in this way were not honorable, then true propriety would command me to be dishonorable.

The most living; in the broadest sense, that rule means nothing. It calls for definition. It seems to begin with the fact that the notion of quantity has not been sufficiently explored. For it can account for a large share of human experience. A man's rule of conduct and his scale of values have no meaning except through the quantity and variety of experiences he has been in a position to accumulate. Now, the conditions of modern life impose on the majority of men the same quantity of experiences and consequently the same profound experience. To be sure, there must also be taken into consideration the individual's spontaneous contribution, the "given" element in him. But I cannot judge of that, and let me repeat that my rule here is to get along with the immediate evidence. I see, then, that the individual character of a common code of ethics lies not so much in the ideal importance of its basic principles as in the norm of an experience that it is possible to measure. To stretch a point somewhat, the Greeks had the code of their leisure just as we have the code of our eight-hour day. But already many men among the most tragic cause us to foresee that a longer experience changes this table of values. They make us imagine that adventurer of the everyday who through mere quantity of experiences would break all records (I am purposely using this sports expression) and

would thus win his own code of ethics. Yet let's avoid roman-
ticism and just ask ourselves what such an attitude may mean
to a man with his mind made up to take up his bet and to
observe strictly what he takes to be the rules of the game.

Breaking all the records is first and foremost being faced
with the world as often as possible. How can that be done
without contradictions and without playing on words? For on
the one hand the absurd teaches that all experiences are unimportant, and on the other it urges toward the greatest
quantity of experiences. How, then, can one fail to do as so
many of those men I was speaking of earlier—choose the
form of life that brings us the most possible of that human
matter, thereby introducing a scale of values that on the other
hand one claims to reject?

But again it is the absurd and its contradictory life that
teaches us. For the mistake is thinking that that quantity of
experiences depends on the circumstances of our life when
it depends solely on us. Here we have to be over-simple. To
two men living the same number of years, the world always
provides the same sum of experiences. It is up to us to be
conscious of them. Being aware of one's life, one's revolt,
one's freedom, and to the maximum, is living, and to the
maximum. Where lucidity dominates, the scale of values becomes useless. Let's be even more simple. Let us say that the
sole obstacle, the sole deficiency to be made good, is constituted by premature death. Thus it is that no depth, no emotion, no passion, and no sacrifice could render equal in the
eyes of the absurd man (even if he wished it so) a conscious
life of forty years and a lucidity spread over sixty years. Madness and death are his irreparables. Man does not choose.
The absurd and the extra life it involves *therefore do not
depend on man's will*, but on its contrary, which is death.
Weighing words carefully, it is altogether a question of luck.
One just has to be able to consent to this. There will never be
any substitute for twenty years of life and experience.

By what is an odd inconsistency in such an alert race, the
Greeks claimed that those who died young were beloved of
the gods. And that is true only if you are willing to believe
that entering the ridiculous world of the gods is forever losing the purest of joys, which is feeling, and feeling on this
earth. The present and the succession of presents before a
constantly conscious soul is the ideal of the absurd man. But

the word "ideal" rings false in this connection. It is not even his vocation, but merely the third consequence of his reasoning. Having started from an anguished awareness of the inhuman, the meditation on the absurd returns at the end of its itinerary to the very heart of the passionate flames of human revolt.

Thus I draw from the absurd three consequences, which are my revolt, my freedom, and my passion. By the mere activity of consciousness I transform into a rule of life what was an invitation to death—and I refuse suicide. I know, to be sure, the dull resonance that vibrates throughout these days. Yet I have but a word to say: that it is necessary.

· · ·

The preceding merely defines a way of thinking. But the point is to live.

The Myth of Sisyphus

The gods had condemned Sisyphus to ceaselessly rolling a rock to the top of a mountain, whence the stone would fall back of its own weight. They had thought with some reason that there is no more dreadful punishment than futile and hopeless labor.

· · ·

You have already grasped that Sisyphus is the absurd hero. He *is*, as much through his passions as through his torture. His scorn of the gods, his hatred of death, and his passion for life won him that unspeakable penalty in which the whole being is exerted toward accomplishing nothing. This is the price that must be paid for the passions of this earth.

· · ·

If this myth is tragic, that is because its hero is conscious. Where would his torture be, indeed, if at every step the hope of succeeding upheld him? The workman of today works every day in his life at the same tasks, and this fate is no less absurd. But it is tragic only at the rare moments when it becomes conscious. Sisyphus, proletarian of the gods, powerless and rebellious, knows the whole extent of his wretched condition: it is what he thinks of during his descent. The lucidity that was to constitute his torture at the same time crowns his victory. There is no fate that cannot be surmounted by scorn.

. . .

All Sisyphus' silent joy is contained therein. His fate belongs to him. His rock is his thing. Likewise, the absurd man, when he contemplates his torment, silences all the idols. In the universe suddenly restored to its silence, the myriad wondering little voices of the earth rise up. Unconscious, secret calls, invitations from all the faces, they are the necessary reverse and price of victory. There is no sun without shadow, and it is essential to know the night. The absurd man says yes and his effort will henceforth be unceasing. If there is a personal fate, there is no higher destiny, or at least there is but one which he concludes is inevitable and despicable. For the rest, he knows himself to be the master of his days. At that subtle moment when man glances backward over his life, Sisyphus returning toward his rock, in that slight pivoting he contemplates that series of unrelated actions which becomes his fate, created by him, combined under his memory's eye and soon sealed by his death. Thus, convinced of the wholly human origin of all that is human, a blind man eager to see who knows that the night has no end, he is still on the go. The rock is still rolling.

I leave Sisyphus at the foot of the mountain! One always finds one's burden again. But Sisyphus teaches the higher fidelity that negates the gods and raises rocks. He too concludes that all is well. This universe henceforth without a master seems to him neither sterile nor futile. Each atom of that stone, each mineral flake of that night-filled mountain, in itself forms a world. The struggle itself toward the heights is enough to fill a man's heart. One must imagine Sisyphus happy.

from
THE FALL

You don't understand what I mean? I'll admit my fatigue. I lose the thread of what I am saying; I've lost that lucidity to which my friends used to enjoy paying respects. I say "my friends," moreover, as a convention. I have no more friends; I have nothing but accomplices. To make up for this their number has increased; they are the whole human race. And within the human race, you first of all. Whoever is at hand is always the first. How do I know I have no friends? It's very easy: I discovered it the day I thought of killing myself to play a trick on them, to punish them, in a way. But punish whom? Some would be surprised, and no one would feel punished. I realized I had no friends. Besides, even if I had had, I shouldn't be any better off. If I had been able to commit suicide and then see their reaction, why then the game would have been worth the candle. But the earth is dark, *cher ami*, the coffin thick, and the shroud opaque. The eyes of the soul —to be sure—if there is a soul and it has eyes! But you see, we're not sure, we can't be sure. Otherwise, there would be a solution; at least one could get oneself taken seriously. Men are never convinced of your reasons, of your sincerity, of the seriousness of your sufferings, except by your death. So long as you are alive, your case is doubtful; you have a right only to their skepticism. So if there were the least certainty that one could enjoy the show, it would be worth proving to them what they are unwilling to believe and thus amazing them. But you kill yourself and what does it matter whether or not they believe you? You are not there to see their amazement and their contrition (fleeting at best), to witness, according to every man's dream, your own funeral. In order to cease being a doubtful case, one has to cease being, that's all.

Besides, isn't it better thus? We'd suffer too much from their indifference. "You'll pay for this!" a daughter said to her father who had prevented her from marrying a too well groomed suitor. And she killed herself. But the father paid for nothing. He loved fly-casting. Three Sundays later he

From *The Fall* by Albert Camus, translated by Justin O'Brien. Copyright © 1956 by Alfred A. Knopf, Inc. Reprinted by permission of Alfred A. Knopf, Inc.

went back to the river—to forget, as he said. He was right; he forgot. To tell the truth, the contrary would have been surprising. You think you are dying to punish your wife and actually you are freeing her. It's better not to see that. Besides the fact that you might hear the reasons they give for your action. As far as I am concerned, I can hear them now: "He killed himself because he couldn't bear . . ." Ah, *cher ami*, how poor in invention men are! They always think one commits suicide for a reason. But it's quite possible to commit suicide for two reasons. No, that never occurs to them. So what's the good of dying intentionally, of sacrificing yourself to the idea you want people to have of you? Once you are dead, they will take advantage of it to attribute idiotic or vulgar motives to your action. Martyrs, *cher ami*, must choose between being forgotten, mocked, or made use of. As for being understood—never!

Besides, let's not beat about the bush; I love life—that's my real weakness. I love it so much that I am incapable of imagining what is not life. Such avidity has something plebeian about it, don't you think? Aristocracy cannot imagine itself without a little distance surrounding itself and its life. One dies if necessary, one breaks rather than bending. But I bend, because I continue to love myself. For example, after all I have told you, what do you think I developed? An aversion for myself? Come, come, it was especially with others that I was fed up. To be sure, I knew my failings and regretted them. Yet I continued to forget them with a rather meritorious obstinacy. The prosecution of others, on the contrary, went on constantly in my heart. Of course—does that shock you? Maybe you think it's not logical? But the question is not to remain logical. The question is to slip through and, above all—yes, above all, the question is to elude judgment. I'm not saying to avoid punishment, for punishment without judgment is bearable. It has a name, besides, that guarantees our innocence: it is called misfortune. No, on the contrary, it's a matter of dodging judgment, of avoiding being forever judged without ever having a sentence pronounced.

* * *

Thus it is that in the end, to take but one example, women cost me dear. The time I used to devote to them I couldn't give to men, who didn't always forgive me this. Is there any way out? Your successes and happiness are forgiven you only if you generously consent to share them. But to be happy it is essential not to be too concerned with others. Consequently, there is no escape. Happy and judged, or absolved and wretched. As for me, the injustice was even greater: I was condemned for past successes. For a long time I had lived in the illusion of a general agreement, whereas, from all sides, judgments, arrows, mockeries rained upon me, inattentive and smiling. The day I was alerted I became lucid; I received all the wounds at the same time and lost my strength all at once. The whole universe then began to laugh at me.

That is what no man (except those who are not really alive —in other words, wise men) can endure. Spitefulness is the only possible ostentation. People hasten to judge in order not to be judged themselves. What do you expect? The idea that comes most naturally to man, as if from his very nature, is the idea of his innocence. From this point of view, we are all like that little Frenchman at Buchenwald who insisted on registering a complaint with the clerk, himself a prisoner, who was recording his arrival. A complaint? The clerk and his comrades laughed: "Useless, old man. You don't lodge a complaint here." "But you see, sir," said the little French-man, "My case is exceptional. I am innocent!"

We are all exceptional cases. We all want to appeal against something! Each of us insists on being innocent at all cost, even if he has to accuse the whole human race and heaven itself. You won't delight a man by complimenting him on the efforts by which he has become intelligent or generous. On the other hand, he will beam if you admire his natural gen-erosity. Inversely, if you tell a criminal that his crime is not due to his nature or his character but to unfortunate circum-stances, he will be extravagantly grateful to you. During the counsel's speech, this is the moment he will choose to weep.

from
"ALBERT CAMUS," BY JEAN-PAUL SARTRE

. . .

He represented in this century, and against History, the present heir of that long line of moralists whose works perhaps constitute what is most original in French letters. His stubborn humanism, narrow and pure, austere and sensual, waged a dubious battle against events of these times. But inversely, through the obstinacy of his refusals, he reaffirmed the existence of moral fact within the heart of our era and against the Machiavellians, against the golden calf of realism.

He *was*, so to speak, this unshakable affirmation. For, as little as people may read or reflect, they collide against the human values which he held in his closed fist. He put the political act in question. He had to be avoided or fought: indispensable, in a word, to this tension which makes the life of the mind. Even his silence, these last years, had a positive aspect: this Cartesian of the absurd refused to leave the sure ground of morality, and to engage upon the uncertain paths of the *practical*. We guessed this, and we also guessed the conflicts which he silenced: because morality, in order to take it up alone, demands revolt and condemns it at the same time.

. . .

I do not believe it [Camus' sudden death in an auto accident]. As soon as it manifests itself, the inhuman becomes part of the human. Every interrupted life—even that of so young a man—is, at the same time, *a record that is broken* and a complete life. For all those who loved him, there was an unbearable absurdity in this death. But we shall have to learn to see this mutilated life-work as a whole life-work. In the same measure that the humanism of Camus contained a humane attitude towards the death that was to take him by surprise, in the measure that his proud quest for human

From *Situations* by Jean-Paul Sartre, translated from the French by Benita Eisler. English translation copyright © 1965 by George Braziller, Inc. Reprinted by permission of the publisher. Originally published in *France-Observateur*, January 7, 1960, after Camus's death.

happiness implied and reclaimed the inhuman necessity of dying, we shall recognize in this work and in the life which is inseparable from it, the pure and victorious endeavor of a man to recover each instant of his existence from his future death.

Jean-Paul Sartre

(b. 1905) ━━━◆●◆━━━ FRENCH

During one series of arrests in the Algerian crisis, de Gaulle himself is said to have refused to have Sartre arrested on the grounds that "Sartre is France, and one cannot arrest France." Such is Sartre's importance, not only in French letters and politics, but in the spirit of the Western world in the twentieth century. It is Sartre who is mainly responsible for both the formulation and the popularization of existentialism. It is Sartre who continues to hold the very identity of existentialism in his actions as well as his writings. He has persisted in his demand that writing have a social conscience, and that the writer be a man of action as well as of words. The central concepts of his philosophy have always been "freedom" and "action," and the goal of his activities has constantly been to hold an honest stance in the struggle for freedom. It has been argued that there are two Sartres, Sartre the existentialist and Sartre the Marxist. Though there has always been tension between the intellectual and committed political action, there has been just one Sartre, whose restless genius has led him to focus now on this problem, now on that one.

In his early Being and Nothingness *(1943) he brings to a climax several years' work in psychology and phenomenology. The theme of that work is individual freedom, and its central intention is to characterize human existence in such a way that it is "without excuse." The work begins with Descartes' cogito, Husserl's phenomenological method, and Heidegger's arguments against the primacy of knowledge. Sartre distinguishes between the being of things—"Being-in-itself" —and the being of consciousness—"Being-for-itself." Only consciousness, not things, has the property of "secreting nothingness," of imagining alternatives, of denying a situation. This ability to negate is also called* freedom, *and Sartre argues that it is the very condition of there being consciousness. Freedom, thus characterized as freedom of intention and not as freedom of successful action (I am always free to try to*

escape; I am not always free to succeed in escaping), is absolute. *Yet this freedom is also always confronted with a specific
situation, its* facticity *(the term is from Heidegger), which
both directs the kinds of actions which are appropriate and
limits the actions which can be successful. Between my freedom and my facticity there is the question who I am. On the
one hand, one might say that I am whatever the facts about
me (i.e., my facticity) say I am. But then, one might say that
I am not those facts, that I am whatever I intend to be.
Neither answer is correct, Sartre tells us, and any attempt to
settle who one is on the basis of only the facts about him or
his intentions is in* bad faith. *The central purpose of* Being
and Nothingness *is to display for us the various pitfalls of
bad faith and to warn us against them. The ideal (though
Sartre, like Heidegger, insists that he is doing "ontology" and
not ethics) is the recognition of both one's freedom and one's
facticity, like, for example, the young Orestes toward the end
of Sartre's play* The Flies. *In addition to bad faith, there is
another serious threat to our attitude toward ourselves: other
people. Sartre follows Hegel's master-slave parable in his description of relations between people which are essentially
conflict. Even love, as well as sadism and hate, is a manifestation of conflict, of the attempt of each person to win the
freedom of the other. In* No Exit *Sartre portrays three people
in hell who discover that "hell is—other people." Similarly,
the young child Jean Genet is reduced to a thing—a thief—
by the accusations of others.*

*For the past twenty years Sartre has focused his attention
more on society than on the isolated individual. The culmina-
tion of his studies is* La Critique de la Raison Dialectique
(not yet translated) with its introduction, Search for a Method
(reprinted in part here). Concepts from Being and Nothingness *have been made at home in this sociological context. For
example, bad faith has its social analogue in* seriality; *the
project (ultimate choice) of the individual remanifests itself
as* praxis. *The two works are complementary, although one
would expect that Sartre has had some changes of mind since
1943. For example, he no longer argues that the notion of
freedom is absolute, largely due to objections raised by
Merleau-Ponty (see the latter's "Freedom," reprinted in this
volume). But Sartre's work—his two main studies plus his
many essays, plays, novels, and discussions—form an integrated whole which has few parallels in this century.*

The following montage of pieces includes several selections from Being and Nothingness *together with selections from contemporaneous novels and plays, such as* Nausea, The Flies, No Exit, *and* The Age of Reason. *The selection from* St. Genet: Actor and Martyr *is a brief illustration of Sartre's brilliant excursions into existential psychoanalysis, most recently applied to Flaubert in a voluminous study. The last selection reflects Sartre's "radical conversion" to Marxism and his political revolution. The opening selection is taken from a popular and somewhat popularized lecture Sartre delivered in 1946–1947.*

from
EXISTENTIALISM IS A HUMANISM

. . . For in truth this is of all teachings the least scandalous and the most austere: it is intended strictly for technicians and philosophers. All the same, it can easily be defined.

The question is only complicated because there are two kinds of existentialists. There are, on the one hand, the Christians, amongst whom I shall name Jaspers and Gabriel Marcel, both professed Catholics; and on the other the existential atheists, amongst whom we must place Heidegger as well as the French existentialists and myself. What they have in common is simply the fact that they believe that *existence* comes before *essence*—or, if you will, that we must begin from the subjective. What exactly do we mean by that?

If one considers an article of manufacture—as, for example, a book or a paper-knife—one sees that it has been made by an artisan who had a conception of it; and he has paid attention, equally, to the conception of a paper-knife and to the pre-existent technique of production which is a part of that conception and is, at bottom, a formula. Thus the paper-knife is at the same time an article producible in a certain manner and one which, on the other hand, serves a definite purpose, for one cannot suppose that a man would produce a

From *Existentialism Is a Humanism* by Jean-Paul Sartre, translated by P. Mairet. Copyright © 1949 by The Philosophical Library, Inc. Reprinted by permission of The Philosophical Library, Inc.

paper-knife without knowing what it was for. Let us say, then, of the paper-knife that its essence—that is to say the sum of the formulae and the qualities which made its production and its definition possible—precedes its existence. The presence of such-and-such a paper-knife or book is thus determined before my eyes. Here, then, we are viewing the world from a technical standpoint, and we can say that production precedes existence.

When we think of God as the creator, we are thinking of him, most of the time, as a supernal artisan. Whatever doctrine we may be considering, whether it be a doctrine like that of Descartes, or of Leibnitz himself, we always imply that the will follows, more or less, from the understanding or at least accompanies it, so that when God creates he knows precisely what he is creating. Thus, the conception of man in the mind of God is comparable to that of the paper-knife in the mind of the artisan: God makes man according to a procedure and a conception, exactly as the artisan manufactures a paper-knife, following a definition and a formula. Thus each individual man is the realisation of a certain conception which dwells in the divine understanding. In the philosophic atheism of the eighteenth century, the notion of God is suppressed, but not, for all that, the idea that essence is prior to existence; something of that idea we still find everywhere, in Diderot, in Voltaire and even in Kant. Man possesses a human nature; that "human nature," which is the conception of human being, is found in every man; which means that each man is a particular example of an universal conception, the conception of Man. In Kant, this universality goes so far that the wild man of the woods, man in the state of nature and the bourgeois are all contained in the same definition and have the same fundamental qualities. Here again, the essence of man precedes that historic existence which we confront in experience.

Atheistic existentialism, of which I am a representative, declares with greater consistency that if God does not exist there is at least one being whose existence comes before its essence, a being which exists before it can be defined by any conception of it. That being is man or, as Heidegger has it, the human reality. What do we mean by saying that existence precedes essence? We mean that man first of all exists, encounters himself, surges up in the world—and defines himself afterwards. If man as the existentialist sees him is not definable, it is because to begin with he is nothing. He will not be anything until later, and then he will be what he makes of himself. Thus, there is no human nature, because there is no God to have a conception of it. Man simply is. Not that he is simply what he conceives himself to be, but he is what he wills, and as he conceives himself after already existing—as he wills to be after that leap towards existence. Man is nothing else but that which he makes of himself. That is the first principle of existentialism. And this is what people call its "subjectivity," using the word as a reproach against us. But what do we mean to say by this, but that man is of a greater dignity than a stone or a table? For we mean to say that man primarily exists—that man is, before all else, something which propels itself towards a future and is aware that it is doing so. Man is, indeed, a project which possesses a subjective life, instead of being a kind of moss, or a fungus or a cauliflower. Before that projection of the self nothing exists; not even in the heaven of intelligence: man will only attain existence when he is what he purposes to be. Not, however, what he may wish to be. For what we usually understand by wishing or willing is a conscious decision taken—much more often than not—after we have made ourselves what we are. I may wish to join a party, to write a book or to marry—but in such a case what is usually called my will is probably a manifestation of a prior and more spontaneous decision. If, however, it is true that existence is prior to essence, man is responsible for what he is. Thus, the first effect of existentialism is that it puts every man in possession of himself as he is, and places the entire responsibility for his existence squarely upon his own shoulders. And, when we say that man is responsible for himself. we do not mean that he is responsible only for his own individuality, but that he is responsible for all men. The word "subjectivism" is to be understood in two senses, and our adversaries play upon only one of them. Subjectivism means, on the one hand, the freedom of the individual subject and, on the other, that man cannot pass beyond human subjectivity. It is the latter which is the deeper meaning of existentialism. When we say that man chooses himself. we do mean that every one of us must choose himself; but by that we also mean that in choosing for himself he chooses for all men. For in effect, of all the actions a man may take in order to create himself as he wills to be, there is not one which is not creative, at the same time, of an image of man such as he believes he ought to be. To choose between this or that is at the same time to affirm the value of that which is chosen; for we are unable ever to choose the worse. What we choose is always the better; and nothing can be better for us unless it is better for all. If, moreover, existence precedes essence and we will to exist at the same time as we fashion our image, that image is valid for all and for the entire epoch in which we find ourselves. Our responsibility is thus much greater than we had supposed, for it concerns mankind as a whole. If I am a worker, for instance, I may choose to join a Christian rather than a Communist trade union. And if, by that membership, I choose to signify that resignation is, after all, the attitude that best becomes a man, that man's kingdom is not upon this earth, I do not commit myself alone to that view. Resignation is my will for everyone, and my action is, in consequence, a commitment on behalf of all mankind. Or if, to take a more personal case, I decide to marry and to have children, even though this decision proceeds simply from my situation, from my passion or my desire, I am thereby committing not only myself, but humanity as a whole, to the practice of monogamy. I am thus responsible for myself and for all men, and I am creating a certain image of man as I would have him to be. In fashioning myself I fashion man.

This may enable us to understand what is meant by such terms—perhaps a little grandiloquent—as anguish, abandonment and despair. As you will soon see, it is very simple. First, what do we mean by anguish? The existentialist frankly states that man is in anguish. His meaning is as follows—When a man commits himself to anything, fully realising that he is not only choosing what he will be, but is thereby at the same time a legislator deciding for the whole of mankind—in such a moment a man cannot escape from the sense of complete and profound responsibility. There are many, indeed, who show no such anxiety. But we affirm that they are merely disguising their anguish or are in flight from it. Certainly, many people think that in what they are doing they commit no one but themselves to anything: and if you ask them, "What would happen if everyone did so?" they shrug their shoulders and reply, "Everyone does not do so." But in truth, one ought always to ask oneself what would happen if everyone did as one is doing; nor can one escape from that disturbing thought except by a kind of self-deception. The man who lies in self-excuse, by saying "Everyone will not do it," must be ill at ease in his conscience, for the act of lying implies the universal value which it denies. By its very disguise his anguish reveals itself. This is the anguish that Kierkegaard called "the anguish of Abraham." You know the story: An angel commanded Abraham to sacrifice his son: and obedience was obligatory, if it really was an angel who had appeared and said, "Thou, Abraham, shalt sacrifice thy son." But anyone in such a case would wonder, first, whether it was indeed an angel and secondly, whether I am really Abraham. Where are the proofs? A certain mad woman who suffered from hallucinations said that people were telephoning to her, and giving her orders. The doctor asked, "But who is it that speaks to you?" She replied: "He says it is God." And what, indeed, could prove to her that it was God? If an angel appears to me, what is the proof that it is an angel; or, if I hear voices, who can prove that they proceed from heaven and not from hell, or from my own subconsciousness or some pathological condition? Who can prove that they are really addressed to me?

Who, then, can prove that I am the proper person to impose, by my own choice, my conception of man upon mankind? I shall never find any proof whatever; there will be no sign to convince me of it. If a voice speaks to me, it is still I myself who must decide whether the voice is or is not that of an angel. If I regard a certain course of action as good, it is only I who choose to say that it is good and not bad. There is nothing to show that I am Abraham: nevertheless I also am obliged at every instant to perform actions which are examples. Everything happens to every man as though the whole human race had its eyes fixed upon what he is doing and regulated its conduct accordingly. So every man ought to say, "Am I really a man who has the right to act in such a manner that humanity regulates itself by what I do?" If a man does not say that, he is dissembling his anguish. Clearly, the anguish with which we are concerned here is not one that could lead to quietism or inaction. It is anguish pure and simple, of the kind well known to all those who have borne responsibilities. When, for instance, a military leader takes upon himself the responsibility for an attack and sends a number of men to their death, he chooses to do it and at bottom he alone chooses. No doubt he acts under a higher command, but its orders, which are more general, require interpretation by him and upon that interpretation depends the life of ten, fourteen or twenty men. In making the decision, he cannot but feel a certain anguish. All leaders know that anguish. It does not prevent their acting, on the contrary it is the very condition of their action, for the action presupposes that there is a plurality of possibilities, and in choosing one of these, they realise that it has value only because it is chosen. Now it is anguish of that kind which existentialism describes, and moreover, as we shall see, makes explicit through direct responsibility towards other men who are concerned. Far from being a screen which could separate us from action, it is a condition of action itself.

And when we speak of "abandonment"—a favourite word of Heidegger—we only mean to say that God does not exist, and that it is necessary to draw the consequences of his absence right to the end. The existentialist is strongly opposed to a certain type of secular moralism which seeks to suppress God at the least possible expense. Towards 1880, when the French professors endeavoured to formulate a secular morality, they said something like this:—God is a useless and costly hypothesis, so we will do without it. However, if we are to have morality, a society and a law-abiding world, it is essential that certain values should be taken seriously; they must have an *a priori* existence ascribed to them. It must be considered obligatory *a priori* to be honest, not to lie, not to beat one's wife, to bring up children and so forth; so we are going to do a little work on this subject, which will enable us to show that these values exist all the same, inscribed in an intelligible heaven although, of course, there is no God. In other words—and this is, I believe, the purport of all that we in France call radicalism—nothing will be changed if God does not exist; we shall re-discover the same norms of honesty, progress and humanity, and we shall have disposed of God as an out-of-date hypothesis which will die away quietly of itself. The existentialist, on the contrary, finds it extremely embarrassing that God does not exist, for there disappears with Him all possibility of finding values in an intelligible heaven. There can no longer be any good *a priori*, since there is no infinite and perfect consciousness to think it. It is nowhere written that "the good" exists, that one must be honest or must not lie, since we are now upon the plane where there are only men. Dostoievsky once wrote "If God did not exist, everything would be permitted"; and that, for existentialism, is the starting point. Everything is indeed permitted if God does not exist, and man is in consequence forlorn, for he cannot find anything to depend upon either within or outside himself. He discovers forthwith, that he is without excuse. For if indeed existence precedes essence, one will never be able to explain one's action by reference to a given and specific human nature; in other words, there is no determinism—man is free, man *is* freedom. Nor, on the other hand, if God does not exist, are we provided with any values or commands that could legitimise our behaviour. Thus we have neither behind us, nor before us in a luminous realm of values, any means of justification or excuse. We are left alone, without excuse. That is what I mean when I say that man is condemned to be free. Condemned, because he did not create himself, yet is nevertheless at liberty, and from the moment that he is thrown into this world he is responsible for everything he does. The existentialist does not believe in the power of passion. He will never regard a grand passion as a destructive torrent upon which a man is swept into certain actions as by fate, and which, therefore, is an excuse for them. He thinks that man is responsible for his passion. Neither will an existentialist think that a man can find help through some sign being vouchsafed upon earth for his orientation: for he thinks that the man himself interprets the sign as he chooses. He thinks that every man, without any support or help whatever, is condemned at every instant to invent man. As Ponge has written in a very fine article, "Man is the future of man." That is exactly true. Only, if one took this to mean that the future is laid up in Heaven, that God knows what it is, it would be false, for then it would no longer even be a future. If, however, it means that whatever man may now appear to be, there is a future to be fashioned, a virgin future that awaits him—then it is a true saying. But in the present one is forsaken.

As an example by which you may the better understand this state of abandonment, I will refer to the case of a pupil of mine, who sought me out in the following circumstances. His father was quarrelling with his mother and was also inclined to be a "collaborator"; his elder brother had been killed in the German offensive of 1940 and this young man, with a sentiment somewhat primitive but generous, burned to avenge him. His mother was living alone with him, deeply afflicted by the semi-treason of his father and by the death of her eldest son, and her one consolation was in this young man. But he, at this moment, had the choice between going to England to join the Free French Forces or of staying near his mother and helping her to live. He fully realised that this woman lived only for him and that his disappearance—or perhaps his death—would plunge her into despair. He also realised that, concretely and in fact, every action he performed on his mother's behalf would be sure of effect in the sense of aiding her to live, whereas anything he did in order to go and fight would be an ambiguous action which might vanish like water into sand and serve no purpose. For instance, to set out for England he would have to wait indefinitely in a Spanish camp on the way through Spain; or, on arriving in England or in Algiers he might be put into an office to fill up forms. Consequently, he found himself confronted by two very different modes of action: the one concrete, immediate but directed towards only one individual; and the other an action addressed to an end infinitely greater, a national collectivity, but for that very reason ambiguous—and it might be frustrated on the way. At the same time, he was hesitating between two kinds of morality; on the one side the morality of sympathy, of personal devotion and, on the other side, a morality of wider scope but of more debatable validity. He had to choose between those two. What could help him to choose? Could the Christian doctrine? No. Christian doctrine says: Act with charity, love your neighbour, deny yourself for others, choose the way which is hardest, and so forth. But which is the harder road? To whom does one owe the more brotherly love, the patriot or the mother? Which is the more useful aim, the general one of fighting in and for the whole community, or the precise aim of helping one particular person to live? Who can give an answer to that *a priori*? No one. Nor is it given in any ethical scripture. The Kantian ethic says, Never regard another as a means, but always as an end. Very well; if I remain with my mother, I shall be regarding her as the end and not as a means: but by the same token I am in danger of treating as means those who are fighting on my behalf; and the converse is also true, that if I go to the aid of the combatants I shall be treating them as the end at the risk of treating my mother as a means.

If values are uncertain, if they are still too abstract to determine the particular, concrete case under consideration, nothing remains but to trust in our instincts. That is what this young man tried to do; and when I saw him he said, "In the end, it is feeling that counts; the direction in which it is really pushing me is the one I ought to choose. If I feel that I love my mother enough to sacrifice everything else for her— my will to be avenged, all my longings for action and adventure—then I stay with her. If, on the contrary, I feel that my love for her is not enough, I go." But how does one estimate the strength of a feeling? The value of his feeling for his mother was determined precisely by the fact that he was standing by her. I may say that I love a certain friend enough to sacrifice such or such a sum of money for him, but I cannot prove that unless I have done it. I may say, "I love my mother enough to remain with her," if actually I have remained with her. I can only estimate the strength of this affection if I have performed an action by which it is defined and ratified. But if I then appeal to this affection to justify my action, I find myself drawn into a vicious circle.

• • •

What is at the very heart and centre of existentialism is the absolute character of the free commitment, by which every man realises himself in realising a type of humanity— a commitment always understandable, to no matter whom in no matter what epoch—and its bearing upon the relativity of the cultural pattern which may result from such absolute commitment. One must observe equally the relativity of Cartesianism and the absolute character of the Cartesian commitment. In this sense you may say, if you like, that every one of us makes the absolute by breathing, by eating, by sleeping or by behaving in any fashion whatsoever. There is no difference between free being—being as self-committal, as existence choosing its essence—and absolute being. And there is no difference whatever between being as an absolute, temporarily localised—that is, localised in history—and universally intelligible being.

• • •

. . . Existentialism is nothing else but an attempt to draw the full conclusions from a consistently atheistic position. . . . Not that we believe God does exist, but we think that the real problem is not that of His existence; what man needs is to find himself again and to understand that nothing can save him from himself, not even a valid proof of the existence of God. In this sense existentialism is optimistic, it is a doctrine of action, and it is only by self-deception, by confusing their own despair with ours that Christians can describe us as without hope.

from
NAUSEA

I have reconsidered my thoughts of yesterday. I was completely dry: it made no difference to me whether there had been no adventures. I was only curious to know whether there could *never be any*.

This is what I thought: for the most banal even to become an adventure, you must (and this is enough) begin to recount it. This is what fools people: a man is always a teller of tales, he lives surrounded by his stories and the stories of others, he sees everything that happens to him through them; and he tries to live his own life as if he were telling a story.

But you have to choose: live or tell. For example, when I was in Hamburg, with that Erna girl I didn't trust and who was afraid of me, I led a funny sort of life. But I was in the middle of it, I didn't think about it. And then one evening, in a little café in San Pauli, she left me to go to the ladies' room. I stayed alone, there was a phonograph playing "Blue Skies". I began to tell myself what had happened since I landed. I told myself, "The third evening, as I was going into a dance hall called *La Grotte Bleue,* I noticed a large woman, half seas over. And that woman is the one I am waiting for now, listening to 'Blue Skies', the woman who is going to come back and sit down at my right and put her arms around my neck." Then I felt violently that I was having an adventure. But Erna came back and sat down beside me, she

From *Nausea* by Jean-Paul Sartre, translated by Lloyd Alexander. All rights reserved. Copyright © 1964 by New Directions Publishing Corporation. Reprinted by permission of New Directions Publishing Corporation.

wound her arms around my neck and I hated her without knowing why. I understand now: one had to begin living again and the adventure was fading out. . . .

Nothing happens while you live. The scenery changes, people come in and go out, that's all. There are no beginnings. Days are tacked on to days without rhyme or reason, an interminable, monotonous addition. From time to time you make a semitotal: you say: I've been travelling for three years, I've been in Bouville for three years. Neither is there any end: you never leave a woman, a friend, a city in one go. And then everything looks alike: Shanghai, Moscow, Algiers, everything is the same after two weeks. There are moments—rarely—when you make a landmark, you realize that you're going with a woman, in some messy business. The time of a flash. After that, the procession starts again, you begin to add up hours and days: Monday, Tuesday, Wednesday. April, May, June. 1924, 1925, 1926.

That's living. But everything changes when you tell about life; it's a change no one notices: the proof is that people talk about true stories. As if there could possibly be true stories; things happen one way and we tell about them in the opposite sense. You seem to start at the beginning: "It was a fine autumn evening in 1922. I was a notary's clerk in Marommes." And in reality you have started at the end. It was there, invisible and present, it is the one which gives to words the pomp and value of a beginning. "I was out walking, I had left the town without realizing it, I was thinking about my money troubles." This sentence, taken simply for what it is, means that the man was absorbed, morose, a hundred leagues from an adventure, exactly in the mood to let things happen without noticing them. But the end is there, transforming everything. For us, the man is already the hero of the story. His moroseness, his money troubles are much more precious than ours, they are all gilded by the light of future passions. And the story goes on in the reverse: instants have stopped piling themselves in a lighthearted way one on top of the other, they are snapped up by the end of the story which draws them and each one of them in turn, draws out the preceding instant: "It was night, the street was deserted." The phrase is cast out negligently, it seems superfluous; but we do not let ourselves be caught and we put it aside: this is a piece of information whose value we shall subsequently appreciate. And we feel that the hero has lived all the details of this night like annunciations, promises, or even that he lived only those that were promises, blind and deaf to all that did not herald adventure. We forget that the future was not yet there; the man was walking in a night without forethought, a night which offered him a choice of dull rich prizes, and he did not make his choice.

I wanted the moments of my life to follow and order themselves like those of a life remembered. You might as well try and catch time by the tail.

PATTERNS OF BAD FAITH

. . . "What must be the being of man if he is to be capable of bad faith?"

Take the example of a woman who has consented to go out with a particular man for the first time. She knows very well the intentions which the man who is speaking to her cherishes regarding her. She knows also that it will be necessary sooner or later for her to make a decision. But she does not want to realize the urgency; she concerns herself only with what is respectful and discreet in the attitude of her companion. She does not apprehend this conduct as an attempt to achieve what we call "the first approach"; that is, she does not want to see possibilities of temporal development which his conduct presents. She restricts this behavior to what is in the present; she does not wish to read in the phrases which he addresses to her anything other than their explicit meaning. If he says to her, "I find you so attractive!" she disarms this phrase of its sexual background; she attaches to the conversation and to the behavior of the speaker, the immediate meanings, which she imagines as objective qualities. The man who is speaking to her appears to be sincere and respectful as the table is round or square, as the wall coloring is blue or gray. The qualities thus attached to the person she is listening to are in this way fixed in a permanence like that of things,

From *Being and Nothingness* by Jean-Paul Sartre. Copyright © 1956 by The Philosophical Library. Reprinted by permission of The Philosophical Library.

which is no other than the projection of the strict present of the qualities into the temporal flux. This is because she does not quite know what she wants. She is profoundly aware of the desire which she inspires, but the desire cruel and naked would humiliate and horrify her. Yet she would find no charm in a respect which would be only respect. In order to satisfy her, there must be a feeling which is addressed wholly to her *personality*—*i.e.*, to her full freedom—and which would be a recognition of her freedom. But at the same time this feeling must be wholly desire; that is, it must address itself to her body as object. This time then she refuses to apprehend the desire for what it is; she does not even give it a name; she recognizes it only to the extent that it transcends itself toward admiration, esteem, respect and that it is wholly absorbed in the more refined forms which it produces, to the extent of no longer figuring anymore as a sort of warmth and density. But then suppose he takes her hand. This act of her companion risks changing the situation by calling for an immediate decision. To leave the hand there is to consent in herself to flirt, to engage herself. To withdraw it is to break the troubled and unstable harmony which gives the hour its charm. The aim is to postpone the moment of decision as long as possible. We know what happens next; the young woman leaves her hand there, but she *does not notice* that she is leaving it. She does not notice because it happens by chance that she is at this moment all intellect. She draws her companion up to the most lofty regions of sentimental speculation; she speaks of Life, of her life, she shows herself in her essential aspect—a personality, a consciousness. And during this time the divorce of the body from the soul is accomplished; the hand rests inert between the warm hands of her companion—neither consenting nor resisting—a thing.

We shall say that this woman is in bad faith. But we see immediately that she uses various procedures in order to maintain herself in this bad faith. She has disarmed the actions of her companion by reducing them to being only what they are; that is, to existing in the mode of the in-itself. But she permits herself to enjoy his desire, to the extent that she will apprehend it as not being what it is, will recognize its transcendence. Finally while sensing profoundly the presence of her own body—to the degree of being disturbed perhaps—she realizes herself as *not being* her own body, and she contemplates it as though from above as a passive object to which events can *happen* but which can neither provoke them nor avoid them because all its possibilities are outside of it. What unity do we find in these various aspects of bad faith? It is a certain art of forming contradictory concepts which unite in themselves both an idea and the negation of that idea. The basic concept which is thus engendered utilizes the double property of the human being, who is at once a *facticity* and a *transcendence*. These two aspects of human reality are and ought to be capable of a valid coordination. But bad faith does not wish either to coordinate them or to surmount them in a synthesis. Bad faith seeks to affirm their identity while preserving their differences. It must affirm facticity as *being* transcendence and transcendence as *being* facticity, in such a way that at the instant when a person apprehends the one, he can find himself abruptly faced with the other.

We can find the prototype of formulae of bad faith in certain famous expressions which have been rightly conceived to produce their whole effect in a spirit of bad faith. Take for example the title of a work by Jacques Chardonne, *Love Is Much More than Love*. We see here how unity is established between *present* love in its facticity—"the contact of two skins," sensuality, egoism, Proust's mechanism of jealousy, Adler's battle of the *sexes, etc.*—and love as transcendence— Mauriac's "river of fire," the longing for the infinite, Plato's *eros*, Lawrence's deep cosmic intuition, *etc.* Here we leave facticity to find ourselves suddenly beyond the present and the factual condition of man, beyond the psychological, in the heart of metaphysics. On the other hand, the title of a play by Sarment, *I Am Too Great for Myself*, which also presents characters in bad faith, throws us first into full transcendence in order suddenly to imprison us within the narrow limits of our factual essence. We will discover this structure again in the famous sentence: "He has become what he was" or in its no less famous opposite: "Eternity at last changes each man into himself." It is well understood that these various formulae have only the appearance of bad faith; they have been conceived in this paradoxical form explicitly to shock the mind and discountenance it by an enigma. But it is precisely this appearance which is of concern to us. What counts here is that the formulae do not constitute new, solidly structured ideas: on the contrary, they are formed so as to remain in perpetual disintegration and so that we may slide at any time from naturalistic present to transcendence and *vice versa*.

We can see the use which bad faith can make of these judgments which all aim at establishing that I am not what I am. If I were only what I *am*, I could, for example, seriously consider an adverse criticism which someone makes of me, question myself scrupulously, and perhaps be compelled to recognize the truth in it. But thanks to transcendence, I am not subject to all that I am. I do not even have to discuss the justice of the reproach. As Suzanne says to Figaro, "To prove that I am right would be to recognize that I can be wrong." I am on a plane where no reproach can touch me since what I really am is my transcendence. I flee from myself, I escape myself, I leave my tattered garment in the hands of the fault-finder. But the ambiguity necessary for bad faith comes from the fact that I affirm here that I *am* my transcendence in the mode of being of a thing. It is only thus, in fact, that I can feel that I escape all reproaches. It is in the sense that our young woman purifies the desire of anything humiliating by being willing to consider it only as pure transcendence, which she avoids even naming. But inversely "I Am Too Great for Myself," while showing our transcendence changed into facticity, is the source of an infinity of excuses for our failures or our weaknesses. Similarly the young coquette maintains transcendence to the extent that the respect, the esteem manifested by the actions of her admirer are already on the plane of the transcendent. But she arrests this transcendence, she glues it down with all the facticity of the present; respect is nothing other than respect, it is an arrested surpassing which no longer surpasses itself toward anything.

But although this *metastable* concept of "transcendence-facticity" is one of the most basic instruments of bad faith, it is not the only one of its kind. We can equally well use another kind of duplicity derived from human reality which we will express roughly by saying that its being-for-itself implies complementarily a being-for-others. Upon any one of my conducts it is always possible to converge two looks, mine and that of the Other. The conduct will not present exactly the same structure in each case. But as we shall see later, as each look perceives it, there is between these two aspects of my being, no difference between appearance and being—as if I were to my self the truth of myself and as if the Other possessed only a deformed image of me. The equal dignity of being, possessed by my being-for-others and by my being-for-myself, permits a perpetually disintegrating synthesis and a perpetual game of escape from the for-itself to the for-others and from the for-others to the for-itself. We have seen also the use which our young lady made of our being-in-the-midst-of-the-world—*i.e.*, of our inert presence as a passive object among other objects—in order to relieve herself suddenly from the functions of her being-in-the-world—that is, from the being which causes there to be a world by projecting itself beyond the world toward its own possibilities. Let us note finally the confusing syntheses which play on the nihilating ambiguity of these temporal ekstases, affirming at once that I am what I have been (the man who deliberately *arrests himself* at one period in his life and refuses to take into consideration the later changes) and that I am not what I have been (the man who in the face of reproaches or rancor dissociates himself from his past by insisting on his freedom and on his perpetual re-creation). In all these concepts, which have only a transitive role in the reasoning and which are eliminated from the conclusion (like hypochondriacs in the calculations of physicians), we find again the same structure. We have to deal with human reality as a being which is what it is not, and which is what it is.

But what exactly is necessary in order for these concepts of disintegration to be able to receive even a pretence of existence, in order for them to be able to appear for an instant to consciousness, even in a process of evanescence? A quick examination of the idea of sincerity, the antithesis of bad faith, will be very instructive in this connection. Actually sincerity presents itself as a demand and consequently is not a *state*. Now what is the ideal to be attained in this case? It is necessary that a man be *for himself* only what he *is*. But is this not precisely the definition of the in-itself—or if you prefer—the principle of identity? To posit as an ideal the being of things, is this not to assert by the same stroke that this being does not belong to human reality and that the principle of identity, far from being a universal axiom universally applied, is only a synthetic principle enjoying a merely regional universality? Thus in order that the concepts of bad faith can put us under illusion at least for an instant, in order that the candor of "pure hearts" (*cf.* Gide, Kessel) can have validity for human reality as an ideal, the principle of identity must not represent a constitutive principle of human reality and human reality must not be necessarily what it is but must be able to be what it is not. What does this mean?

If man is what he is, bad faith is forever impossible and candor ceases to be his ideal and becomes instead his being. But is man what he is? And more generally, how can he *be* what he is when he exists as consciousness of being? If candor or sincerity is a universal value, it is evident that the maxim "one must be what one is" does not serve solely as a regulating principle for judgments and concepts by which I express what I am. It posits not merely an ideal of knowing but an ideal of *being;* it proposes for us an absolute equivalence of being with itself as a prototype of being. In this sense it is necessary that we *make ourselves* what we are. But what *are we* then if we have the constant obligation to make ourselves what we are, if our mode of being is having the obligation to be what we are?

Let us consider this waiter in the café. His movement is quick and forward, a little too precise, a little too rapid. He comes toward the patrons with a step a little too quick. He bends forward a little too eagerly; his voice, his eyes express an interest a little too solicitous for the order of the customer. Finally there he returns, trying to imitate in his walk the inflexible stiffness of some kind of automaton while carrying his tray with the recklessness of a tight-rope-walker by putting it in a perpetually unstable, perpetually broken equilibrium which he perpetually re-establishes by a light movement of the arm and hand. All his behavior seems to us a game. He applies himself to chaining his movements as if they were mechanisms, the one regulating the other; his gestures and even his voice seem to be mechanisms; he gives himself the quickness and pitiless rapidity of things. He is playing, he is amusing himself. But what is he playing? We need not watch long before we can explain it: he is playing at *being* a waiter in a café. There is nothing there to surprise us. The game is a kind of marking out and investigation. The child plays with his body in order to explore it, to take inventory of it; the waiter in the café plays with his condition in order to *realize* it. This obligation is not different from that which is imposed on all tradesmen. Their condition is wholly one of ceremony. The public demands of them that they realize it as a ceremony; there is the dance of the grocer, of the tailor, of the auctioneer, by which they endeavor to persuade their clientele that they are nothing but a grocer, an auctioneer, a tailor. A grocer who dreams is offensive to the buyer, because such a grocer is not wholly a grocer. Society demands that he limit himself to his function as a grocer, just as the soldier at attention makes himself into a soldier-thing with a direct regard which does not see at all, which is no longer meant to see, since it is the rule and not the interest of the moment which determines the point he must fix his eyes on (the sight "fixed at ten paces"). There are indeed many precautions to imprison a man in what he is, as if we lived in perpetual fear that he might escape from it, that he might break away and suddenly elude his condition.

In a parallel situation, from within, the waiter in the café can not be immediately a café waiter in the sense that this inkwell *is* an inkwell, or the glass is a glass. It is by no means that he can not form reflective judgments or concepts concerning his condition. He knows well what it "means"; the obligation of getting up at five o'clock, of sweeping the floor of the shop before the restaurant opens, of starting the coffee pot going, *etc.* He knows the rights which it allows: the right to the tips, the right to belong to a union, *etc.* But all these concepts, all these judgments refer to the transcendent. It is a matter of abstract possibilities, of rights and duties conferred on a "person possessing rights." And it is precisely this person *who I have to be* (if I am the waiter in question) and who I am not. It is not that I do not wish to be this person or that I want this person to be different. But rather there is no common measure between his being and mine. It is a "representation" for others and for myself, which means that I can be he only in *representation*. But if I represent myself as him, I am not he; I am separated from him as the object from the subject, separated *by nothing*, but this nothing isolates me from him. I cannot be he, I can only play *at being* him; that is, imagine to myself that I am he. And thereby I affect him with nothingness. In vain do I fulfill the functions of a café waiter. I can be he only in the neutralized mode, as the actor is Hamlet, by mechanically making the *typical gestures* of my state and by aiming at myself as an imaginary café waiter through those gestures taken as an "analogue." What I attempt to realize is a being-in-itself of the café waiter, as if it were not just in my power to confer their value and their urgency upon my duties and the rights of my position, as if it were not my free choice to get up each morning at five o'clock or to remain in bed, even though it meant getting fired. As if from the very fact that I sustain this role in existence I did not transcend it on every side, as if I did not constitute myself as one *beyond* my condition. Yet there is no doubt that I *am* in a sense a café waiter—otherwise could I not just as well call myself a diplomat or a reporter? But if I am one, this cannot be in the mode of being in-itself. I am a waiter in the mode of *being what I am not*.

Furthermore we are dealing with more than mere social positions; I am never any one of my attitudes, any one of my actions. The good speaker is the one who *plays at* speaking, because he cannot *be* speaking. The attentive pupil who wishes to *be* attentive, his eyes riveted on the teacher, his ears open wide, so exhausts himself in playing the attentive role that he ends up by no longer hearing anything. Perpetually absent to my body, to my acts, I am despite myself that "divine absence" of which Valéry speaks. I cannot say either that I *am* here or that I *am* not here, in the sense that we say "that box of matches *is* on the table"; this would be to confuse my "being-in-the-world" with a "being-in-the-midst-of-the-world." Nor that I *am* standing, nor that I *am* seated; this would be to confuse my body with the idiosyncratic totality of which it is only one of the structures. On all sides I escape being and yet—I am.

But take a mode of being which concerns only myself: I am sad. One might think that surely I am the sadness in the mode of being what I am. What is the sadness, however, if not the intentional unity which comes to reassemble and animate the totality of my conduct? It is the meaning of this dull look with which I view the world, of my bowed shoulders, of my lowered head, of the listlessness in my whole body. But at the very moment when I adopt each of these attitudes, do I not know that I shall not be able to hold on to it? Let a stranger suddenly appear and I will lift up my head, I will assume a lively cheerfulness. What will remain of my sadness except that I obligingly promise it an appointment for later after the departure of the visitor? Moreover is not this sadness itself a *conduct*? Is it not consciousness which affects itself with sadness as a magical recourse against a situation too urgent? And in this case even, should we not say that being sad means first to make oneself sad? That may be, someone will say, but after all doesn't giving oneself the being of sadness mean to *receive* this being? It makes no difference from where I receive it. The fact is that a consciousness which affects itself with sadness is sad precisely for this reason. But it is difficult to comprehend the nature of consciousness; the being-sad is not a ready-made being which I give to myself as I can give this book to my friend. I do not possess the property of *affecting myself with being*. If I make myself sad, I must continue to make myself sad from beginning to end. I cannot treat my sadness as an impulse finally achieved and put it on file without re-creating it, nor can I carry it in the manner of an inert body which continues its movement after the initial shock. There is no inertia in consciousness. If I make myself sad, it is because I *am* not sad—the being of the sadness escapes me by and in the very act by which I affect myself with it. The being-in-itself of sadness perpetually haunts my consciousness (of) being sad, but it is as a value which I cannot realize; it stands as a regulative meaning of my sadness, not as its constitutive modality.

Someone may say that my consciousness at least *is*, whatever may be the object or the state of which it makes itself consciousness. But how do we distinguish my consciousness (of) being sad from sadness? Is it not all one? It is true in a way that my consciousness *is*, if one means by this that for another it is a part of the totality of being on which judgments can be brought to bear. But it should be noted, as Husserl clearly understood, that my consciousness appears originally to the Other as an absence. It is the object always present as the *meaning* of all my attitudes and all my conduct—and always absent, for it gives itself to the intuition of another as a perpetual question—still better, as a perpetual freedom. When Pierre looks at me, I know of course that he is looking at me. His eyes, things in the world, are fixed on my body, a thing in the world—that is the objective fact of which I can say: it *is*. But it is also a fact *in the world*. The meaning of this look is not a fact in the world, and this is what makes me uncomfortable. Although I make smiles, promises, threats, nothing can get hold of the approbation, the free judgment which I seek; I know that it is always beyond. I sense it in my very attitude, which is no longer like that of the worker toward the things he uses as instruments. My reactions, to the extent that I project myself toward the Other, are no longer for myself but are rather mere *presentations;* they await being constituted as graceful or uncouth, sincere or insincere, *etc.*, by an apprehension which is always beyond my efforts to provoke, an apprehension which will be provoked by my efforts only if of itself it lends them force (that is, only in so far as it causes itself to be provoked from the outside), *which is its own mediator with the transcendent.* Thus the objective fact of the being-in-itself of the consciousness of the Other is posited in order to disappear in negativity and in freedom: consciousness of the Other is as not-being; its being-in-itself "here and now" is not-to-be.

Consciousness of the Other is what it is not.

Furthermore the being of my own consciousness does not appear to me as the consciousness of the Other. It *is* because it makes itself, since its being is consciousness of being. But this means that making sustains being; consciousness has to be its own being, it is never sustained by being; it sustains being in the heart of subjectivity, which means once again that it is inhabited by being but that it is not being: *consciousness is not what it is.*

Under these conditions what can be the significance of the ideal of sincerity except as a task impossible to achieve, of which the very meaning is in contradiction with the structure of my consciousness. To be sincere, we said, is to be what one is. That supposes that I am not originally what I am. But here naturally Kant's "You ought, therefore you can" is implicitly understood. I can *become* sincere; this is what my duty and my effort to achieve sincerity imply. But we definitely establish that the original structure of "not being what one is" renders impossible in advance all movement toward being in itself or "being what one is." And this impossibility is not hidden from consciousness; on the contrary, it is the very stuff of consciousness; it is the embarrassing constraint which we constantly experience; it is our very incapacity to recognize ourselves, to constitute ourselves as being what we are. It is this necessity which means that, as soon as we posit ourselves as a certain being, by a legitimate judgment, based on inner experience or correctly deduced from *a priori* or empirical premises, then by that very positing we surpass this being—and that not toward another being but toward emptiness, toward *nothing.*

How then can we blame another for not being sincere or rejoice in our own sincerity since this sincerity appears to us at the same time to be impossible? How can we in conversation, in confession, in introspection, even attempt sincerity since at the very time when we announce it we have a prejudicative comprehension of its futility? In introspection I try to determine exactly what I am, to make up my mind to be my true self without delay—even though it means consequently to set about searching for ways to change myself. But what does this mean if not that I am constituting myself as a thing? Shall I determine the ensemble of purposes and motivations which have pushed me to do this or that action? But this is already to postulate a causal determinism which constitutes the flow of my states of consciousness as a succession of physical states. Shall I uncover in myself "drives," even though it be to affirm them in shame? But is this not deliberately to forget that these drives are realized with my consent, that they are not forces of nature but that I lend them their efficacy by a perpetually renewed decision concerning their value? Shall I pass judgment on my character, on my nature? Is this not to veil from myself at that moment what I know only too well, that I thus judge a past to which by definition my present is not subject? The proof of this is that the same man who in sincerity posits that he is what in actuality he was, is indignant at the reproach of another and tries to disarm it by asserting that he can no longer be what he was. We are readily astonished and upset when the penalties of the court affect a man who in his new freedom *is no longer* the guilty person he was. But at the same time we re quire of this man that he recognize himself as *being* this guilty one. What then is sincerity except precisely a phenomenon of bad faith? Have we not shown indeed that in bad faith human reality is constituted as a being which is what it is not and which is not what it is?

Let us take an example: A homosexual frequently has an intolerable feeling of guilt, and his whole existence is determined in relation to this feeling. One will readily foresee that he is in bad faith. In fact it frequently happens that this man, while recognizing his homosexual inclination, while avowing each and every particular misdeed which he has committed, refuses with all his strength to consider himself *"a paederast."* His case is always "different," peculiar; there enters into it something of a game, of chance, of bad luck, the mistakes are all in the past; they are explained by a certain conception of the beautiful which women cannot satisfy; we should see in them the results of a restless search, rather than the manifestations of a deeply rooted tendency, *etc., etc.*

Here is assuredly a man in bad faith who borders on the comic since, acknowledging all the facts which are imputed to him, he refuses to draw from them the conclusion which they impose. His friend, who is his most severe critic, becomes irritated with this duplicity. The critic asks only one thing—and perhaps then he will show himself indulgent: that the guilty one recognize himself as guilty, that the homosexual declare frankly—whether humbly or boastfully matters little —"I am a paederast." We ask here: Who is in bad faith? The homosexual or the champion of sincerity?

The homosexual recognizes his faults, but he struggles with all his strength against the crushing view that his mistakes constitute for him a *destiny*. He does not wish to let himself be considered as a thing. He has an obscure but strong feeling that a homosexual is not a homosexual as this table is a table or as this red-haired man is red-haired. It seems to him that he has escaped from each mistake as soon as he has posited it and recognized it; he even feels that the psychic duration by itself cleanses him from each misdeed, constitutes for him an undetermined future, causes him to be born anew. Is he wrong? Does he not recognize in himself the peculiar, irreducible character of human reality? His attitude includes then an undeniable comprehension of truth. But at the same time he needs this perpetual rebirth, this constant escape in order to live; he must constantly put himself beyond reach in order to avoid the terrible judgment of collectivity. Thus he plays on the word *being*. He would be right actually if he understood the phrase "I am not a paederast" in the sense of "I am not what I am." That is, if he declared to himself, "To the extent that a pattern of conduct is defined as the conduct of a paederast and to the extent that I have adopted this conduct, I am a paederast. But to the extent that human reality cannot be finally defined by patterns of conduct, I am not one." But instead he slides surreptitiously toward a different connotation of the word "being." He understands "not being" in the sense of "not-being-in-itself." He lays claim to "not being a paederast" in the sense in which this table *is not* an inkwell. He is in bad faith.

But the champion of sincerity is not ignorant of the transcendence of human reality, and he knows how at need to appeal to it for his own advantage. He makes use of it even and brings it up in the present argument. Does he not wish, first in the name of sincerity, then of freedom, that the homosexual reflect on himself and acknowledge himself as a homo-sexual? Does he not let the other understand that such a confession will win indulgence for him? What does this mean if not that the man who will acknowledge himself as a homo-sexual will no longer be *the same* as the homosexual whom he acknowledges being and that he will escape into the region of freedom and of good will? The critic asks the man then to be what he is in order no longer to be what he is. It is the profound meaning of the saying, "A sin confessed is half pardoned." The critic demands of the guilty one that he con-stitute himself as a thing, precisely in order no longer to treat him as a thing. And this contradiction is constitutive of the demand of sincerity. Who cannot see how offensive to the Other and how reassuring for me is a statement such as, "He's just a paederast," which removes a disturbing freedom from a trait and which aims at henceforth constituting all the acts of the Other as consequences following strictly from his es-sence. That is actually what the critic is demanding of his victim—that he constitute himself as a thing, that he should entrust his freedom to his friend as a fief, in order that the friend should return it to him subsequently—like a suzerain to his vassal. The champion of sincerity is in bad faith to the degree that in order to reassure himself, he pretends to judge, to the extent that he demands that freedom as freedom con-stitute itself as a thing. We have here only one episode in that battle to the death of consciousnesses which Hegel calls "the relation of the master and the slave." A person appeals to another and demands that in the name of his nature as con-sciousness he should radically destroy himself as conscious-ness, but while making this appeal he leads the other to hope for a rebirth beyond this destruction.

Very well, someone will say, but our man is abusing sin-cerity, playing one side against the other. We should not look for sincerity in the relation of the *mit-sein* but rather where it is pure—in the relations of a person with himself. But who cannot see that objective sincerity is constituted in the same way? Who cannot see that the sincere man constitutes himself as a thing in order to escape the condition of a thing by the same act of sincerity? The man who confesses that he is evil has exchanged his disturbing "freedom-for-evil" for an inanimate character of evil; he *is* evil, he clings to himself, he is what he is. But by the same stroke, he escapes from that *thing*, since it is he who contemplates it, since it depends on him to maintain it under his glance or to let it collapse in an infinity of particular acts. He derives a *merit* from his sincerity, and the deserving man is not the evil man as he is evil but as he is beyond his evilness. At the same time the evil is disarmed since it is nothing, save on the plane of determinism, and since in confessing it, I posit my freedom in respect to it; my future is virgin; everything is allowed to me.

Thus the essential structure of sincerity does not differ from that of bad faith since the sincere man constitutes himself as what he is *in order not to be it.* This explains the truth recognized by all that one can fall into bad faith through being sincere. As Valéry pointed out, this is the case with Stendhal. Total, constant sincerity as a constant effort to adhere to oneself is by nature a constant effort to dissociate oneself from oneself. A person frees himself from himself by the very act by which he makes himself an object for himself. To draw up a perpetual inventory of what one is means constantly to redeny oneself and to take refuge in a sphere where one is no longer anything but a pure, free regard. The goal of bad faith, as we said, is to put oneself out of reach; it is an escape. Now we see that we must use the same terms to define sincerity. What does this mean?

In the final analysis the goal of sincerity and the goal of bad faith are not so different. To be sure, there is a sincerity which bears on the past and which does not concern us here; I am sincere if I confess *having had* this pleasure or that intention. We shall see that if this sincerity is possible, it is because in his fall into the past, the being of man is constituted as a being-in-itself. But here our concern is only with the sincerity which aims at itself in present immanence. What is its goal? To bring me to confess to myself what I am in order that I may finally coincide with my being; in a word, to cause myself to be, in the mode of the in-itself, what I am in the mode of "not being what I am." Its assumption is that fundamentally I am already, in the mode of the in-itself, what I have to be. Thus we find at the base of sincerity a continual game of mirror and reflection, a perpetual passage from the being which is what it is to the being which is not what it is and inversely from the being which is not what it is to the being which is what it is. And what is the goal of bad faith? To cause me to be what I am, in the mode of "not being what one is," or not to be what I am in the mode of "being what one is." We find here the same game of mirrors. In fact in order for me to have an intention of sincerity, I must at the outset simultaneously be and not be what I am. Sincerity does not assign to me a mode of being or a particular quality, but in relation to that quality it aims at making me pass from one mode of being to another mode of being. This second mode of being, the ideal of sincerity, I am prevented by nature from attaining; and at the very moment when I struggle to attain it, I have a vague prejudicative comprehension that I shall not attain it. But all the same, in order for me to be able to conceive an intention in bad faith, I must have such a nature that within my being I escape from my being. If I were sad or cowardly in the way in which this inkwell is an inkwell, the possibility of bad faith could not even be conceived. Not only should I be unable to escape from my being; I could not even imagine that I could escape from it. But if bad faith is possible by virtue of a simple project, it is because so far as my being is concerned, there is no difference between being and non-being if I am cut off from my project.

Bad faith is possible only because sincerity is conscious of missing its goal inevitably, due to its very nature. I can try to apprehend myself as *"not being cowardly,"* when I *am* so, only on condition that the "being cowardly" is itself "in question" at the very moment when it exists, on condition that it is itself *one* question, that at the very moment when I wish to apprehend it, it escapes me on all sides and annihilates itself. The condition under which I can attempt an effort in bad faith is that in one sense, I *am not* this coward which I do not wish to be. But if I *were not* cowardly in the simple mode of not-being-what-one-is-not, I would be "in good faith" by declaring that I am not cowardly. Thus this inapprehensible coward is evanescent; in order for me not to be cowardly, I must in some way also be cowardly. That does not mean that I must be "a little" cowardly, in the sense that "a little" signifies "to a certain degree cowardly—and not cowardly to a certain degree." No. I must at once both be and not be totally and in all respects a coward. Thus in this case bad faith requires that I should not be what I am; that is, that there be an imponderable difference separating being from non-being in the mode of being of human reality.

But bad faith is not restricted to denying the qualities which I possess, to not seeing the being which I am. It attempts also to constitute myself as being what I am not. It apprehends me positively as courageous when I am not so. And that is possible, once again, only if I am what I am not; that is, if non-being in me does not have being even as non-being. Of course necessarily I *am not* courageous; otherwise bad faith would not be *bad* faith. But in addition my effort in bad faith must include the ontological comprehension that even in my usual being what I *am*, I am not it really and that there is no such difference between the being of "being-sad," for example—which I *am* in the mode of not being what I am—and the "non-being" of not-being-courageous which I wish to hide from myself. Moreover it is particularly requisite that the very negation of being should be itself the object of a perpetual nihilation, that the very meaning of "non-being" be perpetually in question in human reality. If I *were not* courageous in the way in which this inkwell is not a table; that is, if I were isolated in my cowardice, propped firmly against it, incapable of putting it in relation to its opposite, if I were not capable of *determining* myself as cowardly—that is, to deny courage to myself and thereby to escape my cowardice in the very moment that I posit it—if it were not on principle *impossible* for me to coincide with my *not-being-courageous* as well as with my being-courageous—then any project of bad faith would be prohibited me. Thus in order for bad faith to be possible, sincerity itself must be in bad faith. The condition of the possibility for bad faith is that human reality, in its most immediate being, in the intra-structure of the pre-reflective *cogito*, must be what it is not and not be what it is.

from NO EXIT

GARCIN: They shot me.

ESTELLE: I know. Because you refused to fight. Well, why shouldn't you?

GARCIN: I—I didn't exactly refuse. [*In a far-away voice*] I

From *No Exit and Three Other Plays* by Jean-Paul Sartre, translated by Stuart Gilbert. Copyright 1946 by Stuart Gilbert. Reprinted by permission of Alfred A. Knopf, Inc., and Hamish Hamilton, Ltd.

must say he talks well, he makes out a good case against me, but he never says what I should have done instead. Should I have gone to the general and said: "General, I decline to fight"? A mug's game; they'd have promptly locked me up. But I wanted to show my colors, my true colors, do you understand? I wasn't going to be silenced. [*To* Estelle] So I—I took the train. . . . They caught me at the frontier.

Estelle: Where were you trying to go?

Garcin: To Mexico. I meant to launch a pacifist newspaper down there. [*A short silence.*] Well, why don't you speak?

Estelle: What could I say? You acted quite rightly, as you didn't want to fight. [Garcin *makes a fretful gesture.*] But, darling, how on earth can I guess what you want me to answer?

Inez: Can't you guess? Well, *I* can. He wants you to tell him that he bolted like a lion. For "bolt" he did, and that's what's biting him.

Garcin: "Bolted," "went away"—we won't quarrel over words.

Estelle: But you *had* to run away. If you'd stayed they'd have sent you to jail, wouldn't they?

Garcin: Of course. [*A pause.*] Well, Estelle, am I a coward?

Estelle: How can I say? Don't be so unreasonable, darling. I can't put myself in your skin. You must decide that for yourself.

Garcin [*wearily*]: I can't decide.

Estelle: Anyhow, you must remember. You must have had reasons for acting as you did.

Garcin: I had.

Estelle: Well?

Garcin: But were they the real reasons?

Estelle: You've a twisted mind, that's your trouble. Plaguing yourself over such trifles!

Garcin: I'd thought it all out, and I wanted to make a stand. But was that my real motive?

Inez: Exactly. That's the question. Was that your real motive? No doubt you argued it out with yourself, you weighed the pros and cons, you found good reasons for what you did. But fear and hatred and all the dirty little instincts one keeps dark—they're motives too. So carry on, Mr. Garcin, and try to be honest with yourself—for once.

GARCIN: Do I need you to tell me that? Day and night I paced my cell, from the window to the door, from the door to the window. I pried into my heart, I sleuthed myself like a detective. By the end of it I felt as if I'd given my whole life to introspection. But always I harked back to the one thing certain—that I had acted as I did, I'd taken that train to the frontier. But why? Why? Finally I thought: My death will settle it. If I face death courageously, I'll prove I am no coward.

INEZ: And how did you face death?

GARCIN: Miserably. Rottenly. [INEZ *laughs.*] Oh, it was only a physical lapse—that might happen to anyone; I'm not ashamed of it. Only everything's been left in suspense, forever. [*To* ESTELLE] Come here, Estelle. Look at me. I want to feel someone looking at me while they're talking about me on earth. . . . I like green eyes.

INEZ: Green eyes! Just hark to him! And you, Estelle, do you like cowards?

ESTELLE: If you knew how little I care! Coward or hero, it's all one—provided he kisses well.

GARCIN: There they are, slumped in their chairs, sucking at their cigars. Bored they look. Half-asleep. They're thinking: "Garcin's a coward." But only vaguely, dreamily. One's got to think of something. "That chap Garcin was a coward." That's what they've decided, those dear friends of mine. In six months' time they'll be saying: "Cowardly as that skunk Garcin." You're lucky, you two; no one on earth is giving you another thought. But I—I'm long in dying.

• • •

GARCIN [*putting his hands on* (INEZ's) *shoulders*]: Listen! Each man has an aim in life, a leading motive; that's so, isn't it? Well, I didn't give a damn for wealth, or for love. I aimed at being a real man. A tough, as they say. I staked everything on the same horse. . . . Can one possibly be a coward when one's deliberately courted danger at every turn? And can one judge a life by a single action?

INEZ: Why not? For thirty years you dreamt you were a hero, and condoned a thousand petty lapses—because a hero, of course, can do no wrong. An easy method, obviously. Then a day came when you were up against it, the red light of real danger—and you took the train to Mexico.

GARCIN: I "dreamt," you say. It was no dream. When I chose that hardest path, I made my choice deliberately. A man is what he wills himself to be.

INEZ: Prove it. Prove it was no dream. It's what one does, and nothing else, that shows the stuff one's made of.

GARCIN: I died too soon. I wasn't allowed time to—to do my deeds.

INEZ: One always dies too soon—or too late. And yet one's whole life is complete at that moment, with a line drawn neatly under it, ready for the summing up. You are—your life, and nothing else.

BEING-FOR-OTHERS

. . . the upsurge of the Other touches the for-itself in its very heart. By the Other and for the Other the pursuing flight is fixed in in-itself. Already the in-itself was progressively recapturing it; already it was at once a radical negation of fact, an absolute positing of value and yet wholly paralyzed with facticity. But at least it was escaping by temporalization; at least its character as a totality detotalized conferred on it a perpetual "elsewhere." Now it is this very totality which the Other makes appear before him and which he transcends toward his own "elsewhere." It is this totality which is totalized. For the Other I am irremediably what I am, and my very freedom is a given characteristic of my being. Thus the in-self recaptures me at the threshold of the future and fixes me wholly in my very flight, which becomes a flight foreseen and contemplated, a *given* flight. But this fixed flight is never the flight which I am for myself; it is fixed *outside*. The objectivity of my flight I experience as an alienation which I can neither transcend nor know. Yet by the sole fact that I experience it and that it confers on my flight that in-itself

From *Being and Nothingness* by Jean-Paul Sartre. Copyright © 1956 by The Philosophical Library. Reprinted by permission of The Philosophical Library.

which it flees, I must turn back toward it and assume *attitudes* with respect to it.

Such is the origin of my concrete relations with the Other; they are wholly governed by my attitudes with respect to the object which I am for the Other. And as the Other's existence reveals to me the being which I am without my being able either to appropriate that being or even to conceive it, this existence will motivate two opposed attitudes: First—The Other *looks* at me and as such he holds the secret of my being, he knows what I *am*. Thus the profound meaning of my being is outside of me, imprisoned in an absence. The Other has the advantage over me. Therefore in so far as I am fleeing the in-itself which I am without founding it, I can attempt to deny that being which is conferred on me from outside; that is, I can turn back upon the Other so as to make an object out of him in turn since the Other's object-ness destroys my object-ness for him. But on the other hand, in so far as the Other as freedom is the foundation of my being-in-itself, I can seek to recover that freedom and to possess it without removing from it its character as freedom. In fact if I could identify myself with that freedom which is the foundation of my being-in-itself, I should be to myself my own foundation. To transcend the Other's transcendence, or, on the contrary, to incorporate that transcendence within me without removing from it its character as transcendence—such are the two primitive attitudes which I assume confronting the Other. Here again we must understand the words exactly. It is not true that I first am and then later "seek" to make an object of the Other or to assimilate him; but to the extent that the upsurge of my being is an upsurge in the presence of the Other, to the extent that I am a pursuing flight and a pursued-pursuing, I am—at the very root of my being—the project of assimilating and making an object of the Other. I am the proof of the Other. That is the original fact. But this proof of the Other is in itself an attitude toward the Other; that is, I can not *be in the presence of the Other* without being that "in-the-presence" in the form of having to be it. Thus again we are describing the for-itself's structures of being although the Other's presence in the world is an absolute and self-evident fact, but a contingent fact—that is, a fact impossible to deduce from the ontological structures of the for-itself.

These two attempts which I am are opposed to one another.

Each attempt is the death of the other; that is, the failure of the one motivates the adoption of the other. Thus there is no dialectic for my relations toward the Other but rather a circle —although each attempt is enriched by the failure of the other. Thus we shall study each one in turn. But it should be noted that at the very core of the one the other remains always present, precisely because neither of the two can be held without contradiction. Better yet, each of them is in the other and endangers the death of the other. Thus we can never get outside the circle. We must not forget these facts as we approach the study of these fundamental attitudes toward the Other. Since these attitudes are produced and destroyed in a circle, it is as arbitrary to begin with the one as with the other. Nevertheless since it is necessary to choose, we shall consider first the conduct in which the for-itself tries to assimilate the Other's freedom.

First Attitude Toward Others:
Love, Language, Masochism

Everything which may be said of me in my relations with the Other applies to him as well. While I attempt to free myself from the hold of the Other, the Other is trying to free himself from mine; while I seek to enslave the Other, the Other seeks to enslave me. We are by no means dealing with unilateral relations with an object-in-itself, but with reciprocal and moving relations. The following descriptions of concrete behavior must therefore be envisaged within the perspective of *conflict*. Conflict is the original meaning of being-for-others.

If we start with the first revelation of the Other as a *look*, we must recognize that we experience our inapprehensible being-for-others in the form of a *possession*. I am possessed by the Other; the Other's look fashions my body in its nakedness, causes it to be born, sculptures it, produces it as it *is*, sees it as I shall never see it. The Other holds a secret—the secret of what I am. He makes me be and thereby he possesses me, and this possession is nothing other than the consciousness of possessing me. I in the recognition of my object-state have proof that he has this consciousness. By virtue of consciousness the Other is for me simultaneously the one who has stolen my being from me and the one who causes "there to be" a being which is my being. Thus I have a comprehension of this onto-logical structure: I am responsible for my being-for-others, but I am not the foundation of it. It appears to me therefore in the form of a contingent given for which I am nevertheless responsible; the Other founds my being in so far as this being is in the form of the "there is." But he is not responsible for my being although he founds it in complete freedom—in and by means of his free transcendence. Thus to the extent that I am revealed to myself as responsible for my being, I *lay claim* to this being which I am; that is, I wish to recover it, or, more exactly, I am the project of the recovery of my being. I want to stretch out my hand and grab hold of this being which is presented to me as *my being* but at a distance—like the dinner of Tantalus; I want to found it by my very freedom. For if in one sense my being-as-object is an unbearable contingency and the pure "possession" of myself by another, still in another sense this being stands as the indication of what I should be obliged to recover and found in order to be the foundation of myself. But this is conceivable only if I assimilate the Other's freedom. Thus my project of recovering myself is fundamen-tally a project of absorbing the Other.

• • •

from
NO EXIT

GARCIN: . . . [*He swings round abruptly.*] What? Only two of you? I thought there were more; many more. [*Laughs.*] So this is hell. I'd never have believed it. You remember all we were told about the torture-chambers, the fire and brimstone, the "burning marl." Old wives' tales! There's no need for red-hot pokers. Hell is—other people! . . .

From *No Exit and Three Other Plays* by Jean-Paul Sartre, translated by Stuart Gilbert. Copyright 1946 by Stuart Gilbert. Reprinted by permission of Alfred A. Knopf, Inc., and Hamish Hamilton, Ltd.

FREEDOM AND RESPONSIBILITY

Although the considerations which are about to follow are of interest primarily to the ethicist, it may nevertheless be worthwhile after these descriptions and arguments to return to the freedom of the for-itself and try to understand what the fact of this freedom represents for human destiny.

The essential consequence of our earlier remarks is that man being condemned to be free carries the weight of the whole world on his shoulders; he is responsible for the world and for himself as a way of being. We are taking the word "responsibility" in its ordinary sense as "consciousness (of) being the incontestable author of an event or of an object." In this sense the responsibility of the for-itself is overwhelming since he is the one by whom it happens that *there is* a world; since he is also the one who makes himself be, then whatever may be the situation in which he finds himself, the for-itself must wholly assume this situation with its peculiar coefficient of adversity, even though it be insupportable. He must assume the situation with the proud consciousness of being the author of it, for the very worst disadvantages or the worst threats which can endanger my person have meaning only in and through my project; and it is on the ground of the engagement which I am that they appear. It is therefore senseless to think of complaining since nothing foreign has decided what we feel, what we live, or what we are.

Furthermore this absolute responsibility is not resignation; it is simply the logical requirement of the consequences of our freedom. What happens to me happens through me, and I can neither affect myself with it nor revolt against it nor resign myself to it. Moreover everything which happens to me is *mine*. By this we must understand first of all that I am always equal to what happens to me *qua* man, for what happens to a man through other men and through himself can be only human. The most terrible situations of war, the worst tortures do not create a non-human state of things; there is no non-human situation. It is only through fear, flight, and recourse

From *Being and Nothingness* by Jean-Paul Sartre. Copyright © 1956 by The Philosophical Library. Reprinted by permission of The Philosophical Library.

to magical types of conduct that I shall decide on the non-human, but this decision is human, and I shall carry the entire responsibility for it. But in addition the situation is *mine* because it is the image of my free choice of myself, and everything which it presents to me is *mine* in that this represents me and symbolizes me. Is it not I who decide the coefficient of adversity in things and even their unpredictability by deciding myself?

Thus there are no *accidents* in a life; a community event which suddenly bursts forth and involves me in it does not come from the outside. If I am mobilized in a war, this war is *my* war; it is in my image and I deserve it. I deserve it first because I could always get out of it by suicide or by desertion; these ultimate possibles are those which must always be present for us when there is a question of envisaging a situation. For lack of getting out of it, I have *chosen* it. This can be due to inertia, to cowardice in the face of public opinion, or because I prefer certain other values to the value of the refusal to join in the war (the good opinion of my relatives, the honor of my family, *etc.*). Any way you look at it, it is a matter of a choice. This choice will be repeated later on again and again without a break until the end of the war. Therefore we must agree with the statement by J. Romains, "In war there are no innocent victims." If therefore I have preferred war to death or to dishonor, everything takes place as if I bore the entire responsibility for this war. Of course others have declared it, and one might be tempted perhaps to consider me as a simple accomplice. But this notion of complicity has only a juridical sense, and it does not hold here. For it depended on me that for me and by me this war should not exist, and I have decided that it does exist. There was no compulsion here, for the compulsion could have got no hold on a freedom. I did not have any excuse; . . . the peculiar character of human-reality is that it is without excuse. Therefore it remains for me only to lay claim to this war.

But in addition the war is *mine* because by the sole fact that it arises in a situation which I cause to be and that I can discover it there only by engaging myself for or against it, I can no longer distinguish at present the choice which I make of myself from the choice which I make of the war. To live this war is to choose myself through it and to choose it through my choice of myself. There can be no question of considering it as "four years of vacation" or as a "reprieve," as a "recess," the essential part of my responsibilities being elsewhere in my married, family, or professional life. In this war which I have chosen I choose myself from day to day, and I make it mine by making myself. If it is going to be four empty years, then it is I who bear the responsibility for this.

Finally, . . . each person is an absolute choice of self from the standpoint of a world of knowledges and of techniques which this choice both assumes and illumines; each person is an absolute upsurge at an absolute date and is perfectly unthinkable at another date. It is therefore a waste of time to ask what I should have been if this war had not broken out, for I have chosen myself as one of the possible meanings of the epoch which imperceptibly led to war. I am not distinct from this same epoch; I could not be transported to another epoch without contradiction. Thus *I am* this war which restricts and limits and makes comprehensible the period which preceded it. In this sense we may define more precisely the responsibility of the for-itself if to the earlier quoted statement, "There are no innocent victims," we add the words, "We have the war we deserve." Thus, totally free, undistinguishable from the period for which I have chosen to be the meaning, as profoundly responsible for the war as if I had myself declared it, unable to live without integrating it in *my* situation, engaging myself in it wholly and stamping it with my seal, I must be without remorse or regrets as I am without excuse; for from the instant of my upsurge into being, I carry the weight of the world by myself alone without anything or any person being able to lighten it.

Yet this responsibility is of a very particular type. Someone will say, "I did not ask to be born." This is a naïve way of throwing greater emphasis on our facticity. I am responsible for everything. in fact, except for my very responsibility, for I am not the foundation of my being. Therefore everything takes place as if I were compelled to be responsible. I am *abandoned* in the world, not in the sense that I might remain abandoned and passive in a hostile universe like a board floating on the water, but rather in the sense that I find myself suddenly alone and without help, engaged in a world for which I bear the whole responsibility without being able, whatever I do, to tear myself away from this responsibility for an instant. For I am responsible for my very desire of fleeing responsibilities. To make myself passive in the world, to refuse to act upon things and upon Others is still to choose myself, and suicide is one mode among others of being-in-the-world. Yet I find an absolute responsibility for the fact that my facticity (here the fact of my birth) is directly inapprehensible and even inconceivable, for this fact of my birth never appears as a brute fact but always across a projective reconstruction of my for-itself. I am ashamed of being born or I am astonished at it or I rejoice over it, or in attempting to get rid of my life I affirm that I live and I assume this life as bad. Thus in a certain sense I *choose* being born. This choice itself is integrally affected with facticity since I am not able not to choose, but this facticity in turn will appear only in so far as I surpass it toward my ends. Thus facticity is everywhere but inapprehensible; I never encounter anything except my responsibility. That is why I can not ask, "*Why* was I born?" or curse the day of my birth or declare that I did not ask to be born, for these various attitudes toward my birth—*i.e.*, toward the *fact* that I realize a presence in the world—are absolutely nothing else but ways of assuming this birth in full responsibility and of making it *mine*. Here again I encounter only myself and my projects so that finally my abandonment—*i.e.*, my facticity—consists simply in the fact that I am condemned to be wholly responsible for myself. I am the being which *is* in such a way that in its being its being is in question. And this "is" of my being *is* as present and inapprehensible.

Under these conditions since every event in the world can be revealed to me only as an *opportunity* (an opportunity made use of, lacked, neglected, *etc.*), or better yet since everything which happens to us can be considered as a *chance* (*i.e.*, can appear to us only as a way of realizing this being which is in question in our being) and since others as transcendences-transcended are themselves only *opportunities* and *chances*, the responsibility of the for-itself extends to the entire world as a peopled-world. It is precisely thus that the for-itself apprehends itself in anguish; that is, as a being which is neither the foundation of its own being nor of the Other's being nor of the in-itselfs which form the world, but a being which is compelled to decide the meaning of being—within it and everywhere outside of it. The one who realizes in anguish his condition as *being* thrown into a responsibility which extends to his very abandonment has no longer either remorse or regret or excuse; he is no longer anything but a freedom which perfectly reveals itself and whose being resides in this very revelation. But as we pointed out . . ., most of the time we flee anguish in bad faith.

from
THE FLIES

ZEUS: A pity you can't see yourself as you are now, you fool, for all your boasting! What a heroic figure you cut there, cowering between the legs of a protecting god, with a pack of hungry vixen keeping guard on you! If you *can* brag of freedom, why not praise the freedom of a prisoner languishing in fetters, or a slave nailed to the cross?

ORESTES: Certainly. Why not?

. . .

[*The walls draw together.* ZEUS *comes into view, tired and dejected, and he now speaks in his normal voice.*]

ZEUS: Impudent spawn! So I am not your king? Who, then, made you?

ORESTES: You. But you blundered; you should not have made me free.

ZEUS: I gave you freedom so that you might serve me.

ORESTES: Perhaps. But now it has turned against its giver. And neither you nor I can undo what has been done.

ZEUS: Oh, at last! So this is your excuse?

ORESTES: I am not excusing myself.

ZEUS: No? Let me tell you it sounds much like an excuse, this freedom whose slave you claim to be.

ORESTES: Neither slave nor master. I *am* my freedom. No sooner had you created me than I ceased to be yours.

from
THE AGE OF REASON

Mathieu, who was about to get up, subsided into his chair, and the old fraternal resentment took possession of him once more. That firm but gentle pressure on his shoulder was more

From *No Exit and Three Other Plays* by Jean-Paul Sartre, translated by Stuart Gilbert. Copyright 1946 by Stuart Gilbert. Reprinted by permission of Alfred A. Knopf, Inc., and Hamish Hamilton, Ltd.

From *The Age of Reason* by Jean-Paul Sartre, translated by Eric Sutton. Copyright 1947 by Eric Sutton. Reprinted by permission of Alfred A. Knopf, Inc.

than he could stand; he threw his head back and saw Jacques's face foreshortened.

"Tell myself a lie! Look here, Jacques, say you don't want to be mixed up in a case of abortion, that you disapprove of it, or that you haven't the ready money and you're perfectly within your rights, nor shall I resent it. But this talk of lying is nonsense, there's no lying in it at all. I don't want a child: a child is coming, and I propose to suppress it; that's all."

Jacques withdrew his hand and took a few steps with a meditative air. "He's going to make me a speech," thought Mathieu. "I oughtn't to have let myself in for an argument."

"Mathieu," said Jacques in a calm tone, "I know you better than you think, and you distress me. I've long been afraid that something like this would happen: this coming child is the logical result of a situation into which you entered of your own free will, and you want to suppress it because you won't accept all the consequences of your acts. Come, shall I tell you the truth? I dare say you aren't lying to yourself at this precise moment: the trouble is that your whole life is built upon a lie."

"Carry on," said Mathieu. "I don't mind. Tell me what it is I'm trying to evade."

"You are trying," said Jacques, "to evade the fact that you're a bourgeois and ashamed of it. I myself reverted to bourgeoisie after many aberrations and contracted a marriage of convenience with the party, but you are a bourgeois by taste and temperament, and it's your temperament that's pushing you into marriage. For *you are married*, Mathieu," said he forcibly.

"First I heard of it," said Mathieu.

"Oh yes, you are, only you pretend you aren't because you are possessed by theories. You have fallen into a habit of life with this young woman: you go to see her quietly four days a week and you spend the night with her. That has been going on for seven years, and there's no adventure left in it; you respect her, you feel obligations towards her, you don't want to leave her. And I'm quite sure that your sole object isn't pleasure. I even imagine that, broadly speaking, however vivid the pleasure may have been, it has by now begun to fade. In fact, I expect you sit beside her in the evening and tell her long stories about the events of the day and ask her advice in difficulties."

"Of course," said Mathieu, shrugging his shoulders. He was furious with himself.

"Very well," said Jacques, "will you tell me how that differs from marriage—except for cohabitation?"

"Except for cohabitation?" said Mathieu ironically. "Excuse me, but that's a quibble."

"Oh," said Jacques, "being what you are, it probably doesn't cost you much to do without that."

"He has never said so much about my affairs," thought Mathieu, "he is taking his revenge." The thing to do was to go out and slam the door. But Mathieu was well aware that he would stay until the end: he was seized by an aggressive and malicious impulse to discover his brother's true opinion.

"But why do you say it probably doesn't cost me much, *being what I am?*"

"Because you get a comfortable life out of the situation, and an appearance of liberty: you have all the advantages of marriage and you exploit your principles to avoid its inconveniences. You refuse to regularize the position, which you find quite easy. If anyone suffers from all this, it isn't you."

"Marcelle shares my ideas on marriage," said Mathieu acidly; he heard himself pronounce each word and felt extremely ill at ease.

"Oh," said Jacques, "if she didn't share them she would no doubt be too proud to admit it to you. The fact is you're beyond my comprehension: you, so prompt with indignation when you hear of an injustice, you keep this woman for years in a humiliating position, for the sole pleasure of telling yourself that you're respecting your principles. It wouldn't be so bad if it were true, if you really did adapt your life to your ideas. But I must tell you once more, you are as good as married, you have a delightful apartment, you get a competent salary at fixed intervals, you have no anxiety for the future because the State guarantees you a pension . . . and you like that sort of life—placid, orderly, the typical life of an official."

"Listen," said Mathieu, "there's a misunderstanding here; I care little whether I'm a bourgeois or whether I'm not. All I want is"—and he uttered the final words through clenched teeth and with a sort of shame—"to retain my freedom."

"I should myself have thought," said Jacques, "that freedom consisted in frankly confronting situations into which one has deliberately entered, and accepting all one's responsibilities. But that, no doubt, is not your view: you condemn capitalist society, and yet you are an official in that society; you display an abstract sympathy with Communists, but you take care not to commit yourself, you have never voted. You despise the bourgeois class, and yet you are bourgeois, son and brother of a bourgeois, and you live like a bourgeois."

Mathieu waved a hand, but Jacques refused to be interrupted.

"You have, however, reached the age of reason, my poor Mathieu," said he, in a tone of pity and of warning. "But you try to dodge that fact too, you try to pretend you're younger than you are. Well—perhaps I'm doing you an injustice. Perhaps you haven't in fact reached the age of reason, it's really a moral age—perhaps I've got there sooner than you have."

• • •

She felt languid and clammy, still quite disheveled from sleep: the familiar steel helmet gripped her head, there was a taste of blotting-paper in her mouth, a lukewarm feeling down her sides, and beneath her arms, tipping the black hairs, beads of sweat. She felt sick, but restrained herself: her day had not yet begun, it was there, propped precariously against Marcelle, the least movement would bring it crashing down like an avalanche. She laughed sardonically and muttered: "Freedom!"

A human being who wakened in the morning with a queasy stomach, with fifteen hours to kill before next bedtime, had not much use for freedom. Freedom didn't help a person to live. . . .

from
ST. GENET: ACTOR AND MARTYR

A Dizzying Word

> *Our sentence is not severe. Whatever command-*
> *ment the culprit has violated is simply written*
> *upon his skin by the harrow.*
>
> —KAFKA,
> In the Penal Colony

The child was playing in the kitchen. Suddenly he became aware of his solitude and was seized with anxiety, as usual. So he "absented" himself. Once again, he plunged into a kind of ecstasy. There is now no one in the room. An abandoned consciousness is reflecting utensils. A drawer is opening; a little hand moves forward.

Caught in the act. Someone has entered and is watching him. Beneath this gaze the child comes to himself. He who was not yet anyone suddenly becomes Jean Genet. He feels that he is blinding, deafening; he is a beacon, an alarm that keeps ringing. *Who* is Jean Genet? In a moment the whole village will know. . . . The child alone is in ignorance. In a state of fear and shame he continues his signal of distress. Suddenly

> . . . a dizzying word
> From the depths of the world abolishes
> the beautiful order. . . .[1]

A voice declares publicly: "You're a thief." The child is ten years old.

That was how it happened, in that or some other way. In all probability, there were offenses and then punishment, solemn oaths and relapses. It does not matter. The important thing is that Genet lived and has not stopped reliving this period of his life as if it had lasted only an instant.

From *St. Genet: Actor and Martyr* by Jean-Paul Sartre, translated from the French by Bernard Frechtman. English translation copyright © 1963 by George Braziller, Inc. Reprinted by permission of the publisher.
[1] *Genet*, Poèmes, *p. 56.*

It is the moment of awakening. The sleepwalking child opens his eyes and realizes he is stealing. It is revealed to him that he *is* a thief and he pleads guilty, crushed by a fallacy which he is unable to refute; he stole, he is therefore a thief. Can anything be more evident? Genet, thunderstruck, considers his act, looks at it from every angle. No doubt about it, it is a theft. And theft is an offense, a crime. What he *wanted* was to steal; what he *did*, a theft; what he *was*, a thief. A timid voice is still protesting within him; he does not *recognize* his intentions. But soon the voice grows silent. The act is so luminous, so sharply defined, that there is no mistaking its nature. He tries to go back, to understand himself, but it is too late, he has lost his bearings. The dazzlingly evident present confers its meaning on the past; Genet now *recalls* that he cynically decided to steal. What happened? Actually, almost nothing: an action undertaken without reflection, conceived and carried out in the secret, silent inwardness in which he often takes refuge, has just *become objective*. Genet learns what he *is objectively*. It is this *transition* that is going to determine his entire life.

The metamorphosis occurs immediately. He is nothing more than what he was before, yet he is now unrecognizable. Driven from the lost paradise, exiled from childhood, from the immediate, condemned to see himself, suddenly provided with a monstrous and guilty "ego," isolated, separated, in short changed into a bug. An evil principle dwelt in him unperceived, and now it has been discovered. It is this principle which is the source of everything. It produces the slightest impulses of his soul. The child lived at peace with himself; his desires seemed to him limpid and simple. Their transparency now appears to have been deceptive. They had a double bottom. Little Genet's shame reveals eternity to him. He is a thief by birth, he will remain one until his death. Time is only a dream in which his evil nature is refracted into a thousand gleams, a thousand petty thefts, but does not belong to the temporal order. *Genet is a thief*; that is his truth, his eternal essence. And, if he *is* a thief, he must therefore always be one, everywhere, not only when he steals, but when he eats, when he sleeps, when he kisses his foster mother. Each of his gestures betrays him, reveals his vile nature in broad daylight. At any moment the teacher may interrupt the lesson, look Genet in the eyes and cry out: "There's a thief!" It would be vain for him to think he deserved leniency by admitting his errors, by mastering the perversity of his instincts. All the impulses of his heart are equally guilty because all alike express his essence.

. . .

A thief cannot have an intuition of himself *as thief*. The notion of "thief" is on principle incommensurate with the realities of the inner sense. It is of social origin and presupposes a prior definition of society, of the property system, a legal code, a judiciary apparatus and an ethical system of relationships among people. There can therefore be no question of a mind's *encountering* theft within itself, and with immediacy. On the other hand, the *Others*, all the Others, have this intuition at will; a thief is a palpable reality, like a tree, like a Gothic church. Here is a man being dragged along by two cops: "What has he done?" I ask. "He's a crook," answer the cops. The word strikes against its object like a crystal falling into a supersaturated solution. The solution immediately crystallizes, enclosing the word inside itself. In prose, the word dies so that the object may be born. "He's a crook!" I forget the word then and there, I see, I touch, I breathe a crook; with all my senses I feel that secret substance: crime. . . .

. . .

I Will Be the Thief

Pinned by a look, a butterfly fixed to a cork, he is naked, everyone can see him and spit on him. The gaze of the adults is a *constituent power* which has transformed him into a *constituted nature*. He now has to live. In the pillory, with his neck in an iron collar, he still has to live. We are not lumps of clay, and what is important is not what people make of us but what we ourselves make of what they have made of us. By virtue of the option which they have taken on his being, the decent folk have made it necessary for a child to decide about himself prematurely. We can surmise that this decision will be of capital importance. Yes, one *must* decide. To kill oneself is also to decide. He has chosen to live; he has said, in defiance of all, I will be the Thief. I deeply admire this child who grimly *willed* himself at an age when *we* were merely playing the servile buffoon. So fierce a will to survive, such pure courage, such mad confidence within despair will bear their fruit. Twenty years later, this absurd determination will produce the poet Jean Genet.

MARXISM AND EXISTENTIALISM

Philosophy appears to some people as a homogeneous milieu: there thoughts are born and die, there systems are built, and there, in turn, they collapse. Others take Philosophy for a specific attitude which we can freely adopt at will. Still others see it as a determined segment of culture. In our view *Philosophy* does not exist. In whatever form we consider it, this shadow of science, this Gray Eminence of humanity, is only a hypostatized abstraction. Actually, there are *philosophies*. Or rather—for you would never at the same time find more than *one* living philosophy—under certain well-defined circumstances *a* philosophy is developed for the purpose of giving expression to the general movement of the society. So long as a philosophy is alive, it serves as a cultural milieu for its contemporaries. This disconcerting object presents itself *at the same time* under profoundly distinct aspects, the unification of which it is continually effecting.

A philosophy is first of all a particular way in which the "rising" class becomes conscious of itself.[1] This consciousness may be clear or confused, indirect or direct. At the time of the *noblesse de robe*[2] and of mercantile capitalism, a bourgeoisie of lawyers, merchants, and bankers gained a certain self-awareness through Cartesianism; a century and a half

From *Search for a Method* by Jean-Paul Sartre, translated by Hazel E. Barnes. Copyright © 1963 by Alfred A. Knopf, Inc. Reprinted by permission of Alfred A. Knopf, Inc.

[1] *If I do not mention here the* person *who is objectified and revealed in his work, it is because the philosophy of a period extends far beyond the philosopher who first gave it shape—no matter how great he may be. But conversely we shall see that the study of particular doctrines is inseparable from a real investigation of philosophies. Cartesianism illuminates the period and* situates *Descartes within the totalitarian development of analytical reason; in these terms, Descartes, taken as a person and as a philosopher, clarifies the historical (hence the particular) meaning of the new rationality up to the middle of the eighteenth century.*

[2] Noblesse de robe *was originally the designation given in France to those members of the bourgeoisie who were awarded titles of nobility in recognition of outstanding achievement or service to the State. Later it was used loosely to refer to any "new" nobility. (Translator's note.)*

later, in the primitive stage of industrialization, a bourgeoisie of manufacturers, engineers, and scientists dimly discovered itself in the image of universal man which Kantianism offered to it.

. . .

If philosophy is to be simultaneously a totalization of knowledge, a method, a regulative Idea, an offensive weapon, and a community of language, if this "vision of the world" is also an instrument which ferments rotten societies, if this particular conception of a man or of a group of men becomes the culture and sometimes the nature of a whole class—then it is very clear that the periods of philosophical creation are rare. Between the seventeenth century and the twentieth, I see three such periods, which I would designate by the names of the men who dominated them: there is the "moment" of Descartes and Locke, that of Kant and Hegel, finally that of Marx. These three philosophies become, each in its turn, the humus of every particular thought and the horizon of all culture; there is no going beyond them so long as man has not gone beyond the historical moment which they express. I have often remarked on the fact that an "anti-Marxist" argument is only the apparent rejuvenation of a pre-Marxist idea. A so-called "going beyond" Marxism will be at worst only a return to pre-Marxism; at best, only the rediscovery of a thought already contained in the philosophy which one believes he has gone beyond. As for "revisionism," this is either a truism or an absurdity. There is no need to readapt a living philosophy to the course of the world; it adapts itself by means of thousands of new efforts, thousands of particular pursuits, for the philosophy is one with the movement of society. Despite their good intentions, those very people who believe themselves to be the most faithful spokesmen for their predecessors transform the thoughts which they want simply to repeat; methods are modified because they are applied to new objects. If this movement on the part of the philosophy no longer exists, one of two things is true: either the philosophy is dead or it is going through a "crisis." In the first case there is no question of revising, but of razing a rotten building; in the second case the "philosophical crisis" is the particular expression of a social crisis, and its immobility is conditioned by the contradictions which split the society. A so-called "revision," performed by "experts," would be, therefore, only an idealist mystification without real significance. It is the very movement of History, the struggle of men on all planes and on all levels of human activity, which will set free captive thought and permit it to attain its full development.

Those intellectuals who come after the great flowering and who undertake to set the systems in order or to use the new methods to conquer territory not yet fully explored, those who provide practical applications for the theory and employ it as a tool to destroy and to construct—they should not be called philosophers. They cultivate the domain, they take an inventory, they erect certain structures there, they may even bring about certain internal changes; but they still get their nourishment from the living thought of the great dead. They are borne along by the crowd on the march, and it is the crowd which constitutes their cultural milieu and their future, which determines the field of their investigations, and even of their "creation." These *relative* men I propose to call "ideologists." And since I am to speak of existentialism, let it be understood that I take it to be an "ideology." It is a parasitical system living on the margin of Knowledge, which at first it opposed but into which today it seeks to be integrated.

• • •

[Conclusion to *Search for a Method*]

These considerations enable us to understand why we can at the same time declare that we are in profound agreement with Marxist philosophy and yet for the present maintain the autonomy of the existential ideology. There is no doubt, indeed, that Marxism appears today to be the only possible anthropology which can be at once historical and structural. It is the only one which at the same time takes man in his totality—that is, in terms of the materiality of his condition. Nobody can propose to it another point of departure, for this would be to offer to it *another man* as the object of its study. It is *inside* the movement of Marxist thought that we discover a flaw of such a sort that despite itself Marxism tends to eliminate the questioner from his investigation and to make of the questioned the object of an absolute Knowledge. The very notions which Marxist research employs to describe our historical society—exploitation, alienation, fetishizing, reification, etc.—

are precisely those which most immediately refer to existential structures. The very notion of *praxis* and that of dialectic—inseparably bound together—are contradictory to the intellectualist idea of a knowledge. And to come to the most important point, *labor*, as man's reproduction of his life, can hold no meaning if its fundamental structure is not to pro-ject. In view of this default—which pertains to the historical development and not to the actual principles of the doctrine—existentialism, at the heart of Marxism and taking the same givens, the same Knowledge, as its point of departure, must attempt in its turn—at least as an experiment—the dialectical interpretation of History. It puts nothing in question except a mechanistic determinism which is not exactly Marxist and which has been introduced from the outside into this total philosophy. Existentialism, too, wants to situate man in his class and in the conflicts which oppose him to other classes, starting with the mode and the relations of production. But it can approach this "situation" in terms of *existence*—that is, of comprehension. It makes itself the questioned and the question as questioner; it does not, as Kierkegaard did apropos of Hegel, set the irrational singularity of the individual in opposition to universal Knowledge. But into this very Knowledge and into the universality of concepts, it wants to reintroduce the unsurpassable singularity of the human adventure.

Thus the comprehension of existence is presented as the human foundation of Marxist anthropology. Nevertheless, we must beware here of a confusion heavy with consequences. In fact, in the order of Knowledge, what we know concerning the principle or the foundations of a scientific structure, even when it has come—as is ordinarily the case—later than the empirical determinations, is set forth first; and one deduces from it the determinations of Knowledge in the same way that one constructs a building after having secured its foundations. But this is because the foundation is itself a knowing; and if one can deduce from it certain propositions already guaranteed by experience, this is because one has induced it in terms of them as the most general hypothesis. In contrast, the foundation of Marxism, as a historical, structural anthropology, is man himself inasmuch as human existence and the comprehension of the human are inseparable. Historically Marxist Knowledge produces its foundation at a certain moment of its development, and this foundation is presented in a disguised form. It does not appear as the practical foundations of the theory, but as that which, on principle, pushes forward all theoretical knowing. Thus the singularity of existence is presented in Kierkegaard as that which on principle is kept outside the Hegelian system (that is, outside total Knowledge), as that which can in no way be *thought* but only *lived* in the act of faith. The dialectical procedure to reintegrate existence (which is never *known*) as a foundation at the heart of Knowledge could not be attempted then, since neither of the current attitudes—an idealist Knowledge, a spiritual existence—could lay claim to concrete actualization. These two terms outlined abstractly the future contradiction. And the development of anthropological knowing could not lead then to the synthesis of these formal positions: the movement of ideas—as the movement of society—had first to produce Marxism as the only possible form of a really concrete Knowledge. And as we indicated at the beginning, Marx's own Marxism, while indicating the dialectical opposition between knowing and being, contained implicitly the demand for an existential foundation for the theory. Furthermore, in order for notions like reification and alienation to assume their full meaning, it would have been necessary for the questioner and the questioned to be made one. What must be the nature of human relations in order for these relations to be capable of appearing in certain definite societies as the relations of things to each other? If the reification of human relations is possible, it is because these relations, even if reified, are fundamentally distinct from the relations of things. What kind of practical organism is this which reproduces its life by its work so that its work and ultimately its very reality are alienated; that is, so that they, *as others*, turn back upon him and determine him? But before Marxism, itself a product of the social conflict, could turn to these problems, it had to assume fully its role as a practical philosophy—that is, as a theory clarifying social and political *praxis*. The result is a profound *lack* within contemporary Marxism; the use of the notions mentioned earlier—and many others—refers to a comprehension of human reality which is missing. And this lack is not—as some Marxists declare today—a localized void, a hole in the construction of Knowledge. It is inapprehensible and yet everywhere present; it is a general anemia.

. . .

It is precisely this expulsion of man, his exclusion from

Marxist Knowledge, which resulted in the renascence of existentialist thought outside the historical totalization of Knowledge. Human science is frozen in the non-human, and human-reality seeks to understand itself outside of science. But this time the opposition comes from those who directly demand their synthetic transcendence. Marxism will degenerate into a non-human anthropology if it does not reintegrate man into itself as its foundation. But this comprehension, which is nothing other than existence itself, is disclosed at the same time by the historical movement of Marxism, by the concepts which indirectly clarify it (alienation, etc.), and by the new alienations which give birth to the contradictions of socialist society and which reveal to it its abandonment; that is, the incommensurability of existence and practical Knowledge. The movement can *think* itself only in Marxist terms and can *comprehend* itself only as an alienated existence, as a human-reality made into a thing. The moment which will surpass this opposition must reintegrate comprehension into Knowledge as its non-theoretical foundation.

In other words, the foundation of anthropology is man himself, not as the object of practical Knowledge, but as a practical organism producing Knowledge as a moment of its *praxis*. And the reintegration of man as a concrete existence into the core of anthropology, as its constant support, appears necessarily as a stage in the process of philosophy's "becoming-the-world." In this sense the foundation of anthropology cannot precede it (neither historically nor logically). If *existence*, in its free comprehension of itself, preceded the awareness of alienation or of exploitation, it would be necessary to suppose that the free development of the practical organism historically preceded its present fall and captivity. (And if this were established, the historical precedence would scarcely advance us in our comprehension, since the retrospective study of vanished societies is made today with the enlightenment furnished by techniques for reconstruction and by means of the alienations which enchain us.) Or, if one insisted on a logical priority, it would be necessary to suppose that the freedom of the project could be recovered in its full reality *underneath* the alienations of our society and that one could move dialectically from the concrete existence which understands its freedom to the various alterations which distort it in present society. This hypothesis is absurd. To be sure, man can be enslaved only if he is free. But for the historical man who *knows* himself and *comprehends* himself, this practical freedom is grasped only as the permanent, concrete condition of his servitude; that is, across that servitude and by means of it as that which makes it possible, as its foundation. Thus Marxist Knowledge bears on the alienated man; but if it doesn't want to make a fetish of its knowing and to dissolve man in the process of knowing his alienations, then it is not enough to describe the working of capital or the system of colonization. It is necessary that the questioner understand how the questioned—that is, himself—*exists his alienation*, how he surpasses it and is alienated in this very surpassing. It is necessary that his very thought should at every instant surpass the intimate contradiction which unites the comprehension of man-as-agent with the knowing of man-as-object and that it forge new concepts, new determinations of Knowledge which emerge from the existential comprehension and which regulate the movement of their contents by its dialectical procedure. Yet this comprehension—as a living movement of the practical organism—can take place only within a concrete situation, insofar as theoretical Knowledge illuminates and interprets this situation.

Thus the autonomy of existential studies results necessarily from the negative qualities of Marxists (and not from Marxism itself). So long as the doctrine does not recognize its anemia, so long as it founds its Knowledge upon a dogmatic metaphysics (a dialectic of Nature) instead of seeking its support in the comprehension of the living man, so long as it rejects as irrational those ideologies which wish, as Marx did, to separate being from Knowledge and, in anthropology, to found the knowing of man on human existence, existentialism will follow its own path of study. This means that it will attempt to clarify the givens of Marxist Knowledge by indirect knowing (that is, as we have seen, by words which regressively denote existential structures), and to engender within the framework of Marxism a veritable *comprehensive knowing* which will rediscover man in the social world and which will follow him in his *praxis*—or, if you prefer, in the project which throws him toward the social possibles in terms of a defined situation. Existentialism will appear therefore as a fragment of the system, which has fallen outside of Knowledge. From the day that Marxist thought will have taken on the human dimension (that is, the existential project) as the foundation of anthropological Knowledge, existentialism will no longer have any reason for being. Absorbed, surpassed and conserved by the totalizing movement of philosophy, it will cease to be a particular inquiry and will become the foundation of all inquiry. The comments which we have made in the course of the present essay are directed—to the modest limit of our capabilities—toward hastening the moment of that dissolution.

Maurice Merleau-Ponty

(1908–1961) ———◆─◆─◆——— FRENCH

Merleau-Ponty has too often been viewed in the shadow of Sartre, as the younger classmate, as the "other" founder of Les Temps Modernes, *as the "other" French existential phenomenologist and Marxist. In his phenomenological work, Merleau-Ponty far surpasses Sartre in his knowledge and development of Husserl's theory of perception. His early* Structure of Behavior *is an important attempt to argue against the pervasive Cartesian model of man as consciousness + machine-body. His important* Phenomenology of Perception *is the most ambitious attempt to correct certain persistent problems in Husserl's theory of perception. It begins with Husserl's basic techniques of phenomenology, provides an insightful account of the role of "sensation" in phenomenology and psychology, then quickly moves to Husserl's later works, adding a thorough appreciation of Heidegger's* Being and Time *and arguing that perception is primarily more than a relationship between consciousness and its acts and certain objects or meanings. Against Descartes and Husserl, and with Heidegger, Merleau-Ponty holds that essentially human existence is not knowing and thinking, but living, valuing. Against both Husserl and Sartre, Merleau-Ponty argues that it is not consciousness, but the human body that is intentional, through "motility." Our bodies are not simply objects in the world (to which each of us has privileged but yet contingent access). The body is our Being-in-the-world, the perspective from which we perceive, judge, value. Accordingly, Merleau-Ponty adopts a notion of freedom which is also less Cartesian than Sartre's. Freedom is never, as Sartre insists, absolute or total freedom. It is "progressive," a reorientation of our demands on the basis of "pre-evaluated meanings" and motivation. True, one is always free, but to be always free is not to be totally free. One must act in accordance with his motives and interests as well as in obeyance with his situation and facticity (contingency). Politically, Merleau-Ponty was actively in-*

volved in the Left before Sartre. His Humanism and Terror *had a deep effect on Sartre and marked an important break from the Communist party for both of them. Merleau-Ponty remained a moral individualist in his politics, which carried him increasingly further from the orthodox Left and ultimately caused the destruction of his lifelong friendship with Sartre.*

from "MERLEAU-PONTY," BY JEAN-PAUL SARTRE

One day in 1947, Merleau told me that he had never recovered from an incomparable childhood. He had known that private world of happiness from which only age drives us. Pascalian from adolescence, without even having read Pascal, he experienced his singular selfhood as the singularity of an adventure. To be someone, is something which happens and unhappens, but not without first tracing the ribs of a future, always new and always begun anew. What was he, if not this paradise lost, a wild and undeserved piece of luck, a gratuitous gift transformed, after the fall, into adversity, depopulating the world and disenchanting him in advance? This story is both extraordinary and commonplace. Our capacity for happiness is dependent upon a certain equilibrium between what we refuse and concede to our childhood. Completely deprived or completely endowed, we are lost. Thus, there are an infinite number of lots we can draw. His was to have won too soon. He had to live, nonetheless. To the end, it remained for him to make himself as the event had made him. That way and other ways. Seeking the golden age, and with that as his point of departure he forged his myths and what he has since called his "style of life." It established his preferences—choosing, at the same time, the traditions which recalled the rituals of childhood, and the "spontaneity" which evoked childhood's superintended liberty. This naïveté, by starting

From *Situations* by Jean-Paul Sartre, translated from the French by Benita Eisler. English translation copyright © 1965 by George Braziller, Inc. Reprinted by permission of the publisher.

from *what has happened*, also discovered the meaning of *what is happening*, and finally, it made a prophecy based on this inventory and its evaluation. This is what he felt as a young man, without as yet being able to express it. Through these detours, he finally arrived at philosophy. He wondered —nothing more. . . .

PROSPECTUS (A REPORT TO THE COLLÈGE DE FRANCE)

We never cease living in the world of perception, but we go beyond it in critical thought—almost to the point of forgetting the contribution of perception to our idea of truth. For critical thought encounters only *bare propositions* which it discusses, accepts or rejects. Critical thought has broken with the naive evidence of *things*, and when it affirms, it is because it no longer finds any means of denial. However necessary this activity of verification may be, specifying criteria and demanding from our experience its credentials of validity, it is not aware of our contact with the perceived world which is simply there before us, beneath the level of the verified true and the false. Nor does critical thought even define the positive steps of thinking or its most valid accomplishments.

My first two works sought to restore the world of perception. My works in preparation aim to show how communication with others, and thought, take up and go beyond the realm of perception which initiated us to the truth.

The perceiving mind is an incarnated mind. I have tried, first of all, to re-establish the roots of the mind in its body and in its world, going against doctrines which treat perception as a simple result of the action of external things on our body as well as against those which insist on the autonomy of consciousness. These philosophies commonly forget—in favor of a pure exteriority or of a pure interiority—the insertion of the mind in corporeality, the ambiguous relation which we

From *The Primacy of Perception* by Maurice Merleau-Ponty, edited by James M. Edie and translated by Arleen B. Dallery. Northwestern University Press, 1964. Reprinted by permission of Northwestern University Press. First published as an "Unpublished Text" in the *Revue de métaphysique et de morale*, no. 4, 1962.

entertain with our body and, correlatively, with perceived things. When one attempts, as I have in *The Structure of Behavior*, to trace out, on the basis of modern psychology and physiology, the relationships which obtain between the perceiving organism and its milieu one clearly finds that they are not those of an automatic machine which needs an outside agent to set off its pre-established mechanisms. And it is equally clear that one does not account for the facts by superimposing a pure, contemplative consciousness on a thinglike body. In the conditions of life—if not in the laboratory—the organism is less sensitive to certain isolated physical and chemical agents than to the constellation which they form and to the whole situation which they define. Behaviors reveal a sort of prospective activity in the organism, as if it were oriented toward the meaning of certain elementary situations, as if it entertained familiar relations with them, as if there were an "*a priori* of the organism," privileged conducts and laws of internal equilibrium which predisposed the organism to certain relations with its milieu. At this level there is no question yet of a real self-awareness or of intentional activity. Moreover, the organism's prospective capability is exercised only within defined limits and depends on precise, local conditions.

The functioning of the central nervous system presents us with similar paradoxes. In its modern forms, the theory of cerebral localizations has profoundly changed the relation of function to substrate. It no longer assigns, for instance, a pre-established mechanism to each perceptual behavior. "Coordinating centers" are no longer considered as storehouses of "cerebral traces," and their functioning is qualitatively different from one case to another, depending on the chromatic nuance to be evoked and the perceptual structure to be realized. Finally, this functioning reflects all the subtlety and all the variety of perceptual relationships.

The perceiving organism seems to show us a Cartesian mixture of the soul with the body. Higher-order behaviors give a new meaning to the life of the organism, but the mind here disposes of only a limited freedom; it needs simpler activities in order to stabilize itself in durable institutions and to realize itself truly as mind. Perceptual behavior emerges from these relations to a situation and to an environment which are not the workings of a pure, knowing subject.

In my work on the *Phenomenology of Perception* we are

no longer present at the emergence of perceptual behaviors; rather we install ourselves in them in order to pursue the analysis of this exceptional relation between the subject and its body and its world. For contemporary psychology and psychopathology the body is no longer merely *an object in the world*, under the purview of a separated spirit. It is on the side of the subject; it is our *point of view on the world*, the place where the spirit takes on a certain physical and historical situation. As Descartes once said profoundly, the soul is not merely in the body like a pilot in his ship; it is wholly intermingled with the body. The body, in turn, is wholly animated, and all its functions contribute to the perception of objects—an activity long considered by philosophy to be pure knowledge.

We grasp external space through our bodily situation. A "corporeal or postural schema" gives us at every moment a global, practical, and implicit notion of the relation between our body and things, of our hold on them. A system of possible movements, or "motor projects," radiates from us to our environment. Our body is not in space like things; it inhabits or haunts space. It applies itself to space like a hand to an instrument, and when we wish to move about we do not move the body as we move an object. We transport it without instruments as if by magic, since it is ours and because through it we have direct access to space. For us the body is much more than an instrument or a means; it is our expression in the world, the visible form of our intentions. Even our most secret affective movements, those most deeply tied to the humoral infrastructure, help to shape our perception of things.

Now if perception is thus the common act of all our motor and affective functions, no less than the sensory, we must rediscover the structure of the perceived world through a process similar to that of an archaeologist. For the structure of the perceived world is buried under the sedimentations of later knowledge. Digging down to the perceived world, we see that sensory qualities are not opaque, indivisible "givens," which are simply exhibited to a remote consciousness—a favorite idea of classical philosophy. We see too that colors (each surrounded by an affective atmosphere which psychologists have been able to study and define) are themselves different modalities of our co-existence with the world. We also find that spatial forms or distances are not so much relations between different points in objective space as they are relations between these points and a central perspective —our body. In short, these relations are different ways for external stimuli to test, to solicit, and to vary our grasp on the world, our horizontal and vertical anchorage in a place and in a here-and-now. We find that perceived things, unlike geometrical objects, are not bounded entities whose laws of construction we possess *a priori*, but that they are open, inexhaustible systems which we recognize through a certain style of development, although we are never able, in principle, to explore them entirely, and even though they never give us more than profiles and perspectival views of themselves. Finally, we find that the perceived world, in its turn, is not a pure object of thought without fissures or lacunae; it is, rather, like a universal style shared in by all perceptual beings. While the world no doubt co-ordinates these perceptual beings, we can never presume that its work is finished. Our world, as Malebranche said, is an "unfinished task."

If we now wish to characterize a subject capable of this perceptual experience, it obviously will not be a self-transparent thought, absolutely present to itself without the interference of its body and its history. The perceiving subject is not this absolute thinker; rather, it functions according to a natal pact between our body and the world, between ourselves and our body. Given a perpetually new natural and historical situation to control, the perceiving subject undergoes a continued birth; at each instant it is something new. Every incarnate subject is like an open notebook in which we do not yet know what will be written. Or it is like a new language; we do not know what works it will accomplish but only that, once it has appeared, it cannot fail to say little or much, to have a history and a meaning. The very productivity or freedom of human life, far from denying our situation, utilizes it and turns it into a means of expression.

FREEDOM

Again, it is clear that no causal relationship is conceivable between the subject and his body, his world or his society. Only at the cost of losing the basis of all my certainties can I question what is conveyed to me by my presence to myself. Now the moment I turn to myself in order to describe myself, I have a glimpse of an anonymous flux,[1] a comprehensive project in which there are so far no 'states of consciousness', nor, *a fortiori*, qualifications of any sort. For myself I am neither 'jealous', nor 'inquisitive', nor 'hunchbacked', nor 'a civil servant'. It is often a matter of surprise that the cripple or the invalid can put up with himself. The reason is that such people are not for themselves deformed or at death's door. Until the final coma, the dying man is inhabited by a consciousness, he is all that he sees, and enjoys this much of an outlet. Consciousness can never objectify itself into invalid-consciousness or cripple-consciousness, and even if the old man complains of his age or the cripple of his deformity, they can do so only by comparing themselves with others, or seeing themselves through the eyes of others, that is, by taking a statistical and objective view of themselves, so that such complaints are never absolutely genuine: when he is back in the heart of his own consciousness, each one of us feels beyond his limitations and thereupon resigns himself to them. They are the price which we automatically pay for being in the world, a formality which we take for granted. Hence we may speak disparagingly of our looks and still not want to change our face for another. No idiosyncrasy can, seemingly, be attached to the insuperable generality of consciousness, nor can any limit be set to this immeasurable power of escape. In order to be determined (in the two senses of that word) by an external factor, it is necessary that I should be a thing. Neither my freedom nor my universality can admit of any eclipse. It is inconceivable that I should be free in certain of my actions and determined in others: how should we understand a dormant freedom that gave full scope to determin-

From *The Phenomenology of Perception* by Maurice Merleau-Ponty. Reprinted by permission of Humanities Press, Inc., New York, and Routledge & Kegan Paul, Ltd., London.

[1] *In the sense in which, with Husserl, we have taken this word.*

ism? And if it is assumed that it is snuffed out when it is not in action, how could it be rekindled? If *per impossibile* I had once succeeded in *making myself into* a thing, how should I subsequently reconvert myself to consciousness? Once I am free, I am not to be counted among things, and I must then be uninterruptedly free. Once my actions cease to be mine, I shall never recover them, and if I lose my hold on the world, it will never be restored to me. It is equally inconceivable that my liberty should be attenuated; one cannot be to some extent free, and if, as is often said, motives incline me in a certain direction, one of two things happens: either they are strong enough to force me to act, in which case there is no freedom, or else they are not strong enough, and then freedom is complete, and as great in the worst torments as in the peace of one's home. We ought, therefore, to reject not only the idea of causality, but also that of motivation.[2] The alleged motive does not burden my decision; on the contrary my decision lends the motive its force. Everything that I 'am' in virtue of nature or history—hunchbacked, handsome or Jewish—I never am completely for myself, as we have just explained: and I may well be these things for other people, nevertheless I remain free to posit another person as a consciousness whose views strike through to my very being, or on the other hand merely as an object. It is also true that this option is itself a form of constraint: if I am ugly, I have the choice between being an object of disapproval or disapproving of others. I am left free to be a masochist or a sadist, but not free to ignore others. But this dilemma, which is given as part of the human lot, is not one for me as pure consciousness: it is still I who cause the other to be for me, and who cause us both to be as members of mankind. Moreover, even if existence as a human being were imposed upon me, the manner alone being left to my choice, and considering this choice itself and ignoring the small number of forms it might take, it would still be a free choice. If it is said that my temperament inclines me particularly to either sadism or masochism, it is still merely a manner of speaking, for my temperament exists only for the second order knowledge that I gain about myself when I see myself as others see me, and in so far as I recognize it, confer value upon it, and in that

[2] *See J. P. Sartre, L'Être et le Néant, pp. 508 and ff.*

sense, choose it. What misleads us on this, is that we often look for freedom in the voluntary deliberation which examines one motive after another and seems to opt for the weightiest or most convincing. In reality the deliberation follows the decision, and it is my secret decision which brings the motives to light, for it would be difficult to conceive what the force of a motive might be in the absence of a decision which it confirms or to which it runs counter. When I have abandoned a project, the motives which I thought held me to it suddenly lose their force and collapse. In order to resuscitate them, an effort is required on my part to reopen time and set me back to the moment preceding the making of the decision. Even while I am deliberating, already I find it an effort to suspend time's flow, and to keep open a situation which I feel is closed by a decision which is already there and which I am holding off. That is why it so often happens that after giving up a plan I experience a feeling of relief: 'After all, I wasn't so very particular'; the debate was purely a matter of form, and the deliberation a mere parody, for I had decided against from the start.

We often see the weakness of the will brought forward as an argument against freedom. And indeed, although I can will myself to adopt a course of conduct and act the part of a warrior or a seducer, it is not within my power to be a warrior or seducer with ease and in a way that 'comes naturally'; really to *be* one, that is. But neither should we seek freedom in the act of will, which is, in its very meaning, something short of an act. We have recourse to an act of will only in order to go against our true decision, and, as it were, for the purpose of proving our powerlessness. If we had really and truly made the conduct of the warrior or the seducer our own, then we should *be* one or the other. Even what are called obstacles to freedom are in reality deployed by it. An unclimbable rock face, a large or small, vertical or slanting rock, are things which have no meaning for anyone who is not intending to surmount them, for a subject whose projects do not carve out such determinate forms from the uniform mass of the *in itself* and cause an orientated world to arise—a significance in things. There is, then, ultimately nothing that can set limits to freedom, except those limits that freedom itself has set in the form of its various initiatives, so that the subject has simply the external world that he gives himself. Since it is the latter who, on coming into being, brings to light significance and value in things, and since no thing can impinge upon it except through acquiring, thanks to it, significance and value, there is no action of things on the subject, but merely a signification (in the active sense), a centrifugal *Sinngebung*. The choice would seem to lie between scientism's conception of causality, which is incompatible with the consciousness which we have of ourselves, and the assertion of an absolute freedom divorced from the outside. It is impossible to decide beyond which point things cease to be ἐφ ἡμιν. Either they all lie within our power, or none does.

The result, however, of this first reflection on freedom would appear to be to rule it out altogether. If indeed it is the case that our freedom is the same in all our actions, and even in our passions, if it is not to be measured in terms of our conduct, and if the slave displays freedom as much by living in fear as by breaking his chains, then it cannot be held that there is such a thing as *free action*, freedom being anterior to all actions. In any case it will not be possible to declare: 'Here freedom makes its appearance', since free action, in order to be discernible, has to stand out against a background of life from which it is entirely, or almost entirely, absent. We may say in this case that it is everywhere, but equally nowhere. In the name of freedom we reject the idea of acquisition, since freedom has become a primordial acquisition and, as it were, our state of nature. Since we do not have to provide it, it is the gift granted to us of having no gift, it is the nature of consciousness which consists in having no nature, and in no case can it find external expression or a place in our life. The idea of action, therefore, disappears: nothing can pass from us to the world, since we are nothing that can be specified, and since the non-being which constitutes us could not possibly find its way into the world's plenum. There are merely intentions immediately followed by their effects, and we are very near to the Kantian idea of an intention which is tantamount to the act, which Scheler countered with the argument that the cripple who would like to be able to save a drowning man and the good swimmer who actually saves him do not have the same experience of autonomy. The very idea of choice vanishes, for to choose is to choose *something* in which freedom sees, at least for a moment, a symbol of itself. There is free choice only if freedom comes into play in its decision, and posits the situation chosen as a situation of freedom. A freedom which has no need to be exercised because it is already acquired could not commit itself in this way: it knows that the following instant will find it, come what may, just as free and just as indeterminate. The very notion of freedom demands that our decision should plunge into the future, that something should have been *done* by it, that the subsequent instant should benefit from its predecessor and, though not necessitated, should be at least required by it. If freedom is doing, it is necessary that what it does should not be immediately undone by a new freedom. Each instant, therefore, must not be a closed world; one instant must be able to commit its successors and, a decision once taken and action once begun, I must have something acquired at my disposal, I must benefit from my impetus, I must be inclined to carry on, and there must be a bent or propensity of the mind. It was Descartes who held that conservation demands a power as great as does creation; a view which implies a realistic notion of the instant. It is true that the instant is not a philosopher's fiction. It is the point at which one project is brought to fruition and another begun[3] —the point at which my gaze is transferred from one end to another, it is the *Augen-Blick*. But this break in time cannot occur unless each of the two spans is of a piece. Consciousness, it is said, is, though not atomized into instants, at least haunted by the spectre of the instant which it is obliged continually to exorcise by a free act. We shall soon see that we have indeed always the power to interrupt, but it implies in any case a power to *begin*, for there would be no severance unless freedom had taken up its abode somewhere and were preparing to move it. Unless there are cycles of behaviour, open situations requiring a certain completion and capable of constituting a background to either a confirmatory or transformatory decision, we never experience freedom. The choice of an intelligible character is excluded, not only because there is no time anterior to time, but because choice presupposes a prior commitment and because the idea of an initial choice involves a contradiction. If freedom is to have *room*[4] in which to move, if it is to be describable as freedom, there must be something to hold it away from its objectives, it must have a *field*, which means that there must be for it

[3] J. P. Sartre, L'Être et le Néant, p. 544.
[4] 'avoir du champ'; in this sentence there is a play on the word 'champ' = field (Translator's note).

special possibilities, or realities which tend to cling to being. As. J. P. Sartre himself observes, dreaming is incompatible with freedom because, in the realm of imagination, we have no sooner taken a certain significance as our goal than we already believe that we have intuitively brought it into being, in short, because there is no obstacle and nothing *to do*.[5] It is established that freedom is not to be confused with those abstract decisions of will at grips with motives or passions, for the classical conception of deliberation is relevant only to a freedom 'in bad faith' which secretly harbours antagon-istic motives without being prepared to act on them, and so itself manufactures the alleged proofs of its impotence. We can see, beneath these noisy debates and these fruitless efforts to 'construct' us, the tacit decisions whereby we have marked out round ourselves the field of possibility, and it is true that nothing is done as long as we cling to these fixed points, and everything is easy as soon as we have weighed anchor. This is why our freedom is not to be sought in spurious discussion on the conflict between a style of life which we have no wish to reappraise and circumstances suggestive of another: the real choice is that between our whole charac-ter and our manner of being in the world. But either this total choice is never mentioned, since it is the silent upsurge of our being in the world, in which case it is not clear in what sense it could be said to be ours, since this freedom glides over itself and is the equivalent of a fate—or else our choice of ourselves is a genuine choice, a conversion involving our whole existence. In this case, however, there is presupposed a previous acquisition which the choice sets out to modify and it founds a new tradition: this leads us to ask whether the perpetual severance in terms of which we initially defined freedom is not simply the negative aspect of our universal commitment to a world, and whether our indifference to each determinate thing does not express merely our involvement in all; whether the ready-made freedom from which we started is not reducible to a power of initiative which cannot be transformed into *doing* without taking up the world as posited in some shape or form, and whether, in short, concrete and actual freedom is not to be found in this exchange. It is true that nothing has *significance* and value for anyone

[5] J. P. Sartre, L'Être et le Néant, p. 562.

but *me* and through anyone but me, but this proposition remains indeterminate and is still indistinguishable from the Kantian idea of a consciousness which 'finds in things only what it has put into them', and from the idealist refutation of realism, as long as we fail to make clear how we understand significance and the self. By defining ourselves as a universal power of *Sinn-Gebung*, we have reverted to the method of the 'thing without which' and to the analytical reflection of the traditional type, which seeks the conditions of possibility without concerning itself with the conditions of reality. We must therefore resume the analysis of the *Sinngebung*, and show how it can be both centrifugal and centripetal, since it has been established that there is no freedom without a field.

When I say that this rock is unclimbable, it is certain that this attribute, like that of being big or little, straight and oblique, and indeed like all attributes in general, can be conferred upon it only by the project of climbing it, and by a human presence. It is, therefore, freedom which brings into being the obstacles to freedom, so that the latter can be set over against it as its bounds. However, it is clear that, one and the same project being given, one rock will appear as an obstacle, and another, being more negotiable, as a means. My freedom, then, does not so contrive it that this way there is an obstacle, and that way a way through, it arranges for there to be obstacles and ways through in general; it does not draw the particular outline of this world, but merely lays down its general structures. It may be objected that there is no difference; if my freedom conditions the structure of the 'there is', that of the 'here' and the 'there', it is present wherever these structures arise. We cannot distinguish the quality of 'obstacle' from the obstacle itself, and relate one to freedom and the other to the world in itself which, without freedom, would be merely an amorphous and unnameable mass. It is not, therefore, outside myself that I am able to find a limit to my freedom. But should I not find it in myself? We must indeed distinguish between my express intentions, for example the plan I now make to climb those mountains, and general intentions which evaluate the potentialities of my environment. Whether or not I have decided to climb them, these mountains appear high to me, because they exceed my body's power to take them in its stride, and even if I have just read *Micromégas*, I cannot so contrive it that they are small for me. Underlying myself as a thinking subject, who am able to take my place at will on Sirius or on the earth's surface, there is, therefore, as it were a natural self which does not budge from its terrestrial situation and which constantly adumbrates absolute valuations. What is more, my projects as a thinking being are clearly modelled on the latter; if I elect to see things from the point of view of Sirius, it is still to my terrestrial experience that I must have recourse in order to do so; I may say, for example, that the Alps are *molehills*. In so far as I have hands, feet, a body, I sustain around me intentions which are not dependent upon my decisions and which affect my surroundings in a way which I do not choose. These intentions are general in a double sense: firstly in the sense that they constitute a system in which all possible objects are simultaneously included; if the mountain appears high and upright, the tree appears small and sloping; and furthermore in the sense that they are not of my own making, they originate from outside me, and I am not surprised to find them in all psycho-physical subjects organized as I am.

. . .

The rationalist's dilemma—either the free act is possible, or it is not, either the event originates in me or is imposed on me from outside, does not apply to our relations with the world and with our past. Our freedom does not destroy our situation, but gears itself to it: as long as we are alive, our situation is open, which implies both that it calls up specially favoured modes of resolution, and also that it is powerless to bring one into being by itself.

We shall arrive at the same result by considering our relations with history. Taking myself in my absolute concreteness, as I am presented to myself in reflection, I find that I am an anonymous and prehuman flux, as yet unqualified as, for instance, 'a working man' or 'middle class'. If I subsequently think of myself as a man among men, a bourgeois among bourgeois, this can be, it would seem, no more than a second order view of myself; I am never in my heart of hearts a worker or a bourgeois, but a consciousness which freely evaluates itself as a middle class or proletarian consciousness. And indeed, it is never the case that my objective position in the production process is sufficient to awaken class consciousness. There was exploitation long before there were revolutionaries. Nor is it always in periods of economic difficulty that the working class movement makes headway. Revolt is, then, not the outcome of objective conditions, but it is rather the decision taken by the worker to will revolution that makes a proletarian of him. The evaluation of the present operates through one's free project for the future. From which we might conclude that history by itself has no significance, but only that conferred upon it by our will. Yet here again we are slipping into the method of 'the indispensable condition failing which . . .': in opposition to objective thought, which includes the subject in its deterministic system; we are setting idealist reflection which makes determinism dependent upon the constituting activity of the subject. Now, we have already seen that objective thought and analytical reflection are two aspects of the same mistake, two ways of overlooking the phenomena. Objective thought derives class-consciousness from the objective condition of the proletariat. Idealist reflection reduces the proletarian condition to the awareness of it, which the proletarian arrives at. The former traces class-consciousness to the class defined in terms of objective characteristics, the latter on the other hand reduces 'being a workman' to the consciousness of being one. In each case we are in the realm of abstraction, because we remain torn between the *in itself* and the *for itself*. If we approach the question afresh with the idea of discovering, not the causes of the act of becoming aware, for there is no cause which can act from outside upon a consciousness—nor the conditions of its possibility, for we need to know the conditions which actually produce it—but class-consciousness itself, if, in short, we apply a genuinely existential method, what do we find? I am not conscious of being working class or middle class simply because, as a matter of fact, I sell my labour or, equally as a matter of fact, because my interests are bound up with capitalism, nor do I become one or the other on the day on which I elect to view history in the light of the class struggle: what happens is that 'I exist as working class' or 'I exist as middle class' in the first place, and it is this mode of dealing with the world and society which provides both the motives for my revolutionary or conservative projects and my explicit judgements of the type: 'I am working class' or 'I am middle class', without its being possible to deduce the former from the latter, or *vice versa*. What makes me a proletarian is not the economic system or society considered as systems of impersonal forces, but these institutions as I carry them within me and experience them; nor is it an intellectual operation devoid of motive, but my way of being in the world within this institutional framework.

. . .

. . . class is a matter neither for observation nor decree; like the appointed order of the capitalistic system, like revolution, before being thought it is lived through as an obsessive presence, as possibility, enigma and myth. To make class-consciousness the outcome of a decision and a choice is to say that problems are solved on the day they are posed, that every question already contains the reply that it awaits; it is, in short, to revert to immanence and abandon the attempt to understand history. In reality, the intellectual project and the positing of ends are merely the bringing to completion of an existential project. It is I who give a direction, significance and future to my life, but that does not mean that these are concepts; they spring from my present and past and in particular from my mode of present and past co-existence. Even in the case of the intellectual who turns revolutionary, his decision does not arise *ex nihilo*; it may follow upon a prolonged period of solitude: the intellectual is in search of a doctrine which shall make great demands on him and cure him of his subjectivity; or he may yield to the clear light thrown by a Marxist interpretation of history, in which case he has given knowledge pride of place in his life, and that in itself is understandable only in virtue of his past and his childhood. Even the decision to become a revolutionary without motive, and by an act of pure freedom, would express a certain way of being in the natural and social world, which is typically that of the intellectual. He 'throws in his lot with the working class' from the starting point of his situation as an intellectual and from nowhere else (and this is why even fideism, in his case, remains rightly suspect). Now with the worker it is *a fortiori* the case that his decision is elaborated in the course of his life. This time it is through no misunderstanding that the horizon of a particular life and revolutionary aims coincide: for the worker revolution is a more immediate possibility. and one closer to his own interests than for the intellectual. since he is at grips with the economic system in his very life. For this reason there are, statistically, more workers than middle class people in a revolutionary party. Motivation, of course, does not do away with freedom. Working class parties of the most unmistakable kind have had many intellectuals among their leaders, and it is likely that a man such as Lenin identified himself with revolution and eventually transcended the distinction between intellectual and worker. But these are the virtues proper to action and commitment; at the outset, I am not an individual beyond class, I am situated in a social environment, and my freedom, though it may have the power to commit me elsewhere, has not the power to transform me instantaneously into what I decide to be. Thus to be a bourgeois or a worker is not only to be aware of being one or the other, it is to identify oneself as worker or bourgeois through an implicit or existential project which merges into our way of patterning the world and co-existing with other people. My decision draws together a spontaneous meaning of my life which it may confirm or repudiate, but not annul. Both idealism and objective thinking fail to pin down the coming into being of class-consciousness, the former because it deduces actual existence from consciousness, the latter because it derives consciousness from *de facto* existence, and both because they overlook the relationship of motivation.

• • •

What then is freedom? To be born is both to be born of the world and to be born into the world. The world is already constituted, but also never completely constituted; in the first case we are acted upon, in the second we are open to an infinite number of possibilities. But this analysis is still abstract, for we exist in both ways *at once*. There is, therefore, never determinism and never absolute choice, I am never a thing and never bare consciousness. In fact, even our own pieces of initiative, even the situations which we have chosen, bear us on, once they have been entered upon by virtue of a state rather than an act. The generality of the 'rôle' and of the situation comes to the aid of decision, and in this exchange between the situation and the person who takes it up, it is impossible to determine precisely the 'share contributed by the situation' and the 'share contributed by freedom'. Let us suppose that a man is tortured to make him talk. If he refuses to give the names and addresses which it is desired to extract from him, this does not arise from a solitary and unsupported decision: the man still feels himself to be with his comrades, and, being still involved in the common struggle, he is as it were incapable of talking. Or else, for months or years, he has, in his mind, faced this test and staked his whole life upon it. Or finally, he wants to prove, by coming through it, what he has always thought and said about freedom. These motives do not cancel out freedom, but at least ensure that it does not go unbuttressed in being. What withstands pain is not, in short, a bare consciousness, but the prisoner with his comrades or with those he loves and under whose gaze he lives; or else the awareness of his proudly willed solitude, which again is a certain mode of the *Mit-Sein*. And probably the individual in his prison daily reawakens these phantoms, which give back to him the strength he gave to them. But conversely, in so far as he has committed himself to this action, formed a bond with his comrades or adopted this morality, it is because the historical situation, the comrades, the world around him seemed to him to expect that conduct from him. The analysis could be pursued endlessly in this way. We choose our world and the world chooses us. What is certain, in any case, is that we can at no time set aside within ourselves a redoubt to which being does not find its way through, without seeing this freedom, immediately and by the very fact of being a living experience, take on the appearance of being and become a motive and a buttress. Taken concretely, freedom is always a meeting of the inner and the outer—even the prehuman and prehistoric freedom with which we began—and it shrinks without ever disappearing altogether in direct proportion to the lessening of the *tolerance* allowed by the bodily and institutional data of our lives. There is, as Husserl says, on the one hand a 'field of freedom' and on the other a 'conditioned freedom';[6] not that freedom is absolute within the limits of this field and non-existent outside it (like the perceptual field, this one has no traceable boundaries), but because I enjoy immediate and remote possibilities. Our commitments sustain our power and there is no freedom without some power. Our freedom, it is said, is either total or non-existent. This dilemma belongs to objective thought and its stable-companion. analytical reflection. If indeed we place ourselves within being, it must necessarily be the case that our actions must have their origin outside us, and if we revert to constituting consciousness, they must originate within. But we have learnt precisely to recognize the order of phenomena.

6 *Fink*, Vergegenwärtigung und Bild, *p. 285.*

We are involved in the world and with others in an inextricable tangle. The idea of situation rules out absolute freedom at the source of our commitments, and equally, indeed, at their terminus. No commitment, not even commitment in the Hegelian State, can make me leave behind all differences and free me for anything. This universality itself, from the mere fact of its being experienced, would stand out as a particularity against the world's background, for existence both generalizes and particularizes everything at which it aims, and cannot ever be finally complete.

The synthesis of *in itself* and *for itself* which brings Hegelian freedom into being has, however, its truth. In a sense, it is the very definition of existence, since it is effected at every moment before our eyes in the phenomenon of presence, only to be quickly re-enacted, since it does not conjure away our finitude. By taking up a present, I draw together and transform my past, altering its significance, freeing and detaching myself from it. But I do so only by committing myself somewhere else. Psychoanalytical treatment does not bring about its cure by producing direct awareness of the past, but in the first place by binding the subject to his doctor through new existential relationships. It is not a matter of giving scientific assent to the psychoanalytical interpretation, and discovering a notional significance for the past; it is a matter of reliving this or that as significant, and this the patient succeeds in doing only by seeing his past in the perspective of his co-existence with the doctor. The complex is not dissolved by a non-instrumental freedom, but rather displaced by a new pulsation of time with its own supports and motives. The same applies in all cases of coming to awareness: they are real only if they are sustained by a new commitment. Now this commitment too is entered into in the sphere of the implicit, and is therefore valid only for a certain temporal cycle. The choice which we make of our life is always based on a certain givenness. My freedom can draw life away from its spontaneous course, but only by a series of unobtrusive deflections which necessitate first of all following its course —not by any absolute creation. All explanations of my conduct in terms of my past. my temperament and my environment are therefore true, provided that they be regarded not as separable contributions, but as moments of my total being, the significance of which I am entitled to make explicit in various ways, without its ever being possible to say whether

I confer their meaning upon them or receive it from them. I am a psychological and historical structure, and have received, with existence, a manner of existing, a style. All my actions and thoughts stand in a relationship to this structure, and even a philosopher's thought is merely a way of making explicit his hold on the world, and what he is. The fact remains that I am free, not in spite of, or on the hither side of, these motivations, but by means of them. For this significant life, this certain significance of nature and history which I am, does not limit my access to the world, but on the contrary is my means of entering into communication with it. It is by being unrestrictedly and unreservedly what I am at present that I have a chance of moving forward; it is by living my time that I am able to understand other times, by plunging into the present and the world, by taking on deliberately what I am fortuitously, by willing what I will and doing what I do, that I can go further. I can pass freedom by, only if I try to get over my natural and social situation by refusing, in the first place, to take it up, instead of using it as a way into the natural and human world. Nothing determines me from outside, not because nothing acts upon me, but, on the contrary, because I am from the start outside myself and open to the world. We are *true* through and through, and have with us, by the mere fact of belonging to the world, and not merely being in the world in the way that things are, all that we need to transcend ourselves. We need have no fear that our choices or actions restrict our liberty, since choice and action alone cut us loose from our anchorage. Just as reflection borrows its wish for absolute sufficiency from the perception which causes a thing to appear, and as in this way idealism tacitly uses that 'primary opinion' which it would like to destroy as opinion, so freedom flounders in the contradictions of commitment, and fails to realize that, without the roots which it thrusts into the world, it would not be freedom at all. Shall I make this promise? Shall I risk my life for so little? Shall I give up my liberty in order to save liberty? There is no theoretical reply to these questions. But there are these *things* which stand, irrefutable, there is before you this person whom you love, there are these men whose existence around you is that of slaves, and *your* freedom cannot be willed without leaving behind its singular relevance, and without willing freedom *for all*. Whether it is a question of things or of historical situations, philosophy has no function

other than to teach us once more to see them clearly, and
it is true to say that it comes into being by destroying itself
as separate philosophy. But what is here required is silence,
for only the hero lives out his relation to men and the world.
'Your son is caught in the fire; you are the one who will save
him. . . . If there is an obstacle, you would be ready to give
your shoulder provided only that you can charge down that
obstacle. Your abode is your act itself. Your act is you. . . .
You give yourself in exchange. . . . Your significance shows
itself, effulgent. It is your duty, your hatred, your love, your
steadfastness, your ingenuity. . . . Man is but a network of
relationships, and these alone matter to him.'[7]

from
HUMANISM AND TERROR

Communism is often discussed in terms of the contrast between
deception, cunning, violence, propaganda, and the respect for
truth, law, and individual consciousness—in short, the opposition between political realism and liberal values. Communists reply that in democracies cunning, violence, propaganda,
and *realpolitik* in the guise of liberal principles are the substance of foreign or colonial politics and even of domestic
politics. Respect for law and liberty has served to justify police
suppression of strikes in America; today[1] it serves even to
justify military suppression in Indochina or in Palestine and
the development of an American empire in the Middle East.
The material and moral culture of England presupposes the
exploitation of the colonies. The purity of principles not only
tolerates but even requires violence. Thus there is a mystification in liberalism. Judging from history and by everyday
events, liberal ideas belong to a system of violence of which,

[7] *A. de Saint-Exupéry*, Pilote de Guerre, *pp. 171 and 174.*

From *Humanism and Terror* by Maurice Merleau-Ponty. English translation
Copyright © 1969 by Beacon Press; first published in French as *Humanisme
et Terreur, Essai sur le Problème Communiste* 1947, Editions Gallimard.
Reprinted by permission of Beacon Press.
[1] *1947.*

as Marx said, they are the "spiritual *point d'honneur*," the "solemn complement" and the "general basis of consolation and justification."[2]

It is a powerful argument. In refusing to judge liberalism in terms of the ideas it espouses and inscribes in constitutions and in demanding that these ideas be compared with the prevailing relations between men in a liberal state, Marx is not simply speaking in the name of a debatable materialist philosophy—he is providing a formula for the concrete study of society which cannot be refuted by idealist arguments. Whatever one's philosophical or even theological position, a society is not the temple of value-idols that figure on the front of its monuments or in its constitutional scrolls; the value of a society is the value it places upon man's relation to man. It is not just a question of knowing what the liberals have in mind but what in reality is done by the liberal state within and beyond its frontiers. Where it is clear that the purity of principles is not put into practice, it merits condemnation rather than absolution. To understand and judge a society, one has to penetrate its basic structure to the human bond upon which it is built; this undoubtedly depends upon legal relations, but also upon forms of labor, ways of loving, living, and dying. The theologian will observe that human relations have a religious significance and are under God's eye. But he will not refuse to adopt them as a touchstone and, on pain of degrading religion to a daydream, he is ultimately obliged to admit that principles and the inner life are alibis the moment they cease to animate external and everyday life. A regime which is nominally liberal can be oppressive in reality. A regime which acknowledges its violence *might* have in it more genuine humanity. To counter Marxism on this with "ethical arguments" is to ignore what Marxism has said with most truth and what has made its fortune in the world; it is to continue a mystification and to bypass the problem. Any serious discussion of communism must therefore pose the problem in Communist terms, that is to say, not on the ground of principles but on the ground of human relations. It will not

---

[2] Contribution to the Critique of Hegel's Philosophy of Right. *Introduction, Karl Marx*, Early Writings, *translated and edited by T. B. Bottomore, New York, McGraw-Hill Book Co., 1964.*

brandish liberal principles in order to topple communism; it will examine whether it is doing anything to resolve the problem rightly raised by communism, namely, to establish among men relations that are human.

. . .

Only then does the discussion begin. It does not consist in looking to see if communism respects the rules of liberal thought—it is too evident that it does not—but in asking whether the violence it exercises is revolutionary and capable of creating human relations between men. The Marxist critique of liberal ideas is so powerful that if communism were on the way to create by world revolution a classless society in which the causes of war and decadence had disappeared, along with the exploitation of man by man, then one would have to be a Communist. But is it on this path? Does the violence in today's communism have the same sense it had in Lenin's day? Is communism still equal to its humanist intentions? That is the real question.

Its intentions are beyond question. Marx draws a radical distinction between human and animal life inasmuch as man creates his means of life, culture, history, and thus evinces a capacity for initiative which is his absolute originality. Marxism looks toward the horizon of the future in which "man is the supreme being for man." The reason Marx does not adopt this intuition of man as the first principle of political action is that in advocating nonviolence one reinforces established violence, or a system of production which makes misery and war inevitable. At the same time, in the return to the play of violence there is the risk of permanent involvement. Thus the essential task of Marxism is to find a violence which recedes with the approach of man's future. This is what Marx believed he had found in proletarian violence, namely, the power of that class of men who, because they are expropriated in present society from their country, their labor, and their very life, are capable of recognizing one another aside from all differences, and thus of founding humanity. Cunning, deception, bloodshed, and dictatorship are justified if they bring the proletariat into power and to that extent alone.

Marxist politics is formally dictatorial and totalitarian. But it is a dictatorship of men who are men first and foremost and a totalitarianism of workers of all kinds who repossess the State and the means of production. The dictatorship of the proletariat is not the will of a few officials who are the only ones initiated in the secret of history, as in Hegel; it follows the spontaneous movement of the proletariat in every country and relies upon the "instinct" of the masses. Lenin may well have insisted upon the authority of the Party to guide the proletariat, who would otherwise, as he says, remain syndicalist and not move on to political action. He nevertheless grants much to the instinct of the masses, at least once the capitalist machine has been smashed, and at the beginning of the Revolution he even goes so far as to say: "There is not nor can there be a concrete plan for the organization of economic life. No one knows how to issue it. Only the masses are capable of that, thanks to their experience . . ." Since he subscribes to class action, the Leninist abandons universal ethics; but he will have it restored in the new universe of the world proletariat. Not just any means is good for the realization of this universe and, for example, there can be no question of systematically deceiving the proletariat and hiding the real issue for very long; in principle that is out because it would diminish class consciousness and compromise the victory of the proletariat. The proletariat and class consciousness are fundamental to the character of Marxist politics; they can to some extent be put in the background if circumstances demand it, but too long or too extensive a shift of this kind would destroy its character. Marx is hostile to the liberal posture of nonviolence, but the violence which he prescribes is not indiscriminate.

Can we say the same of today's communism? In the last ten years in the U.S.S.R. the social hierarchy has become considerably accentuated. The proletariat plays an insignificant role in the Party Congresses. Perhaps political discussion goes on in the cells but it never appears publicly. National Communist parties struggle for power without a proletarian platform and without always avoiding chauvinism. Political differences which previously did not involve the death penalty are not only punished as crimes but are even dressed up as crimes against common law. Terror no longer seeks to advance itself as revolutionary Terror. In the cultural order the dialectic is effectively replaced by the scientific rationalism of the last generation apparently because the dialectic leaves too great a margin for ambiguity and too much scope for divergences. There is an increasing difference between what Communists think and what they write because there is a widening gap between their intentions and their deeds. A

Communist who declared himself warmly in agreement with us, having read the first part of this essay, three days later wrote that it is an example of what might be called a solitary vice of the mind, and that we were playing the game of French neo-Fascism. If one tries to evaluate the general orientation of the Communist system, it would be difficult to maintain that it is moving toward the recognition of man by man, internationalism, or the withering away of the State and the realization of proletarian power. Communist behavior has not changed: it is still the same attitude of conflict, the same warlike cunning, the same methodical wickedness, the same distrust, but underwritten less and less by class spirit and revolutionary brotherhood, relying less and less upon the spontaneous convergence of proletarian movements and the truth of its own historical perspective; communism is increasingly strained, more and more it shows its dark side. There is still the same absolute devotion, the same fidelity, and when the need arises, the same heroism. But this selfless gift, these virtues which appeared in all their purity during the war and have since been the unforgettable grandeur of communism are less visible in peacetime because the defense of the U.S.S.R. now demands a cunning politics. All the facts, varying in significance from the scale of salaries in the U.S.S.R. to the double truth of a Parisian journalist, are signs of a growing tension between intentions and action, between behavior and the thought behind it. The Communist has launched the conscience and values of private man in a public undertaking which should return them a hundredfold. He is still waiting for the returns.

Thus we find ourselves in an inextricable situation. The Marxist critique of capitalism is still valid and it is clear that anti-Sovietism today resembles the brutality, hybris, vertigo, and anguish that already found expression in fascism. On the other side, the Revolution has come to a halt: it maintains and aggravates the dictatorial apparatus while renouncing the revolutionary liberty of the proletariat in the Soviets and its Party and abandoning the humane control of the State. It is impossible to be an anti-Communist and it is not possible to be a Communist.

From the Proletarian to the Commissar

The foundations of Marxist politics are to be found *simultaneously* in the inductive analysis of the economic process and in a certain intuition of man and the relations between men. "To be radical," says Marx in a well-known passage, "is to grasp things by the root. But for man the root is man himself."[3] Marx's innovation does not lie in the reduction of philosophical and human problems to problems of economics but in drawing from economics the real equivalents of these questions. It has been remarked without paradox that *Capital* is a concrete *Phenomenology of Mind*, that is to say, that it is inseparably concerned with the working of the economy and the realization of man. The point of connection between these two problem areas lies in the Hegelian idea that every system of production and property implies a system of relations between men such that their social relations become imprinted upon their relations to nature, and these in turn imprint upon *their* social relations. There can be no definitive understanding of the whole import of Marxist politics without going back to Hegel's description of the fundamental relations between men.

"Each self-consciousness aims at the destruction and death of the other," says Hegel.[4] Inasmuch as self-consciousness gives meaning and value to every object that we can grasp, it is by nature in a state of vertigo and it is a permanent temptation for it to assert itself at the expense of other consciousnesses who dispute its privilege. But consciousness can do nothing without its body and can only act upon others by acting on their bodies. It can only reduce them to slavery by making nature an appendix of its body, by appropriating nature to itself and establishing in nature its instruments of power. Thus history is essentially a struggle—the struggle of the master and the slave, the struggle between classes—and this is a necessity of the human condition; because of the fundamental paradox that man is an indivisible consciousness no one is able to affirm himself except by reducing the others to objects.

---

[3] Contribution to the Critique of Hegel's Philosophy of Right.
[4] The Phenomenology of Mind, p. 232. (Translator.)

What accounts for there being a human history is that man is a being who externalizes himself, who needs others and nature to fulfill himself, who individualizes himself by appropriating certain goods and thereby enters into conflict with other men. Man's self-oppression may appear unmasked, as in despotism, where the absolute subjectivity of one individual transforms all others into objects; it may be disguised in the dictatorship of objective truth, as in those regimes which imprison, burn, and hang their citizens for their salvation (though the disguise is useless since an imposed truth is only the truth of a few, i.e., the instrument of their power); finally, violence, as in the liberal state, may be put outside the law and, in effect, suppressed in the commerce of ideas though maintained in daily life in the form of colonization, unemployment, and wages. In every case we are only dealing with different modalities of the same fundamental situation. What Marxism undertakes is a radical solution to the problem of human coexistence beyond the oppression of absolute subjectivity and absolute objectivity, and beyond the pseudo-solution of liberalism.

To the extent that it gives a pessimistic picture of our starting point—conflict and struggle to the death—Marxism will always contain an element of violence and Terror. If it is true that history is a struggle, if rationalism is itself a class ideology, there is no possibility of reconciling men very soon through an appeal to what Kant called a "good will," or a universal ethic free from conflict. "We must be able to stand up to all this, agree to make any sacrifice, and even—if need be—to resort to various stratagems, artifices and illegal methods, to evasions and subterfuges, as long as we get into the trade unions, remain in them and carry on communist work within them at all costs."[5] And Trotsky has the following comment: "The life and death struggle is unthinkable without military craftiness, in other words, without lying and deceit."[6]

To tell the truth and to act out of conscience are nothing but alibis of a false morality; true morality is not concerned with what we think or what we want but obliges us to take an historical view of ourselves. Thus the Communist dis-

[5] V. I. Lenin, Left-Wing Communism—An Infantile Disorder, Collected Works, Vol. 31, p. 55.

[6] "Their Morals and Ours," The Basic Writings of Trotsky. Edited and introduced by Irving Howe, New York, Random House, 1963, p. 394.

turbs conscience: in himself and in others. Consciousness is not a good judge of what we are *doing* since we are involved in the struggle of history and in this we achieve more, less, or something else than we thought we were doing. As a rule, the Communist does not allow himself to trust others at their word or to treat them as free and rational subjects. How could he, since they are exposed as he himself is to mystification? He wants to uncover what they are behind what they think and say deliberately, the role they are playing, perhaps unwittingly, in the clash of forces and the class struggle. He has to learn to recognize the play of opposing forces, and those writers, even the reactionary ones, who have described it are more precious for communism than those, however progressive, who have masked it with liberal illusions. Machiavelli is worth more than Kant. Engels said that Machiavelli was "the first writer of modern times worth mention." Marx said of the *History of Florence* that it was a "master-piece." He considered Machiavelli, with Spinoza, Rousseau, and Hegel, in the company of those who had discovered the working laws of the State.[7] As social life in general affects each individual beyond his deliberate thoughts and decisions down to the very manner of his being in the world, the Revolution in the Marxist sense is not exhausted by the legislative actions it takes; it takes a long time for it to extend from its economic and legal infrastructures into the lived relations of men—a long time therefore before it can really be indisputable and guaranteed against harmful reversals to the old world. During this transitional period the application of the philosophical rule that "man is the supreme being for man" (Marx) would be a reversion to utopia and would in reality achieve the opposite of what we intended.

If it is true that the State as we know it is the instrument of a class, we may assume that it "will wither away" with the disappearance of classes. But Lenin carefully points out that "it has never entered the head of any socialist to 'promise' that the higher phase of the development of Communism will arrive."[8] This means that Marxism, rather than an affirmation of a future that is necessary, is much more a judgment of the present as contradictory and intolerable. It operates in the tangle of the present and with the means of action offered by

[7] Kolnische Zeitung, *No. 179.*
[8] V. I. Lenin. *"The State and Revolution."* loc. cit. Vol. 25. p. 469.

the present. The proletariat cannot destroy the machinery of bourgeois oppression without first seizing it and turning it against the bourgeoisie. The result is that Communist action disavows at the outset the formal rules of the bourgeoisie. "So long as the proletariat still uses the state," says Engels, "it does not use it in the interests of freedom but in order to hold down its adversaries, and as soon as it becomes possible to speak of freedom the state as such does not exist."[9] And Lenin remarks: "It is clear that there is no freedom and no democracy where there is suppression and where there is violence."[10]

• • •

To such questions the immediate response of Marxism is: it is either that or nothing. Either one wants to do something, but it is on condition of using violence—or else one respects formal liberty and renounces violence, but one can only do this by renouncing socialism and the classless society, in other words by consolidating the rule of "Quaker hypocrisy." The Revolution takes on and directs a violence which bourgeois society tolerates in unemployment and in war and disguises with the name of misfortune. But successful revolutions taken altogether have not spilled as much blood as the empires. All we know is different kinds of violence and we ought to prefer revolutionary violence because it has a future of humanism.

All the same, what does the future of the Revolution matter if its present remains under the law of violence? Even if in the end it produces a society without violence, in respect of those whom it crushes today, each of whom is a world to himself, it is absolutely evil. Even if those who will inhabit the future can one day talk of success, those who live at present and are unable to make the transition have only a failure to record. Revolutionary violence does not make itself distinct *for us* from other kinds of violence and social life only involves failures.

The argument and its conclusion would be valid if history were the simple encounter and discreet succession of absolutely autonomous individuals, without roots, without posterity, without any interaction. In this case, the good of some could

[9] *Engels to Bebel, 18-28 March, 1875, in Karl Marx and Friedrich Engels,* Correspondence, *1846-1895. Translated by Dona Torr, London, Lawrence and Wishart Ltd., 1936.*
[10] V. I. Lenin. *"The State and Revolution."* loc. cit. *p. 462.*

not redeem the evil to others and where each conscience is a totality unto itself, the violence done to a single conscience would suffice, as Péguy thought, to damn the society that caused it. There would be no sense in preferring a regime which employed violence for humanist aims since from the viewpoint of the conscience which suffers it, violence is absolutely unacceptable, being the negation of conscience; and in such a philosophy there can be no other standpoint than that of self-consciousness, the world and history being only the sum of such viewpoints. But these are precisely the axioms that Marxism, following Hegel, questions by introducing the perspective of one consciousness upon another. What we find in the private life of a couple, or in a society of friends, or, with all the more reason, in history, is not a series of juxtaposed "self-consciousnesses."

I never encounter face to face another person's consciousness any more than he meets mine. I am not for him and nor is he for me a pure existence for itself. We are both for one another situated beings, characterized by a certain type of relation to men and the world, by a certain activity, a certain way of treating other people and nature. Of course, a pure consciousness would be in such a state of *original innocence* that any harm done to him would be irreparable. But to start with a pure consciousness is beyond my grasp; even if I tortured his body I could not do him any violence. In such a case the problem of violence does not arise. It only arises with respect to a consciousness originally committed in the world, that is to say, with violence, and thus can only be solved beyond utopia. We only know of situated consciousnesses which blend themselves with the situation they take and are unable to complain at being identified with it or at the neglect of the incorruptible innocence of conscience. When one says that there is a history one means precisely that each person committing an act does so not only in his own name, engages not only himself, but also others whom he makes use of, so that as soon as we begin to live, we lose the alibi of good intentions; we are what we do to others, we yield the right to be respected as noble souls. To respect one who does not respect others is ultimately to despise them; to abstain from violence toward the violent is to become their accomplice.

We do not have a choice between purity and violence but between different kinds of violence. Inasmuch as we are incarnate beings, violence is our lot. There is no persuasion even without seduction, or in the last analysis, contempt. Violence is the common origin of all regimes. Life, discussion, and political choice occur only against a background of violence. What matters and what we have to discuss is not violence but its sense or its future. It is a law of human action that the present encroaches upon the future, the self upon other people. This intrusion is not only a fact of political life, it also happens in private life. Just as in love, in affection, or in friendship we do not encounter face to face "consciousnesses" whose absolute individuality we could respect at every moment, but beings qualified as "my son," "my wife," "my friend" whom we carry along with us into common projects where they receive (like ourselves) a definite role, with specific rights and duties, so in collective history the spiritual atoms train after them their historical role and are tied to one another by the threads of their actions; what is more, they are blended with the totality of actions, whether or not deliberate, which they exert upon others and the world so that there exists not a plurality of subjects, but an intersubjectivity, and that is why there exists a common measure of the evil inflicted upon certain people and of the good gotten out of it by others.

He who condemns all violence puts himself outside the domain to which justice and injustice belong. He puts a curse upon the world and humanity—a hypocritical curse, since he who utters it has already accepted the rules of the game from the moment that he has begun to live. Between men considered as pure consciousnesses there would indeed be no reason to choose. But between men considered as the incumbents of situations which together compose a single *common situation* it is inevitable that one has to choose—it is allowable to sacrifice those who according to the logic of their situation are a threat and to promote those who offer a promise of humanity. This is what Marxism does when it creates its politics on the basis of an analysis of the situation of the proletariat.

Political problems come from the fact that we are all subjects and yet we look upon other people and treat them as objects. Coexistence among men seems therefore doomed to failure. For either some men exercise their absolute right as subjects in which case the others submit to their will and are not recognized as subjects. Or else the whole social body is devoted to some providential destiny, some philosophical mission, but then this case reverts to the first; objective politics becomes subjective politics since it is really necessary that only a few be the incumbents of this destiny or mission. Or finally it is agreed that all men have the same rights and that there is no truth in the State. But this equality of principle remains nominal; at decisive moments the government continues to be violent and the majority of men remain objects of history. Marxism seeks to destroy the alternative of subjective or objective politics by submitting history neither to the arbitrary will of certain men nor to the exigencies of an ungraspable World Spirit, but to the exigencies of a certain condition considered human by all men, namely, the condition of the proletariat.

. . .

Simone de Beauvoir

(b. 1908)   ━━━━━◆━━━━━   FRENCH

Simone de Beauvoir shares with Merleau-Ponty the disadvantage of frequently being viewed in the shadow of Sartre, in her case often with doubly barbed comments that she is Sartre's "companion" or "disciple." De Beauvoir has long been one of France's foremost novelists, and far from reiterating Sartre's views, she has provided us with an "existential ethics" which Sartre himself has never given us. In her Ethics of Ambiguity *freedom is again the central concept, but in an explicitly ethical role. Freedom and morality are paired, as they are not in Sartre ("To will freedom and to will to be moral are one and the same"). A free action is also a universalizable action, an action which essentially takes account of social values and institutions as well as personal interests and consequences.*

In The Second Sex *de Beauvoir has applied the concepts of freedom and universality to a concrete though universal ethical problem in what must count as one of the most insightful socio-philosophical treatises of the century. The problem is woman; What is a woman? What is it for a woman to be a woman as well as a human being? What is it for a woman to be a woman as opposed to a human being? In de Beauvoir's analysis the apparatus of existential philosophy is used to destroy both the views that a woman is a woman (has an essence which defines her actions, feelings, and roles) and the equally deceptive doctrine that a woman is only a human being, without distinctive features that distinguish her from men. The following selections are from* The Ethics of Ambiguity *and* The Second Sex, *respectively.*

from
THE ETHICS OF AMBIGUITY

As for us, whatever the case may be, we believe in freedom. Is it true that this belief must lead us to despair? Must we grant this curious paradox: that from the moment a man recognizes himself as free, he is prohibited from wishing for anything?

On the contrary, it appears to us that by turning toward this freedom we are going to discover a principle of action whose range will be universal. The characteristic feature of all ethics is to consider human life as a game that can be won or lost and to teach man the means of winning. Now, we have seen that the original scheme of man is ambiguous: he wants to be, and to the extent that he coincides with this wish, he fails. All the plans in which this will to be is actualized are condemned; and the ends circumscribed by these plans remain mirages. Human transcendence is vainly engulfed in those miscarried attempts. But man also wills himself to be a disclosure of being, and if he coincides with this wish, he wins, for the fact is that the world becomes present by his presence in it. But the disclosure implies a perceptual tension to keep being at a certain distance, to tear oneself from the world, and to assert oneself as a freedom. To wish for the disclosure of the world and to assert oneself as freedom are one and the same movement. Freedom is the source from which all significations and all values spring. It is the original condition of all justification of existence. The man who seeks to justify his life must want freedom itself absolutely and above everything else. At the same time that it requires the realization of concrete ends, of particular projects, it requires itself universally. It is not a ready-made value which offers itself from the outside to my abstract adherence, but it appears (not on the plane of facility, but on the moral plane) as a cause of itself. It is necessarily summoned up by the values which it sets up and through which it sets itself up. It can not establish a denial of itself, for in denying itself, it would deny the possibility of any foundation. To will oneself moral and to will oneself free are one and the same decision.

. . .

From *The Ethics of Ambiguity* by Simone de Beauvoir. Copyright © 1949 by The Philosophical Library, Inc. Reprinted by permission of The Philosophical Library.

Every man is originally free, in the sense that he spontaneously casts himself into the world. But if we consider this spontaneity in its facticity, it appears to us only as a pure contingency, an upsurging as stupid as the clinamen of the Epicurean atom which turned up at any moment whatsoever from any direction whatsoever. And it was quite necessary for the atom to arrive somewhere. But its movement was not justified by this result which had not been chosen. It remained absurd. Thus, human spontaneity always projects itself toward something. The psychoanalyst discovers a meaning even in abortive acts and attacks of hysteria. But in order for this meaning to justify the transcendence which discloses it, it must itself be founded, which it will never be if I do not choose to found it myself. Now, I can evade this choice. We have said that it would be contradictory deliberately to will oneself not free. But one can choose not to will himself free. In laziness, heedlessness, capriciousness, cowardice, impatience, one contests the meaning of the project at the very moment that one defines it. The spontaneity of the subject is then merely a vain living palpitation, its movement toward the object is a flight, and itself is an absence. To convert the absence into presence, to convert my flight into will, I must assume my project positively. It is not a matter of retiring into the completely inner and, moreover, abstract movement of a given spontaneity, but of adhering to the concrete and particular movement by which this spontaneity defines itself by thrusting itself toward an end. It is through this end that it sets up that my spontaneity confirms itself by reflecting upon itself. Then, by a single movement, my will, establishing the content of the act, is legitimized by it. I realize my escape toward the other as a freedom when, assuming the presence of the object, I thereby assume myself before it as a presence. But this justification requires a constant tension. My project is never founded; it founds itself. To avoid the anguish of this permanent choice, one may attempt to flee into the object itself, to engulf one's own presence in it. In the servitude of the serious, the original spontaneity strives to deny itself. It strives in vain, and meanwhile it then fails to fulfill itself as moral freedom.

· · ·

However, man does not create the world. He succeeds in disclosing it only through the resistance which the world opposes to him. The will is defined only by raising obstacles, and by the contingency of facticity certain obstacles let themselves be conquered, and others do not. This is what Descartes expressed when he said that the freedom of man is infinite, but his power is limited. How can the presence of these limits be reconciled with the idea of a freedom confirming itself as a unity and an indefinite movement?

In the face of an obstacle which it is impossible to overcome, stubbornness is stupid. If I persist in beating my fist against a stone wall, my freedom exhausts itself in this useless gesture without succeeding in giving itself a content. It debases itself in a vain contingency. Yet, there is hardly a sadder virtue than resignation. It transforms into phantoms and contingent reveries projects which had at the beginning been set up as will and freedom. A young man has hoped for a happy or useful or glorious life. If the man he has become looks upon these miscarried attempts of his adolescence with disillusioned indifference, there they are, forever frozen in the dead past. When an effort fails, one declares bitterly that he has lost time and wasted his powers. The failure condemns that whole part of ourselves which we had engaged in the effort. It was to escape this dilemma that the Stoics preached indifference. We could indeed assert our freedom against all constraint if we agreed to renounce the particularity of our projects. If a door refuses to open, let us accept not opening it and there we are free. But by doing that, one manages only to save an abstract notion of freedom. It is emptied of all content and all truth. The power of man ceases to be limited because it is annulled. It is the particularity of the project which determines the limitation of the power, but it is also what gives the project its content and permits it to be set up. There are people who are filled with such horror at the idea of a defeat that they keep themselves from ever doing anything. But no one would dream of considering this gloomy passivity as the triumph of freedom.

The truth is that in order for my freedom not to risk coming to grief against the obstacle which its very engagement has raised, in order that it might still pursue its movement in the face of the failure, it must, by giving itself a particular content, aim by means of it at an end which is nothing else but precisely the free movement of existence. Popular opinion is quite right in admiring a man who, having been ruined or having suffered an accident, knows how to gain the upper hand, that is, renew his engagement in the world, thereby strongly asserting the independence of freedom in relation to thing. Thus, when the sick Van Gogh calmly accepted the prospect of a future in which he would be unable to paint any more, there was no sterile resignation. For him painting was a personal way of life and of communication with others which in another form could be continued even in an asylum. The past will be integrated and freedom will be confirmed in a renunciation of this kind. It will be lived in both heartbreak and joy. In heartbreak, because the project is then robbed of its particularity—it sacrifices its flesh and blood. But in joy, since at the moment one releases his hold, he again finds his hands free and ready to stretch out toward a new future. But this act of passing beyond is conceivable only if what the content has in view is not to bar up the future, but, on the contrary, to plan new possibilities. This brings us back by another route to what we had already indicated. My freedom must not seek to trap being but to disclose it. The disclosure is the transition from being to existence. The goal which my freedom aims at is conquering existence across the always inadequate density of being.

. . .

. . . not only do we assert that the existentialist doctrine permits the elaboration of an ethics, but it even appears to us as the only philosophy in which an ethics has its place. For, in a metaphysics of transcendence, in the classical sense of the term, evil is reduced to error; and in humanistic philosophies it is impossible to account for it, man being defined as complete in a complete world. Existentialism alone gives—like religions—a real role to evil, and it is this, perhaps, which makes its judgments so gloomy. Men do not like to feel themselves in danger. Yet, it is because there are real dangers, real failures and real earthly damnation that words like victory, wisdom, or joy have meaning. Nothing is decided in advance, and it is because man has something to lose and because he can lose that he can also win.

from
THE SECOND SEX

For a long time I have hesitated to write a book on woman. The subject is irritating, especially to women; and it is not new. Enough ink has been spilled in the quarreling over feminism, now practically over, and perhaps we should say no more about it. It is still talked about, however, for the voluminous nonsense uttered during the last century seems to have done little to illuminate the problem. After all, is there a problem? And if so, what is it? Are there women, really? Most assuredly the theory of the eternal feminine still has its adherents who will whisper in your ear: "Even in Russia women still are *women*"; and other erudite persons—sometimes the very same—say with a sigh: "Woman is losing her way, woman is lost." One wonders if women still exist, if they will always exist, whether or not it is desirable that they should, what place they occupy in this world, what their place should be. "What has become of women?" was asked recently in an ephemeral magazine.

But first we must ask: what is a woman? "*Tota mulier in utero*," says one, "woman is a womb." But in speaking of certain women, connoisseurs declare that they are not women, although they are equipped with a uterus like the rest. All agree in recognizing the fact that females exist in the human species; today as always they make up about one half of humanity. And yet we are told that femininity is in danger; we are exhorted to be women, remain women, become women. It would appear, then, that every female human being is not necessarily a woman; to be so considered she must share in that mysterious and threatened reality known as femininity. Is this attribute something secreted by the ovaries? Or is it a Platonic essence, a product of the philosophic imagination? Is a rustling petticoat enough to bring it down to earth? Although some women try zealously to incarnate this essence, it is hardly patentable. It is frequently described in vague and dazzling terms that seem to have been borrowed from the vocabulary of the seers, and indeed in the times of St. Thomas

From *The Second Sex* by Simone de Beauvoir, translated by H. M. Parshley. Copyright 1952 by Alfred A. Knopf, Inc. Reprinted by permission of Alfred A. Knopf, Inc.

it was considered an essence as certainly defined as the somnif-
erous virtue of the poppy.

But conceptualism has lost ground. The biological and
social sciences no longer admit the existence of unchangeably
fixed entities that determine given characteristics, such as
those ascribed to woman, the Jew, or the Negro. Science
regards any characteristic as a reaction dependent in part
upon a *situation*. If today femininity no longer exists, then it
never existed. But does the word *woman*, then, have no
specific content? This is stoutly affirmed by those who hold
to the philosophy of the enlightenment, or rationalism, of
nominalism; women, to them, are merely the human beings
arbitrarily designated by the word *woman*. Many American
women particularly are prepared to think that there is no
longer any place for woman as such; if a backward individual
still takes herself for a woman, her friends advise her to be
psychoanalyzed and thus get rid of this obsession. In regard to a work, *Modern Woman: The Lost Sex*, which in
other respects has its irritating features, Dorothy Parker has
written: "I cannot be just to books which treat of woman as
woman. . . . My idea is that all of us, men as well as women,
should be regarded as human beings." But nominalism is
a rather inadequate doctrine, and the antifemininists have
had no trouble in showing that women simply *are not* men.
Surely woman is, like man, a human being, but such a declaration is abstract. The fact is that every concrete human being is always a singular, separate individual. To decline to
accept such notions as the eternal feminine, the black soul, the
Jewish character, is not to deny that Jews, Negroes, women
exist today—this denial does not represent a liberation for
those concerned, but rather a flight from reality. Some years
ago, a well-known woman writer refused to permit her por-
trait to appear in a series of photographs especially devoted
to women writers; she wished to be counted among the men.
But in order to gain this privilege she made use of her husband's influence! Women who assert that they are men lay
claim none the less to masculine consideration and respect.
I recall also a young Trotskyite standing on a platform at a
boisterous meeting and getting ready to use her fists, in spite
of her evident fragility. She was denying her feminine weakness; but it was for love of a militant male whose equal
she wished to be. The attitude of defiance of many Amer
ican women proves that they are haunted by a sense of thei

femininity. In truth, to go for a walk with one's eyes open is enough to demonstrate that humanity is divided into two classes of individuals whose clothes, faces, bodies, smiles, gaits, interests, and occupations are manifestly different. Perhaps these differences are superficial, perhaps they are destined to disappear. What is certain is that right now they do most obviously exist.

If her functioning as a female is not enough to define woman, if we decline also to explain her through "the eternal feminine," and if nevertheless we admit, provisionally, that women do exist, then we must face that question: what is a woman?

To state the question is, to me, to suggest, at once, a preliminary answer. The fact that I ask it is in itself significant. A man would never get the notion of writing a book on the peculiar situation of the human male. But if I wish to define myself, I must first of all say: "I am a woman"; on this truth must be based all further discussion. A man never begins by presenting himself as an individual of a certain sex; it goes without saying that he is a man. The terms *masculine* and *feminine* are used symmetrically only as a matter of form, as on legal papers. In actuality the relation of the two sexes is not quite like that of two electrical poles, for man represents both' tne positive and the neutral, as is indicated by the common use of *man* to designate human beings in general: whereas woman represents only the negative, defined by limiting criteria, without reciprocity. In the midst of an abstract discussion it is vexing to hear a man say: "You think thus and so because you are a woman"; but I know that my only defense is to reply: "I think thus and so because it is true," thereby removing my subjective self from the argument. It would be out of the question to reply: "And you think the contrary because you are a man," for it is understood that the fact of being a man is no peculiarity. A man is in the right in being a man; it is the woman who is in the wrong. It amounts to this: just as for the ancients there was an absolute vertical with reference to which the oblique was defined, so there is an absolute human type, the masculine. Women has ovaries, a uterus, these peculiarities imprison her in her subjectivity, circumscribe her within the limits of her own nature. It is often said that she thinks with her glands: Man superbly ignores the fact that his anatomy also includes glands, such as the testicles, and that they secrete hormones. He thinks of his body as a direct and normal connection with the world, which he believes he apprehends objectively, whereas he regards the body of woman as a hindrance, a prison, weighed down by everything peculiar to it. "The female is a female by virtue of a certain *lack* of qualities," said Aristotle: "we should regard the female nature as afflicted with a natural defectiveness." And St. Thomas for his part pronounced woman to be an "imperfect man," an "incidental" being. This is symbolized in Genesis where Eve is depicted as made from what Bossuet called "a supernumerary bone" of Adam.

Thus humanity is male and man defines woman not in herself but as relative to him; she is not regarded as an autonomous being. Michelet writes: "Woman, the relative being. . . ." And Benda is most positive in his *Rapport d'Uriel*: "The body of man makes sense in itself quite apart from that of woman, whereas the latter seems wanting in significance by itself. . . . Man can think of himself without woman. She cannot think of herself without man." And she is simply what man decrees; thus she is called "the sex," by which is meant that she appears essentially to the male as a sexual being. For him she is sex—absolute sex, no less. She is defined and differentiated with reference to man and not he with reference to her; she is the incidental, the inessential as opposed to the essental. He is the Subject, he is the Absolute—she is the Other.

The category of the *Other* is as primordial as consciousness itself. In the most primitive societies, in the most ancient mythologies, one finds the expression of a duality—that of the Self and the Other. This duality was not originally attached to the division of the sexes; it was not dependent upon any empirical facts. It is revealed in such works as that of Granet on Chinese thought and those of Dumézil on the East Indies and Rome. The feminine element was at first no more involved in such pairs as Varuna-Mitra, Uranus-Zeus, Sun-Moon, and Day-Night than it was in the contrasts between Good and Evil, lucky and unlucky auspices, right and left, God and Lucifer. Otherness is a fundamental category of human thought.

Thus it is that no group ever sets itself up as the One without at once setting up the Other over against itself. If three travelers chance to occupy the same compartment, that is enough to make vaguely hostile "others" out of all the rest

of the passengers on the train. in small-town eyes all persons
not belonging to the village are "strangers" and suspect; to the
native of a country all who inhabit other countries are
"foreigners"; Jews are "different" for the anti-Semite, Negroes
are "inferior" for American racists, aborigines are "natives" for
colonists, proletarians are the "lower class" for the privileged.

Lévi-Strauss, at the end of a profound work on the various
forms of primitive societies, reaches the following conclusion:
"Passage from the state of Nature to the state of Culture is
marked by man's ability to view biological relations as a
series of contrasts; duality, alternation, opposition, and sym-
metry, whether under definite or vague forms, constitute not
so much phenomena to be explained as fundamental and immediately given data of social reality." These phenomena
would be incomprehensible if in fact human society were
simply a *Mitsein* or fellowship based on solidarity and friendliness. Things become clear, on the contrary, if, following
Hegel, we find in consciousness itself a fundamental hostility
toward every other consciousness; the subject can be posed
only in being opposed—he sets himself up as the essential, as
opposed to the other, the inessential, the object.

But the other consciousness, the other ego, sets up a
reciprocal claim. The native traveling abroad is shocked to
find himself in turn regarded as a "stranger" by the natives
of neighboring countries. As a matter of fact, wars, festivals,
trading, treaties, and contests among tribes, nations, and
classes tend to deprive the concept *Other* of its absolute sense
and to make manifest its relativity; willy-nilly, individuals and
groups are forced to realize the reciprocity of their relations.
How is it, then, that this reciprocity has not been recognized
between the sexes, that one of the contrasting terms is set
up as the sole essential, denying any relativity in regard to
its correlative and defining the latter as pure otherness? Why
is it that women do not dispute male sovereignty? No subject
will readily volunteer to become the object, the inessential; it
is not the Other, who, in defining himself as the Other, establishes the One. The Other is posed as such by the One in
defining himself as the One. But if the Other is not to regain
the status of being the One, he must be submissive enough
to accept this alien point of view. Whence comes this submission in the case of woman?

There are, to be sure, other cases in which a certain category has been able to dominate another completely for a time.

Very often this privilege depends upon inequality of numbers
—the majority imposes its rule upon the minority or persecutes
it. But women are not a minority, like the American Negroes
or the Jews; there are as many women as men on earth. Again,
the two groups concerned have often been originally independent; they may have been formerly unaware of each other's
existence, or perhaps they recognized each other's autonomy.
But a historical event has resulted in the subjugation of the
weaker by the stronger. The scattering of the Jews, the introduction of slavery into America, the conquests of imperialism
are examples in point. In these cases the oppressed retained at
least the memory of former days; they possessed in common
a past, a tradition, sometimes a religion or a culture.

The parallel drawn by Bebel between women and the
proletariat is valid in that neither ever formed a minority or
a separate collective unit of mankind. And instead of a single
historical event it is in both cases a historical development
that explains their status as a class and accounts for the
membership of *particular individuals* in that class. But
proletarians have not always existed, whereas there have always been women. They are women in virtue of their anatomy
and physiology. Throughout history they have always been
subordinated to men, and hence their dependency is not the
result of a historical event or a social change—it was not
something that *occurred*. The reason why otherness in this
case seems to be an absolute is in part that it lacks the contingent or incidental nature of historical facts. A condition
brought about at a certain time can be abolished at some other
time, as the Negroes of Haiti and others have proved; but it
might seem that a natural condition is beyond the possibility
of change. In truth, however, the nature of things is no more
immutably given, once for all, than is historical reality. If
woman seems to be the inessential which never becomes the
essential, it is because she herself fails to bring about this
change. Proletarians say "We"; Negroes also. Regarding themselves as subjects, they transform the bourgeois, the whites,
into "others." But women do not say "We," except at some
congress of feminists or similar formal demonstration; men
say "women," and women use the same word in referring to
themselves. They do not authentically assume a subjective
attitude. The proletarians have accomplished the revolution
in Russia, the Negroes in Haiti, the Indo-Chinese are battling
for it in Indo-China; but the women's effort has never been

anything more than a symbolic agitation. They have gained only what men have been willing to grant; they have taken nothing, they have only received.

The reason for this is that women lack concrete means for organizing themselves into a unit which can stand face to face with the correlative unit. They have no past, no history, no religion of their own; and they have no such solidarity of work and interest as that of the proletariat. They are not even promiscuously herded together in the way that creates community feeling among the American Negroes, the ghetto Jews, the workers of Saint-Denis, or the factory hands of Renault. They live dispersed among the males, attached through residence, housework, economic condition, and social standing to certain men—fathers or husbands—more firmly than they are to other women. If they belong to the bourgeoisie, they feel solidarity with men of that class, not with proletarian women; if they are white, their allegiance is to white men, not to Negro women. The proletariat can propose to massacre the ruling class, and a sufficiently fanatical Jew or Negro might dream of getting sole possession of the atomic bomb and making humanity wholly Jewish or black; but woman cannot even dream of exterminating the males. The bond that unites her to her oppressors is not comparable to any other. The division of the sexes is a biological fact, not an event in human history. Male and female stand opposed within a primordial *Mitsein*, and woman has not broken it. The couple is a fundamental unity with its two halves riveted together, and the cleavage of society along the line of sex is impossible. Here is to be found the basic trait of woman: she is the Other in a totality of which the two components are necessary to one another.

• • •

. . . it is doubtless impossible to approach any human problem with a mind free from bias. The way in which questions are put, the points of view assumed, presuppose a relativity of interest, all characteristics imply values, and every objective description, so called, implies an ethical background. Rather than attempt to conceal principles more or less definitely implied, it is better to state them openly at the beginning. This will make it unnecessary to specify on every page in just what sense one uses such words as *superior, inferior, better, worse, progress, reaction,* and the like. If we survey some of the works on women, we note that one of the points of view most frequently adopted is that of the public good, the general interest; and one always means by this the benefit of society as one wishes it to be maintained or established. For our part, we hold that the only public good is that which assures the private good of the citizens; we shall pass judgment on institutions according to their effectiveness in giving concrete opportunities to individuals. But we do not confuse the idea of private interest with that of happiness, although that is another common point of view. Are not women of the harem more happy than women voters? Is not the housekeeper happier than the working-woman? It is not too clear just what the word *happy* really means and still less what true values it may mask. There is no possibility of measuring the happiness of others, and it is always easy to describe as happy the situation in which one wishes to place them.

In particular those who are condemned to stagnation are often pronounced happy on the pretext that happiness consists in being at rest. This notion we reject, for our perspective is that of existentialist ethics. Every subject plays his part as such specifically through exploits or projects that serve as a mode of transcendence, he achieves liberty only through a continual reaching out toward other liberties. There is no justification for present existence other than its expansion into an indefinitely open future. Every time transcendence falls back into immanence, stagnation, there is a degradation of existence into the *"en-soi"*—the brutish life of subjection to given conditions—and of liberty into constraint and contingence. This downfall represents a moral fault if the subject consents to it: if it is inflicted upon him, it spells frustration and oppression. In both cases it is an absolute evil. Every individual concerned to justify his existence feels that his existence involves an undefined need to transcend himself, to engage in freely chosen projects.

Now, what peculiarly signalizes the situation of woman is that she—a free and autonomous being like all human creatures—nevertheless finds herself living in a world where men compel her to assume the status of the Other. They propose to stabilize her as object and to doom her to immanence since her transcendence is to be overshadowed and forever transcended by another ego (*conscience*) which is essential and sovereign. The drama of woman lies in this conflict between the fundamental aspirations of every subject (ego)—who always regards the self as the essential—and the compulsions of a situation in which sne is the inessential. How can a human being in woman's situation attain fulfillment? What roads are open to her? Which are blocked? How can independence be recovered in a state of dependency? What circumstances limit woman's liberty and how can they be overcome? These are the fundamental questions on which I would fain throw some light. This means that I am interested in the fortunes of the individual as defined not in terms of happiness but in terms of liberty.

• • •

A world where men and women would be equal is easy to visualize, for that precisely is what the Soviet Revolution *promised*: women raised and trained exactly like men were to work under the same conditions and for the same wages. Erotic liberty was to be recognized by custom, but the sexual act was not to be considered a "service" to be paid for; woman was to be *obliged* to provide herself with other ways of earning a living; marriage was to be based on a free agreement that the spouses could break at will; maternity was to be voluntary, which meant that contraception and abortion were to be authorized and that, on the other hand, all mothers and their children were to have exactly the same rights, in or out of marriage; pregnancy leaves were to be paid for by the State, which would assume charge of the children, signifying not that they would be *taken away* from their parents, but that they would not be *abandoned* to them.

But is it enough to change laws, institutions, customs, public opinion, and the whole social context, for men and women to become truly equal? "Women will always be women," say the skeptics. Other seers prophesy that in casting off their femininity they will not succeed in changing themselves into men and they will become monsters. This would be to admit that the woman of today is a creation of nature; it must be repeated once more that in human society nothing is natural and that woman, like much else, is a product elaborated by civilization. The intervention of others in her destiny is fundamental: if this action took a different direction, it would produce a quite different result. Woman is determined not by her hormones or by mysterious instincts, but by the manner in which her body and her relation to the world are modified through the action of others than herself. The abyss that separates the adolescent boy and girl has been deliberately opened out between them since earliest childhood; later on, woman could not be other than what she *was made*, and that past was bound to shadow her for life. If we appreciate its influence, we see clearly that her destiny is not predetermined for all eternity.

We must not believe, certainly, that a change in woman's economic condition alone is enough to transform her, though this factor has been and remains the basic factor in her evolution; but until it has brought about the moral, social, cultural, and other consequences that it promises and requires, the new woman cannot appear. At this moment they have been realized nowhere, in Russia no more than in France or the United States, and this explains why the woman of today is torn between the past and the future. She appears most often as a "true woman" disguised as a man, and she feels herself as ill at ease in her flesh as in her masculine garb. She must shed her old skin and cut her own new clothes. This she could do only through a social evolution. No single educator could fashion a *female human being* today who would be the exact homologue of the *male human being*; if she is raised like a boy, the young girl feels she is an oddity and thereby she is given a new kind of sex specification. Stendhal understood this when he said: "The forest must be planted all at once." But if we imagine, on the contrary, a society in which the equality of the sexes would be concretely realized, this equality would find new expression in each individual.

. . .

As a matter of fact, man, like woman, is flesh, therefore passive, the plaything of his hormones and of the species, the restless prey of his desires. And she, like him, in the midst of the carnal fever, is a consenting, a voluntary gift, an activity; they live out in their several fashions the strange ambiguity of existence made body. In those combats where they think they confront one another, it is really against the self that each one struggles, projecting into the partner that part of the self which is repudiated; instead of living out the ambiguities of their situation, each tries to make the other bear the abjection and tries to reserve the honor for the self. If, however, both should assume the ambiguity with a clear-sighted modesty, correlative of an authentic pride, they would see each other as equals and would live out their erotic drama in amity. The fact that we are human beings is infinitely more important than all the peculiarities that distinguish human beings from one another; it is never the given that confers superiorities: "virtue," as the ancients called it, is defined at the level of "that which depends on us." In both sexes is played out the same drama of the flesh and the spirit, of finitude and transcendence; both are gnawed away by time and laid in wait for by death, they have the same essential need for one another; and they can gain from their liberty the same glory. If they were to taste it, they would no longer be tempted to dispute fallacious privileges, and fraternity between them could then come into existence.

I shall be told that all this is utopian fancy, because woman cannot be "made over" unless society has first made her really the equal of man. Conservatives have never failed in such circumstances to refer to that vicious circle; history, however, does not revolve. If a caste is kept in a state of inferiority, no doubt it remains inferior; but liberty can break the circle. Let the Negroes vote and they become worthy of having the vote; let woman be given responsibilities and she is able to assume them. The fact is that oppressors cannot be expected to make a move of gratuitous generosity; but at one time the revolt of the oppressed, at another time even the very evolution of the privileged caste itself, creates new situations; thus men have been led, in their own interest, to give partial emancipation to women: it remains only for women to continue their ascent, and the successes they are obtaining are an encouragement for them to do so. It seems almost certain that sooner or later they will arrive at complete economic and social equality, which will bring about an inner metamorphosis.

. . .

To begin with, there will always be certain differences between man and woman; her eroticism, and therefore her sexual world, have a special form of their own and therefore cannot fail to engender a sensuality, a sensitivity, of a special nature. This means that her relations to her own body, to that of the male, to the child, will never be identical with those the male bears to his own body, to that of the female and to the child; those who make much of "equality in difference" could not with good grace refuse to grant me the possible existence of differences in equality. Then again, it is institutions that create uniformity. Young and pretty, the slaves of the harem are always the same in the sultan's embrace; Christianity gave eroticism its savor of sin and legend when it endowed the human female with a soul; if society restores her sovereign individuality to woman, it will not thereby destroy the power of love's embrace to move the heart.

It is nonsense to assert that revelry, vice, ecstasy, passion, would become impossible if man and woman were equal in concrete matters; the contradictions that put the flesh in opposition to the spirit, the instant to time, the swoon of immanence to the challenge of transcendence, the absolute of pleasure to the nothingness of forgetting, will never be resolved; in sexuality will always be materialized the tension, the anguish, the joy, the frustration, and the triumph of existence. To emancipate woman is to refuse to confine her to the relations she bears to man, not to deny them to her; let her have her independent existence and she will continue none the less to exist for him *also*: mutually recognizing each other as subject, each will yet remain for the other an *other*. The reciprocity of their relations will not do away with the miracles—desire, possession, love, dream, adventure—worked by the division of human beings into two separate categories; and the words that move us—giving, conquering, uniting—will not lose their meaning. On the contrary, when we abolish the slavery of half of humanity, together with the whole system of hypocrisy that it implies, then the "division" of humanity will reveal its genuine significance and the human couple will find its true form. "The direct, natural, necessary relation of human creatures is the *relation of man to woman*," Marx has said.[1] "The nature of this relation determines to what point man himself is to be considered as a *generic being*, as mankind; the relation of man to woman is the most natural relation of human being to human being. By it is shown, therefore, to what point the *natural* behavior of man has become *human* or to what point the *human* being has become his *natural* being, to what point his *human nature* has become his *nature*."

The case could not be better stated. It is for man to establish the reign of liberty in the midst of the world of the given. To gain the supreme victory, it is necessary, for one thing, that by and through their natural differentiation men and women unequivocally affirm their brotherhood.

---

[1] *Philosophical Works, Vol. VI (Marx's italics).*

Paul Ricoeur

(b. 1913) ————◆◆◆———— FRENCH

*Ricoeur entered philosophy as a student of Marcel, soon fell
under the influence of Husserl, and later became a devotee of
Freud. Now the most prominent interpreter of Husserl and
the leading phenomenologist in France, he has recently published one of the most insightful philosophical studies of Freud
available. His central work, however, is an original study of a
segment of philosophy which has been left unexplored in most
phenomenological investigations. In Kant there is a rigid cleavage between nature—the world of science and knowledge—
and freedom—the world of the will. Husserlian phenomenologists have concentrated heavily on the "cognitive" world of
knowledge; the existential phenomenologists have devoted
themselves primarily to freedom and choice, but they typically
leave uncharted the link between them—the details of choice,
motivation and volition. It is to this area that Ricoeur de-
votes his mammoth study,* The Voluntary and the Involuntary
(Part I of Freedom and Nature*), an analysis of the will, motivation, and action, a selection of which is included here.*

MOTIVE AND VALUE

. . .

A motive represents and, so to speak, "historializes" values
and their relations.[1] To give a reason is not to explain, but to

From *Freedom and Nature: The Voluntary and the Involuntary* by Paul
Ricoeur, translated by Erazim V. Kohák. Reprinted by permission of Northwestern University Press.

[1] *This abbreviated formula is freely inspired by Max Scheler,* Der Formalis-
mus in der Ethik und die materiale Wertethik *(Halle, 1927), from which
we have retained two ideas: (1) there is a way between formalism of duty
and hedonism of the good (that is, utilitarianism and affectively oriented*

justify, to legitimize, that is, to appeal to a right. But the values entailed by the thrust of the project do not necessarily take the form of value judgments, just as my self-imputation in a decision is only available to a reflection which would then make it explicit as a judgment of responsibility. Such reflection, while raising a motive to the level of a judged value, also makes it an occasion of contact between myself and the other. Thus I justify myself before . . . , in the eyes of, seek approval, contest or prevent disapproval, and in turn I learn to evaluate my acts in evaluating those of others. In brief, I reflect on value in the social context of praise and blame.[2] But reflection on the "they" and its inauthentic valuations, similar to those which elicited our considerations with regard to imputative judgment, leads to analogous considerations here. Social valuation is only the occasion, sometimes an opportunity and often a degradation, of a more elementary power of valuation which constitutes the individual will. It is the nature of the will to seek reasons; in terms of them it moves beyond social valuation and finds roots and context in them.

Thus the reflexive character of valuation gives to the value judgment a significance comparable to judgments of responsibility. Implicit evaluation, which movement brings out before consciousness, remains a feeling contained *in* the project itself: it is the project which has a value. When I reflect on the value of the project, I partially set aside its thrust. Thus valuation is a drawing back to question the legitimacy of my project and my own value because the project is myself. Such recoil, such turning back toward value, can remain a

---

theories in general); (2) the material (non-formal) a prioris can reveal themselves only in terms of psychological feelings and the unfolding of history. . . . The relation of the a priori to history transcends the narrowly psychological framework of this work. Yet it is the most important problem of ethics. For what would have to be shown systematically in order to justify our expression, "historialization" of values, is that there are no moral constants, alongside of or above various judgments, feelings, and mores, but that, rather, varying history is a mode of appearance of a moral a priori. More than Scheler, we shall stress the necessary mediation through action and through history which prevents us from treating values as contemplative essences. That is why we refuse to harden our opposition to J.-P. Sartre's conception of value. It is no exaggeration to say that we decipher the good by our own devotion: an a prioristic interpretation of values will stretch that far.

[2] Concerning approbation, see Le Senne, Traité de morale (Paris, 1942), pp. 325–29.

moment of broader dialectic of thrust and reflection. But if the return to value is lasting, if the project is suspended for a longer time or even abandoned entirely, valuation becomes isolated from the thrust of consciousness toward action. This is why value judgments do not share the future orientation of a project but rather express present value, as "this is good." As they more generally lose any reference to an imminent or postponed insertion of the project into the world, their grammatical mode is no longer the imperative or the gerundative, but the indicative of value.[3]

Under these conditions, where is the line between pure description of willing and ethics?

First of all it seems clear that ethics begins by abstracting away the thrust of the project in which prereflexive valuation is embedded. Consciousness constitutes itself as moral consciousness as it makes itself entirely a valuation, a reflection concerning values. Such explicit valuation is undoubtedly a judgment, or, more precisely, a comparison: this is better than that, right now this is the best. This judgment, at the lowest rung of a situation, has as a horizon or backdrop landmarks or value references which are not valuated actively each time, but rather form, for a given consciousness at a given time of its development, a concrete, more or less ordained table, or better, a configuration or a constellation of fixed stars. These non-revaluated values form, so to speak, its ethical firmament, its moral "habitus." The term "horizon of value" well suggests what an ethical consciousness is: it is a consciousness which, unlike a willing consciousness, moves from the reason for its project to the reasons for its reasons, reopening the question of its value references and unceasingly questioning its proximate, remote, penultimate, and ultimate values and reevaluating its ethical firmament. To the extent to which it thus removes itself from its present project it places all its problems in a radical light and evaluates its life and its action as a whole. Ethics is such a radicalization. Now such questioning does not take place without another type of anxiety, which is no longer the anxiety of potential

---

[3] *In this sense the scholastics distinguished speculative-practical judgments (lying is wrong) and practical-practical judgments (I shall tell him all) tied to the imperium of decision: between abstract injunction of the rule and the effective suggestion of concrete action there is the same distance as between the* infima *species and the individual apprehended* hic et nunc.

willing or potential doing but an anxiety of ultimate goals. In effect every project activates only a sector of values with respect to which the whole field of value serves as reference. In a given situation, I seek a point on which to base myself. I ordinarily find it in the totality of values not reevaluated at that moment, which in the course of the debate with myself reveal their motivating power in *that* situation. All my other values function as variables in a partial evaluation. This is what Bergson described in *Two Sources of Morality and Religion* under the name of the whole obligation. But in great crises, on the occasion of a trial which radicalizes my very self, in face of a commotion which attacks me in my ultimate reasons, I turn to my fixed stars. Everything is changed. I can no longer ask for the horizon of value of *this* valuation. Suddenly, my ultimate values are no longer something which refers to. . . . But are my fixed stars fixed? How can we trace the ultimate tangents of reference, and what does "ultimate" mean? Anxiety about the ground of value seizes me; for the question "what does ultimate mean?" inevitably leads to another—"is there an ultimate in value?" The "ἀνάγκη στῆναι" becomes suspect. The *Grund* becomes *Abgrund*.

This anxiety, also is an anxiety within reflection, and it is not certain that it could be unraveled within reflection. It could, if there existed something like a Platonic intuition of values and if the receptive aspect of reflection represented a closed field of an absolutely pure apperception in which absolute values would become manifest. Such intuition would in a sense mask the abyss which widens and becomes more radical as the question of my aims itself swells and grows to the proportions of an ultimate question.

For my part, I believe that there exists a certain emotional revelation of values in a given situation and that Max Scheler gave ethics a satisfactory orientation by his conception of the emotional *a priori*. But I also believe that he deceived himself when he conceived of that emotional intuition as independent of the thrust of my dedication, that is, of a project in act, and so could entertain illusions concerning the possibility of a pure ethics. This emotional intuition to which we shall return in time appears to be subjected to a peculiar condition which makes it unusual. Values only appear to me in proportion to my loyalty, that is, my active dedication. In our language of pure description we can say that value is valuable in relation to an eventual project, which means that values only appear to me in a historical, qualified situation within which I orient myself and seek to motivate my action. Motivation of a specific project is the basic context where moral judgments enter in. This is why we have said above that a motive "presents" or, so to speak, "historializes" a value or a value-context: following Josiah Royce and Gabriel Marcel, I should say that values are not timeless ideas but suprapersonal existences, thereby stressing that their appearance is tied to a definite *history* on which I collaborate actively with all the power of my dedication, briefly, a history which I invent. Yes, that is the paradox of value: it is not completely a product of history, it is not invented, it is recognized, respected, and discovered—but only to the extent of my capacity for making history, for inventing history. Royce especially insisted that only a loyalty of a collective (or rather community) character to what he calls a cause can bring forth the values which legitimize that cause; and the closer that cause comes to being a universally human cause, the closer we come to universal values. It is not certain that such loyalty is the only way along which values are historialized, or rather the way along which we *make* them historically present in our *making* of history. But it is enough for us to say, at the level of abstraction which we have adopted, that I encounter values in motivating a project (this project being itself a moment of a militant consciousness). If there is such a thing as a contemplation of the good, it is sustained only by the thrust of consciousness which incorporates its values in a project. Detached from this living dialectic of contemplation and decision, of legitimization and invention, a value judgment loses not only its function, but even its possibility. It is of the essence of value not to appear except as a possible motive of decision. I testify to a value only as its champion. This is the source of a certain deception which seems to accompany all theory of values. I do not see values as I see things. I see only those values which I am willing to serve. The very nature of value and of the seeing appropriate to it seems to enclose all theory of value in a circle. On the one hand, will seeks its justification in values and turns to them to receive a blessing of the good; on the other hand valuation is only a moment in the initiative of the will which enlists in its service. I do not will unless I see, but I cease to see if I absolutely cease to will. That is the difference in principle which separates the truth of the good from the truth of an object. The attention which the latter requires activates only a pure understanding shorn of passions, while the attention demanded by the former mobilizes my whole being. Values are never given to an observer-consciousness. Impartiality and objectivity have no longer the same meaning in relation to value as in relation to empirical objects. This explains the gaps and the more or less lasting blindness which afflict our perception of the good.

Perhaps we shall now understand why pure reflection dealing with values, in the margins of any commitment, should be an undiminishing anxiety. For the second time, reflection appears as the subversion of a certain living relation which I must constantly rediscover as reflection annuls it. Just as self-imputation in a project cannot exile itself from that project without losing itself in the bad infinite of reflection, so evaluation, separated from loyalty, can only disappear in an endless question. We must constantly return to a second naïveté, suspend the reflection which itself suspends the living relation between valuation and project.

Nikolai Berdyaev

(1874–1948)   ————◆————   RUSSIAN

*Berdyaev is a logical if radical step after Dostoevsky. Follow-
ing through Ivan Karamazov's parables, Berdyaev becomes
a Marxist and an existential Christian. In place of the sanctions of God, whose disappearance Ivan feared would leave
everything permitted, Berdyaev, perhaps like the later Dostoevsky himself, substituted purely interpersonal ideals of
human dignity and shared personal values. His Marxism was
sufficiently radical to win him a professorship at the University
of Moscow in the early days of the Revolution, but his
existential spirit produced a Marxism sufficiently unorthodox
to result in his later being exiled from Russia. The short
selection here is taken from Berdyaev's* The Destiny of Man.

from
THE DESTINY OF MAN

The very existence of moral life with its distinctions and
valuations presupposes freedom. Hence ethics is a philosophy
of freedom. The traditional scholastic doctrine of free will
does not touch on the real problem of freedom. That doctrine
was invented in order to find a culprit, someone who could be
held responsible and so vindicate the idea of punishment in
this life and in eternity. The doctrine of free will was
modelled to suit a normative, legalistic morality. It implies
that man is confronted with the choice between good and
evil, and may or may not fulfil the law or norm imposed
upon him. Man will be justified if he chooses the good and

From *The Destiny of Man* by Nikolai Berdyaev, translated by N. Duddington.
Reprinted by permission of Geoffrey Bles, Publishers, London.

fulfils the law, and condemned if he chooses evil and fails to fulfil the law. In spite of a certain confusion of thought, there is profound truth in Luther's rebellion against justification by works connected with free will. It is paradoxical that so-called "free will" should be the source of man's enslavement. Man is enslaved by the necessity to choose between that which is forced upon him and carrying out the law under fear of penalties. He proves to be least free in that which is connected with his "free will". Yet freedom may be understood not merely as the possibility given to man of fulfilling the law and justifying himself by good works due to his free will, but as man's creative energy resulting in the production of values. Freedom may lead man to evil; it is tragic in character and does not come under any pedagogical or morally legalistic categories. Freedom is the essential condition of moral life—freedom in evil as well as in good. There can be no moral life without freedom in evil, and this renders moral life a tragedy and makes ethics a philosophy of tragedy. Legalistic, normative ethics, for which freedom is merely the condition of fulfilling the moral law, leaves out of account the tragic aspect of moral life. Tragedy is an essential element of morality and a fundamental ethical category. It is the tragic that leads us to the depths and heights, beyond good and evil in the normative sense. The tragic springs from freedom and is neither "good" nor "evil" in the sense in which these terms are usually defined in ethics, yet ethics must inquire into it. Ethics has to deal both with the tragic and the paradoxical. Moral life is made up of paradoxes in which good and evil are intertwined. They cannot be solved rationally, but have to be lived through to the end. The tragic and paradoxical character of ethics is due to the fact that its fundamental problem is not that of the moral norm or of the good, but of the relation between the Divine and the human freedom.

Martin Buber

(1878–1965)   AUSTRIAN
                                               (ISRAELI)

The central focus of Martin Buber's philosophy is on "dialogue," between man and man, between man and God. He
draws a sharp cleavage between our relationships with things
as objects of experience, contemplation, and use, and our
relationships with others. The first relation, I-It, is essentially
"detached." The second relation, I-Thou, essentially "involves
the whole person." In the first relation, one sees the It in its
context in the world, as something that is interesting or useful.
In the second relation, one "addresses" a Thou and is "addressed" in return. In relating to a Thou, one sees the world
in the context of the Thou. One experiences an It in a
causal, deterministic context: one addresses a Thou "beyond
causality." Of course, to be another person is not yet to be a
Thou. One typically treats others as Its, as interesting or
useful. In an "age of sickness," such treatment is the rule.
Against such reduction of Thou to It, of I-Thou to I-It, Buber
insists that it is only through I-Thou that one is a man. On
the political side, Buber saw the emerging state of Israel as
a living community of I-Thou relationships and developed a
concept of socialism—later realized in Israeli kibbutzim—
which he opposed to the deterministic socialism of Marxism.
Buber's I-Thou relations have an ultimate theological aspect,
of course. Every I-Thou, he tells us, leads us to the Ultimate
Thou, the one Thou that cannot become an It for us. In his
later works Buber moves further from traditional political
Zionism and further toward the Jewish mysticism of Hasidism.
   The selection here is edited from Buber's best-known work,
I and Thou.

from
I AND THOU

The world is twofold for man in accordance with his twofold attitude.

The attitude of man is twofold in accordance with the two basic words he can speak.

The basic words are not single words but word pairs.

One basic word is the word pair I-You.

The other basic word is the word pair I-It; but this basic word is not changed when He or She takes the place of it.

Thus the I of man is also twofold.

For the I of the basic word I-You is different from that in the basic word I-It.

Basic words do not state something that might exist outside them; by being spoken they establish a mode of existence.

Basic words are spoken with one's being.

When one says You, the I of the word pair I-You is said, too.

When one says It, the I of the word pair I-It is said, too.

The basic word I-You can only be spoken with one's whole being.

The basic word I-It can never be spoken with one's whole being.

There is no I as such but only the I of the basic word I-You and the I of the basic word I-It.

When a man says I, he means one or the other. The I he means is present when he says I. And when he says You or It, the I of one or the other basic word is also present.

Being I and saying I are the same. Saying I and saying one of the two basic words are the same.

Whoever speaks one of the basic words enters in the world and stands in it.

The life of a human being does not exist merely in the

From *I and Thou* by Martin Buber, translated by Walter Kaufmann. Copyright © 1970 Charles Scribner's Sons. Reprinted by permission of Charles Scribner's Sons.

sphere of goal-directed verbs. It does not consist merely of activities that have something for their object.

I perceive something. I feel something. I imagine something. I want something. I sense something. The life of a human being does not consist merely of all this and its like.

All this and its like is the basis of the realm of It.

But the realm of You has another basis.

Whoever says You does not have something for his object. For wherever there is something there is also another something; every It borders on other Its; It is only by virtue of bordering on others. But where You is said there is no something. You has no borders.

Whoever says You does not have something; he has nothing. But he stands in relation.

. . .

The world as experience belongs to the basic word I-It. The basic word I-You establishes the world of relation.

Three are the spheres in which the world of relation arises.

The first: life with nature. Here the relation vibrates in the dark and remains below language. The creatures stir across from us, but they are unable to come to us, and the You we say to them sticks to the threshold of language.

The second: life with men. Here the relation is manifest and enters language. We can give and receive the You.

The third: life with spiritual beings. Here the relation is wrapped in a cloud but reveals itself, it lacks but creates language. We hear no You and yet feel addressed; we answer —creating, thinking, acting: with our being we speak the basic word, unable to say You with our mouth.

But how can we incorporate into the world of the basic word what lies outside language?

In every sphere, through everything that becomes present to us, we gaze toward the train of the eternal You; in each we perceive a breath of it; in every You we address the eternal You, in every sphere according to its manner.

. . .

—What, then, does one experience of the You?

—Nothing at all. For one does not experience it.

—What, then, does one know of the You?

—Only everything. For one no longer knows particulars.

The You encounters me by grace—it cannot be found by seeking. But that I speak the basic word to it is a deed of my whole being, is my essential deed.

The You encounters me. But I enter into a direct relationship to it. Thus the relationship is election and electing, passive and active at once: An action of the whole being must approach passivity, for it does away with all partial actions and thus with any sense of action, which always depends on limited exertions.

The basic word I-You can be spoken only with one's whole being. The concentration and fusion into a whole being can never be accomplished by me, can never be accomplished without me. I require a You to become; becoming I, I say You.

All actual life is encounter.

. . .

In the history of the primitive mind the fundamental difference between the two basic words appears in this: even in the original relational event, the primitive man speaks the basic word I-You in a natural, as it were still unformed manner, not yet having recognized himself as an I; but the basic word I-It is made possible only by this recognition, by the detachment of the I.

The former word splits into I and You, but it did not originate as their aggregate, it antedates any I. The latter originated as an aggregate of I and It, it postdates the I.

Owing to its exclusiveness, the primitive relational event includes the I. For by its nature this event contains only two partners, man and what confronts him, both in their full actuality, and the world becomes a dual system; and thus man begins to have some sense of that cosmic pathos of the I without as yet realizing this.

In the natural fact, on the other hand, that will give way to the basic word I-It and I-related experience, the I is not yet included. This fact is the discreteness of the human body as the carrier of its sensations, from its environment. In this particularity the body learns to know and discriminate itself, but this discrimination remains on the plane where things are next to each other, and therefore it cannot assume the character of implicit I-likeness.

But once the I of the relation has emerged and has become existent in its detachment, it somehow etherializes and functionalizes itself and enters into the natural fact of the discreteness of the body from its environment, awakening I-likeness in it. Only now can the conscious I-act, the first form of the basic word I-It, of experience by an I, come into being. The I that has emerged proclaims itself as the carrier of sensations and the environment as their object. Of course, this happens in a "primitive" and not in an "epistemological" manner; yet once the sentence "I see the tree" has been pronounced in such a way that it no longer relates a relation between a human I and a tree You but the perception of the tree object by the human consciousness, it has errected the crucial barrier between subject and object; the basic word I-It, the word of separation, has been spoken.

• • •

One cannot live in the pure present: it would consume us if care were not taken that it is overcome quickly and thoroughly. But in pure past one can live; in fact, only there can a life be arranged. One only has to fill every moment with experiencing and using, and it ceases to burn.

And in all the seriousness of truth, listen: without It a human being cannot live. But whoever lives only with that is not human.

• • •

In the It-world causality holds unlimited sway. Every event that is either perceivable by the senses and "physical" or discovered or found in introspection and "psychological" is considered to be of necessity caused and a cause. Those events which may be regarded as purposive form no exception insofar as they also belong in the continuum of the It-world: this continuum tolerates a teleology, but only as a reversal that is worked into one part of causality without diminishing its complete continuity.

The unlimited sway of causality in the It-world, which is of fundamental importance for the scientific ordering of nature, is not felt to be oppressive by the man who is not confined to the It-world but free to step out of it again and again into the world of relation. Here I and You confront each other freely in a reciprocity that is not involved in or tainted by any causality; here man finds guaranteed the freedom of his being and of being. Only those who know relation and who know of the presence of the You have the capacity for decision. Whoever makes a decision is free because he has stepped before the countenance.

The fiery matter of all my capacity to will surging intractably, everything possible for me revolving primevally, intertwined and seemingly inseparable, the alluring glances of potentialities flaring up from every corner, the universe as a temptation, and I, born in an instant, both hands into the fire, deep into it, where the one that intends me is hidden, my deed, seized: now! And immediately the menace of the abyss is subdued; no longer a coreless multiplicity at play in the iridescent equality of its claims; but only two are left alongside each other, the other and the one, delusion and task. But now the actualization commences within me. Having decided cannot mean that the one is done while the other remains lying there, an extinguished mass, filling my soul, layer upon layer, with its dross. Only he that funnels all the force of the other into the doing of the one, absorbing into the actualization of what was chosen the undiminished passion of what was not chosen, only he that "serves God with the evil impulse," decides—and decides what happens. Once one has understood this, one also knows that precisely this deserves to be called righteous: that which is set right, toward which a man directs himself and for which he decides; and if there were a devil he would not be the one who decided against God but he that in all eternity did not decide.

The man to whom freedom is guaranteed does not feel oppressed by causality. He knows that his mortal life is by its very nature an oscillation between You and It, and he senses the meaning of this. It suffices him that again and again he may set foot on the threshold of the sanctuary in which he could never tarry. Indeed, having to leave it again and again is for him an intimate part of the meaning and destiny of this life. There, on the threshold, the response, the spirit is kindled in him again and again; here, in the unholy and indigent land the spark has to prove itself. What is here called necessity cannot frighten it; for there he recognized true necessity: fate.

Fate and freedom are promised to each other. Fate is encountered only by him that actualizes freedom. That I discovered the deed that intends me, that, this movement of my freedom, reveals the mystery to me. But this, too, that I cannot accomplish it the way I intended it, this resistance also reveals the mystery to me. He that forgets all being caused as he decides from the depths, he that puts aside possessions and cloak and steps bare before the countenance —this free human being encounters fate as the counter-image of his freedom. It is not his limit but his completion; freedom and fate—with its eyes, hitherto severe, suddenly full of light —looks like grace itself.

No, the man who returns into the It-world, carrying the spark, does not feel oppressed by causal necessity. And in healthy ages, confidence flows to all the people from the men of the spirit; to all of them, even the most obtuse, the encounter, the presence has happened somehow, if only in the dimension of nature, impulse, and twilight; all of them have somewhere felt the You; and now the spirit interprets this guarantee to them.

But in sick ages it happens that the It-world, no longer irrigated and fertilized by the living currents of the You-world, severed and stagnant, becomes a gigantic swamp phantom and overpowers man. As he accommodates himself to a world of objects that no longer achieve any presence for him, he succumbs to it. Then common causality grows into an oppressive and crushing doom.

Every great culture that embraces more than one people rests upon some original encounter, an event at the source when a response was made to a You, an essential act of the spirit. Reinforced by the energy of subsequent generations that points in the same direction, this creates a distinctive conception of the cosmos in the spirit; only thus does a human cosmos become possible again and again; only now can man again and again build houses of worship and human houses in a distinctive conception of space and from a confident soul— and fill vibrant time with new hymns and songs and give the human community itself a form. But only as long as he possesses this essential act in his own life, acting and suffering, only as long as he himself enters into the relation is he free and thus creative. When a culture is no longer centered in a living and continually renewed relational process, it freezes into the It-world which is broken only intermittently by the eruptive, glowing deeds of solitary spirits. From that point on, common causality, which hitherto was never able to disturb the spiritual conception of the cosmos, grows into an oppressive and crushing doom. Wise, masterful fate which, as long as it was attuned to the abundance of meaning in the cosmos, held sway over all causality, has become transformed into demonic absurdity and has collapsed into causality. The same karma that appeared to earlier generations as a beneficial dispensation—for our deeds in this life raise us into higher spheres in the next—now is seen as tyranny; for the deeds of a former life of which we are unconscious have imprisoned us in a dungeon from which we cannot escape in this life. Where the meaningful law of a heaven used to arch, with the spindle of necessity hanging from its bright vault, the meaningless, tyrannical power of the planets now holds sway. It used to be merely a matter of entering *Dike*, the heavenly "path" that aimed to be ours, too, and one could live with a free heart in the total measure of destiny. Now we feel, whatever we do, the compulsion of *heimarmene*,[1] a stranger to spirit who bends every neck with the entire burden of the dead mass of the world. The craving for redemption grows by leaps and bounds and remains unsatisfied in the end, in spite of all kinds of experiments, until it is finally assuaged by one who teaches men how to escape from the wheel of rebirth, or by one who saves the souls enslaved by the powers into the freedom of the children of God. Such accomplishments issue from a new encounter that becomes substantial, a new response of one human being to his You, an event that comes to determine fate. The repercussions of such a central essential act may include the supersession of one culture by another that is devoted to this ray, but it is also possible for a culture to be thus renewed.

The sickness of our age is unlike that of any other and yet belongs with the sicknesses of all. The history of cultures is not a stadium of eons in which one runner after another must cover the same circle of death, cheerfully and unconsciously. A nameless path leads through their ascensions and declines. It is not a path of progress and development. It is a descent through the spirals of the spiritual underworld but could also be called an ascent to the innermost, subtlest, most intricate turn that knows no Beyond and even less any Backward but only the unheard of return—the breakthrough. Shall we have to follow this path all the way to the end, to the test of the final darkness? But where there is danger what saves grows, too.

The biologistic and the historiosophical orientations of this age, which made so much of their differences, have combined to produce a faith in doom that is more obdurate and anxious than any such faith has ever been. It is no longer the power of karma nor the power of the stars that rules man's lot ineluctably; many different forces claim this dominion, but

---

[1] A Greek word for fate, used by Plato, Phaedo 115a and Gorgias 512e.

upon closer examination it appears that most of our contemporaries believe in a medley of forces, as the late Romans believed in a medley of gods. The nature of these claims facilitates such a faith. Whether it is the "law of life"—a universal struggle in which everybody must either join the fight or renounce life—or the "psychological law" according to which innate drives constitute the entire human soul; or the "social law" of an inevitable social process that is merely accompanied by will and consciousness; or the "cultural law" of an unalterably uniform genesis and decline of historical forms; or whatever variations there may be: the point is always that man is yoked into an inescapable process that he cannot resist, though he may be deluded enough to try. From the compulsion of the stars the ancient mysteries offered liberation; from the compulsion of karma, the Brahmanic sacrifice, accompanied by insight. Both were preparations for salvation. But the medley idol does not tolerate any faith in liberation. It is considered foolish to imagine any freedom; one is supposed to have nothing but the choice between resolute and hopelessly rebellious slavery. Although all these laws are frequently associated with long discussions of teleological development and organic evolution, all of them are based on the obsession with some running down, which involves unlimited causality. The dogma of a gradual running down represents man's abdication in the face of the proliferating It-world. Here the name of fate is misused: fate is no bell that has been jammed down over man; nobody encounters it, except those who started out from freedom. But the dogma of some running down leaves no room for freedom or for its most real revelation whose tranquil strength changes the countenance of the earth: returning. The dogma does not know the human being who overcomes the universal struggle by returning; who tears the web of drives, by returning; who rises above the spell of his class by returning; who by returning stirs up, rejuvenates, and changes the secure historical forms. The dogma of running down offers you only one choice as you face its game: to observe the rules or drop out. But he that returns knocks over the men on the board. The dogma will at most permit you to carry out conditionality with your life and to "remain free" in your soul. But he that returns considers this freedom the most ignominious slavery.

Nothing can doom man but the belief in doom, for this prevents the movement of return.

The belief in doom is a delusion from the start. The scheme of running down is appropriate only for ordering that which is nothing-but-having-become, the severed world-event, objecthood as history. The presence of the You, that which is born of association, is not accessible to this approach, which does not know the actuality of spirit; and this scheme is not valid for spirit. Divination based on objecthood is valid only for those who do not know presentness. Whoever is overpowered by the It-world must consider the dogma of an ineluctable running down as a truth that creates a clearing in the jungle. In truth, this dogma only leads him deeper into the slavery of the It-world. But the world of the You is not locked up. Whoever proceeds toward it, concentrating his whole being, with his power to relate resurrected, beholds his freedom. And to gain freedom from the belief in unfreedom is to gain freedom.

. . .

Extended, the lines of relationships intersect in the eternal You.

Every single You is a glimpse of that. Through every single You the basic word addresses the eternal You. The mediatorship of the You of all beings accounts for the fullness of our relationships to them—and for the lack of fulfillment. The innate You is actualized each time without ever being perfected. It attains perfection solely in the immediate relationship to the You that in accordance with its nature cannot become an it.

Paul Tillich

(1886–1965) ━━━━━━◆━━━━━━ **GERMAN**
(AMERICAN)

*Paul Tillich is one of the most influential religious philosophers
of this century. However, his "religion" must be carefully
qualified. He does not believe in a supreme personal deity, and
thus he moves away from Kierkegaard and Buber, for whom a
personal God is the essential mark of the religious. Yet Tillich's
"Ultimate Concern" is neither a return to pantheism nor a
reversion to mysticism before an impersonal transcendent
force. His "faith" is first of all a living answer to the anxieties
of life, the (ontic) anxiety of death and fate, the (spiritual)
anxiety of meaninglessness and emptiness, and the (moral)
anxiety of guilt and condemnation. Like Kierkegaard, Tillich
stresses the* how, *that is, the* dynamics, *of faith and deem-
phasizes the* what, *or objects of faith. His Christianity is
neither a set of doctrines nor a focal point for an existential
"leap" so much as it is the foremost symbol of Ultimate Concern, and existential courage.*

*The following discussion of anxiety and courage is excerpted
from Tillich's* The Courage to Be.

from
THE COURAGE TO BE

The Interdependence
of Fear and Anxiety

Anxiety and fear have the same ontological root but they are
not the same in actuality. This is common knowledge, but it
has been emphasized and overemphasized to such a degree

From *The Courage to Be* by Paul Tillich. Copyright 1952 by Yale University
Press. Reprinted by permission of Yale University Press.

that a reaction against it may occur and wipe out not only the exaggerations but also the truth of the distinction. Fear, as opposed to anxiety, has a definite object (as most authors agree), which can be faced, analyzed, attacked, endured. One can act upon it, and in acting upon it participate in it—even if in the form of struggle. In this way one can take it into one's self-affirmation. Courage can meet every object of fear, because it is an object and makes participation possible. Courage can take the fear produced by a definite object into itself, because this object, however frightful it may be, has a side with which it participates in us and we in it. One could say that as long as there is an *object* of fear love in the sense of participation can conquer fear.

But this is not so with anxiety, because anxiety has no object, or rather, in a paradoxical phrase, its object is the negation of every object. Therefore participation, struggle, and love with respect to it are impossible. He who is in anxiety is, insofar as it is mere anxiety, delivered to it without help. Helplessness in the state of anxiety can be observed in animals and humans alike. It expresses itself in loss of direction, inadequate reactions, lack of "intentionality" (the being related to meaningful contents of knowledge or will). The reason for this sometimes striking behavior is the lack of an object on which the subject (in the state of anxiety) can concentrate. The only object is the threat itself, but not the source of the threat, because the source of the threat is "nothingness."

One might ask whether this threatening "nothing" is not the unknown, the indefinite possibility of an actual threat? Does not anxiety cease in the moment in which a known object of fear appears? Anxiety then would be fear of the unknown. But this is an insufficient explanation of anxiety. For there are innumerable realms of the unknown, different for each subject, and faced without any anxiety. It is the unknown of a special type which is met with anxiety. It is the unknown which by its very nature cannot be known, because it is nonbeing.

Fear and anxiety are distinguished but not separated. They are immanent within each other: The sting of fear is anxiety, and anxiety strives toward fear. Fear is being afraid of something, a pain, the rejection by a person or a group, the loss of something or somebody, the moment of dying. But in the anticipation of the threat originating in these things, it is not the negativity itself which they will bring upon the subject that is frightening but the anxiety about the possible implications of this negativity. The outstanding example—and more than an example—is the fear of dying. Insofar as it is *fear* its object is the anticipated event of being killed by sickness or an accident and thereby suffering agony and the loss of everything. Insofar as it is *anxiety* its object is the absolutely unknown "after death," the nonbeing which remains nonbeing even if it is filled with images of our present experience. The dreams in Hamlet's soliloquy, "to be or not to be," which we may have after death and which make cowards of us all are frightful not because of their manifest content but because of their power to symbolize the threat of nothingness, in religious terms of "eternal death." The symbols of hell created by Dante produce anxiety not because of their objective imagery but because they express the "nothingness" whose power is experienced in the anxiety of guilt. Each of the situations described in the *Inferno* could be met by courage on the basis of participation and love. But of course the meaning is that this is impossible; in other words they are not real situations but symbols of the objectless, of nonbeing.

The fear of death determines the element of anxiety in every fear. Anxiety, if not modified by the fear of an object, anxiety in its nakedness, is always the anxiety of ultimate nonbeing. Immediately seen, anxiety is the painful feeling of not being able to deal with the threat of a special situation. But a more exact analysis shows that in the anxiety about any special situation anxiety about the human situation as such is implied. It is the anxiety of not being able to preserve one's own being which underlies every fear and is the frightening element in it. In the moment, therefore, in which "naked anxiety" lays hold of the mind, the previous objects of fear cease to be definite objects. They appear as what they always were in part, symptoms of man's basic anxiety. As such they are beyond the reach of even the most courageous attack upon them.

This situation drives the anxious subject to establish objects of fear. Anxiety strives to become fear, because fear can be met by courage. It is impossible for a finite being to stand naked anxiety for more than a flash of time. People who have experienced these moments, as for instance some mystics in their visions of the "night of the soul," or Luther under the despair of the demonic assaults, or Nietzsche-Zarathustra in the experience of the "great disgust," have told of the unimaginable horror of it. This horror is ordinarily avoided by the transformation of anxiety into fear of something, no matter what. The human mind is not only, as Calvin has said, a permanent factory of idols, it is also a permanent factory of fears—the first in order to escape God, the second in order to escape anxiety; and there is a relation between the two. For facing the God who is really God means facing also the absolute threat of nonbeing. The "naked absolute" (to use a phrase of Luther's) produces "naked anxiety"; for it is the extinction of every finite self-affirmation, and not a possible object of fear and courage. . . . But ultimately the attempts to transform anxiety into fear are vain. The basic anxiety, the anxiety of a finite being about the threat of nonbeing, cannot be eliminated. It belongs to existence itself.

• • •

Sartre draws consequences from the earlier Heidegger which the later Heidegger did not accept. But it remains doubtful whether Sartre was historically right in drawing these consequences. It was easier for Sartre to draw them than for Heidegger, for in the background of Heidegger's ontology lies the mystical concept of being which is without significance for Sartre. Sartre carried through the consequences of Heidegger's Existentialist analyses without mystical restrictions. This is the reason he has become the symbol of present-day Existentialism, a position which is deserved not so much by the originality of his basic concepts as by the radicalism, consistency, and psychological adequacy with which he has carried them through. I refer above all to his proposition that "the essence of man is his existence." This sentence is like a flash of light which illuminates the whole Existentialist scene. One could call it the most despairing and the most courageous sentence in all Existentialist literature. What it says is that there is no essential nature of man, except in the one point that he can make of himself what he wants. Man creates what he is. Nothing is given to him to determine his creativity. The essence of his being—the "should-be," "the ought-to-be,"—is not something which he finds; he makes it. Man is what he makes of himself. And the courage to be as oneself is the courage to make of oneself what one wants to be.

There are Existentialists of a less radical point of view. Karl Jaspers recommends a new conformity in terms of an all-embracing "philosophical faith"; other speak of a *philosophia perennis*; while Gabriel Marcel moves from an Existentialist radicalism to a position based on the semicollectivism of medieval thought. Existentialism in philosophy is represented more by Heidegger and Sartre than by anybody else.

The Courage of Despair in the Noncreative Existentialist Attitude

I have dealt in the last sections with people whose creative courage enables them to express existential despair. Not many people are creative. But there is a noncreative Existentialist attitude called cynicism. A cynic today is not the same person the Greeks meant by the term. For the Greeks the cynic was a critic of contemporary culture on the basis of reason and natural law; he was a revolutionary rationalist, a follower of Socrates. Modern cynics are not ready to follow anybody. They have no belief in reason, no criterion of truth, no set of values, no answer to the question of meaning. They try to undermine every norm put before them. Their courage is expressed not creatively but in their form of life. They courageously reject any solution which would deprive them of their freedom of rejecting whatever they want to reject. The cynics are lonely although they need company in order to show their loneliness. They are empty of both preliminary meanings and an ultimate meaning, and therefore easy victims of neurotic anxiety. Much compulsive self-affirmation and much fanatical self-surrender are expressions of the noncreative courage to be as oneself.

The Limits of the Courage to be as Oneself

This leads to the question of the limits of the courage to be as oneself in its creative as well as its uncreative forms. Courage is self-affirmation "in spite of," and the courage to be as oneself is self-affirmation of the self as itself. But one must ask: What is this self that affirms itself? Radical Existentialism answers: What it makes of itself. This is all it can say, because anything more would restrict the absolute freedom of the self. The self, cut off from participation in its world, is an empty shell, a mere possibility. It must act because it lives, but it must redo every action because acting involves him who acts in that upon which he acts. It gives content and for this reason it restricts his freedom to make of himself what he wants. In classical theology, both Catholic and Protestant, only God has this prerogative: He is $\bar{a}$ $s\bar{e}$ (from himself) or absolute freedom. Nothing is in him which is not by him. Existentialism, on the basis of the message that God is dead, gives man the divine "a-se-ity." Nothing shall be in man which is not by man. But man is finite, he is given to himself as what he is. He has received his being and with it the structure of his being, including the structure of finite freedom. And finite freedom is not aseity. Man can affirm himself only if he affirms not an empty shell, a mere possibility, but the structure of being in which he finds himself before action and nonaction. Finite freedom has a definite structure, and if the self tries to trespass on this structure it ends in the loss of itself. The nonparticipating hero in Sartre's *The Age of Reason* is caught in a net of contingencies, coming partly from the subconscious levels of his own self, partly from the environment from which he cannot withdraw. The assuredly empty self is filled with contents which enslave it just because it does not know or accept them as contents. This is true too of the cynic, as was said before. He cannot escape the forces of his self which may drive him into complete loss of the freedom that he wants to preserve.

This dialectical self-destruction of the radical forms of the courage to be as oneself has happened on a world-wide scale in the totalitarian reaction of the 20th century against the revolutionary Existentialism of the 19th century. The Existentialist protest against dehumanization and objectivation, together with its courage to be as oneself, have turned into the most elaborate and oppressive forms of collectivism that have appeared in history. It is the great tragedy of our time that Marxism, which had been conceived as a movement for the liberation of everyone, has been transformed into a system of enslavement of everyone. even of those who enslave the others. It is hard to imagine the immensity of this tragedy in terms of psychological destruction, especially within the intelligentsia. The courage to be was undermined in innumerable people because it was the courage to be in the sense of the revolutionary movements of the 19th century. When it broke down, these people turned either to the neocollectivist system, in a fanatic-neurotic reaction against the cause of their tragic disappointment, or to a cynical-neurotic indifference to all systems and every content.

It is obvious that similar observations can be made on the transformation of the Nietzschean type of the courage to be as oneself into the fascist-Nazi forms of neocollectivism. The totalitarian machines which these movements produced embodied almost everything against which the courage to be as oneself stands. They used all possible means in order to make such courage impossible. Although, in distinction to communism, this system fell down, its aftermath is confusion, indifference, cynicism. And this is the soil on which the longing for authority and for a new collectivism grows.

* * *

The Courage
to Accept Acceptance

Courage is the self-affirmation of being in spite of the fact of nonbeing. It is the act of the individual self in taking the anxiety of nonbeing upon itself by affirming itself either as part of an embracing whole or in its individual selfhood. Courage always includes a risk, it is always threatened by nonbeing, whether the risk of losing oneself and becoming a thing within the whole of things or of losing one's world in an empty self-relatedness. Courage needs the power of being, a power transcending the nonbeing which is experienced in the anxiety of fate and death, which is present in the anxiety of emptiness and meaninglessness, which is effective in the anxiety of guilt and condemnation. The courage which takes this threefold anxiety into itself must be rooted in a power of being that is greater than the power of oneself and the power of one's world. Neither self-affirmation as a part nor self-affirmation as oneself is beyond the manifold threat of nonbeing. Those who are mentioned as representatives of these forms of courage try to transcend themselves and the world in which they participate in order to find the power of being-itself and a courage to be which is beyond the threat of nonbeing. There are no exceptions to this rule; and this means that every courage to be has an open or hidden religious root. For religion is the state of being grasped by the power of being-itself. In some cases the religious root is carefully covered, in others it is passionately denied; in some it is deeply hidden and in others superficially. But it is never completely absent. For everything that is participates in being-itself, and everybody has some awareness of this participation, especially in the moments in which he experiences the threat of nonbeing. . . .

Harold Pinter

(b. 1930) ENGLISH

Harold Pinter is England's foremost playwright and an advocate of that peculiar British brand of existentialism which says—or rather shows—that we really have nothing to say to each other. The following extract is from The Dwarfs.

from
THE DWARFS

LEN: Do you believe in God?
MARK: What?
LEN: Do you believe in God?
MARK: Who?
LEN: God.
MARK: God?
LEN: Do you believe in God?
MARK: Do I believe in God?
LEN: Yes.
MARK: Would you say that again?

From *Three Plays* by Harold Pinter. Copyright © 1961 by Harold Pinter. Reprinted by permission of Grove Press, Inc.

Samuel Beckett

(b. 1906) ━━━◆◆◆━━━ **IRISH**

From our perspective, Samuel Beckett's theater is a paradigm of existentialist literature. Two of his best-known plays, Waiting for Godot *and* Endgame, *capture the nameless despair and unavoidable religious hope of vulgar man as well as any plays by Camus or Sartre. Because it is the overall effect of such plays, rather than any particular dialogue or action within them, that makes them so effective, no selections from them could do them justice. What follows is a short but complete one-act play without words that illustrates Beckett's existentialism.*

ACT WITHOUT WORDS

Desert. Dazzling light.

The man is flung backwards on stage from right wing. He falls, gets up immediately, dusts himself, turns aside, reflects.

Whistle from right wing.

He reflects, goes out right.

Immediately flung back on stage he falls, gets up immediately, dusts himself, turns aside, reflects.

Whistle from left wing.

He reflects, goes out left.

Immediately flung back on stage he falls, gets up immediately, dusts himself, turns aside, reflects.

Act Without Words by Samuel Beckett. Copyright © 1958, by Grove Press, Inc. Reprinted by permission of Grove Press, Inc.

Whistle from left wing.

He reflects, goes towards left wing, hesitates, thinks better of it, halts, turns aside, reflects.

A little tree descends from flies, lands. It has a single bough some three yards from ground and at its summit a meager tuft of palms casting at its foot a circle of shadow.

He continues to reflect.

Whistle from above.

He turns, sees tree, reflects, goes to it, sits down in its shadow, looks at his hands.

A pair of tailor's scissors descends from flies, comes to rest before tree, a yard from ground.

He continues to look at his hands.

Whistle from above.

He looks up, sees scissors, takes them and starts to trim his nails.

The palms close like a parasol, the shadow disappears.

He drops scissors, reflects.

A tiny carafe, to which is attached a huge label inscribed WATER, descends from flies, comes to rest some three yards from ground.

He continues to reflect.

Whistle from above.

He looks up, sees carafe, reflects, gets up, goes and stands under it, tries in vain to reach it, renounces, turns aside, reflects.

A big cube descends from flies, lands.

He continues to reflect.

Whistle from above.

He turns, sees cube, looks at it, at carafe, reflects, goes to cube, takes it up, carries it over and sets it down under carafe, tests its stability, gets up on it, tries in vain to reach carafe, renounces, gets down, carries cube back to its place, turns aside, reflects.

A second smaller cube descends from flies, lands.

He continues to reflect.

Whistle from above.

He turns, sees second cube, looks at it, at carafe, goes to second cube, takes it up, carries it over and sets it down under carafe, tests its stability, gets up on it, tries in vain to reach carafe, renounces, gets down, takes up second cube to carry it back to its place, hesitates, thinks better of it, sets it down, goes to big cube, takes it up, carries it over and puts it on small one, tests their stability, gets up on them, the cubes collapse, he falls, gets up immediately, brushes himself, reflects.

He takes up small cube, puts it on big one, tests their stability, gets up on them and is about to reach carafe when it is pulled up a little way and comes to rest beyond his reach.

He gets down, reflects, carries cubes back to their place, one by one, turns aside, reflects.

A third still smaller cube descends from flies, lands.

He continues to reflect.

Whistle from above.

He turns, sees third cube, looks at it, reflects, turns aside, reflects.

The third cube is pulled up and disappears in flies.

Beside carafe a rope descends from flies, with knots to facilitate ascent.

He continues to reflect.

Whistle from above

He turns, sees rope, reflects, goes to it, climbs up it and is about to reach carafe when rope is let out and deposits him back on ground.

He reflects, looks around for scissors, sees them, goes and picks them up, returns to rope and starts to cut it with scissors.

The rope is pulled up, lifts him off ground, he hangs on, succeeds in cutting rope, falls back on ground, drops scissors, falls, gets up again immediately, brushes himself, reflects.

The rope is pulled up quickly and disappears in flies.

With length of rope in his possession he makes a lasso with which he tries to lasso carafe.

The carafe is pulled up quickly and disappears in flies.

He turns aside, reflects.

He goes with lasso in his hand to tree, looks at bough, turns and looks at cubes, looks again at bough, drops lasso, goes to cubes, takes up small one, carries it over and sets it down under bough, goes back for big one, takes it up and carries it over under bough, makes to put it on small one, hesitates, thinks better of it, sets it down, takes up small one and puts it on big one, tests their stability, turns aside and stoops to pick up lasso.

The bough folds down against trunk.

He straightens up with lasso in his hand, turns and sees what has happened.

He drops lasso, turns aside, reflects.

He carries back cubes to their place, one by one, goes back for lasso, carries it over to cubes and lays it in a neat coil on small one.

He turns aside, reflects.

Whistle from right wing.

He reflects, goes out right.

Immediately flung back on stage he falls, gets up immediately, brushes himself, turns aside, reflects.

Whistle from left wing.

He does not move.

He looks at his hands, looks around for scissors, sees them, goes and picks them up, starts to trim his nails, stops, reflects, runs his finger along blade of scissors, goes and lays them on small cube, turns aside, opens his collar, frees his neck and fingers it.

The small cube is pulled up and disappears in flies, carrying away rope and scissors.

He turns to take scissors, sees what has happened.

He turns aside, reflects.

He goes and sits down on big cube.

The big cube is pulled from under him. He falls. The big cube is pulled up and disappears in flies.

He remains lying on his side, his face towards auditorium, staring before him.

The carafe descends from flies and comes to rest a few feet from his body.

He does not move.

Whistle from above.

He does not move.

The carafe descends further, dangles and plays about his face.

He does not move.

The carafe is pulled up and disappears in flies.

The bough returns to horizontal, the palms open, the shadow returns.

Whistle from above.

He does not move.

The tree is pulled up and disappears in flies.

He looks at his hands.

Curtain

Norman Mailer

(b. 1923) ————◆———— AMERICAN

Overriding all the contemporary concern over whether the novel is dead, Norman Mailer has kept one fact clear for us: the novelist is not. In a long series of brilliant and discomforting novels and essays Norman Mailer has given us the first explicit formulation of what might well be called American existentialism. This is not to say that it has held an appropriate position in American intellectual life. But given the difference between the role of the intellect in French and American life, it is not surprising that American existentialism should find its home in jazz and in the streets, Whether or not we consider it worthwhile to attempt a comparison between Mailer's existentialism and the philosophical theses we have presented, it is undeniable that Mailer's writings offer us the best American expression of the existential attitude we have to date. The following selection is from his essay "The White Negro," included in his Advertisements for Myself.

from
THE WHITE NEGRO

It is on this bleak scene that a phenomenon has appeared: the American existentialist—the hipster, the man who knows that if our collective condition is to live with instant death by atomic war, relatively quick death by the State as *l'univers concentrationnaire,* or with a slow death by conformity with every creative and rebellious instinct stifled (at what damage

From *Advertisements for Myself* by Norman Mailer. Copyright © 1959 by Norman Mailer. Reprinted by permission of G. P. Putnam's Sons, the author, and his agents, Scott Meredith Literary Agency, Inc., 580 Fifth Avenue, New York, N.Y.

to the mind and the heart and the liver and the nerves no research foundation for cancer will discover in a hurry), if the fate of twentieth-century man is to live with death from adolescence to premature senescence, why then the only life-giving answer is to accept the terms of death, to live with death as immediate danger, to divorce oneself from society, to exist without roots, to set out on that uncharted journey into the rebellious imperatives of the self. In short, whether the life is criminal or not, the decision is to encourage the psychopath in oneself, to explore that domain of experience where security is boredom and therefore sickness, and one exists in the present, in that enormous present which is without past or future, memory or planned intention, the life where a man must go until he is beat, where he must gamble with his energies through all those small or large crises of courage and unforeseen situations which beset his day, where he must be with it or doomed not to swing. The unstated essence of Hip, its psychopathic brilliance, quivers with the knowledge that new kinds of victories increase one's power for new kinds of perception; and defeats, the wrong kind of defeats, attack the body and imprison one's energy until one is jailed in the prison air of other people's habits, other people's defeats, boredom, quiet desperation, and muted icy self-destroying rage. One is Hip or one is Square (the alternative which each new generation coming into American life is beginning to feel), one is a rebel or one conforms, one is a frontiersman in the Wild West of American night life, or else a Square cell, trapped in the totalitarian tissues of American society, doomed willy-nilly to conform if one is to succeed.

A totalitarian society makes enormous demands on the courage of men, and a partially totalitarian society makes even greater demands, for the general anxiety is greater. Indeed if one is to be a man, almost any kind of unconventional action often takes disproportionate courage. So it is no accident that the source of Hip is the Negro for he has been living on the margin between totalitarianism and democracy for two centuries. But the presence of Hip as a working philosophy in the sub-worlds of American life is probably due to jazz, and its knifelike entrance into culture, its subtle but so penetrating influence on an avant-garde generation—that postwar generation of adventurers who (some consciously, some by osmosis) had absorbed the lessons of disillusionment and disgust of the twenties, the depression, and the war. Sharing a collective disbelief in the words of men who had too much money and controlled too many things, they knew almost as powerful a disbelief in the socially monolithic ideas of the single mate, the solid family and the respectable love life. If the intellectual antecedents of this generation can be traced to such separate influences as D. H. Lawrence, Henry Miller, and Wilhelm Reich, the viable philosophy of Hemingway fit most of their facts: in a bad world, as he was to say over and over again (while taking time out from his parvenu snobbery and dedicated gourmandize), in a bad world there is no love nor mercy nor charity nor justice unless a man can keep his courage, and this indeed fitted some of the facts. What fitted the need of the adventurer even more precisely was Hemingway's categorical imperative that what made him feel good became therefore The Good.

So no wonder that in certain cities of America, in New York of course, and New Orleans, in Chicago and San Francisco and Los Angeles, in such American cities as Paris and Mexico, D.F., this particular part of a generation was attracted to what the Negro had to offer. In such places as Greenwich Village, a ménage-à-trois was completed—the bohemian and the juvenile delinquent came face-to-face with the Negro, and the hipster was a fact in American life. If marijuana was the wedding ring, the child was the language of Hip for its argot gave expression to abstract states of feeling which all could share, at least all who were Hip. And in this wedding of the white and the black it was the Negro who brought the cultural dowry. Any Negro who wishes to live must live with danger from his first day, and no experience can ever be casual to him, no Negro can saunter down a street with any real certainty that violence will not visit him on his walk. The cameos of security for the average white: mother and the home, job and the family, are not even a mockery to millions of Negroes; they are impossible. The Negro has the simplest of alternatives: live a life of constant humility or ever-threatening danger. In such a pass where paranoia is as vital to survival as blood, the Negro had stayed alive and begun to grow by following the need of his body where he could. Knowing in the cells of his existence that life was war, nothing but war, the Negro (all exceptions admitted) could rarely afford the sophisticated inhibitions of civilization, and so he kept for his survival the art of the primitive, he lived in the enormous present, he subsisted for his Saturday night kicks,

relinquishing the pleasures of the mind for the more obligatory pleasures of the body, and in his music he gave voice to
the character and quality of his existence, to his rage and the
infinite variations of joy, lust, languor, growl, cramp, pinch,
scream and despair of his orgasm. For jazz is orgasm, it is the
music of orgasm, good orgasm and bad, and so it spoke across
a nation, it had the communication of art even where it was
watered, perverted, corrupted, and almost killed, it spoke in
no matter what laundered popular way of instantaneous existential states to which some whites could respond, it was
indeed a communication by art because it said, "I feel this,
and now you do too."

So there was a new breed of adventurers, urban adventurers who drifted out at night looking for action with a black
man's code to fit their facts. The hipster had absorbed the
existentialist synapses of the Negro, and for practical purposes
could be considered a white Negro.

To be an existentialist, one must be able to feel oneself—
one must know one's desires, one's rages, one's anguish, one
must be aware of the character of one's frustration and know
what would satisfy it. The overcivilized man can be an existentialist only if it is chic, and deserts it quickly for the next
chic. To be a real existentialist (Sartre admittedly to the contrary) one must be religious, one must have one's sense of the
"purpose"—whatever the purpose may be—but a life which
is directed by one's faith in the necessity of action is a life
committed to the notion that the substratum of existence is
the search, the end meaningful but mysterious; it is impossible to live such a life unless one's emotions provide their
profound conviction. Only the French, alienated beyond alienation from their unconscious could welcome an existential
philosophy without ever feeling it at all; indeed only a
Frenchman by declaring that the unconscious did not exist
could then proceed to explore the delicate involutions of consciousness, the microscopically sensuous and all but ineffable
frissons of mental becoming, in order finally to create the
theology of atheism and so submit that in a world of absurdi-
ties the existential absurdity is most coherent.

In the dialogue between the atheist and the mystic, the
atheist is on the side of life, rational life, undialectical life—
since he conceives of death as emptiness, he can, no matter
how weary or despairing, wish for nothing but more life; his
pride is that he does not transpose his weakness and spiritual

fatigue into a romantic longing for death, for such appreciation of death is then all too capable of being elaborated by his
imagination into a universe of meaningful structure and moral
orchestration.

Yet this masculine argument can mean very little for the
mystic. The mystic can accept the atheist's description of his
weakness, he can agree that his mysticism was a response to
despair. And yet . . . and yet his argument is that he, the
mystic, is the one finally who has chosen to live with death,
and so death is his experience and not the atheist's, and the
atheist by eschewing the limitless dimensions of profound
despair has rendered himself incapable to judge the experience. The real argument which the mystic must always advance is the very intensity of his private vision—his argument
depends from the vision precisely because what was felt in
the vision is so extraordinary that no rational argument, no
hypotheses of "oceanic feelings" and certainly no skeptical
reductions can explain away what has become for him the
reality more real than the reality of closely reasoned logic.
His inner experience of the possibilities within death is his
logic. So, too, for the existentialist. And the psychopath. And
the saint and the bullfighter and the lover. The common de-
nominator for all of them is their burning consciousness of
the present, exactly that incandescent consciousness which the
possibilities within death has opened for them. There is a
depth of desperation to the condition which enables one to
remain in life only by engaging death, but the reward is their
knowledge that what is happening at each instant of the elec-
tric present is good or bad for them, good or bad for their
cause, their love, their action, their need.

It is this knowledge which provides the curious community
of feeling in the world of the hipster, a muted cool religious
revival to be sure, but the element which is exciting, disturbing, nightmarish perhaps, is that incompatibles have come to
bed, the inner life and the violent life, the orgy and the
dream of love, the desire to murder and the desire to create,
a dialectical conception of existence with a lust for power, a
dark, romantic, and yet undeniably dynamic view of existence for it sees every man and woman as moving individually
through each moment of life forward into growth or backward into death.

• • •

It is impossible to conceive a new philosophy until one

creates a new language, but a new popular language (while it must implicitly contain a new philosophy) does not necessarily present its philosophy overtly. It can be asked then what really is unique in the life-view of Hip which raises its argot above the passing verbal whimsies of the bohemian or the lumpenproletariat.

The answer would be in the psychopathic element of Hip which has almost no interest in viewing human nature, or better, in judging human nature, from a set of standards conceived a priori to the experience, standards inherited from the past. Since Hip sees every answer as posing immediately a new alternative, a new question, its emphasis is on complexity rather than simplicity (such complexity that its language without the illumination of the voice and the articulation of the face and body remains hopelessly incommunicative). Given its emphasis on complexity, Hip abdicates from any conventional moral responsibility because it would argue that the results of our actions are unforeseeable, and so we cannot know if we do good or bad, we cannot even know (in the Joycean sense of the good and the bad) whether we have given energy to another, and indeed if we could, there would still be no idea of what ultimately the other would do with it.

Therefore, men are not seen as good or bad (that they are good-and-bad is taken for granted) but rather each man is glimpsed as a collection of possibilities, some more possible than others (the view of character implicit in Hip) and some humans are considered more capable than others of reaching more possibilities within themselves in less time, provided, and this is the dynamic, provided the particular character can swing at the right time. And here arises the sense of context which differentiates Hip from a Square view of character. Hip sees the context as generally dominating the man, dominating him because his character is less significant than the context in which he must function. Since it is arbitrarily five times more demanding of one's energy to accomplish even an inconsequential action in an unfavorable context than a favorable one, man is then not only his character but his context, since the success or failure of an action in a given context reacts upon the character and therefore affects what the character will be in the next context. What dominates both character and context is the energy available at the moment of intense context.

Character being thus seen as perpetually ambivalent and

dynamic enters then into an absolute relativity where there are no truths other than the isolated truths of what each observer feels at each instant of his existence. To take a perhaps unjustified metaphysical extrapolation, it is as if the universe which has usually existed conceptually as a Fact (even if the Fact were Berkeley's God) but a Fact which it was the aim of all science and philosophy to reveal, becomes instead a changing reality whose laws are remade at each instant by everything living, but most particularly man, man raised to a neo-medieval summit where the truth is not what one has felt yesterday or what one expects to feel tomorrow but rather truth is no more nor less than what one feels at each instant in the perpetual climax of the present.

What is consequent therefore is the divorce of man from his values, the liberation of the self from the Super-Ego of society. The only Hip morality (but of course it is an ever-present morality) is to do what one feels whenever and wherever it is possible, and—this is how the war of the Hip and the Square begins—to be engaged in one primal battle: to open the limits of the possible for oneself, for oneself alone, because that is one's need. Yet in widening the arena of the possible, one widens it reciprocally for others as well, so that the nihilistic fulfillment of each man's desire contains its antithesis of human co-operation.

If the ethic reduces to Know Thyself and Be Thyself, what makes it radically different from Socratic moderation with its stern conservative respect for the experience of the past is that the Hip ethic is immoderation, childlike in its adoration of the present (and indeed to respect the past means that one must also respect such ugly consequences of the past as the collective murders of the State). It is this adoration of the present which contains the affirmation of Hip, because its ultimate logic surpasses even the unforgettable solution of the Marquis de Sade to sex, private property, and the family, that all men and women have absolute but temporary rights over the bodies of all other men and women—the nihilism of Hip proposes as its final tendency that every social restraint and category be removed, and the affirmation implicit in the proposal is that man would then prove to be more creative than murderous and so would not destroy himself. Which is exactly what separates Hip from the authoritarian philosophies which now appeal to the conservative and liberal temper —what haunts the middle of the twentieth century is that faith in man has been lost, and the appeal of authority has been that it would restrain us from ourselves. Hip, which would return us to ourselves, at no matter what price in individual violence, is the affirmation of the barbarian, for it requires a primitive passion about human nature to believe that individual acts of violence are always to be preferred to the collective violence of the State; it takes literal faith in the creative possibilities of the human being to envisage acts of violence as the catharsis which prepares growth.

R. D. Laing

(b. 1927) ————◆●◆———— SCOTTISH

Ronald Laing has been recently discovered by the psychedelic movement for his somewhat wild social phenomenology in The Politics of Experience *and his experimentation with mescaline and lysergic acid. More important, however, he pioneered a revolution in the psychiatry of schizophrenia and is leading an attack on traditional concepts of mental illness and treatment. With David Cooper he has written an exposition of Sartre's later work, including* St. Genet *and* La Critique de la Raison Dialectique (Reason and Violence). *His psychiatric and psychological theories may properly be called existential for their heavy emphasis on choice rather than "disease," the individual rather than the "syndrome," the self and self-consciousness rather than etiology. The following selection is taken from* The Divided Self.

SELF-CONSCIOUSNESS

Self-consciousness, as the term is ordinarily used, implies two things: an awareness of oneself by oneself, and *an awareness of oneself as an object of someone else's observation.*

These two forms of awareness of the self, as an object in one's own eyes and as an object in the other's eyes, are closely related to each other. In the schizoid individual both are enhanced and both assume a somewhat compulsive nature. The schizoid individual is frequently tormented by the compulsive nature of his awareness of his own processes, and also by the equally compulsive nature of his sense of his body as an

From *The Divided Self* by R. D. Laing. Copyright © 1960 by Tavistock Publications. Copyright © 1969 by R. D. Laing. Reprinted by permission of Pantheon Books, a Division of Random House, Inc.

object in the world of others. The heightened sense of being always seen, or at any rate of being always potentially seeable, may be principally referable to the body, but the preoccupation with being seeable may be condensed with the idea of the mental self being penetrable, and vulnerable, as when the individual feels that one can look right through him into his 'mind' or 'soul'. Such 'plate-glass' feelings are usually spoken about in terms of metaphor or simile, but in psychotic conditions the gaze or scrutiny of the other can be experienced as an actual penetration into the core of the 'inner' self.

The heightening or intensifying of the awareness of one's own being, both as an object of one's own awareness and of the awareness of others, is practically universal in adolescents, and is associated with the well-known accompaniments of shyness, blushing, and general embarrassment. One readily invokes some version of 'guilt' to account for such awkwardness. But to suggest, say, that the individual is self-conscious 'because' he has guilty secrets (e.g. masturbation) does not take us far. Most adolescents masturbate, and not uncommonly they are frightened that it will show in some way in their faces. But why, if 'guilt' is the key to this phenomenon, does guilt have these particular consequences and not others, since there are many ways of being guilty, and a heightened sense of oneself as an embarrassed or ridiculous object in the eyes of others is not the only way. 'Guilt' in itself is inadequate to help us here. Many people with profound and crushing guilt do not feel unduly self-conscious. Moreover, it is possible, for instance, to tell a lie and feel guilt at doing so without being frightened that the lie will show in one's face, or that one will be struck blind. It is indeed an important achievement for the child to gain the assurance that the adults have no means of knowing what he does, if they do not see him; that they cannot do more than guess at what he thinks to himself if he does not tell them; that actions that no one has seen and thoughts that he has 'kept to himself' are in no way accessible to others unless he himself 'gives the show away'. The child who *cannot* keep a secret or who *cannot* tell a lie because of the persistence of such primitive magical fears has not established his full measure of autonomy and identity. No doubt in most circumstances good reasons can be found against telling lies, but the *inability* to do so is not one of the best reasons.

The self-conscious person feels he is more the object of

other people's interest than, in fact, he is. Such a person walking along the street approaches a cinema queue. He will have to 'steel himself' to walk past it: preferably, he will cross to the other side of the street. It is an ordeal to go into a restaurant and sit down at a table by himself. At a dance he will wait until two or three couples are already dancing before he can face taking the floor himself, and so on.

Curiously enough, those people who suffer from intense anxiety when performing or acting before an audience are by no means necessarily 'self-conscious' in general, and people who are usually extremely self-conscious may lose their compulsive preoccupations with this issue when they are performing in front of others—the very situation, on first reflection, one might suppose would be most difficult for them to negotiate.

Further features of such self-consciousness may seem again to point to guilt being the key to the understanding of the difficulty. The look that the individual expects other people to direct upon him is practically always imagined to be unfavourably critical of him. He is frightened that he will look a fool, or he is frightened that other people will think he wants to show off. When a patient expresses such phantasies it is easy to suppose that he has a secret unacknowledged desire to show off, to be the centre of attraction, to be superior, to make others look fools beside him, and that this desire is charged with guilt and anxiety and so is unable to be experienced as such. Situations, therefore, which evoke phantasies of this desire being gratified lose all pleasure. The individual would then be a concealed exhibitionist, whose body was unconsciously equated with his penis. Every time his body is on show, therefore, the neurotic guilt associated with this potential avenue of gratification exposes him to a form of castration anxiety which 'presents' phenomenologically as 'self-consciousness'.

An understanding of self-consciousness in some such terms eludes, I believe, the central issue facing the individual whose basic existential position is one of ontological insecurity and whose schizoid nature is partly a direct expression of, and occasion for, his ontological insecurity, and partly an attempt to overcome it; or, putting the last remark in slightly different terms, partly an attempt to defend himself against the dangers to his being that are the consequences of his failure to achieve a secure sense of his own identity.

Self-consciousness in the ontologically insecure person plays a double role:

1. Being aware of himself and knowing that other people are aware of him are a means of assuring himself that he exists, and also that they exist. Kafka clearly demonstrates this in his story called 'Conversation with a Suppliant': the suppliant starts from the existential position of ontological insecurity. He states, 'There has never been a time in which I have been convinced from within myself that I am alive.' The need to gain a conviction of his own aliveness and the realness of things is, therefore, the basic issue in his existence. His way of seeking to gain such conviction is by feeling himself to be an object in the real world; but, since *his* world is unreal, he must be an object in the world of someone else, for objects to other people seem to be real, and even calm and beautiful. At least, '. . . it must be so, for I often hear people talking about them as though they were.' Hence it is that he makes his confession '. . . don't be angry if I tell you that *it is the aim of my life to get people to look at me*' (italics mine).

A further factor is the discontinuity in the temporal self. When there is uncertainty of identity in time, there is a tendency to rely on spatial means of identifying oneself. Perhaps this goes some way to account for the frequently pre-eminent importance to the person of being *seen*. However, sometimes the greatest reliance may be placed on the awareness of oneself in time. This is especially so when time is experienced as a succession of moments. The loss of a section of the linear temporal series of moments through inattention to one's time-self may be felt as a catastrophe. Dooley (1941) gives various examples of this temporal self-awareness arising as part of the person's 'struggle against fear of obliteration' and his attempt at the preservation of his integrity 'against threats of being engulfed, crushed, of losing . . . identity . . . .' One of her patients said: 'I forgot myself at the Ice Carnival the other night. I was so absorbed in looking at it that I forgot what time it was and who and where I was. When I suddenly realized I hadn't been thinking about myself I was frightened to death. The unreality feeling came. I must never forget myself for a single minute. I watch the clock and keep busy, or else I won't know who I am' (p. 17).

2. In a world full of danger, to be a potentially seeable object is to be constantly exposed to danger. Self-consciousness, then, may be the apprehensive awareness of oneself as

potentially exposed to danger by the simple fact of being visible to others. The obvious defence against such a danger is to make oneself invisible in one way or another.

In an actual instance, the issue is thus always necessarily complex. Kafka's suppliant makes it the aim of his life to get people to look at him, since thereby he mitigates his state of depersonalization and derealization and inner deadness. He needs other people to experience him as a real live person because he has never been convinced from within himself that he was alive. This, however, implies a trust in the benign quality of the other person's apprehension of him which is not always present. Once he becomes aware of something it becomes unreal, although 'I always feel that they were once real and are now flitting away.' One would not be surprised to find that such a person would have in some measure a distrust of other people's awareness of him. What, for instance, if they had, after all, the same 'fugitive awareness' of him as he had of them? Could he place any more reliance on their consciousness than on his own to lend him a conviction that he was alive? Quite often, in fact, the balance swings right over so that the individual feels that his greatest risk is to be the object of another person's awareness. The myth of Perseus and the Medusa's head, the 'evil eye', delusions of death rays and so on are I believe referable to this dread.

. . .

The 'self-conscious' person is caught in a dilemma. He may *need* to be seen and recognized, in order to maintain his sense of realness and identity. Yet, at the same time, the other represents a threat to his identity and reality. One finds extremely subtle efforts expended in order to resolve this dilemma in terms of the secret inner self and the behavioural false-self systems already described. James, for instance, feels that 'other people provide me with my existence'. On his own, he feels that he is empty and nobody. 'I can't feel real unless there is someone there. . . .' Nevertheless, he cannot feel at ease with another person, because he feels as 'in danger' with others as by himself.

He is, therefore, driven compulsively to seek company, but never allows himself to 'be himself' in the presence of anyone else. He avoids social anxiety by never really *being with* others. He never quite says what he means or means what he says. The part he plays is always not quite himself. He takes care to laugh when he thinks a joke is *not* funny, and look bored when he is amused. He makes friends with people he does not really like and is rather cool to those with whom he would 'really' like to be friends. No one, therefore, really knows him, or understands him. He can be *himself* in safety only in isolation, albeit with a sense of emptiness and unreality. With others, he plays an elaborate game of pretence and equivocation. His social self is felt to be false and futile. What he longs for most is the possibility of 'a moment of recognition', but whenever this by chance occurs, when he has by accident 'given himself away', he is covered in confusion and suffused with panic.

The more he keeps his 'true self' in hiding, concealed, unseen, and the more he presents to others a false front, the more compulsive this false presentation of himself becomes. He appears to be extremely narcissistic and exhibitionistic. In fact he hates himself and is terrified to reveal himself to others. Instead, he compulsively exhibits what he regards as mere extraneous trappings to others; he dresses ostentatiously, speaks loudly and insistently. He is constantly drawing attention to himself, and at the same time drawing attention *away* from his self. His behaviour is compulsive. All his thoughts are occupied with being seen. His longing is to be known. But this is also what is most dreaded.

Saul Bellow

(b. 1915)   ————◆————   CANADIAN-
AMERICAN

Saul Bellow is another of the best contemporary American novelists. If Mailer has celebrated and Americanized the adventurous aspects of French existentialism, Bellow has brought home the gloomier aspects of German existentialism, with its stress on guilt and anxiety. Accordingly, his novels display a painful sensitivity to human frailty and failure which are completely absent from Mailer's heroic existentialism. Dangling Man *was his first novel.*

from DANGLING MAN

December 15, 1942

There was a time when people were in the habit of addressing themselves frequently and felt no shame at making a record of their inward transactions. But to keep a journal nowadays is considered a kind of self-indulgence, a weakness, and in poor taste. For this is an era of hardboiled-dom. Today, the code of the athlete, of the tough boy—an American inheritance, I believe, from the English gentleman—that curious mixture of striving, asceticism, and rigor, the origins of which some trace back to Alexander the Great—is stronger than ever. Do you have feelings? There are correct and incorrect ways of indicating them. Do you have an inner life? It is nobody's business but your own. Do you have emotions? Strangle them. To a degree, everyone obeys this code. And it does admit of a limited kind of candor, a closemouthed straightforwardness.

From *Dangling Man* by Saul Bellow. Copyright 1944 by Vanguard Press, Inc. Reprinted by permission of the publisher, Vanguard Press, Inc.

But on the truest candor, it has an inhibitory effect. Most serious matters are closed to the hard-boiled. They are unpracticed in introspection, and therefore badly equipped to deal with opponents whom they cannot shoot like big game or outdo in daring.

If you have difficulties, grapple with them silently, goes one of their commandments. To hell with that! I intend to talk about mine, and if I had as many mouths as Siva has arms and kept them going all the time, I still could not do myself justice. In my present state of demoralization, it has become necessary for me to keep a journal—that is, to talk to myself—and I do not feel guilty of self-indulgence in the least. The hard-boiled are compensated for their silence; they fly planes or fight bulls or catch tarpon, whereas I rarely leave my room.

John Barth

(b. 1930) ━━━━◆◆◆━━━━ **AMERICAN**

John Barth's first novel, The Floating Opera, *was a straight-forwardly existentialist work. It concerned a young man who had come to view the world through the eyes of Camus and saw no reason not to commit suicide. (By the end of the novel, he sees that there is no reason to commit suicide either.) In Barth's later works the existentialist themes become more refined.* Giles Goat-Boy *weaves slender existentialist threads through the complex patterns of a cosmic parable.* The End of the Road, *a piece of which appears here, introduces us to Jacob Horner, an existentialist nonhero who has grown sufficiently sophisticated to face a Sartrian rather than a Camusian dilemma, and receives therapy in the hands of a most peculiar super-Laingian therapist. Jacob Horner sees himself as a void (Sartre's nothingness), finds himself catatonically immobile (since every movement is equally arbitrary), but then begins to see the Sartrian way out.*

from
THE END OF THE ROAD

I Got Up,
Stiff from Sleeping in the Chair

I got up, stiff from sleeping in the chair, showered, changed my clothes, and went out for breakfast. Perhaps because the previous day had been, for me, so unusually eventful, or perhaps because I'd had relatively little sleep (I must say I take no great interest in causes), my mind was empty. All

From *The End of the Road* by John Barth. Copyright © 1958, 1967 by John Barth. Reprinted by permission of Doubleday & Company, Inc.

the way to the restaurant, all through the meal, all the way home, it was as though there were no Jacob Horner today. After I'd eaten I returned to my room, sat in my rocker, and rocked, barely sentient, for a long time, thinking of nothing.

Once I had a dream in which it became a matter of some importance to me to learn the weather prediction for the following day. I searched the newspapers for the weather report, but couldn't find it in its usual place. I turned the radio on, but the news broadcasters made no mention of tomorrow's weather. I dialed the Weather number on the telephone (this dream took place in Baltimore), but although the recording described the current weather conditions it told me nothing about the forecast for the next day. Finally I called the Weather Bureau directly, but it was late at night and no one answered. I happened to know the chief meteorologist's name, and so I called his house. The telephone rang many times before he answered; it seemed to me that I detected an uneasiness in his voice.

"What is it?" he asked.

"I want to know what weather we'll be having tomorrow," I demanded. "It's terribly important."

"There's no use your trying to impress me," the meteorologist said. "No use at all. What made you suspicious?"

"I assure you, sir, I just want to know what the weather will be tomorow. I can't say I see anything suspicious in that question."

"There isn't going to be any weather tomorrow."

"What?"

"You heard me. There isn't going to be any weather tomorrow. All our instruments agree. No weather."

"But that's impossible!"

"I've said what I've said," the weatherman grumbled. "No weather tomorrow, and that's that. Leave me alone; I have to sleep."

That was the end of the dream, and I woke up very much upset. I tell it now to illustrate a difference between moods and the weather, their usual analogy; a day without weather is unthinkable, but for me at least there were frequently days without any mood at all. On these days Jacob Horner, except in a meaningless metabolistic sense, ceased to exist, for I was without a personality. Like those microscopic specimens that biologists must dye in order to make them visible at all, I had to be colored with some mood or other if there was to be a recognizable self to me. The fact that my sucessive and discontinuous selves were linked to one another by the two unstable threads of body and memory; the fact that in the nature of Western languages the word *change* presupposes something upon which the changes operate; the fact that although the specimen is invisible without the dye, the dye is not the specimen—these are considerations of which I was aware, but in which I had no interest.

. . .

The Doctor spent two or three one-hour sessions with me each day. He asked me virtually nothing about myself; the conversations consisted mostly of harangues against the medical profession for its stupidity in matters of paralysis, and imputations that my condition was the result of defective character and intelligence.

"You claim to be unable to choose in many situations," he said once. "Well, I claim that the inability is only theoretically inherent in situations, when there's no chooser. Given a particular chooser, it's unthinkable. So, since the inability *was* displayed in your case, the fault lies not in the situation but in the fact that there was no chooser. Choosing is existence: to the extent that you don't choose, you don't exist. Now, everything we do must be oriented toward choice and action. It doesn't matter whether this action is more or less reasonable than inaction; the point is that it is its opposite."

"But why should anyone prefer it?" I asked.

"There's no reason why you should prefer it," he said, "and no reason why you shouldn't. One is a patient simply because one chooses a condition that only therapy can bring one to, not because any one condition is inherently better than another. All my therapies for a while will be directed toward making you conscious of your existence. It doesn't matter whether you act constructively or even consistently, so long as you act. It doesn't matter to the case whether your character is admirable or not, so long as you think you have one."

"I don't understand why you should choose to treat anyone, Doctor," I said.

"That's my business, not yours."

And so it went. I was charged, directly or indirectly, with everything from intellectual dishonesty and vanity to nonexistence. If I protested, the Doctor observed that my protests indicated my belief in the truth of his statements. If I only listened glumly, he observed that my glumness indicated my belief in the truth of his statements.

"All right, then," I said at last, giving up. "Everything you say is true. All of it is the truth."

The Doctor listened calmly. "You don't know what you're talking about," he said. "There's no such thing as truth as you conceive it."

These apparently pointless interviews did not constitute my only activity at the farm. Before every meal the other patients and I were made to perform various calisthenics under the direction of Mrs. Dockey. For the older patients these were usually very simple—perhaps a mere nodding of the head or flexing of the arms—although some of the old folks could execute really surprising feats: one gentleman in his seventies was an excellent rope climber, and two old ladies turned agile somersaults. For each Mrs. Dokey prescribed different activities; my own special prescription was to keep some sort of visible motion going all the time. If nothing else, I was constrained to keep a finger wiggling or a foot tapping, say, during mealtimes, when more involved movements would have made eating difficult. And I was told to rock from side to side in my bed all night long: not an unreasonable request, as it happened, for I did this habitually anyhow, even in my sleep—a habit carried over from childhood.

"Motion! Motion!" the Doctor would say, almost exalted. "You must be always *conscious* of motion!"

There were special diets and, for many patients, special drugs. I learned of Nutritional Therapy, Medicinal Therapy, Surgical Therapy, Dynamic Therapy, Informational Therapy, Conversational Therapy, Sexual Therapy, Devotional Therapy, Occupational and Preoccupational Therapy, Virtue and Vice Therapy, Theotherapy and Atheotherapy—and later, Mythotherapy, Philosophical Therapy, Scriptotherapy, and many, many other therapies practiced in various combinations and sequences by the patients. Everything, to the Doctor, is either therapeutic, anti-therapeutic, or irrelevant. He is a kind of super-pragmatist.

At the end of my last session—it had been decided that I was to return to Baltimore experimentally, to see whether and how soon my immobility might recur—the Doctor gave me some parting instructions.

"It would not be well in your particular case to believe in

God," he said. "Religion will only make you despondent. But until we work out something for you it will be useful to subscribe to some philosophy. Why don't you read Sartre and become an existentialist? It will keep you moving until we find something more suitable for you. Study the *World Almanac*: it is to be your breviary for a while. Take a day job, preferably factory work, but not so simple that you are able to think coherently while working. Something involving sequential operations would be nice. Go out in the evenings; play cards with people. I don't recommend buying a television set just yet. If you read anything outside the *Almanac*, read nothing but plays—no novels or non-fiction. Exercise frequently. Take long walks, but always to a previously determined destination, and when you get there, walk right home again, briskly. And move out of your present quarters; the association is unhealthy for you. Don't get married or have love affairs yet: if you aren't courageous enough to hire prostitutes, then take up masturbation temporarily. Above all, act impulsively: don't let yourself get stuck between alternatives, or you're lost. You're not that strong. If the alternatives are side by side, choose the one on the left; if they're consecutive in time, choose the earlier. If neither of these applies, choose the alternative whose name begins with the earlier letter of the alphabet. These are the principles of Sinistrality, Antecedence, and Alphabetical Priority—there are others, and they're arbitrary, but useful. Good-by."

"Good-by, Doctor," I said, a little breathless, and prepared to leave.

"If you have another attack, contact me as soon as you can. If nothing happens, come back in three months. My services will cost you ten dollars a visit—no charge for this one. I have a limited interest in your case, Jacob, and in the vacuum you have for a self. That *is* your case. Remember, keep moving all the time. Be *engagé*. Join things."

I left, somewhat dazed, and took the bus back to Baltimore. There, out of it all, I had a chance to attempt to decide what I thought of the Doctor, the Remobilization Farm, the endless list of therapies, and my own position. One thing seemed fairly clear: the Doctor was operating either outside the law or on its very fringes. Sexual Therapy, to name only one thing, could scarcely be sanctioned by the American Medical Association. This doubtless was the reason for the farm's frequent relocation It was also apparent that he was a crank—though perhaps not an ineffective one—and one wondered whether he had any sort of license to practice medicine at all. Because—his rationalization aside—I was so clearly different from his other patients, I could only assume that he had some sort of special interest in my case: perhaps he was a frustrated psychoanalyst. At worst he was some combination of quack and prophet—Father Divine, Sister Kenny, and Bernard MacFadden combined (all of them quite effective people), with elements of faith healer and armchair Freud thrown in—running a semi-legitimate rest home for senile ecentrics; and yet one couldn't easily laugh off his forcefulness, and his insights frequently struck home. As a matter of fact, I was unable to make any judgment one way or the other about him or the farm or the therapies.

A most extraordinary Doctor. Although I kept telling myself that I was just going along with the joke, I actually did move down to East Chase Street; I took a job as an assembler on the line of the Chevrolet factory out on Broening Highway, where I operated an air wrench that bolted leaf springs on the left side of Chevrolet chassis, and I joined the U.A.W. I read Sartre but had difficulty deciding how to apply him to specific situations (How did existentialism help one decide whether to carry one's lunch to work or buy it in the factory cafeteria? I had no head for philosophy). I played poker with my fellow assemblers, took walks from Chase Street down to the waterfront and back, and attended B movies. Temperamentally I was already pretty much of an atheist most of the time, and the proscription of women was a small burden, for I was not, as a rule, heavily sexed. I applied Sinistrality, Antecedence, and Alphabetical Priority religiously (though in some instances I found it hard to decide which of those devices best fitted the situation). And every quarter for the next two years I drove over to the Remobilization Farm for advice. It would be idle for me to speculate further on why I assented to this curious alliance, which more often than not is insulting to me—I presume that anyone interested in causes will have found plenty to pick from by now in this account.

I left myself sitting in the Progress and Advice Room, I believe, in September of 1953, waiting for the Doctor. My mood on this morning was an unusual one; as a rule I am almost "weatherless" the moment I enter the farmhouse, and I suppose that weatherlessness is the ideal condition for receiving advice, but on this morning, although I felt unemotional, I was not without weather. I felt dry, clear, and competent, for some reason or other—quite sharp and not a bit humble. In meteorological terms, my weather was *sec Supérieur*.

"How are you these days, Horner?" the Doctor asked affably as he entered the room.

"Just fine, Doctor," I replied breezily. "How's yourself?"

The Doctor took his seat, spread his knees, and regarded me critically, not answering my question.

"Have you begun teaching yet?"

"Nope. Start next week. Two sections of grammar and two of composition."

"Ah." He rolled his cigar around in his mouth. He was studying me, not what I said. "You shouldn't be teaching composition."

"Can't have everything," I said cheerfully, stretching my legs out under his chair and clasping my hands behind my head. "It was that or nothing, so I took it." The Doctor observed the position of my legs and arms.

"Who is this confident fellow you've befriended?" he asked. "One of the teachers? He's terribly sure of himself!"

I blushed: it occurred to me that I *was* imitating Joe Morgan. "Why do you say I'm imitating somebody?"

"I didn't," the Doctor smiled. "I only asked who was the forceful fellow you've obviously met."

"None of your business, sir."

"Oh, my. Very good. It's a pity you can't take over that manner consistently—you'd never need my services again! But you're not stable enough for that yet, Jacob. Besides, you couldn't act like him when you're in his company, could you? Anyway I'm pleased to see you assuming a role. You do it, evidently, in order to face up to me: a character like your friend's would never allow itself to be insulted by some crank with his string of implausible therapies, eh?"

"That's right, Doctor," I said, but much of the fire had gone out of me under his analysis.

"This indicates to me that you're ready for Mythotherapy, since you seem to be already practicing it without knowing it, and therapeutically, too. But it's best you be aware of what you're doing, so that you won't break down through ignorance. Some time ago I told you to become an existentialist. Did you read Sartre?"

"Some things. Frankly I really didn't get to be an existentialist."

"No? Well, no matter now. Mythotherapy is based on two assumptions: that human existence precedes human essence, if either of the two terms really signifies anything; and that a man is free not only to choose his own essence but to change it at will. Those are both good existentialist premises, and whether they're true or false is of no concern to us—they're *useful* in your case."

He went on to explain Mythotherapy.

"In life," he said, "there are no essentially major or minor characters. To that extent, all fiction and biography, and most historiography, are a lie. Everyone is necessarily the hero of his own life story. *Hamlet* could be told from Polonius's point of view and called *The Tragedy of Polonius, Lord Chamberlain of Denmark.* He didn't think he was a minor character in anything, I daresay. Or suppose you're an usher in a wedding. From the groom's viewpoint he's the major character; the others play supporting parts, even the bride. From your viewpoint, though, the wedding is a minor episode in the very interesting history of *your* life, and the bride and groom both are minor figures. What you've done is choose to *play the part* of a minor character: it can be pleasant for you to *pretend to be* less important than you are, as Odysseus does when he disguises as a swineherd. And every member of the congregation at the wedding sees himself as the major character, condescending to witness the spectacle. So in this sense fiction isn't a lie at all, but a true representation of the distortion that everyone makes of life.

"Now, not only are we the heroes of our own life stories —we're the ones who conceive the story, and give other people the essences of minor characters. But since no man's life story as a rule is ever one story with a coherent plot, we're always reconceiving just the sort of hero we are, and consequently just the sort of minor roles that other people are supposed to play. This is generally true. If any man displays almost the same character day in and day out, all day long, it's either because he has no imagination, like an actor who can play only one role, or because he has an imagination so comprehensive that he sees each particular situation of his life as an episode in some grand over-all plot, and can so distort the situations that the same type of hero can deal with them all. But this is most unusual.

"This kind of role-assigning is myth-making, and when it's done consciously or unconsciously for the purpose of aggrandizing or protecting your ego—and it's probably done for this purpose all the time—it becomes Mythotherapy. Here's the point: an immobility such as you experienced that time in Penn Station is possible only to a person who for some reason or other has ceased to participate in Mythotherapy. At that time on the bench you were neither a major nor a minor character: you were no character at all. It's because this has happened once that it's necessary for me to explain to you something that comes quite naturally to everyone else. It's like teaching a paralytic how to walk again.

"Now many crises in people's lives occur because the hero role that they've assumed for one situation or set of situations no longer applies to some new situation that comes up, or—the same thing in effect—because they haven't the imagination to distort the new situation to fit their old role. This happens to parents, for instance, when their children grow older, and to lovers when one of them begins to dislike the other. If the new situation is too overpowering to ignore, and they can't find a mask to meet it with, they may become schizophrenic—a last-resort mask—or simply shattered. All questions of integrity involve this consideration, because a man's integrity consists in being faithful to the script he's writter for himself.

"I've said you're too unstable to play any one part all the time—you're also too unimaginative—so for you these crises had better be met by changing scripts as often as necessary. This should come naturally to you; the important thing for you is to realize what you're doing so you won't get caught without a script, or with the wrong script in a given situation. You did quite well, for example, for a beginner, to walk in here so confidently and almost arrogantly a while ago, and assign me the role of a quack. But you must be able to change masks at once if by some means or other I'm able to make the one you walked in with untenable. Perhaps—I'm just suggesting an offhand possibility—you could change to thinking of me as The Sagacious Old Mentor, a kind of Machiavellian Nestor, say, and yourself as The Ingenuous But Promising Young Protégé, a young Alexander, who someday will put all these teachings into practice and far outshine the master. Do you get the idea? Or—this is repugnant, but it could be used as a last resort—The Silently Indignant Young Man, who tolerates the ravings of a Senile Crank but who will leave this house unsullied by them. I call this repugnant because if you ever used it you'd cut yourself off from much that you haven't learned yet.

"It's extremely important that you learn to assume these masks wholeheartedly. Don't think there's anything behind them: *ego* means *I*, and *I* means *ego*, and the ego by definition is a mask. Where there's no ego—this is you on the bench—there's no *I*. If you sometimes have the feeling that your mask is *insincere*—impossible word!—it's only because one of your masks is incompatible with another. You mustn't put on two at a time. There's a source of conflict, and conflict between masks, like absence of masks, is a source of immobility. The more sharply you can dramatize your situation, and define your own role and everybody else's role, the safer you'll be. It doesn't matter in Mythotherapy for paralytics whether your role is major or minor, as long as it's clearly conceived, but in the nature of things it'll normally always be major. Now say something."

Peter Weiss

(b. 1916) ———————◆◆◆◆——————— GERMAN
(SWEDISH)

Peter Weiss is best known for his play The Persecution and Assassination of Jean-Paul Marat as Performed by the Inmates of the Asylum at Charenton under the Direction of the Marquis de Sade, *the winner of the 1965–1966 New York Drama Critics Circle and Tony awards. He is also a novelist, painter, and film director. The Marquis de Sade was a perverse individualist who spent most of his mature life in prisons and asylums during the French Revolution, the "Reign of Terror," and the rise of Napoleon. Jean-Paul Marat was an ultraradical theoretician and chief engineer of the "Terror," who was murdered ungloriously in his medicinal bathtub by a vengeful young girl from the provinces. In the running dialogue between Marat and de Sade, there develops a dialectic between life and death, between Marat's dedication to violent action and the hopes of the revolution and de Sade's celebration of death and cruelty, the "indifference of the universe" and the priority of experience—even horrible or destructive experience—over the futility of action. It is not difficult to find Sartre's philosophy supporting Marat (Weiss, like Sartre, is a Marxist) and to find Heidegger and Camus uncomfortably standing behind de Sade's grim passions.*

from
MARAT/SADE

Conversation Concerning
Life and Death

> [*Order is restored at the back.*
> *The* SISTERS *murmur a short litany.*]

MARAT:
> [*speaking to* SADE *across the empty arena*]
> I read in your books de Sade
> in one of your immortal works
> that the basis of all of life is death

SADE:
> Correct Marat
> But man has given a false importance to death
> Any animal plant or man who dies
> adds to Nature's compost heap
> becomes the manure without which
> nothing could grow nothing could be created
> Death is simply part of the process
> Every death even the cruellest death
> drowns in the total indifference of Nature
> Nature herself would watch unmoved
> if we destroyed the entire human race
> > [*rising*]

> I hate Nature
> this passionless spectator this unbreakable iceberg-face
> that can bear everything
> this goads us to greater and greater acts
> > [*breathing heavily*]
> Haven't we always beaten down those weaker than
> ourselves

From *The Persecution and Assassination of Jean-Paul Marat As Performed by the Inmates of the Asylum of Charenton Under the Direction of the Marquis de Sade* by Peter Weiss; English version by Geoffrey Skelton; verse adaptation by Adrian Mitchell. Copyright © 1965 by John Calder Ltd. Reprinted by permission of Atheneum Publishers.

Haven't we torn at their throats
with continuous villainy and lust
Haven't we experimented in our laboratories
before applying the final solution
Let me remind you of the execution of Damiens
after his unsuccessful attempt to assassinate
Louis the Fifteenth (now deceased)
Remember how Damiens died
How gentle the guillotine is
compared with his torture
It lasted four hours while the crowd goggled
and Casanova at an upper window
felt under the skirts of the ladies watching
        [*pointing in the direction of the tribunal
        where* COULMIER *sits*]
His chest arms thighs and calves were slit open
Molten lead was poured into each slit
boiling oil they poured over him burning tar wax sulphur
They burnt off his hands
tied ropes to his arms and legs
harnessed four horses to him and geed them up
They pulled at him for an hour but they'd never done it
    before
and he wouldn't come apart
Until they sawed through his shoulders and hips
So he lost the first arm then the second
and he watched what they did to him and then turned
    to us
and shouted so everyone could understand
And when they tore off the first leg and then the second
    leg
he still lived though his voice was getting weak
and at the end he hung there a bloody torso with a
    nodding head
just groaning and staring at the crucifix
which the father confessor was holding up to him
        [*In the background a half-murmured litany is heard.*]
That
was a festival with which
today's festivals can't compete
Even our inquisition gives us no pleasure
nowadays
Although we've only just started

there's no passion in our post-revolutionary murders
Now they are all official
We condemn to death without emotion
and there's no singular personal death to be had
only an anonymous cheapened death
which we could dole out to entire nations
on a mathematical basis
until the time comes
for all life
to be extinguished

MARAT:

Citizen Marquis
you may have fought for us last September
when we dragged out of the gaols
the aristocrats who plotted against us
but you still talk like a grand seigneur
and what you call the indifference of Nature
is your own lack of compassion

SADE:

Compassion
Now Marat you are talking like an aristocrat
Compassion is the property of the privileged classes
When the pitier lowers himself
to give to a beggar
he throbs with contempt
To protect his riches he pretends to be moved
and his gift to the beggar amounts to no more than a kick
    [lute chord]
No Marat
no small emotions please
Your feelings were never petty
For you just as for me
only the most extreme actions matter

MARAT:

If I am extreme I am not extreme in the same way as you
Against Nature's silence I use action
In the vast indifference I invent a meaning
I don't watch unmoved I intervene
and say that this and this are wrong
and I work to alter them and improve them

The important thing
is to pull yourself up by your own hair
to turn yourself inside out
and see the whole world with fresh eyes

   . . .

Continuation of the Conversation between Marat and Sade

SADE:

Before deciding what is wrong and what is right
first we must find out what we are
I
do not know myself
No sooner have I discovered something
than I begin to doubt it
and I have to destroy it again
What we do is just a shadow of what we want to do
and the only truths we can point to
are the ever-changing truths of our own experience
I do not know if I am hangman or victim
for I imagine the most horrible tortures
and as I describe them I suffer them myself
There is nothing that I could not do and everything fills
me with horror

   . . .

Arthur Miller

(b. 1915) ——————◆—◆—◆—————— AMERICAN

Death of a Salesman *is Arthur Miller's classic American tragedy. Its protagonist, Willy Loman, is destroyed in the abyss between the American promise of success and the realities of failure. He is a firm believer in individual initiative, a broad smile, and polished shoes. But he has grown old and ineffective, and, like his two sons, reared on the same ethic of success, he is a failure. When he is fired from his job and deserted by his sons, he is forced to confront himself, and he makes a final heroic gesture. He kills himself in the family car to provide the insurance money for his wife.* Requiem *is the epilogue of the play, with Willy's wife and sons and his sole friend Charley standing before the simple grave. If existentialism is to force us "to know who we are,"* Requiem *is a fitting epilogue to our collection as well.*

from DEATH OF A SALESMAN

Requiem

CHARLEY: It's getting dark, Linda.

Linda doesn't react. She stares at the grave.

BIFF: How about it, Mom? Better get some rest, heh? They'll be closing the gate soon.

Linda makes no move. Pause.

From *Death of a Salesman* by Arthur Miller. Copyright 1949 by Arthur Miller. All rights reserved. Reprinted by permission of The Viking Press, Inc

HAPPY, *deeply angered:* He had no right to do that. There was no necessity for it. We would've helped him.

CHARLEY, *grunting:* Hmmm.

BIFF: Come along, Mom.

LINDA: Why didn't anybody come?

CHARLEY: It was a very nice funeral.

LINDA: But where are all the people he knew? Maybe they blame him.

CHARLEY: Naa. It's a rough world, Linda. They wouldn't blame him.

LINDA: I can't understand it. At this time especially. First time in thirty-five years we were just about free and clear. He only needed a little salary. He was even finished with the dentist.

CHARLEY: No man only needs a little salary.

LINDA: I can't understand it.

BIFF: There were a lot of nice days. When he'd come home from a trip; or on Sundays, making the stoop; finishing the cellar; putting on the new porch; when he built the extra bathroom; and put up the garage. You know something, Charley, there's more of him in that front stoop than in all the sales he ever made.

CHARLEY: Yeah. He was a happy man with a batch of cement.

LINDA: He was so wonderful with his hands.

BIFF: He had the wrong dreams. All, all, wrong.

HAPPY, *almost ready to fight Biff:* Don't say that!

BIFF: He never knew who he was.

CHARLEY, *stopping Happy's movement and reply. To Biff*: Nobody dast blame this man. You don't understand: Willy was a salesman. And for a salesman, there is no rock bottom to the life. He don't put a bolt to a nut, he don't tell you the law or give you medicine. He's a man way out there in the blue, riding on a smile and a shoeshine. And when they start not smiling back— that's an earthquake. And then you get yourself a couple of spots on your hat, and you're finished. Nobody dast blame this man. A salesman is got to dream, boy. It comes with the territory.

BIFF: Charley, the man didn't know who he was.

HAPPY, *infuriated*: Don't say that!

BIFF: Why don't you come with me, Happy?

HAPPY: I'm not licked that easily. I'm staying right in this city, and I'm gonna beat this racket! *He looks at Biff, his chin set.* The Loman Brothers!

BIFF: I know who I am, kid.

HAPPY: All right, boy. I'm gonna show you and everybody else that Willy Loman did not die in vain. He had a good dream. It's the only dream you can have—to come out number-one man. He fought it out here, and this is where I'm gonna win it for him.

BIFF, *with a hopeless glance at Happy, bends toward his mother*: Let's go, Mom.

LINDA: I'll be with you in a minute. Go on, Charley. *He hesitates.* I want to, just for a minute. I never had a chance to say good-by.

Charley moves away, followed by Happy. Biff remains a slight distance up and left of Linda. She sits there, summoning herself. The flute begins, not far away, playing behind her speech.

LINDA. Forgive me, dear. I can't cry. I don't know what it is, but I can't cry. I don't understand it. Why did you ever do that? Help me, Willy, I can't cry. It seems to me that you're just on another trip. I keep expecting you. Willy, dear, I can't cry. Why did you do it? I search and search and I search, and I can't understand it, Willy. I made the last payment on the house today. Today, dear. And there'll be nobody home. *A sob rises in her throat.* We're free and clear. *Sobbing more fully, released:* We're free. *Biff comes slowly toward her.* We're free . . . We're free . . .

Biff lifts her to her feet and moves out up right with her in his arms. Linda sobs quietly. Bernard and Charley come together and follow them, followed by Happy. Only the music of the flute is left on the darkening stage as over the house the hard towers of the apartment buildings rise into sharp focus, and

The Curtain Falls